Deleuze and the Postcolonial

Deleuze Connections

'It is not the elements or the sets which define the multiplicity. What defines it is the AND, as something which has its place between the elements or between the sets. AND, AND, AND – stammering.'

Gilles Deleuze and Claire Parnet, *Dialogues*

General Editor
Ian Buchanan

Editorial Advisory Board

Keith Ansell-Pearson	Gregg Lambert
Rosi Braidotti	Adrian Parr
Claire Colebrook	Paul Patton
Tom Conley	Patricia Pisters

Titles Available in the Series
Ian Buchanan and Claire Colebrook (eds), *Deleuze and Feminist Theory*
Ian Buchanan and John Marks (eds), *Deleuze and Literature*
Mark Bonta and John Protevi (eds), *Deleuze and Geophilosophy*
Ian Buchanan and Marcel Swiboda (eds), *Deleuze and Music*
Ian Buchanan and Gregg Lambert (eds), *Deleuze and Space*
Martin Fuglsang and Bent Meier Sørensen (eds), *Deleuze and the Social*
Ian Buchanan and Adrian Parr (eds), *Deleuze and the Contemporary World*
Constantin V. Boundas (ed.), *Deleuze and Philosophy*
Ian Buchanan and Nicholas Thoburn (eds), *Deleuze and Politics*
Chrysanthi Nigianni and Merl Storr (eds), *Deleuze and Queer Theory*
Jeffrey A. Bell and Claire Colebrook (eds), *Deleuze and History*
Laura Cull (ed.), *Deleuze and Performance*
Mark Poster and David Savat (eds), *Deleuze and New Technology*
Simone Bignall and Paul Patton (eds), *Deleuze and the Postcolonial*

Forthcoming Titles in the Series
Ian Buchanan and Laura Guillaume (eds), *Deleuze and the Body*
Simon O'Sullivan and Stephen Zepke (eds), *Deleuze and Contemporary Art*

Deleuze and the Postcolonial

Edited by Simone Bignall and Paul Patton

Edinburgh University Press

We dedicate this collection to a 'future form, for a new earth and a people that do not yet exist' – and to 'the now of our becoming'.

© in this edition, Edinburgh University Press, 2010
© in the individual contributions is retained by the authors

Edinburgh University Press Ltd
22 George Square, Edinburgh

www.euppublishing.com

Typeset in 10.5/13 Sabon
by Servis Filmsetting Ltd, Stockport, Cheshire

A CIP record for this book is available from the British Library

ISBN 978 0 7486 3699 0 (hardback)
ISBN 978 0 7486 3700 3 (paperback)

The right of the contributors
to be identified as authors of this work
has been asserted in accordance with
the Copyright, Designs and Patents Act 1988.

Contents

Acknowledgements	vii
Introduction: Deleuze and the Postcolonial: Conversations, Negotiations, Mediations Simone Bignall and Paul Patton	1
1 Living in Smooth Space: Deleuze, Postcolonialism and the Subaltern Andrew Robinson and Simon Tormey	20
2 Postcolonial Theory and the Geographical Materialism of Desire John K. Noyes	41
3 Postcolonial Visibilities: Questions Inspired by Deleuze's Method Rey Chow	62
4 Affective Assemblages: Ethics beyond Enjoyment Simone Bignall	78
5 The Postcolonial Event: Deleuze, Glissant and the Problem of the Political Nick Nesbitt	103

6 Postcolonial Haecceities
   Réda Bensmaïa
   Translated by Paul Gibbard
	119

7 'Another Perspective on the World': Shame and Subtraction in Louis Malle's *L'Inde fantôme* Timothy Bewes	163
8 Becoming-Nomad: Territorialisation and Resistance in J. M. Coetzee's *Waiting for the Barbarians* Grant Hamilton	183

9 Violence and Laughter: Paradoxes of Nomadic Thought in Postcolonial Cinema Patricia Pisters	201
10 The Production of *Terra Nullius* and the Zionist-Palestinian Conflict Marcelo Svirsky	220
11 Virtually Postcolonial? Philip Leonard	251
12 In Search of the Perfect Escape: Deleuze, Movement and Canadian Postcolonialism Jennifer Blair	272
Notes on Contributors	297
Index	301

Acknowledgements

Like all books, this collection is a 'group work', which has emerged from a virtual state of existence into formal actuality only through the efforts of the many people who have been involved in the process of its becoming. We are grateful for the assistance given by the editorial team at EUP, and especially wish to thank Carol MacDonald and Ian Buchanan for their advice and support. Christopher Miller, Rey Chow, Dipesh Chakrabarty, Peter Hallward, Françoise Lionnet and Bill Ashcroft provided us with valuable early suggestions about potential contributors with an interest in the connections between Deleuze and postcolonialism. Our sincere thanks are due to Paul Gibbard for his expert translation of the chapter by Réda Bensmaïa. We are indebted to Nabile Farès for kindly allowing us to reprint pages of illustrative text from his book *L'État perdu* (1982), published by Actes Sud. Princeton University Press gave us kind permission to include material previously published in Réda Bensmaïa's book *Experimental Nations* (2003). The Thomas Fisher Rare Book library at the University of Toronto and the Canadian Centre for Architecture in Montreal generously authorised the reproduction of archived images of early fire escapes. Simone would especially like to thank Greg Dayman for his care and support. Paul would like to thank Moira Gatens, as always, for her advice and support. Finally, we wish to thank each of the contributors for making the shared journey so enjoyable and illuminating.

Introduction

Deleuze and the Postcolonial: Conversations, Negotiations, Mediations

Simone Bignall and Paul Patton

Conversations

The collection of essays assembled in this volume constructs a series of conversations between Deleuzian philosophy and postcolonial theory,[1] canvassing the relationship between Deleuze's concepts, the phenomena of the postcolony and the project of decolonisation. As an act of engagement, a 'conversation' may take various forms, including 'speaking with', 'speaking to', 'speaking about' and 'speaking for'. In different ways, the contributions participate in each of these aspects of conversational interaction. The starting premise for this collection, also defining the rationale for its production, concerns the problematic lack of mutuality, or else the mutual disregard, which previous scholarship has highlighted as characteristic of the relationship between Deleuze and the postcolonial. Deleuze does not directly 'speak with' the thinkers and writers of the postcolony, and postcolonial theory seldom engages with Deleuzian philosophy in a sustained or comprehensive way, despite the abundance of Deleuzian *motifs* in postcolonial discourse. When theorists *have* directly considered postcolonial influences of/upon Deleuzian philosophy, they have usually done so in a critical and dismissive fashion.

For some, his failure to relate expressly to postcolonial issues does not simply suggest a careless lack of concern on Deleuze's part, but also the more worrying possibility that his silence on colonialism conceals a certain Eurocentric self-interest, a neo-imperial motivation or a hidden or unacknowledged desire to deflect attention away from the political concerns of the postcolony. Deleuze is accordingly condemned for his lack of explicit engagement with the body of postcolonial thought and with colonialism as a problematic site of analysis. Furthermore, certain Deleuzian concepts – nomadology in particular – are seen to appropriate and intellectualise indigenous experience and ways of life, extracting these from their concrete formulations and maintaining blindness to the devastating impact of colonialism on actually existing nomadic peoples (Miller 1993; Wuthnow 2002; see also Holland 2003; Noyes 2004). This tendency has at times been read as evidence for Deleuze's indifference to the real historical experiences of colonised peoples and their struggles for justice. This apparent indifference is thought to be compounded by Deleuze's failure to provide concepts of resistance, critique and political society that address the concerns of formerly colonised peoples. Worse, on occasion his indifference is seen to indicate a cultivated or 'interested' disinterest; rather than enabling the authentic expression of the subjective agency of formerly colonised peoples, his concepts are perceived to contribute to the demolition of consistent expressions of selfhood and structures of common identification – including human rights – widely understood as necessary platforms for co-ordinating strategies of resistance. Caren Kaplan argues that Deleuze and Guattari's use of nomadism perpetuates a long tradition of Eurocentric primitivism and a fascination for the other. She further argues that they perpetuate colonial discourse by not allowing the other to speak for itself: 'The Third World functions simply as a metaphorical margin for European oppositional strategies, an imaginary space, rather than a location of theoretical production itself' (Kaplan 1996: 88). Deleuze's perceived penchant for philosophical and historical abstractions – his preference for virtual creativity over the analysis of actually existing political situations – is thought to disable scope for concrete acts of engagement with the world, and therefore with the actual scars that continue to mark societies in the post-colonial world (Hallward 2006).

However, more sympathetic readers or nuanced readings might well consider such criticisms to be misguided. After all, the texts and interviews collected in *Desert Islands* (2004) and *Two Regimes of Madness* (2007) document Deleuze's supportive interest and active involvement in struggles for decolonisation and the return of appropriated territory in colonised regions including Algeria and Palestine.[2] François Dosse documents Deleuze and Guattari's engagement with the Palestinian cause and Deleuze's friendship with Elias Sanbar, Palestinian intellectual and founder of the *Revue d'Études Palestiniennes* in 1981 (Dosse 2007: 308–11). In an interview with Dosse, Sanbar described the work of Deleuze and Guattari as an essential resource for his own thought. Deleuze facilitated the publication of the *Revue* by Éditions de Minuit and published a long interview with Sanbar in *Libération* in 1982. Far from not allowing the colonised other to speak, Deleuze's remarks in this interview draw attention to the emergence of an intellectually rich and politically mature Palestinian voice capable of speaking to the world as an equal (Deleuze 2007: 194). Guillaume Sibertin-Blanc comments that, instead of the traditional positioning of a French intellectual addressing or speaking for the Middle East, Deleuze presents 'a deliberately marginal position which is authorized only by its own decentring in relation to the position won by "the Palestinians" themselves and expressed by the editors of this journal addressing their *own* historical and geopolitical situation' (Sibertin-Blanc 2008).

Over and above such specific interventions in support of decolonisation, many of Deleuze's philosophical writings, both alone and with Guattari, develop concepts and frameworks of discussion that resonate with themes and issues pertinent to postcolonialism. Among other examples, we might point to their comments about the imperialism of normative Western forms of Oedipal subjectivity; movements of de/reterritorialisation describing a conceptual politics of capture and relative liberation; the creation of hybrid and migratory forms of selfhood through relational processes of becoming; and of course nomads and their relation to the 'war-machines' that embody acts of resistance against the imperial 'state-form'. We might also note the concepts of minoritarian subjectivities and minor languages that introduce a deconstructive 'stuttering' into majoritarian identities, discourses and literary forms. Sibertin-Blanc points out that Deleuze had been interested in the status of minorities at least since his work on Kafka in 1975–6. This led him to study the socio-linguistic situation of Jewish communities in the declining Hapsburg empire (Sibertin-Blanc 2008). The question of 'minorities' reappears at the end of Plateau 13 '7000 B.C.: Apparatus of Capture' when Deleuze and Guattari declare that they are living in a period characterised by the proliferation of minoritarian movements (Deleuze and Guattari 1987: 469–73).

These and other aspects of Deleuze's work have long been taken up by others in their efforts to think about colonialism and postcolonial experiences. For example, Robert Young (1994; 1995) considers the Deleuzo-Guattarian concept of desiring-production in the context of capitalist colonialism, emphasising the usefulness of their materialist conceptualisation of desire in thinking about politics of colonial social construction. In his *Poetics of Relation* (1991), Édouard Glissant develops a conception of creolised Caribbean subjectivity by reference to a concept of 'relation' that owes much to Deleuze and Guattari's 'rhizome'. Réda Bensmaïa (2003) draws from Deleuzian concepts and philosophical approaches in his work on the Francophone literature of the Maghreb its their postcolonial inventions of 'Experimental

Nations'. In their different ways, Arjun Appadurai (1996; see also Bell 1999) and Graham Huggan (1989) make use of the Deleuzian notion of de/reterritorialisation. Paul Patton (2000; 2006b; 2010) considers aspects of Deleuze's work in relation to the legal forms and political structures constituting the internal colonisation of indigenous peoples, drawing from the nomad image of thought underpinning Deleuzian political philosophy in order to describe the 'event' of colonisation and the possibility of its counter-actualisation. Simone Bignall makes use of Deleuze's concepts of different/ciation and becoming in considering the requirements of a postcolonial philosophy of transformative agency (Bignall 2010). The Deleuzean *motif* of nomad subjects defined and destabilised by lines of flight, influential in a range of work on diaspora, exile and identity produced by postcolonial theorists, has also been taken up in related fields of study such as cultural feminism, for example by Françoise Lionnet (2005; 1993) in writing about subjects that resonate with postcolonial concerns: paths of migration, trajectories of exile and the nature of belonging. Similarly, writing in Canada, Laura U. Marks (1999) draws from Deleuze's writings on cinema and memory to consider how intercultural filmmakers can help to link people living in postcolonial diasporas by creating, through cinema, an embodied sense of place and culture.

However, with the notable exception of Martinican poet and novelist Glissant, these few examples describe work being produced mainly in the West, by theorists who are interested in postcolonial issues but who do not generally identify as postcolonial subalterns. This returns us to the question succinctly formulated by Réda Bensmaïa in his contribution to this volume: 'How do we interpret the *gap* that exists between the "influence" of Deleuze and Guattari's work on theorists of the postcolony and the absence we have already referred to of any direct relation between them?' Why, on the rare occasions when he is considered as a focus of postcolonial investigation, is Deleuze most commonly criticised and dismissed within postcolonial theory, despite evidence in his writings that he was sympathetic to postcolonial approaches and concerns, and despite the frequent use of his concepts and approaches as 'tools' in postcolonial projects? Such criticisms surface repeatedly over time in various works that have considered Deleuze's place within Western imperialism and postcolonial philosophy.

Deleuze's most discernible entry into the arena of postcolonial thought occurred with the publication of Gayatri Chakravorty Spivak's celebrated essay, 'Can the Subaltern Speak?' (1988), in which she criticises Deleuze and Foucault for their disinclination to 'speak for' the subaltern other, and renders problematic their rather facile assumption that the other can 'speak for' herself. Spivak insists that Deleuze and Foucault are guilty of a Eurocentrism that fails to acknowledge how such 'speech' must be presented within the privileged structures of Western epistemology and representation in order to be comprehended or perceived as sensible. Accordingly, she points to the troubling forms of exclusion that arise when resistance to domination must be normatively 'spoken' through the same terms of subjective representation that have historically been the cause of imperial oppression; and furthermore, that as formally 'other' in this system of representation, the authentic or 'true speech' of the subaltern remains always already outside the bounds of 'what can be heard'.

Arguably, Spivak's critique in 'Can the Subaltern Speak?' remains influential not solely because of the scathing reading she offers of Deleuze and Foucault, but more precisely because she signals (and complicates) the political and ethical issue of Western responsibility in the face of postcolonial projects of representation. This issue of Western responses to non-Western forms of resistance to colonialism is problematic precisely because of the trenchant contradiction inherent in forms of post-colonial 'speech', which articulate but simultaneously capture and delimit the protests and resistance struggles of formerly colonised peoples by reducing these to terms assimilable to the colonising ear they are directed towards (Memmi 1965; Fanon 1967; see also Bensmaïa 2003). It is not enough for Western intellectuals to resist the imperial temptation to 'speak for' the colonised other, since this response carries with it the danger that the other will remain inarticulate, having already been silenced within colonial history. If she is to speak 'for herself' in ways that are not fully captured by Western forms of discourse and structures of representation, then alternative forms of 'listening' are also required so that the particular sound of her 'voice' and the heterogeneous and irreducible 'sense' she conveys is able to be adequately heard and properly acknowledged on its own terms.

The intractable problem, of course, is that the act of 'speaking about' oneself, others or particular aspects of the world involves constructing and delimiting a representation of the object of one's speech, which renders it manageable and comprehensible, but also threatens to ossify into a set of assumptions and understandings, a habitual knowledge outside of which one eventually finds hard to think. It also becomes difficult to 'hear' alternative representations when they are spoken, because they do not neatly fit with established ways of making sense. In the context of postcolonialism, the problem of representation is highly politicised because many of the world's established and ossified forms of representation emerged and were consolidated with colonialism; for the 'West', to think outside of these established structures of meaning and 'hear' the alternative sense of the Other involves a certain effort and a political and ethical choice, which rarely seems to be made – either because the effort required to register the existence of the problem and then to act upon it is 'too great', or because the West has a vested interest in remaining 'deaf' to the alternative worlds 'spoken' by postcolonial subjects. The consequence of this is that post-colonial responses to the continuing forms of colonialism that exist as a contemporary legacy of global histories of imperialism often necessarily involve 'resorting to the language of their colonizers' in order to be heard at all (Bensmaïa 2003: 1), and so, in some ways at least, remain complicit with the structures they seek to disrupt.

While the tendency of representative forms of 'speech' to capture, delimit and suppress the diversity of subaltern meanings and interpretations is of particular concern for postcolonialism, the contributors to this collection are also concerned with the narrow way Deleuze has often been represented within the field of postcolonial theory. This is particularly problematic because Deleuze's work is so rich and varied; it traverses various terrains of engagement and shifts form and focus at various stages in his intellectual and political development. In his contribution to this collection, Réda Bensmaïa discusses how a narrow representation of this amorphous and extensive body of ideas is therefore singularly constraining upon the multiple names of Deleuze. However, it is also problematic because Deleuze's work comprises a consistent method of thought as creative assemblage, which 'opens up the way to a general logic' (Deleuze 2007: 177) that informs his concepts and the use to which they may be employed in a manner consistent with his way of doing philosophy. This is not to imply that Deleuze's work comprises a unified philosophical system; in so far as his work can be thought of as systematic, for Deleuze, 'the system must not only be in perpetual heterogeneity, it must also be a heterogenesis' (Deleuze 2007: 365). Deleuze's commitment to the idea of philosophy as creative assemblage makes clear his conviction that philosophical concepts should be mobile, both in themselves and in their relations with other concepts, which clearly complicates the claim that the various texts comprising 'Deleuzian philosophy' might enjoy a systemic consistency. Indeed, in much of Deleuze's work, there is a notable absence of systemic closure even within particular texts, as can be observed in the example of *A Thousand Plateaus*, which is an assemblage of a range of problematic investigations, with no overall argumentative or narrative structure that links them in any particular order. In this work, the concepts undergo continuous variation as components are modified in the passage from one plateau to the next. The book ends without a conclusion but instead with a set of definitions and rules for the construction of concepts. Clearly, the 'system' of concepts laid out in the course of the book could be continued without limits to the variation it employs.

There is always movement and discontinuity in Deleuze's thinking from one problem or series of problems to the next, and changing the problems on which these concepts are brought to bear, or changing the network of other concepts within which they appear, has consequences for the identity of the concepts themselves. However, this kind of historical sensitivity need not deny the existence of 'local' continuities within some of Deleuze's works, nor can it excuse the lack of rigour that results when his concepts are extracted from their local contexts as they occur in Deleuze's *oeuvre*, and then discretely deployed in postcolonial analyses without due attention to the Deleuzian image of thought that gives them their consistency and form. As is the case with the critical discussions of 'nomads' in postcolonial theory, it is common to read Deleuze in a more traditional way, which insists upon an essentialised interpretation or fixed definition of a concept he has created, extracting it from the discrete conditions of the problematic in which it was initially defined. When this is done, the 'sense' and political effects of both the concepts themselves, and the way they have been deployed within local problematics explored within Deleuzian philosophy, can be lost. As Patricia Pisters suggests in her contribution, the misinterpretation that has been made of the Deleuzian concepts of the actual and the virtual may be seen as another exemplary case in point. That Deleuze himself encouraged the piecemeal use of his and Guattari's concepts, which he hoped others would find of 'some use, however small . . . in their own work, in their life and in their projects' (2007: 180), does not stop the appropriation, interpretive reduction and assimilation of Deleuze from being a problem relevant to postcolonial theory.

Postcolonial criticisms of Deleuze, postcolonial uses of Deleuze and the essays collected here discussing the complex relationship between Deleuze and the postcolonial all involve a 'speaking about' Deleuze and a 'speaking about' postcolonialism – necessarily employing a particular representation of each. The chapters collected in this volume attest that Spivak's essay remains an important benchmark for understanding Deleuze's relationship with postcolonialism. Over time, and through the many and various readings and applications of the problems concerning subaltern agency that Spivak discusses in this early essay, the criticism she directs towards Deleuze has been taken up by others and developed into a kind of *doxa* or a stratified set of assumptions and understandings, which capture Deleuze and 'designate a character' (Deleuze 2007: 158). This *doxa* tends to take his approach as naturally complicit with the sort of Western epistemological and cultural imperialism that postcolonial philosophy commonly takes as its focus of critique. Each of the chapters in this collection aims to unsettle this *doxa* in order to open up a more reflexive rapprochement between Deleuzian philosophy and postcolonial theory. Collectively, they work to free the constraints that currently exist upon 'what can be thought' and 'what can be said' about the relationship between Deleuze and the postcolonial. Indeed, the collection begins with Andrew Robinson's and Simon Tormey's sustained engagement with Spivak's essay in order to perform a 'ground clearing' exercise, which they argue is necessary to enable the reassessment of Deleuze's usefulness in thinking about and practically engaging with postcolonial issues.

Accordingly, this collection 'speaks to' the fields of postcolonialism and Deleuze scholarship and to constructivism more broadly. In different ways, and with different foci of concern and engagement, the respective authors of each chapter ask how these fields of thought might be transformed when they are brought into a closer interrogative proximity or dialogue. What new concepts and understandings might be produced? What new understandings of the 'problems' and 'practices' defining each field might emerge from the encounter between Deleuze and postcolonialism?

Negotiations

What *method* of conversation befits an encounter between Deleuze and the postcolonial? For Deleuze, a conversation is best seen as a negotiation, which involves the participants in something beyond the symbolic exchange of their corresponding points of view. For him, conversations are acts of creation occurring *between* participants and *between* the respective terms and stances they bring to the discussion. Participants in a conversation are joined in a form of active engagement, a set of 'nuptials', which involve them in 'blocs' of becoming that happen between them and which effect the transformation of each (Deleuze and Parnet 1987: 1–19); in the process of this transformation, something new and different, which comes from both of them but exceeds them both, is created. This mutual and creative process of becoming is possible because the participants have something in common – a mutual concern, a mutual interest, a mutual antagonism or conflict of opinions – that draws them together, causing them to combine and enter into discussion. This mutual interest, concern or antagonism always relates to a common problem, which prompts the engagement and is itself shaped and redefined through the act of conversation. Thus, Deleuze explains that even participants with very disparate characters and outlooks can enjoy 'a felicitous encounter. Kurosawa can adapt Dostoyevsky at least because he can say: "I share a concern with him, a shared problem, this problem"' (Deleuze 2007: 322).

As we see it, defining the contours of an encounter between Deleuze and the postcolonial is to define the shared problem of finding lines of escape from forms of capture and containment, but also to identify some of the ways in which these lines of escape might come together, mutually reinforcing one another. In philosophy, the problem is to get away from established concepts and ways of thinking and understanding, including ways of thinking about thinking and understanding. In postcolonialism, the problem is to find ways of subverting the colonial control of peoples and territories, or to overcome colonial ways of producing and expressing worldly relations of being and belonging. For Deleuze, thinking is stifled by the philosophical inflexibility of rigid concepts and a stultifying image of thought that interrupts and blocks the creative flow of the new that he insists is the task of philosophy, properly conceived. He considers that when 'thinking's fettered, any analysis in terms of movement is blocked', and in fact, this is the source of the many contemporary forms of oppression: '[I]f we're so oppressed, it's because our movement is being restricted' (Deleuze 1995: 122). His approach to philosophy accordingly describes a 'conceptual politics' of resistance and liberation, which responds to the problem of conceptual capture by constructing 'intellectually mobile concepts' (Deleuze 1995: 122; see Patton 2006a, 2010). For Deleuze, because it actively creates the real, rather than simply reflecting upon it, philosophy is inherently material and political, and so may be employed with different political intents and material effects: 'Embracing movement, or blocking it: politically, two completely different methods of negotiation' (Deleuze 1995: 127). Deleuzian philosophy is a political practice that actively resists forms of conceptual capture by creating movement in thought, beginning lines of flight that prompt an established representation of worldly reality to flee.

Similarly for Fanon, postcolonialism interjects and attempts to 'solve' the problem of colonial capture, which has produced:

> A world divided into compartments, a motionless, Manichaeistic world, a world of statues. The statue of the general who carried out the conquest, the statue of the engineer who built the bridge, a world which is sure of itself, which crushes with its stories the backs flayed by whips: this is the colonial world. The native is a being hemmed in . . . the first thing which the native learns is to stay in his place, and not to go beyond certain limits. (Fanon 1967: 40)

Informed by a common problem, Deleuze and postcolonialism also share sympathy of approach, exhibiting a common desire to invent and explore 'worlds less sure' but permanently open to renewal and transformation. Deleuze and postcolonialism thus share not only a common problem, but also a certain understanding of the kinds of 'solutions' that are needed. As Rey Chow argues in her contribution, both seek to contact an 'outside' of established structures, revealing that nothing is 'hemmed in'. It is always possible to develop alternative ways of regarding both self and other, thereby creating the possibility of inventing alternative, postcolonial forms of self, sociability and 'worldliness'. Common to both is the emphasis on creating movement, as a way out of capture and containment:

> I dream I am jumping, swimming, running, climbing; I dream that I burst out laughing, that I span a river in one stride, or that I am followed by a flood of motor-cars that never catch up with me . . . the presence of an obstacle accentuates the tendency towards motion. (Fanon 1967: 40–1)

For Deleuze, the method of 'negotiation' is vital because it enriches the process of problematic conversation; each participant brings insights to bear on the problem they share, which impact upon the forms of the solution that each might individually propose. Without taking care to negotiate one's position concerning a problem, one is limited to 'speaking on one's own', identifying the problem from one's own inevitably limited, because insular, point of view; the danger here is that one 'won't get away from a "Master's or colonists discourse", an established discourse' (Deleuze 1995: 125). We have seen how Spivak insists upon the need for a different 'solution' to the problem of subaltern resistance when she criticises Deleuze's reluctance to 'speak for' the other. In response, Deleuze might well have pointed to his work on the importance of a particular quality of listening as an alternative solution, relevant to the postcolonial project of making subaltern speech audible: 'There is no absolute ear; the problem is to have an impossible one – making audible forces that are not audible in themselves' (Deleuze 2007: 160). Through this process of negotiation that arises when commentators are brought into engaged contact, postcolonialism and Deleuzian philosophy enrich one another, adding new dimensions of interpretation that shed new light on the problem and the viability of the solutions called for.

This collection performs a series of negotiations of this sort, and we can imagine there are many more possible negotiations aroused by an engagement between Deleuze and the postcolonial. For example, brought into conversation, Deleuze and Bhabha might well share an emphasis on the relational and interstitial nature of postcolonial subjectivities whose combinations thrust them into hybrid becomings as a way of resolving the problematic fixture of identities and representations established through colonial discourse. However, Deleuze's (1994) critique of the repetition of the Same (in philosophy) and his emphasis on the eternal return of difference as a creative force of affirmation and novelty complicates Bhabha's presentation of mimicry as a form of hybrid 'solution' that disrupts the power of colonial representations. A problematic conversation of this sort between Deleuze and Bhabha opens up the potential for 'negotiating' a different understanding of the solution described by the postcolonial; no longer simply as that which destabilises and contests colonialism by playing on its internal dissonances, but more positively as a method of actively engendering 'a new horizon' of sociality (cf. Bhabha 1994: 1).

An encounter between usually unrelated theories also potentially facilitates the internal negotiation, within each field of study, of new understandings concerning the problems that constitute and define each field. For example, postcolonial theory has often been caught between a poststructuralist or deconstructivist impulse concerned with the subjective desires underlying colonial identity and discourse, and a Marxist impulse concerned with the material conditions of production and the need to assert collective forms of grounded and coherent resistance to colonial ideologies, economies and cultures of productive practice (Gandhi 1998). This rift has increasingly come to define the debates and concerns that describe the broad field of postcolonial study. An engagement with Deleuzian philosophy potentially illuminates a 'way out' of this seemingly irresolvable argument and associated philosophical hiatus, through Deleuze and Guattari's materialist conceptualisation of desiring-production, which they describe as an ontological force of composition and decomposition that produces and effects the transformation of all modes of reality (subjective, conceptual, material, ideological, social). The quibble within postcolonialism over the correct focus and location of critical engagement (subjective or social, individual or collective) might then be revealed as a 'false' or 'badly posed' problem. Taking a Deleuzian perspective on colonialism enables a re-vision of the problem, such that the correct focus and location of critique is understood to be the causal force of desire itself, and more particularly the depraved kinds of desire (possessive, appropriative, assimilating) that have caused the actualisation of problematic forms of existence, including colonial subjects and sociality (Bignall 2010).

Brought into direct communion with postcolonialism, Deleuzian philosophy is required to *become* adequate to the practical task of postcolonisation, and may be evaluated according to its successful application to this task. Conversely, communication with Deleuzian concepts may prompt a critical *becoming* of postcolonial theory, providing a useful philosophical perspective for evaluating and improving the adequacy of the existing solutions proposed to resist and transform the conditions defining the problem of colonialism. Properly mutual negotiations witness the simultaneous becoming-Deleuzian of postcolonialism and the becoming-postcolonial of Deleuze.

Mediations

The art of negotiation takes place through the act of mediation. For Deleuze, 'Mediators are fundamental. Creation's all about mediators. Without them nothing happens . . . I need my mediators to express myself, and they'd never express themselves without me: you're always working in a group, even when you seem to be on your own' (Deleuze 1995: 125). According to Deleuze, in order to avoid becoming trapped in a 'black hole' of established discourse in which 'nothing happens', 'what we have to do is catch someone else "telling tales", "caught in the act of telling tales". Then a minority discourse, with one or many speakers, takes shape' (1995: 125).

The 'tales' told by our contributors mediate the figure of Deleuze and the field of postcolonial theory. In this process, each chapter enters into an assemblage with Deleuze and with postcolonialism; the authors carve out a conceptual territory that sets out the plane of their engagement (philosophy, culture, politics), and they effect a creation, which is a becoming-postcolonial of Deleuze and a becoming-Deleuzian of the postcolonial. This act of creation is also the 'constitution of a people', a 'future-people' that may come to occupy the planes of thought defined by the overlapping fields of Deleuzian philosophy and postcolonialism (Deleuze 1995: 126). The following are the story-lines of the tales the contributors will tell.

The opening chapters address issues of philosophy and ethics. Andrew Robinson and Simon Tormey revisit and respond to Spivak's early critique of Deleuze. They identify and explore 'five distinct claims' made by Spivak: that Deleuze and Foucault covertly reintroduce the transcendent European subject; that they lack a theory of ideology and, consequently, a theory of interest; that they foreclose the need for counter-hegemonic ideological production and dialogue with the other by assuming the other can speak for itself; that their points of reference, the problems they seek to solve and the texts they refer to are entirely caught within a self-contained West or Europe; and that their refusal of constitutive contradiction reintroduces an undivided subject and is essentialist.

The problem investigated by John K. Noyes concerns the 'temporality of the post- in postcolonialism', which threatens to depoliticise postcolonial theory when it is understood to represent a periodisation 'following-colonialism'. This is a charge similarly directed towards Deleuzian philosophy, whose conception of the subject is criticised for disabling political action. Noyes finds a solution to these twinned problems concerning the political in Deleuze's attempts to describe a geographical materialism of desire.

Rey Chow considers new possibilities for thinking postcolonial resistance opened up by 'Deleuze's Foucault'. She attends particularly to the concept of 'visibility', which has the function of capture and entrapment in Foucault's work on disciplinary power, but which Deleuze 'cracks open' to reveal an 'invisible' Outside that has been excluded. This, Chow believes, 'offers infinite inspiration for the postcolonial as a type of liberatory thought' that strives to move beyond the 'cultural logic of repression-resistance'. Chow discusses this alternative style of resistance in the context of the 'newly multiplied visibilities' produced by the contemporary frames of 'shadow media' – small, mobile media devices that simultaneously capture, disperse and fragment images and representations.

Simone Bignall considers the Deleuzian concepts of assemblage and affectivity in relation to the 'Stolen Generations' of indigenous Australians removed from their land and their communities as a result of colonialist state policy. She suggests that these aspects of Deleuzian philosophy privilege a certain idea of careful sociability, which expands the realm of practical ethics beyond rights-based and state-mediated discourses of justice, to include unmediated qualities of interpersonal relationship as defining aspects of the style of political and ethical life called for by the idea of the postcolonial. Accordingly, she notes Deleuze's work is part of an alternative tradition of Western thought, offering potentially non-imperial conceptualisations of sociability, motivation and self-comportment, freeing it from the dominant emphases and the entrenched terms of debate of much Western political theory.

14 Deleuze and the Postcolonial

Deleuze and Guattari are commonly referenced in the work of Édouard Glissant, the foremost theorist of colonialism and postcolonialism in the Caribbean. Nick Nesbitt here explores some of the less visible, subterranean conceptual linkages between Deleuze and Glissant, and in so doing, traces the complex and often problematic image of the political that emerges at the intersection of the triplet Deleuze/Glissant/postcolonialism. Through the figure of Glissant, Nesbitt engages with Peter Hallward's influential criticisms of Deleuze (2006) and postcolonial theory (2001). While Hallward insists both are fatally deficient because they neglect a necessary concrete engagement with the political, Nesbitt claims that investigation of the complex intersection of the works of Gilles Deleuze and Édouard Glissant offers a 'concentrated opportunity' to grapple with the political problem of 'the event' and its 'eternal truth', providing an opening onto a renewed notion of the political aspects of the '*post*colonial' and of associated processes of transformative change.

At this point, the focus of the collection shifts to consider postcolonial issues concerning cultural production and representation. Réda Bensmaïa asks about the conditions of thinking about Deleuze and about postcolonialism that have allowed the multiple names of Deleuze to be taken up and employed in various, often contradictory, ways within postcolonial theory. He suggests that the figure of Deleuze is in important ways *virtual*, a 'differentiator' permitting multiple actualisations according to the practical contexts and problems that call him forth. Bensmaïa describes this in terms of the Deleuzian concept of 'haecceity', as a particular type of 'philosophical event' that describes the complex nature of certain encounters – between philosophy and non-philosophy, between Deleuze and the postcolony – and the creative becomings they incite. This discussion is subsequently grounded in terms of the 'postcolonial haecceities' Bensmaïa identifies in the work of the Algerian writer Nabile Farès, and also in Farès' subsequent response to Bensmaïa's analysis. In this response – a letter to Bensmaïa, which is included here as an appendix – Farès affirms the role played by Deleuze as a kind of 'differentiator', active in the creative process of his writing.

Timothy Bewes investigates the ontological source of the shame with which writers of the 'West' so frequently seem to approach their interactions with the 'non-West', in order to enquire about the possibility of engaging in a 'form of writing that would be free of the shame of the post-colonial epoch, a truly postcolonial literature'. Arguing that 'to free ourselves of this most intimate residue of the colonial enterprise it is necessary to overcome the models of thought and perception that made colonialism possible in the first place', Bewes observes the different styles of ontological engagement and perception represented in Michel Leiris' ethnographic journal *L'Afrique fantôme* (1934), and in the documentary series filmed by Louis Malle, titled *L'Inde fantôme* (1993). He draws from Deleuze's philosophy of perception and the concept of 'subtraction', here found in Deleuze's cinema books, so as to 'grasp the inseparability of shame from perception in order to decentre, even vacate both'.

Grant Hamilton offers a Deleuzian reading of J. M. Coetzee's novel *Waiting for the Barbarians* (1980), drawing on the set of Deleuzian concepts of 'smooth' and 'striated' space, relative movements of de/reterritorialisation defining these spaces, and the nomad war-machines that effect this shift between the 'two combative conceptualisations of the earth that seem to characterise the colonial encounter'. Hamilton accordingly discusses the way in which Coetzee uses the dynamic that develops between these two conceptualisations of the earth to describe the complex ontological character of the protagonist: the Magistrate enters into a process of 'becoming-nomad' that ultimately casts him in opposition to the colonial power that he serves. As such, Hamilton explains how the figure of the Magistrate stages a powerful resistance to colonial practice, involving a deterritorialisation of the self that simultaneously instructs the self-destructive drive of the state apparatus.

Patricia Pisters seeks to address the objections raised against Deleuze by postcolonial and political theory by focusing on Deleuzian concepts including the 'politics of the impersonal' and 'nomadology'. The focus of her attention is colonial Palestine. Through her Deleuzian reading of Elia Suleiman's films *Chronicle of a Disappearance* (1996) and *Divine Intervention* (2002), she argues that in order to understand the political accountability of Deleuzian philosophy it is necessary to grasp the paradoxical implications of nomadic thought and immanent philosophy, in which virtual existence simultaneously exceeds, and is carried within, every instance of concrete actualisation.

Marcelo Svirsky also considers the problem of colonisation in Palestine but, in concert with the final chapters of the collection, he shifts our attention towards the political processes of colonial and postcolonial nationalisation. He adopts the Deleuzo-Guattarian notion of a 'politics of desire' in order to investigate the practical function of the concept of *Terra Nullius* in the context of the colonisation of Palestine by Israel. This concept is identified, not simply as an 'ideal' fantasy of an empty land, but as a productive series of desiring-machines that actively produce the 'real' by manufacturing dispossession and oppression. Svirsky persuasively evidences how these desiring-machines have been historically assembled over time through the different connections and relations made from within the Zionist-Palestinian structure.

The final two chapters similarly consider issues of postcolonial nationhood. Philip Leonard addresses the 'misrecognition of subjectivity, agency, cultural location, materiality, and transcendence' occurring with an uncritical celebration of globalisation that neglects the persistence and significance of the nation-state. Leonard argues that Deleuze's writing on the 'state-form' that constantly reasserts itself against both internal and external threats 'offers an antidote both to the notion that new technologies necessarily overcome the uneven distribution of power that has continued to shape postcolonial cultures and to the idea that a new virtuality has initiated a smooth space of global community'. However, by emphasising the incessant reshaping of territorial space that allows oppressed groups and minorities to interrupt the functioning of the majoritarian nation-state, Deleuze's work simultaneously promises to 'expose the ambivalent contingency that constantly haunts narratives of the nation-state's fixity'.

In the final contribution to the collection, Jennifer Blair reviews the trend toward discourse analysis in Canadian postcolonial criticism and its associated enactment of a linguistic displacement of the material processes of nation-building. She takes a series of nineteenth-century fire-escape designs as her object of analysis, considering these not just as historical curiosities, but as engagements with the material environment that question the extent to which Canadian postcolonial criticism has considered the relation between time, memory, affectivity and movement in the construction of the nation. If the preoccupation with nation-building remains a defining feature of postcolonial analysis, even if 'the nation' itself has suffered a deconstruction of sorts (with increased attention now paid to multinationals, transnationals, nations within and First Nations), then a Deleuzian reading of 'nation-building' that focuses on the affectivity of the virtual in the course of material construction reveals the becoming of the Canadian nation as something much more heterogeneous and open-ended in character than has yet been acknowledged in postcolonial renderings of the nation as a primarily discursive phenomenon. According to Blair, the early Canadian fire escapes offer postcolonial studies some key examples of becoming in time and movement, which promise to expand established notions of causality, agency, responsibility and embodied subjectivity.

This collection forges connections between Deleuze and the postcolonial, in the form of conversations, negotiations and mediations. In doing so, it does not attempt to establish a consensus on the nature of the relationship between Deleuzian philosophy and postcolonial theory. Rather, it aims to open up new possibilities for inventing the postcolonial world, as well as new ways of creating the names of Deleuze. We see this process of 'creation as tracing a path between impossibilities' (Deleuze 1995: 133), which begins with the problem at the heart of postcolonialism: 'the impossibility of not speaking, of speaking in English, of speaking in French' (Deleuze 1995: 133) – the impossibility, for postcolonialism, of simultaneously speaking 'within' and from 'without' established forms of representation. We hope the creative connections produced here between Deleuze and the postcolonial will begin new lines of thought and understanding that mediate this impossibility. We see that the encounter between Deleuze and the postcolonial is an event which offers innovative ways to think about the invention of new kinds of subjectivity and society, new ways of speaking and listening arising from the invention of an 'impossible ear' that makes possible the audibility of alternative kinds of postcolonial sense and sensibility. We hope the contributions will assist readers in this development: '[T]o the established fictions that are always rooted in a colonist's discourse, we oppose a minority discourse, with mediators' (Deleuze 1995: 126).

References

Appadurai, A. (1996), *Modernity at Large: Cultural Dimensions of Globalisation*, Minneapolis: University of Minnesota Press.
Bell, V. (1999), 'Historical Memory, Global Movements and Violence: Paul Gilroy and Arjun Appadurai in Conversation', *Theory, Culture, Society* 16 (2): 21–40.
Bensmaïa, R. (2003), *Experimental Nations or the Invention of the Maghreb*, trans. A. Waters, Princeton: Princeton University Press.
Bhabha, H. (1994), *Location of Culture*, London and New York: Routledge.
Bignall, S. (2010), *Postcolonial Agency*, Edinburgh: Edinburgh University Press.
Deleuze, G. (1994), *Difference and Repetition*, trans. P. Patton, London: Athlone Press; and New York: Columbia University Press.
Deleuze, G. (1995), *Negotiations 1972–1990*, trans. Martin Joughin, Columbia: Columbia University Press.
Deleuze, G. (2004), *Desert Islands and Other Texts 1953–1974*, trans. M. Taormina, New York: Semiotext(e).
Deleuze, G. (2007), *Two Regimes of Madness: Texts and Interviews 1975–1995*, trans. Ames Hodges and Mike Taormina, revd edn, New York: Semiotext(e).
Deleuze, G. and F. Guattari (1987), *A Thousand Plateaus*, trans. B. Massumi, Minneapolis: University of Minnesota Press.
Deleuze, G. and C. Parnet (1987), *Dialogues*, trans. H. Tomlinson and B. Habberjam, London: Athlone.
Dosse, F. (2007) *Gilles Deleuze et Félix Guattari: Biographie Croisée*, Paris: Éditions de la Découverte.
Fanon, F. (1967), *The Wretched of the Earth*, Harmondsworth: Penguin.
Gandhi, L. (1998), *Postcolonial Theory: A Critical Introduction*, Sydney: Allen and Unwin.

Glissant, E. (1991), *Poétique de la relation*, Paris: Gallimard.
Hallward, P. (2001), *Absolutely Postcolonial: Writing between the Singular and the Specific*, Manchester: Manchester University Press.
Hallward, P. (2006), *Out of this World: Deleuze and the Philosophy of Creation*, London: Verso.
Holland, E. (2003), 'Representation and Misrepresentation in Postcolonial Literature and Theory', *Research in African Literatures* 34 (1): 159–73.
Huggan, G. (1989), 'Decolonizing the Map: Post-Colonialism, Post-Structuralism, and the Cartographic Connection', *Ariel* 20 (4): 115–29.
Kaplan, C. (1996), *Questions of Travel: Postmodern Discourses of Displacement*, Durham: Duke University Press.
Lionnet, F. (ed.) (1993), 'Post/Colonial Conditions: Exiles, Migrations, Nomadisms', *Special Double Issue of Yale French Studies* 82 and 83.
Lionnet, F. and S. Shih (eds) (2005), *Minor Transnationalism*, Durham: Duke University Press.
Marks, L. U. (1999), *The Skin of the Film: Intercultural Cinema, Embodiment, and the Senses*, Durham: Duke University Press.
Memmi, A. (1965), *The Colonizer and the Colonized*, New York: Orion.
Miller, C. L. (1993), 'The Post-Identitarian Predicament in the Footnotes of *A Thousand Plateaus*: Nomadology, Anthropology and Authority', *Diacritics* 23 (3): 6–35.
Noyes, J. K. (ed.) (2004), 'Special Issue: Nomadism, Nomadology, Empire', *Interventions* 6 (2).
Patton, P. (2000), *Deleuze and the Political*, London and New York: Routledge.
Patton, P. (2006a), 'Mobile Concepts, Metaphor and the Problem of Referentiality in Deleuze and Guattari', in Maria Margaroni and Effie Yiannopoulou (eds), *Metaphoricity and the Politics of Mobility*, Amsterdam and New York: Rodopi, pp. 27–47.
Patton, P. (2006b), 'The Event of Colonisation', in Ian Buchanan and Adrian Parr (eds), *Deleuze and the Contemporary World*, Edinburgh: Edinburgh University Press, pp. 108–25.
Patton, P. (2010), *Deleuzian Concepts: Philosophy, Colonization, Politics*, Stanford: Stanford University Press.
Sibertin-Blanc, G. (2008) 'Peuple et territoire: Deleuze lecteur de la *Revue d'Études Palestiniennes*'. To appear in Catherine Mayaux (ed.), *Écrivains et intellectuels français face au monde arabe*, Actes du Colloque de l'Université de Cergy-Pontoise, 31 janv.–2 fév.
Spivak, G. C. (1988), 'Can the Subaltern Speak?', in C. Nelson and L. Grossberg (eds), *Marxism and the Interpretation of Culture*, Urbana: University of Illinois Press, pp. 271–313.
Wuthnow, J. (2002), 'Deleuze in the Postcolonial: On Nomads and Indigenous Politics,' *Feminist Theory* 3 (2): 183–200.
Young, R. (1994), 'Colonialism and The Desiring-Machine', in T. D'haen and H. Bertens (eds), *Liminal Postmodernisms*, Amsterdam and Atlanta: Rodopi Press, pp. 11–34.
Young, R. (1995), *Colonial Desire: Hybridity in Theory, Culture and Race*, Routledge: London.

Notes

1. Throughout this collection, unless indicated otherwise, we use the terms 'post-imperial' and 'post-colonial' to signify a historical state of worldly existence

experienced (in different ways) by both former colonisers and the formerly colonised, in the sense of self-concepts or societies 'following colonisation', which remain defined by past imperial modes of representation and conditions of production. We intend the unhyphenated term 'postcolonial' to signal a form of subjectivity and society that is qualitatively different from colonial forms. We consider that 'postcolonial' subjectivity is a 'future-form' of selfhood, not structured by imperial ontology or by imperial relations of power and social engagement, which therefore currently exists as a virtual (though real), rather than actual form, and is involved in a process of 'becoming' that takes place in relation to the becoming-postcolonial of society. In comparison with Homi Bhabha's formulation of the postcolonial as 'neither a new horizon, nor a leaving behind of the past' (1994: 1), which we believe properly refers to the historical condition of 'postcoloniality', our understanding of the term 'postcolonial' is more positive: it signals 'a new horizon' which qualitatively differs from past forms, even though the colonial past as world memory is indelibly contained and contracted in the future-present form of this new horizon.

2. In particular, see the series of articles on the plight of the Palestinian people including 'Les gêneurs' in *Le Monde*, 7 avril 1978, translated as 'Spoilers of Peace', (Deleuze 2007: 161–3); 'Les Indiens de Palestine' in *Libération*, 8–9 May 1982, translated as 'The Indians of Palestine', (Deleuze 2007: 194–200); 'Grandeur de Yasser Arafat' in the *Revue d'Études Palestiniennes* 10, 1984, translated as 'The Importance of Being Arafat' (Deleuze 2007: 241–5); and 'Les Pierres' in *Al-Karmel* 29, 1988, translated as 'Stones' (Deleuze 2007: 338–9).

Chapter 1

Living in Smooth Space: Deleuze, Postcolonialism and the Subaltern

Andrew Robinson and Simon Tormey

Any attempt to situate Deleuze in relation to the postcolonial, and in particular to postcolonial theory, will inevitably involve a reckoning with Gayatri Spivak's well-known critique of Deleuze (and Foucault) in 'Can the Subaltern Speak?' (1988).[1] Spivak is, of course, an exemplary figure as far as the development of postcolonial theory is concerned. Her brutal dissection of the interview between Deleuze and Foucault, 'The Intellectuals and Power', remains an emblematic encounter between the claims of a certain wing of 'French theory' – particularly the Nietzschean inflected variant of it – and a nascent postcolonial critique which Spivak has been so instrumental in establishing. Here, famously, Spivak demolishes the pretensions of Deleuze and Foucault to offer an escape from the universalising ambitions of post-Enlightenment thought, demonstrating how their admonition to give up representing the oppressed ends up enacting the very same logic of subordination to the Western 'global-local' they claimed to confront in their own work. Deleuze and Foucault are revealed as post-Kantian avatars preparing to subordinate otherness to the claims of cosmopolitical reasoning, and the subaltern periphery to the globalising empire of liberal-capitalism.

Spivak has not to our knowledge disavowed her analysis of Deleuze, which implies that the latter's work and approach remains in some important sense a valid subject of the critiques she develops in the piece; that what Deleuze offers is 'Eurocentric', teleological, totalising and so forth. It is clear that unless the claims advanced by Spivak are examined on their own terms, there will continue to be a significant barrier to the reception of Deleuze – and indeed Deleuze and Guattari – as 'postcolonial' thinkers. This is notwithstanding the evident influence their work has had on contemporary theorists operating within the postcolonial frame, such as Arjun Appadurai, Achille Mbembe and Uday Singh Mehta. Perhaps because Deleuze and Guattari have also influenced strongly modernist neo-Marxist thinkers such as Michael Hardt and Antonio Negri, there appears to be a residual hostility towards the idea that Deleuze and Guattari are quite properly postcolonial thinkers, which we would argue they are.

Accordingly, we think that there is a need for a reckoning with Spivak's piece as a ground clearing exercise.[2] The thrust of this chapter is thus to show that Spivak's claims concerning the nature of Deleuze's work are mistaken. We argue that her critique is based on a somewhat cursory examination of Deleuze's *oeuvre*, especially the co-authored work with Guattari, which is replete with analyses of non-Western, indigenous and subaltern practices and discourses. Getting beyond Spivak's early analysis is crucial for assessing the usefulness of Deleuze and Guattari's work for the kinds of critical intervention which postcolonial theory seeks to develop. Clearing the theoretical horizon in this way allows for a much needed rapprochement between a Spivakian inflected critique of occidental thought – which is the very locus of postcolonial theory at one level – and Deleuze and Guattari's approach, which stresses the possibility of advancing an outside, not only of Eurocentric ways of thinking, but also of Eurocentric 'statism'. Such an exercise is, we think, a necessary prelude to the development of a properly postcolonial *politics* to complement the impact of theorisations that have hitherto been largely confined to the world of theory itself.

Spivak's critique of Deleuze can be broken down into five distinct claims, which we explore one at a time. The first of these is that Deleuze and Foucault covertly reintroduce the transcendent European subject by making their own position 'transparent' and by means of overly general conceptions of the subject of power and the subject of oppression. The second is that they lack a theory of ideology and, consequently, a theory of interest. The third is that they foreclose the need for counter-hegemonic ideological production and dialogue with the other, by assuming the other can speak for itself. The fourth is that their points of reference, the problems they seek to solve and the texts they refer to are entirely caught within a self-contained West or Europe. The fifth is that their refusal of constitutive contradiction reintroduces an undivided subject and is essentialist. In sum, Deleuze is guilty of erecting a 'global-local' in which a distinct form of subjectivity and logic of being in the world is rendered invisible or 'unmarked', whilst other terms are 'marked' as local or subordinate to them.

The 'Transparent' Subject

Spivak's principal claim in 'Can the Subaltern Speak?' concerns the 'transparency' of the subject. In her view, Deleuze 'restore[s] the category of the sovereign subject' (278), by which she means that in the manner of classical Western philosophy, he deploys an essentialised subject of oppression, which acts with respect to the object of a singular emancipatory project. The task of the intellectual is to allow this subject to speak, in turn making it impossible to engage with those others who do not resemble or sound like this oppressed figure. From this standpoint the unmarked intellectual claims to speak truth, revealing to the reader 'the surreptitious subject of power and desire marked by the transparency of the intellectual' (280). Deleuze is thus a 'dangerous . . . first world intellectual masquerading as the absent non-representor who lets the oppressed speak for themselves' (292), in whose work 'a postrepresentationalist vocabulary hides an essentialist agenda'(285). In short, the claim that subaltern subjects are able to represent themselves merely disguises a form of 'substitutionism' in which the intellectual elides difference in the name of a universal subject of oppression. This in turn implies Deleuze is indifferent to difference; he is oblivious to the complex forms of differentiation that cannot be encompassed within Western notions of oppression or domination. Given that many sympathisers with Deleuze feel these concerns lie at the heart of the Deleuzian enterprise, the accusation is damaging to say the least. But does it stand up?

Spivak attempts, in Lacanian fashion, to discern a 'subject of desire' in Deleuze. However Deleuze's view is not only that desire can be differentiated from subjectivity, but also that desire alone does not produce a unified subject. Desire for Deleuze is not an attribute of a desiring subject but is a matter of flows and becomings which traverse the entire social, and indeed material or ecological field. Hence, desire is not something 'possessed' by the sovereign subject but something inter-, sub- and extra-subjective. The subject, where it exists, is a product of *certain forms* of desire, but only one of the possible outcomes of what is termed 'desiring-production'. It arises from a certain kind of 'molar', 'majoritarian' or 'reactive' construction of desire which produces self-other boundaries and identities. But it arises only from this specific configuration of desire, it is a product (not producer) of desire, and its genesis is in the trapping or capture of desire and not in the kind of affirmative, free-flowing desire Deleuze and Guattari seek. As Deleuze and Guattari explain in their *Anti-Oedipus* (which Spivak largely ignores), desiring-machines are always molecular, engaged in their own assembly, and their function and formation are indiscernible from one another (1983: 1–9). On the other hand, molar machines are structurally unified: each appears as a single object or subject, and they have limited and exclusive connections and exclusions. Molar aggregates are products of paranoiac desire, engineered into existence by pitting 'packs' and 'masses' against one another (Deleuze and Guattari 1983: 286–7, 279). The molecular is taken as primary, always existing as a vibrant multitude beneath any molar formation. Hence, beneath limiting schemas and couples there are bundles of networks and radiations in all directions; '[a]n entire multiplicity rumbles under the sameness of the Idea' (Deleuze 1994: 51, 274).

Deleuze and Guattari thus reject dominant 'humanist' models of subjectivity focused on the integrity and unity of a single self, instead positing what Brian Massumi has termed the 'dividual', the divided and divisible subject of desire (Massumi 1993). Their theory of subjectivity (for whatever Spivak may say, they do have such a theory) views the modern subject as a molar outgrowth of capitalism. Indeed, they theorise that subjectivity arises from 'subjection', a specifically capitalist linguistic/representational process (distinct from earlier 'machinic enslavement'), and devote considerable space to demonstrating its mechanisms (Deleuze and Guattari 1987: 456–9; Guattari 1996: 141–7).

Nor is it clear that Deleuze and Guattari celebrate 'any desire' resisting 'any power'. Their theory, advanced over many thousands of pages, is far more nuanced than this. For instance, they distinguish between types of desire (active and reactive, 'schizophrenic' and 'paranoiac'), siding clearly with those which perform certain functions rather than others. All desires infuse the social field, but divide into two types of 'delirium' or psychological complex, the 'fascisizing [*fascisant*]' type which disinvests every 'free' figure of desire and invests central sovereignty, and the 'schizorevolutionary type or pole that follows the lines of escape of desire; breaches the wall and causes flows to move; assembles its machines and its groups-in-fusion in the enclaves or at the periphery', producing an inverse effect (Deleuze and Guattari 1983: 277). Active forces are connected to affirmative desire, and reactive forces to nihilistic desire; affirmation and negation are 'becoming-active' and 'becoming-reactive', respectively (Deleuze 1983: 54). They are locked in combat as two poles between which society vacillates. The two poles can be distinguished radically, identified respectively with the enslavement of desire by sovereignty, and its inverse, the overthrow of power (Deleuze and Guattari 1983: 260, 266).

Hence, there is not one 'subject of desire' but at least two (one a force of subjection and subjectivation and the other of deterritorialisation), the reactive/paranoiac and the active/schizoid. These could also be termed a majoritarian subject and a minoritarian becoming. Here majority and minority are not matters of relative quantity; rather, majority refers to 'the determination of a state or standard'. It necessarily 'implies a state of domination'. 'Majority implies a constant . . . serving as a standard measure' (Deleuze and Guattari 1987: 291, 105). A minoritarian force is an expression of singularity and intensity, and hence is a qualitative phenomenon, pitted against the denumerable, quantitative regime of majorities (and quantitative minorities). A minority is defined not by smallness but by its expression of the process of becoming (rather than the fixity of being), and by the gap of its situation from the majority axiom or benchmark (Deleuze and Guattari 1987: 469). By the nondenumerable, qualitative process of becoming, it threatens to destroy the very concept of majority.

One can thus see how this account intersects with Deleuzian ideas of smooth and striated space, or rhizomatic and arborescent thought, in analysing the qualities of dominant systems. The Western subject, Spivak rightly observes, is constructed by particular striations – 'strong passport', 'hard currency' – which make certain movements possible (273). This marks the Western subject very clearly as a *majoritarian* subject. Not that one needs to go via Spivak to reach this conclusion; Deleuze and Guattari have already stated it explicitly. Their analysis of becoming includes a sophisticated analysis of marked and unmarked terms, including the white male European as subject (Deleuze and Guattari 1987: 292). Spivak claims that both the figure of resistance and the figure of the intellectual in Deleuzian theory are Western and transparent. Yet in their work, these figures are defined against the majoritarian positioning of the Western subject. It therefore follows that the 'subject of [active] desire', to the extent that one emerges, is a molecular, nomadic subject who seeks to escape the striations of power – precisely the striations Spivak specifies as constitutive of the Western subject. The 'subject' (more often specified as a de-subjectified becoming or flow) must either already be a minority, or else must become-minoritarian, rejecting its majoritarian inscriptions.

Hence, the agency of the oppressed, the voice of the subaltern, is not characterised by true representation or self-presence. Rather, it concerns *original production*, an expression of the primacy of desiring-production over social production (Deleuze and Guattari 1983: 348). What is important is that the other speaks, not whether they speak 'truly' or not. Hence, Deleuze and Guattari are not really concerned with whether the voice which emerges is 'authentic' or not. They are concerned with whether, and how, the 'subaltern' is constructing its own voice – for instance, with whether the subaltern is 'speaking' so as to be added as an axiom, or is 'speaking' in a manner disruptive of processes of capture and control. And why would Deleuze be unable to imagine an 'other' subject? In fact such 'others' frequently emerge in Deleuze's work, for instance as nomad, minoritarian and so on. Radical difference as the emergence or becoming of new subjects in the plural is arguably the rationale of Deleuze and Guattari's project, certainly as it is expressed in *A Thousand Plateaus*.

Deleuze's rejection of representation also extends to the theorist, who should then speak only on her or his own behalf, and form connections and relays, not represent others. Here, the point Foucault and Deleuze seek to make is about constructing a non-representational type of relation. 'On the contrary, when people begin to speak and act on their own behalf, they do not oppose their representation (even as its reversal) to another; they do not oppose a new representativity to the false representativity of power' (211). In other words, those who resist and those who side with them precisely do *not* claim to be speaking in a truly representative voice, against the false representative voice of power. They do something entirely different, which is not about representation at all, but about flows, relays and connections. The colonial subaltern is irreducibly heterogeneous – but so are the Deleuzian figures of oppression and otherness: multiplicities, minorities, haecceities and so on.

This apparent heterogeneity contests the supposed homogeneity of the oppressed, the 'list' of equivalent subjects that Spivak accuses Deleuze of constructing. What her reading misunderstands is that Deleuzian theory aims for open space, not a specific system of categorisation. Open or smooth space is 'equivalent' in being available for use by many different people with different desires, but it does not at all render these groups equivalent or similar; indeed, their radical heterogeneity is a central claim of Deleuzian theory. If they have something 'in common', it is only in the negative sense of resisting overarching oppressive structures, which are not at all identical in all places and times, but do have certain structural isomorphisms. Deleuze and Guattari emphasise that, while states are isomorphic and realise a similar imaginary project in each case, they are not homogeneous – one of their fundamental bipolarities being between North and South (1987: 464–5). The unitary nature of the global system emerges not at the level of power but at the level of capitalism. On another level, while 'power' does not produce a unitary system in this vocabulary, certain arrangements of power and desire – as the stateform or 'Urstaat' for example – are necessarily oppressive, and engender something akin to an 'abstract interest' in resisting forms of domination in general, that is, the various reactive and molar forces in whatever forms they take, despite the irreducible multiplicity of forms which the becoming of active desire takes. Hence, power, like desire, takes active and reactive forms. This echoes Foucault's distinction between power and domination, and prefigures Holloway's 'power-over' and 'power to' (Holloway 2005). The rigid segmentarities and arborescent subordinations of capitalism and the state are deemed to be repressive to everyone, in their uniqueness and singularity, so everyone has an ultimate 'interest', at the level of active desire, in resisting – even though, one must add immediately, some have more 'interest' than others, as some are assigned to marked 'minorities' while others are not. This is a theoretical problem if one assumes some people are 'naturally' in accord with dominant majoritarian categories, or that the reactive interest-bearing subject is a universal construct. Once these dubious essentialist claims are rejected, it is not clear how it is a theoretical problem.

What about the third figure of the subject, the intellectual? Given the number of pages Deleuze and Guattari devote to defining the 'task' of schizoanalysis, philosophy, thought and so on, it is hard to maintain that the intellectual vanishes into the background or becomes transparent (see Deleuze 1994: 149–59; Deleuze and Guattari 1983: 307ff.; Deleuze and Guattari 1994: 5–42). On the contrary, they are frequently given to excursuses on the function of the intellectual, shaman, thinker, culminating in their joint work, *What is Philosophy?* (1994), which puts in play the issue of the relationship of ideas to processes of change and transformation. However, the specific function of whatever Deleuze and Guattari are trying to do in any particular text is always explicitly asserted. This entirely visible function can be generalised as the task of creating connections (hence not of representing or 'discovering' truth). It is a work of building, of *bricolage*, a 'scouring' or 'curettage' of the unconscious to clear out Oedipus and its correlates, untying the knots of the representations and territorialisations of a subject so that transversal connections and molecular flows become possible, 'undoing all the reterritorializations that transform madness into mental illness' and 'liberating the schizoid movement of deterritorialization in all the flows', 'causing the desiring-machines to start up again', introducing 'a bit of a relation to the outside', including awareness of social forces and structures beyond the family (1983: 311, 318, 321, 339, 334, 366–7). And between the two 'subjects' as Spivak calls them, between active and reactive forces, the theorist is not mere analyst, but in the act of creation becomes-minoritarian, becomes part of the construction of agency of the 'oppressed' (the minoritarian). In fact we are dealing not with two subjects but with two structures of desire, active versus reactive, and for Deleuze, the radical philosopher's desire is active and constructive. One could not be further from the 'transparent intellectual' identified in

Spivak's critique, loftily gazing down on the oppressed subject from a position of Archimedean splendour.

Theorising Ideology and Interest

The second criticism Spivak makes is that Deleuze and Foucault do not have a theory of ideology or of interest (273–4). Or to put the same point in more direct terms, they lack the Althusserian categories which construct Spivak's theory of North–South epistemological relations. This is not simply a difference of perspective. For Spivak, in order to account for micro-functioning of power one *must* move towards theories of ideology (279). A theory of ideology, in this context, means an Althusserian type of theory in which ideology expresses itself in lacunae, in what is not said, in which ideology resides in ways of living and acting rather than in thought, and in which ideological production is arranged in a rigid apparatus at an extra-subjective level. It is linked to the idea of 'sanctioned ignorance' which is Spivak's take on Althusser's lacunae (291).

For Spivak, Deleuzian theory not only fails to take the steps towards this kind of approach, but contains elements which impede it. Deleuze and Guattari's orientation to post-representational theory leads them to overlook, or dismiss, the functioning of representation (279). It is a barrier, not an enabling factor: 'The refusal of the sign-system blocks the way to a developed theory of ideology' (280). Furthermore, theories of power and desire serve to help keep the economic 'under erasure', and hence secure a new balance of hegemonic relations (280). Issues of power and desire are here more a distraction than a help; 'interest', writes Spivak, operates 'in terms of the social rather than the libidinal being' (285). This is also a political question. According to Spivak, 'without a theory of ideology', what is otherwise 'an admirable program of localized resistance . . . can lead to a dangerous utopianism' based on an 'unacknowledged privileging of the subject' (290). We should embrace representation, not only because 'post-representation' is naively complicit in the maintenance of the status quo, but also because those who cannot speak *must* be represented. Endorsing Marx, Spivak thus asserts that there can be no outside of representation, occurring as both *Vertreten* and *Darstellen*.

Contrary to Spivak's analysis, Deleuze and Guattari do have a theory of interest, though it is not articulated in the same terms as Althusser's – which is perhaps why Spivak dismisses it. They briefly articulate such a theory, although they distinguish this from their theory of desire, and largely render it secondary to this theory (1983: 343–6). They also have a theory of systematic knowledge-production by/for the status quo, expressed in ideas such as the image of thought, royal science, axiomatisation, history versus nomadology and so on (see 1987: 372–3; Deleuze 1994: 129–68). Spivak makes a crucial error in assuming that a post-representational position implies an inability or unwillingness to investigate or theorise the working of representation. Large sections of *Anti-Oedipus* and *Difference and Repetition* are devoted to exactly this question (1983: 184–92, 200–17, 240–62; 1994: Chap. 1). One could take as an example Deleuze's theory of the four 'iron collars' of identity, opposition, analogy and resemblance, and the analysis of the role of the despotic signifier as 'repressing representation' (Deleuze 1994: 262; Deleuze and Guattari 1983: 206–9). A post-representational position does not at all imply a refusal to recognise the political effects of representation. It simply entails that one deny the constitutivity and necessity of representation (distinguished for example from repetition, concept-formation, nomadology) – which is a rather different matter.

Interest does not have the centrality it does for Spivak because Deleuze and Guattari do not presume it has primary motivating force. For Althusser, 'interest' figures as a result of a direct, unmediated relationship between socio-economic positions and libidinal attachments. Following Reich, Deleuze and Guattari embrace the idea of a relationship, but deny that it is unmediated, adding the third figure of desire – socio-economic systems must obtain attachments of desire in order to function, in order to constitute 'interests'. This is an additional layering, an increased subtlety which acts as a safeguard against a too-easy 'reading-off'. And there is a specific reason in their problematic for this selection. It is of great importance to Deleuze and Guattari that people can come to desire things which are absolutely counter to their interests. '[T]hose who have an interest . . . are always of a smaller number than those whose interest, in some fashion, "is had" or represented: the class from the standpoint of praxis is infinitely less numerous or less extensive than the class taken in its theoretical determination' (1987: 344). In other words, there are more adherents of ruling-class ideology, more people who react against threats to ruling-class interests, than there are practical members of the ruling class. Desire supplants 'interest' at the heart of Deleuzo-Guattarian theory partly because of the persistence of non-self-interested attachments, as in micro-fascism (see Guattari 1984). Why, Deleuze and Guattari ask, do people in a wide range of contexts so often put the imagined antagonism with a small, often quite harmless or imaginary other, at the forefront of action and attachment, at the expense of stepping on their own 'interests' at a socio-economic level? (1983: 257)

Perhaps when it is a matter of Western fascists and anti-immigrant sentiment, one can go on pretending that there is no more at stake than 'privilege' and 'complicity', and that people are simply following their 'interests'. But this tendency to act contrary to political interests does not only emerge in Western movements – it also occurs in political Islam, autochthony in Côte d'Ivoire, ethnic chauvinism, xenophobia in South Africa . . . And is it not also true of India? Can one discuss the rise of Hindu communalism – its complicity with neoliberalism, its connections to male Brahmin power, and in spite of this its appeal to some among the worse-off, even at the expense of the left – without a theory of reactive desire which goes against interests? In a recent work addressing these various phenomena, Arjun Appadurai (2006) provides an explanation, in terms of active and reactive structures, remarkably similar to Deleuze's. In Appadurai, as in Deleuze, one finds the focus shifted from economic interests to libidinal attachments; categories of rhizomatic and arborescent (here rephrased as vertebrate and cellular) come to the fore. Can one really explain the paradoxes of such 'predatory' movements without venturing outside the field of 'interests'? When Spivak herself discusses Hindu communalism, it is noticeable that she, too, quietly replaces interest-derivation with a theory of complex symbolic motivation (304). Hence, we would argue, Deleuze's privileging of desire over interest is entirely apt.

It is also entirely possible to theorise sanctioned ignorance or lacunae from within a Deleuzian frame. That dominant systemic discourses contain lacunae is implicit in the Deleuzian rendering of Lacanian theory as a reductive depiction of neurotic or 'paranoiac' thought. To be within 'Oedipus', to be trapped without the 'little bit of the outside', is to be within 'reality' in the (negatively-loaded) Lacanian sense of a closed imaginary/symbolic construct, which is also to be within Althusserian 'ideology', a concept largely modelled after Lacan's. Where Deleuze and Guattari break with Lacan is not in the depth and complexity of his inner account of neurosis, but rather in his (or his followers') insistence that this underlying neurosis is 'necessary', 'constitutive' and ethically desirable. For Deleuze and Guattari, echoing Sahlins, lack is constituted by the dominant system, organised through social production so as to prop up a system which requires scarcity (Deleuze and Guattari 1983: 28; Sahlins 2004). They can thus import unaltered much of the explanatory structure of Lacanian or Althusserian theory, dropping simply the supplementary claims of constitutivity. Their account of 'subjection', for example, is remarkably similar to Althusserian interpellation. And isn't Deleuze's account of the 'image of thought', of the imaginary relationship of philosophy to its 'object', an exemplary parallel of Althusserian ideology-critique? (Deleuze 1994: Chap. 3, 129–67).[3]

Spivak implies that Deleuze and Guattari ignore what is unsaid, and hence also the production of the colonial system through lacunae. But Deleuze and Guattari do discuss lacunae – the way in which psychoanalysis reduces the pack to the family for instance, and the way in which nomadic invention is unthinkable for many historians (Deleuze and Guattari 1987: 38, 404–5). But why do they not deal with lacunae more often – as often, say, as Spivak does? That they do not do so explicitly more often is a function of their approach, as well as their different focus. How Deleuze deals with 'sanctioned ignorance' is to reveal the limits of what is said by speaking something 'other'. Hence, the dominant model insists on sameness, so Deleuze shows difference; the dominant model assumes arborescence, so Deleuze posits the rhizome; the dominant model assumes molar aggregates, so Deleuze points to the molecular level. One could easily show that ignorance of the rhizome (which in fact underlies everyday life) is an interested 'sanctioned ignorance' of hierarchical power, and that the 'sanctioned ignorance' of becoming-minoritarian motivates the too-easy reduction of minorities to representable categories. But Deleuze's procedure is much quicker, more abrupt, more 'cruel' – 'look, here is the other that is not spoken'. However one puts it, the notion that Deleuze disavows the complex processes underpinning representation in the name of some naive 'let the people speak' line is too absurd to let pass here. 'What is said' is itself the subject for schizo-analysis, nomadology, interrogation on the basis of active/reactive desires and so forth. Desire can be theorised, as can the subject of desire, but this alone does not necessitate representation as a *political* strategy, which of course Spivak, following Althusser and Marx (of *The Civil War in France*) before him, argues it must.

Foreclosing the Need for Counterhegemony

As a consequence of positing a near-transparent subject of oppression, Spivak further alleges that Deleuze 'foreclos[es] the necessity of the difficult task of counterhegemonic ideological production' (275) with foreclosure theorised elsewhere as the 'interested denial' of something 'present in excess' (Spivak 1990: 125–6). This position is more ambiguous than the others, since it is principally derivative. We later learn there is nothing all that bad about seeking a 'voice-consciousness' of the muted other, as long as one realises it is not 'ideology-transcendent or "fully" subjective' (297). However, for Spivak, one is ethically obliged to develop a certain kind of dialogical or communicative stance in relation to the subaltern other, to 'learn to speak to (rather than listen to or speak for) the historically muted subject of the subaltern woman' (295). This 'speaking to' appears to involve an achievement of voice. The project of unlearning is the development of the ability to speak to the subaltern other without being dismissed as a colonial missionary, and without dumbing-down. The point is also to occupy the subject-position of the other. If the subaltern can speak, then she or he ceases to be subaltern, and the idea of Spivak's praxis is to make the subaltern disappear (Spivak 1990: 56, 121, 158). She takes it as obvious that Deleuze fails to do any such thing and as such falls short of what a theorist should do.

As we have seen, Deleuze and Guattari do not assume that the 'subaltern' is a transparent subject which can automatically speak 'authentically'. Hence, there is no reason why their approach would preclude educative, therapeutic or political projects to 'counter-hegemonise' the other. Spivak's claim is easily rebutted by the discussion of the 'tasks of schizoanalysis', which are defined in terms of introducing otherness and creating new flows. This is a production of discursive otherness of an almost Freirean type. We doubt Deleuze and Guattari would be at all hostile to something like the Freirean project.[4]

The phrase Spivak uses, however, is overdetermined. 'Hegemony' has connotations from Gramsci and Laclau of a counter-power which becomes a state, a leading group or idea, or a master-signifier – all implications which go against Deleuze and Guattari's approach. So, while Deleuze and Guattari certainly have a counter-project, whether it is 'ideological' or 'counterhegemonic' is more doubtful; but in this case, the response might be: why should it be? Ideology by its very structure requires the reproduction of the lacking subject; (counter)hegemony requires the reproduction of arborescent integration. The point is rather to create alternatives which do not lead back into this same trap – to replace the 'hegemony of hegemony' with an 'affinity for affinity', in Richard Day's phrase (Day 2005).

Spivak's phrase 'speak to (not listen to or speak for)' is unclear. On a generous reading, it is a call for dialogism of a Freirean case – a communicative process in which the 'subaltern' learns to formulate a voice and the 'teacher' unlearns assumptions. One might 'earn' a voice with the subaltern by means of entering the specificity of social contexts, rejecting the urge to colonise or hegemonise. This kind of praxis is certainly not anti-Deleuzian. That people become 'submerged' and 'culturally colonised' (via overcoding, axiomatisation, the Oedipal trap and so on) is hardly alien to Deleuzian theory. To the extent that this happens, they are not so much subaltern – minoritarian – as co-opted into majoritarian forms of Being.

Deleuze and Guattari have a specific way of conceiving the relationship to the excluded, nomadic, minor other. This other is summoned forth by art and philosophy, but is disavowed by dominant reason, and for them, the point is to write *for* this other – not 'for their benefit' and not 'in their place', but 'before', as a question of becoming. 'The thinker . . . becomes Indian, and never stops becoming so – perhaps "so that" the Indian who is himself Indian becomes something else and tears himself away from his own agony' (Deleuze and Guattari 1994: 109). The procedure of allowing or enabling to speak arises for instance in the Ndembu case – at a very marginal point, among the most peripheral people in the colonial world system; here, the intellectual (the doctor or medicine-man) does not simply 'allow to speak' but performs an entire group therapy through which the 'sick' subject, the social others and the ghost of the past all 'speak' (Deleuze and Guattari 1983: 168). Such a writing-for would seem to be implicitly similar to a Freirean dialogical process, where the other 'speaking her/his own word' is the end rather than the beginning of the process, and the teacher speaks to and of this other in order to 'speak before', to put in motion the 'conscientization' of the other, its becoming-other through rejecting submersion and cultural colonisation, its formation as a distinct voice (Freire 1996). One can therefore view Freire as a node connecting Deleuze and Spivak. If Ilan Kapoor is right, key Spivakian tropes such as 'learning to learn from below' and 'unlearning one's privilege' are dialogical processes demanding a direct engagement with the subaltern, a process which is also key to Deleuze's notion of becoming-minor (Kapoor 2004: 641–2).

A Eurocentric Definition of Questions, Texts and Frameworks

A fourth accusation is that Deleuze is caught in a European way of thinking: 'Everything they read . . . is caught within the debate of the production of [the non-European] Other' (280). These authors 'buy a self-contained version of the west' (291), ignoring the effects of global imperialism on Western integration (290–1). Hence, they make claims and assumptions in general (global-local) terms which are applicable only to the West. To compound the problem, 'Deleuze and Foucault ignore both the epistemic violence of imperialism and the international division of labour' (289). In contrast, Derrida is praised for situating his questions as specifically European, as issues of European ethnocentrism – '*Not* a general problem, but a *European* problem' (293). Derrida's position is offered as a positive model in relation to which Deleuze falls short. The subaltern cannot speak within a Western framework, and hence according to Spivak, remains voiceless. According to Spivak, 'the general nonspecialist, non-academic population' of India (and the South) is inaccessible to the likes of Deleuze because the colonial episteme 'operates its silent programming function' on such people. Deleuze, says Spivak, assumes that the oppressed, if given the chance, *can speak and know their conditions*, at least in the North; but the Southern or marginal subaltern, she contends, cannot (283). Subalternity is thus a condition of inaccessibility and radical otherness that in turn escapes the clutches of anthropology and the 'human sciences'. They cannot speak and we cannot 'know' them – though of course the subaltern can be *represented*.

A cursory reading of the work of Deleuze and Guattari would confirm reference to a staggering range of non-European authors, peoples and traditions, from Ndembu doctors, Amazonian warriors and Mongolian invaders to Ibn Khaldūn, the Bantu and Hopi, the Ancient Chinese and so forth. If Deleuze and Guattari are drawing on a philosophical history, a history of ideas, it is not simply that of the Eurocentric canon. Not only does it figure the other side of European thought, the 'minor' figures (Clastres, Sahlins, Dumézil), but it also prominently figures non-European theorists, and more diffuse narratives of theoretical import refracted through anthropology and sociology. This is rather unsurprising given the emphasis in their thought on the relationship to an 'outside', on not being caught in a fantasy-frame.

However, this is not quite good enough for Spivak, who of course insists that one can remain Eurocentric while referring to non-European others, for example by reducing them to the figure of the 'native informant' or to inferior models or past stages. Against the idea of the 'native informant', Spivak insists that the indigenous other is also a theorist, philosopher and person with history, hence is just as problematic as the Western self. In Eurocentric thought, a few recurring token figures provide the intellectual with an alibi of having 'covered' certain groups. The difficulty is that the post-colonial elite has constructed itself as the colonial subject, producing epistemological violence as a by-product by identifying with the colonial regime (Spivak 1990: 66, 60–1, 102, 77). Hence, a theory that seems to avoid Eurocentrism can still fall into a trap of reproducing it.

Looking more closely at Deleuze and Guattari's work, we see that numerous examples of the centrality of non-Western concepts are offered, often juxtaposed in a manner designed to show the availability of different, that is, non-Western, ways of thinking and being in the world. So they do not merely show the existence of other ways of conceiving the world; these other ways are mobilised in support of a more general thesis that the existence of an outside of Eurocentrism has subsisted and could form the basis for a different form of being in the world. In *Difference and Repetition*, Deleuze's distinction between repetition and representation is largely drawn from Levi-Strauss study of masks (Deleuze 1994: 19–20). Hence, it is among the Native Americans that Deleuze finds an answer to the perennial critique of poststructuralism – how one can recognise constructedness and contingency without a loss of social meaning-production and comprehensibility. In *Anti-Oedipus* Deleuze and Guattari explore how indigenous peoples, suddenly invaded by flows of money, make sense of this new flow in spite of its disruptive effect on their prior codings (Deleuze and Guattari 1983: 176). They also look specifically at the effects of the superimposition of Islam onto older indigenous belief-systems in Senegal, discussing how Islamic rituals become infused with older beliefs so that the sign becomes something which one can drink (Deleuze and Guattari 1983: 206). Indigenous peoples return in *A Thousand Plateaus*, as bearers of a 'supple' segmentarity infinitely preferable to the 'rigid' segmentarities of the state and disciplinary apparatuses. It is the ethnographers' studies of indigenous segmentarities which make it possible to theorise metropolitan segmentarities also (Deleuze and Guattari 1987: 208ff.).[5] Deleuze and Guattari could here be accused of simply making use of the other to aid the self-becoming of the West, but the engagement in this case is rather more subversive, breaking down the dominant claims of Western epistemology by showing them to be based on false binaries ('only the Other is segmentary') and a privileging of rigidity. The West is here to learn from the other, but not in the modality of Western thought – rather, in the form of its collapse, its return to 'provincial' status as one among many transversal becomings.

As for the reliance on anthropology, it is hard to see how else a scholar outside an indigenous community can gain even a partial access to indigenous epistemologies and ways of life. One can thus compare Deleuze and Guattari's use of anthropology to the work of another scholar, Ranajit Guha, who in the absence of direct testimonies, turned to the colonial archive as his source on peasant insurgency. Spivak notes that for Guha the sender of the message is 'marked only as a pointer to an irretrievable consciousness', inaccessible because of colonial privilege (287). Yet this is also how Deleuze and Guattari use figures of otherness – unrepresentable, singular, one can discern the figures through whatever pointers are left – one can certainly map how they function, which is basically what Guha does of insurgents. It is interesting that in both cases, what remains once the colonial imposition is (partially) stripped away is not so much a direct voice as a structure.

Of course we are not denying here that Deleuze and Guattari could have gone further in theorising the global South, that some of their concepts may require reworking in light of peripheral phenomena they were unaware of, even that their theoretical framework needs to be constantly reassessed in terms of its responsiveness to different kinds of otherness. But we do query the notion that an affirmative conception of desire should be rejected in advance because it assumes a sovereign subject. We do not see any reason to posit the existence of such an assumption in Deleuze and Guattari's work. We are also sceptical of whether the alternative 'lackist' framework is able to handle otherness as it appears. Deleuze and Guattari may well make contingent, quantitative errors in terms of overestimating global subsumption for example; such empirical claims are easily rectified. But the more general claim that their work is pervasively Eurocentric does not stand up to close analysis.

Refusing to Accept Constitutive Antagonism and Lack

We come finally to what we believe is the crux of Spivak's objection. On this point, she is indeed right – Deleuze and Guattari reject the idea that lack or antagonism is constitutive of subjectivity and the social field. This does not, however, make them advocates of what she takes to be the only alternative, the authentic self-present subject. As we have already seen, their approach is based on *non-subjective* molecular multiplicities. Spivak's critique is thus based on a false binary – either the transparent, self-knowing subject, or the barred, Lacanian subject. Deleuze and Guattari reject the latter so they must (it is hypothesised) embrace the former. But this denies the availability of a third alternative, which is precisely what Deleuze and Guattari offer. In Deleuzian theory, there is an 'other' of the neurotic 'barred subject'. This other is the schizophrenic (or nomad, molecular becoming and so on). Yet the schizophrenic is also 'divided', cross-cut with flows, schizzes and multiple positions. In other words, Deleuze posits against the lacking divided self, not an undivided self, but a non-lacking divided self. This is not the sovereign subject of Eurocentrism, it is an entirely different kind of figure.

Spivak rehashes the divide between negative and affirmative theory – between her own preference for Lacan, Hegel and Derrida on the one hand, and the 'refusal of negation' of Deleuze, Guattari, Foucault and their forebears on the other. The philosophical stakes of this dispute are certainly real; but Spivak wishes to add extra stakes to the dispute by claiming that affirmative theory is connected to a Western model of subjectivity, a 'global-local', and is somehow unable to obtain relevance to the 'third world' or the 'subaltern'. However the insistence on negation and 'constitutive lack' is hardly a postcolonial project. Take three examples: Hegel's reduction of world history to European history, the reductionism of psychoanalysis as exposed by Fanon, or the recent 'leftist Eurocentrism' of Slavoj Žižek . What has any of them to do with the project of combating Eurocentrism? We have rehearsed elsewhere a response to this kind of theorising and its inadequacy for theorising difference, resistance and emancipation (Robinson 2005; Robinson and Tormey 2007, 2005). What Spivak adds to the wider *milieu* of 'lackist' theory is mainly the claim that the 'subaltern' specifically is affected by the 'foreclosure' of lack. But this foreclosure should not be seen as the *sine qua non* of a postcolonial approach, as is demonstrated in the work of Mbembe (2001), Appadurai (1996), Hecht and Simone (1994) and others.

This claim that the struggle against colonialism requires such an approach is tendentious. It is all very well to insist on the necessity of various dominant structures. But what if these are the same structures which render one ineffective in other ways, and/or which silence others and render them ineffective? Surely we should seek to do more than using narratives which require the 'crimes' of colonialism as supplements, hence reproducing these 'crimes'? Spivak seems to assume that colonialism can be ameliorated without destroying its basic generative structure, through a kind of slippage of the signified under the signifier. Since colonialism is arborescent, and the 'trunk' thus retains a certain rigidity relative to the rest of its construction, we seriously doubt if this is possible. If it is not, then a 'lackist' approach to colonialism simply reproduces it.

We could go further at this point, and argue that Spivak is covertly re-inserting a global-local into her theory (against the impetus of her entire project) by adopting the position of ontological lack. After all, are not Althusser, or Lacan or Derrida, also rooted in their time and place and thus elaborating yet another global-local? These approaches evince an elaboration from European conditions of a perspective, a single way of reading and seeing, which reveals partial truths but is limited by its context; it generalises itself into a global-local by positing its own universality, insisting that 'man', the 'subject', everywhere has the same structure of lack, of Oedipus. The irony is that this is precisely the line of critique pursued in the *Anti-Oedipus* which, following a wide array of commentators such as Leach, Malinowski and Reich, argues that constitutive lack is the interpellatory project of the Freudian-Lacanian analyst operating as a limit point on thinking about how human subjectivity and social relations might otherwise be configured. This is notwithstanding the wealth of alternative conceptualisations and theorisations of the 'primordial' condition many with an origin in subaltern or indigenous cosmologies. The thesis of the necessity of lack and alienation is itself part of the Western power-apparatus.

Spivak is thus working on the basis of a problematic dualism of her own. The binary of existing structures or nothing involves a 'sanctioned ignorance' of a third option, the formation of different kinds of structures – for instance, smooth instead of striated spaces. Spivak paradoxically silences the subaltern with her own refusal of the possibility of radical antagonism from outside. A Deleuzian approach stresses the possibility of creating new social relations through a 'line of flight' which moves outside existing social relations and which ultimately makes possible their elimination, dissolution, overthrow or 'counter-actualisation'. The forces which emerge in resistance to the present are not inexorably tied to it; rather, they can emerge into forces of opposition, machineries of metamorphosis which create situations of dual or fragmented power and which open possibilities of entirely new and unexplored becomings.

Conclusion

Given the limitations of space it is not possible to describe here the ways in which Deleuze and Guattari's work has been and can be developed positively in the service of a postcolonial critique. However, we hope to have established that the 'Deleuze' Spivak attacks in 'Can the Subaltern Speak?' bears very little relation to the position advanced by Deleuze in his own work. It bears even less relation to his joint work with Guattari. Far from a position that reinforces or supports an occidental or Eurocentric perspective, we find an analysis that is not only overtly hostile to the presuppositions of this perspective, but whose evidential base, points of reference and principal counterexamples are rooted in an array of subaltern, indigenous and minoritarian practices and cultures. Thus the charge that Deleuze repackages the sovereign subject under a new guise largely ignores that large proportion of *Anti-Oedipus* which is expressly designed to show how, on the contrary, the subject is dividuated through multiple flows, schizzes and machines that lack unity – and which thus have to be assembled under the dominant *socius* to create 'the subject'. The assertion that Deleuze has no theory of ideology or interests similarly ignores Deleuze and Guattari's extended examination of the function of reactive desire in creating interests which helps us analyse the means by which social structures are able to maintain themselves on the basis of 'fascistic' desire, that is, desire that is used against the subject in the interests of a ruling statist project. The derivative point that Deleuze's approach prevents a foreclosure of counterhegemonic claims ignores the extended analyses Deleuze and Guattari give of the function of art and philosophy, for example, and how such discourses foster, create, catalyse the emergence of new becomings, possibilities and futures. Spivak's accusation that Deleuze commits the sin of Eurocentricity would be more compelling coming from a theorist who is not so obviously herself influenced by the loftiest peaks of occidental thought. It is also difficult to take seriously, given that *A Thousand Plateaus* sets in motion an astonishing array of non-occidental and non-European sources and references with the express purpose of showing the many lines of flight beyond Eurocentric notions of subjectivity, space, consciousness and action.

Finally, Deleuze's refusal to accept the ontological premise of constitutive lack animating Spivak's own approach is hardly a cause for regret, as such an approach is located in a Eurocentric account of the function of language, of the constitution of subjectivity and the trajectory of social life and its antagonisms. We think it is clear that Spivak's approach, which is grounded in ontological negativity, is almost guaranteed to discount what is most at stake in a postcolonial critique: demonstrating the historicity and contingency of notions of primordial lack, antagonism and alienation, and thus the possibility of other worlds that escape the preoccupations and excesses of the narcissistic Oedipal subject. This is one of the projects (among many) that animated Deleuze and Guattari and which provides an astonishingly rich reservoir of materials for theorising difference, multiplicity and otherness, as the work of a growing array of cultural theorists illustrates. It is also a fertile source for generating political strategies in which the subaltern comes to speak and act in ways that expand the possibilities of and for the subaltern.

References

Appadurai, A. (1996), *Modernity at Large: Cultural Dimensions of Globalisation*, Minneapolis: University of Minnesota Press.
Appadurai, A. (2006), *The Fear of Small Numbers*, Durham: Duke University Press.
Day, R. (2005), *Gramsci is Dead*, London: Pluto.
Deleuze, G. (1983), *Nietzsche and Philosophy*, trans. H. Tomlinson, London: Athlone.
Deleuze, G. (1994), *Difference and Repetition*, trans. P. Patton, London: Athlone.

Deleuze, G. and F. Guattari (1983), *Anti-Oedipus: Capitalism and Schizophrenia 1*, trans. R. Hurley, M. Seem and H. R. Lane, Minneapolis: University of Minnesota Press.
Deleuze, G. and F. Guattari (1987), *A Thousand Plateaus: Capitalism and Schizophrenia 2*, trans. B. Massumi, Minneapolis: University of Minnesota Press.
Deleuze, G. and F. Guattari (1994), *What is Philosophy?*, trans. G. Burchell and H. Tomlinson, London: Verso.
Freire, P. (1996), *Pedagogy of the Oppressed*, London: Penguin.
Guattari F. (1984), 'The Micro-Politics of Fascism', in *Molecular Revolution*, London: Penguin, pp. 217–33.
Guattari, F. (1996), 'Semiological Subjection, Semiotic Enslavement', in G. Genosko (ed.), *The Guattari Reader*, Oxford: Blackwell, pp. 141–8.
Hecht, D. and M. Simone (1994), *Invisible Governance: The Art of African Micropolitics*, New York: Autonomedia.
Holland, E. (2003), 'Representation and Misrepresentation in Postcolonial Literature and Theory', *Research in African Literatures* 34 (1): 159–73.
Holloway, J. (2005), *Change the World without Taking Power: The Meaning of Revolution Today*, London: Pluto.
Kapoor, I. (2004), 'Hyper Self-Reflexive Development: Spivak on Representing the Third World "Other"', *Third World Quarterly* 25 (4): 627–47.
Massumi, B. (1993), 'Everywhere You Want to Be: Introduction to Fear', in *The Politics of Everyday Fear*, Minneapolis: University of Minnesota Press. Viewed at http://www.anu.edu.au/HRC/first_and_last/works/feareverywhere.htm
Mbembe, A. (2001), *On the Postcolony*, Berkeley: University of California Press.
Robinson, A. (2005), 'The Political Theory of Constitutive Lack: A Critique', *Theory & Event* 8 (1). Viewed at http://muse.jhu.edu/journals/theory_and_event/v008/8.1robinson.html
Robinson, A. and S. Tormey (2005), 'Horizontals, Verticals and the Conflicting Logics of Transformative Politics', in P. Hayden and C. el-Ojeili (eds), *Confronting Globalisation: Humanity, Justice and the Renewal of Politics after Postmodernism*, London: Palgrave, pp. 208–27.
Robinson, A. and S. Tormey (2007), 'Beyond Representation? A Rejoinder', *Parliamentary Affairs* 60 (1): 127–37.
Sahlins, M. (2004), *Stone Age Economics*, London: Routledge.
Spivak, G. C. (1988), 'Can the Subaltern Speak?', in C. Nelson and L. Grossberg (eds), *Marxism and the Interpretation of Culture*, Urbana: University of Illinois Press, pp. 271–313.
Spivak, G. C. (1990), *The Post-Colonial Critic*, London: Routledge.

Notes

1. All unaccompanied page references in the text are to Spivak (1988).
2. This is not to say that there is no commentary on Spivak's critique of Deleuze, merely that it rarely has as its object a direct rebuttal of Spivak's claims. So for example Eugene Holland offers an immanent critique of 'anti-Deleuzian' postcolonial theory, but limits his comments on Spivak to some robust comments in the footnotes (Holland 2003).
3. Of course, the parallel with Althusser is only partial: the critique of the imaginary construction is present in Deleuze, but the contrast with an alternative truth of 'science' possessed by the theorist is not. In a sense, therefore, Deleuze counterposes image to image (fantasmatic image to creative image), rather than image to

truth. This aside, the nature of the *critique* (as opposed to the alternative suggested) is very similar.
4. Freirean pedagogy is based on a dialogical process of 'learning with' the other by constructing an ability to 'speak one's own word' through critical literacy; it echoes both Deleuzian and Spivakian concerns. See Freire (1996).
5. That supple segmentarity is preferable is not to say that it is without its own dangers and limits.

Chapter 2
Postcolonial Theory and the Geographical Materialism of Desire

John K. Noyes

In the mid-1990s, with postcolonialism beginning to gain currency as a powerful new concept for understanding the role of culture in globalisation, a number of voices expressed their troubled response to this term and the ideas behind it. If we are to ask what the works of Gilles Deleuze might offer to the interrogation of postcolonialism and postcolonial theory, it is worth briefly following one strand of this sense of discontent with the idea of the postcolonial: the problem of its periodisation. This question concerned the temporality of the post- in postcolonialism, a temporality which, in the minds of many commentators, aimed at absolving theory of any complicity in the wrongs of colonialism, since these had purportedly been put to rest. At the same time, but in a largely disconnected debate, Deleuzian theory was being charged with a similar omission – that its conception of the subject disabled political action. In this chapter I will suggest that the errors in the charges against both theoretical fields can best be addressed via Deleuze's attempts to describe a geographical materialism of desire.

On the face of it, the temporal question in postcolonialism should have been an easy question, perhaps even a non-question. As Stuart Hall succinctly (and rhetorically) put it, the post-colonial as an epochal marker surely denotes 'the time after colonialism', where 'colonialism is defined in terms of the binary division between the colonisers and the colonised' (Hall 1996: 242). And yet, as he so pointedly goes on to show, the time of the postcolonial cannot be understood only in these terms. The postcolonial is not 'one of those periodisations based on epochal "stages"; when everything is reversed at the same moment'. The reason is that the age of the 'colonial' is 'not dead, since it lives on in its "after-effects"' (Hall 1996: 247, 248).

One reason why the postcolonial resists this simple periodisation is deeply inscribed in the Marxian tradition of the dialectic – the profound mistrust for the conceptual binaries required by the power structures of international capital. This mistrust is succinctly expressed in a letter Friedrich Engels wrote to Joseph Bloch in September 1890. Engels rails against the philosopher Paul Barth and others who accuse Marx and Engels of denying:

> any and every reaction of the political, etc., reflexes of the economic movement upon the movement itself . . . What these gentlemen all lack is dialectics. They always see only here cause, there effect. That this is a hollow abstraction, that such metaphysical polar opposites exist in the real world only during crises, while the whole vast process goes on in the form of interaction – though of very unequal forces, the economic movement being by far the strongest, most primeval, most decisive – that here everything is relative and nothing absolute – this they never begin to see. Hegel has never existed for them. (Engels 1978: 765)

This is not the place to pursue the Hegelian bent in Engels' observation, nor to ask how it might form the political unconscious of the intellectual climate out of which Deleuze's anti-Hegelianism emerged (see Noyes 2003). Instead, let us take note of the persistent attempts of Marxian and post-Marxian theory to escape simple binaries of power, for this tradition has informed the postcolonialism debates in important ways. Any attempt to define postcolonialism epochally by the transitory binaries of power is subverted in its very foundation by the Hegelian-Marxian unsettling of these binaries. This is why, in the opening paragraphs of Book 3 of *Anti-Oedipus*, Deleuze and Guattari state that 'it is correct to retrospectively understand all history in the light of capitalism, provided that the rules formulated by Marx are followed exactly' (Deleuze and Guattari 1977: 140).

There is another reason for postcolonialism's resistance to periodisation, and it has to do with what Benita Parry has called the concept's 'constant slippage' between 'significations of an historical transition, a cultural location, a discursive stance, and an epochal condition' (Parry 1997: 3). Or, as Ella Shohat writes, the post- in postcolonialism is different from that in post-modernism or post-feminism (and so on), in that it not only aspires to surpass an outmoded theoretical model; 'the "post-colonial" implies both going beyond anti-colonial nationalist theory as well as a movement beyond a specific point in history, that of colonialism and Third World nationalist struggles' (Shohat 1992: 101). Extending this line of reasoning, Anne McClintock argues that if 'post-colonial *theory* has sought to challenge the grand march of western historicism with its entourage of binaries (self-other, metropolis-colony, centre-periphery, etc.), the *term* "post-colonialism" nonetheless re-orients the globe once more around a single, binary opposition: colonial/postcolonial' (McClintock 1992: 85).

The objection that Shohat, McClintock, Parry and others bring to bear on this conceptual slippage at the heart of the postcolonial has to do mainly with their conviction that it stands in the way of any effective engagement with the political: it views the globe 'within generic abstractions voided of political nuance' (McClintock 1992: 86). Arif Dirlik goes so far as to state that 'with rare exceptions, postcolonial critics have been silent on the relationship of the idea of postcolonialism to its context in contemporary capitalism' (Dirlik 1994: 331).

Shohat, Dirlik, McClintock, Parry and others are all careful to caution against this slippage between historical description and meta-theory; and yet, the idea of postcolonialism has become so popular precisely because it will not abandon the slippery ground on which these two levels of description refuse to part ways. Stuart Hall puts it well when he observes that 'it is possible to argue that the tension between the epistemological and the chronological is not disabling but productive' (Hall 1996: 254).

In response to those who lament the political ineffectiveness (or even regressiveness) of the idea of the postcolonial, I would argue that the field of its political potential is given by this very slippage and by the tension Hall describes: by its refusal to make a sharp distinction between historical modelling of globalisation and epistemological modelling of colonial subjectivity. What is contested in both cases is the primacy of the metaphysical polar opposites of crisis. This refusal to erase the tension between the epistemological and the chronological is one of the hallmarks of Derrida's politics of deconstruction (it could also be described as a recognition that the epistemological is enabled by the enchantment of the chronological), and it is the reason why Spivak in a seminal statement of the postcolonial project insisted on the presence of Derrida in her thought (Spivak 1988).

This is where Deleuze comes in. And not simply because exactly the same criticism of political ineffectiveness has been levelled against him.[1] More important is that a careful reading of Deleuze will help to unlock the ideological nature of the very distinction on which this critique is founded. The refusal of the distinction between historical and epistemological modelling goes beyond a Foucauldian blurring of the boundaries between discursive action and the political. We can, by way of a Deleuzian reading, show how postcolonial theory attempts to realise the political implications of a materialist theory of desire by developing what I will be calling a geographical materialism of desire. A Deleuzian reading of postcolonialism's slippages reveals that, if the 'post' in postcolonialism addresses anything that might lead to a political position beyond colonialism, it is precisely the slippage it enacts. Or to put it differently, the political force of the postcolonial idea lies in its attempts to disable the global economy's easy displacement of socio-political and economic disparities into the heart of the subject.

This is the core idea behind Deleuze and Guattari's conception of desire, and enables a discussion of desire's history and its geography in light of the changing face of imperialism. Stuart Hall's question: 'When was the postcolonial?' enacts postcolonial theory's resistance to the separation of the political field from the field of historical time and the ontogenesis of the subject. In a strong reading of postcolonial theory's slippages, it performs the political work it is accused of neglecting. In the model of capitalism put forward by Deleuze and Guattari, the critical position that attempts an alternative history and an alternative geography of capitalism cannot be divorced from the critical position that has continually to re-invent and re-compose itself alongside and outside the disciplined, well-structured subject of capitalism. It is this blended critical position in flight that enables the political, which Deleuze calls the 'different politics of assemblages' (Deleuze 1993: 137).

What is the difference between a politics of assemblages and the kind of politics that is held up as a deficit in postcolonialism? While the practical difference has yet to be worked out (or perhaps is currently being worked out along the lines suggested by Antonio Negri [2008] to name but one example), the theoretical difference rests on the conceptualisation of desire, or what might be called a geographical materialism of desire.

The possibility of such a politics is propped up on Deleuze's understanding of desire. In *Anti-Oedipus*, Deleuze and Guattari begin the discussion of desire as a materiality with a revisionary reference to Kant (something they generally enjoy doing). Kant, they write, 'must be credited with effecting a critical revolution as regards the theory of desire' (1977: 25). This assessment rests on Kant's comments on desire as a productive instance in the life of the psyche. Their final analysis rejects Kant's views on desire as production for this very reason – it remains bound to the conviction that the life of the psyche is driven by negativity. What they wish to retain from Kant is the idea of desire's productivity. And they do this by underlining his understanding of desire as intimately connected to representation. Referring to the Introduction to the *Critique of Judgement*, they quote him as stating that desire possesses 'the faculty of being, through its representation, the cause of the reality of the objects of these representations' (Deleuze and Guattari 1977: 25).[2]

As Deleuze and Guattari explain in *Anti-Oedipus*, production is never organised on the basis of a lack for which subjects feel a need. The organisation of production and social production creates lack as empty spaces in the organisation of production. 'Social production is purely and simply desiring-production itself under determinate conditions' (1977: 28). And this conception of desire which produces social relations can only be understood in materialist terms. As Deleuze and Guattari emphasise, if desire produces, 'its product is real. If desire is productive, it can be productive only in the real world and can produce only reality' (1977: 26).

As Simone Bignall (2008) has pointed out, this materialist conception of desire has important consequences for a strategic political philosophy in the context of postcolonialism. This includes rethinking the unevenness in postcolonial society and asking how to effect reconciliation and redistribution according to a different understanding of what lack is and where it comes from (Bignall 2008: 138). Such a project is institutional, conceptual and practical – it is representational in the sense that a map is representational (Bignall 2008: 140; Deleuze and Guattari 1987: 13). Deleuzian desire refuses to represent the subject of lack, choosing instead to name and activate strategic links between conception, representation and action.

I think Spivak is correct to call Deleuze to account on his pronouncements on representation in his conversation with Foucault (Spivak 1988). However, it is precisely on the point of representation that I think Spivak misreads the potential of a Deleuzian politics. The materiality of desire leads not to 'the generalized ideological subject of the theorist' but to an attempt to conceptualise action beyond the dual moments of representation Spivak discusses as '*Darstellung*' and '*Vertretung*' (Spivak 1988: 273, 276–80). Political action is not a struggle of the absent and occluded subject to gain representation. If political action is to be possible, it requires political agency 'assembled' in what Deleuze and Guattari describe as a machinic manner. This agency emerges out of representational moments that refuse the dynamics of interest inscribed in representational practice. Where Spivak laments the absence of a theory of ideology in Deleuze and Guattari, they see a strategy for bypassing the representational regime of interests. Where Spivak accuses them of erasing geographical difference in evoking 'the worker', they see a potentially liberating distribution of unaffiliated (unrepresented) bodies in space. The political potential of the geographical materialism of desire lies in this conception of bodies outside the impasses of represented subjects and subjective lack. As Deleuze put it in conversation with Claire Parnet: 'Far from presupposing a subject, desire cannot be attained except at the point where someone is deprived of the power of saying "I". Far from directing itself towards an object, desire can only be reached at the point where someone no longer reaches for or grasps an object any more than he grasps himself as subject' (Deleuze and Parnet 2007: 89).

Throughout their entire project, Deleuze and Guattari grapple with the same central problem that will not leave postcolonialism alone – the place of representation in the distributions and movement of bodies in space; to engage this aspect of representation is to enable political practice under the conditions of capitalism. For the postcolonial project, this goes beyond Dirlik's laments concerning the third-world intellectual or the purported universalisation of the third world. The project of postcolonialism is a writing project, and as such it involves a shift in the understanding of representation, 'a move from one conception of difference to another' (Hall 1996: 247). This shift does not simply superimpose historiography's narrative uncertainty onto a pre-existing geographical order of the world, it implicates this uncertainty within the specific geographical order of late capitalism. Precisely for this reason, Dirlik undoes all that the writing project of postcolonialism strives for when he insists on distinguishing 'postcolonial' as 'a description of intellectuals of Third World origin . . . from postcolonial as a description of this world situation' (Dirlik 1994: 331). Responding to and refuting Dirlik, Stuart Hall calls the 'post-colonial' a 're-narrativisation' that 'displaces the "story" of capitalist modernity from its European centring to its dispersed global "peripheries"'; and, he continues, it is in the 'reconstitution of the epistemic and power/knowledge fields around the relations of globalisation, through its various historical forms, that the "periodisation" of the "post-colonial" is really challenging' (Hall 1996: 250).

Deleuze and Guattari address this reconstitution via a geographical materialism of social production in their description of the world-historical processes surrounding territorialisation, deterritorialisation and reterritorialisation. I call it a geographical materialism in the sense outlined above – a linking of thought to the spatialised materiality of its production; this is achieved not in the manner detailed by the young Marx – as a dialectic of nature and history,[3] but by spatialising received relations of bodies to the traditional arrangements of production in any one *socius,* and by recasting the temporal scale of production in such wide terms that the fundamental relationship of thought and nature (energy and material) has to be revisited (see Sellars 1999). This reconceptualisation of thought is necessary in order to bypass what Deleuze regards as the pitfalls of the dialectic – its conception as a 'relation of forces dominated by reactive bodies and a negative will to power' (Bignall 2008: 131) and its ability to reduce thought to the historical interaction of personalities constructed out of interlinked opinions.[4] The processes of territorialisation and deterritorialisation are first and foremost geographical processes linked to subject-formation. Robert Young has described them as a conceptualisation of 'the appropriation of land and its confiscation from those who have formerly worked on it, with or without legal title.' In this view, reterritorialisation describes 'the violent dynamics of the colonial or imperial propagation of economic, cultural, and social transformation of the indigenous culture, at the same time as characterizing the successful process of resistance to deterritorialization through the anti-colonial movements' (Young 2003: 52).

But it cannot stop there. While thinking of territory in geographical terms, it is important to retain the multi-dimensionality of the idea of territory in Deleuze and Guattari, a layering of ideas that allows them to tie land management and appropriation in world history to the problem of writing, and to the onto- and phylogenesis of the subject. Territory is not reducible to 'a principle of residence or of geographic distribution' (Deleuze and Guattari 1977: 145). And yet the two are relatable via a layering of materiality and abstraction. In *Anti-Oedipus*, the layering that moves between geographical territory and individuation, between world history and subjectification, looks something like this:

Layer 1: The materiality of thought. Thought is enabled by the physicality of territory, abstracting from territory's materiality and returning to that materiality. This is indicated in the pages of *Anti-Oedipus* devoted to the initial exposition of desire (1977: 22–35); and it receives a more explicit treatment in the discussion on the rhizome in the introduction to *A Thousand Plateaus*. Here, thought is said to 'lag behind nature', in a manner perhaps not dissimilar to the way Marx intended. But the consequences are very different (1987: 5). In the words of Eleanor Kaufman, the concept of the rhizome as a figure of thought forges 'linkages or connections between different systems of knowledge-formation. In this fashion, Deleuze and Guattari outline an expansive cartography of living, one that is coterminous with real time and space'(Kaufman 1998: 5). This is the principle of cartography outlined in *A Thousand Plateaus*, where the map is distinguished from the tracing on the basis of the map's orientation 'toward an experimentation in contact with the real' (1987: 12).

Layer 2: The linking of thought to territoriality and the earth demands a reconceptualisation of subjectivity. In Chapter 4 of *What is Philosophy?* (1991), entitled 'Geophilosophy', Deleuze and Guattari begin with the observation that the subject/object distinction gives 'a poor approximation of thought. Thinking is neither a line drawn between subject and object, nor a revolving of one around the other. Rather, thinking takes place in the relationship of territory and the earth' (1994: 85).

Layer 3: The narration of macro- and micro-history. In the backward and forward movement of thought's materiality, writing history becomes an engagement with the universal, and yet the cartographic writing of history requires the contact with the real to be foregrounded. This is to a large extent the problem both addressed and enacted in the chapter 'Savages, Barbarians, Civilized Men' in *Anti-Oedipus*. The chapter begins with the question: 'If the universal comes at the end – the body without organs and desiring-production – under the conditions determined by an apparently victorious capitalism, where do we find enough innocence for generating universal history?' (1977: 139). This question founds the historiography of *Capitalism and Schizophrenia*. And the initial answer is that 'universal history is not only retrospective, it is also contingent, singular, ironic, and critical' (1977: 140). It is at this point that the significance of territory is introduced in the project of writing universal history. The contingency of universal history is given by the 'primitive, savage unity of desire and production' that is the earth, or more precisely what I would call the earth-yet-to-become-territory.

Layer 4: The narration of flight. The reconceptualisation of subjectivity in terms of a geographical materialism of desire means that critical discourse becomes a matter of flight. The flight of capital from the land and its return to abstractions of land development is mirrored in the dematerialisation of desire and its rematerialisation in the body of the split subject. To narrate this process is the aim not only of Deleuze and Guattari's *Capitalism and Schizophrenia*, but of postcolonial theory. What is being narrated is how the materiality of thought relates to 'non-localizable space' (Kaufman 1998: 12). The narration of the contingent, singular, ironical, critical edifices of history is a shared project that is at once Deleuzian and postcolonial.

In describing the layers of world historical processes, the changing codification of flows, and the vicissitudes of desiring production, Deleuze and Guattari explain how subjectivity emerges from the material organisation of desire. If critical discourse is to come to terms with this changing codification, it has to view history in retrospect, and it has to follow Marx's rules. That means thought cannot reveal itself in a voice reduced to pure history or to pure nature. Marxian natural history cannot speak of nature without speaking of history, and vice versa. Capitalism's game is: ask a history question and you get a history answer, ask a nature question and you get a nature answer. This reduction is typical of what Spivak calls 'ideology at work' – it involves obscuring the polyphonic nature of the Marxian subject, only to dismiss Marx wholesale (Spivak 1982: 260).

The language in which Deleuze and Guattari frame the polyphony of Marx is an attempt to describe subjectivity outside of the dialectic of nature and history. In this language, critical discourse has to set itself up as a flight from the capitalist codification of desire. As John S. Howard observes, Deleuze believes that any attempt to return thought to the problems posed by the new world order of globalisation and to reinvest subjectivity in its contradictions

> forces a desire for the very thing that dominates and exploits us. Hence, if we are seriously and playfully to invest Deleuze and Guattari's ideas against the liquid assets of late capitalism, we must look for the interstices, for the nomad only exists in the intermezzo. So we must look for the way out – to get out is the most important thing – and we must do that by looking in-between. (Howard 1998: 115)

'Looking in-between' as an alternative to epistemological structures of late-capitalism is the strategy that inhabits the intersection between Deleuze/Guattari and postcolonialism. This is the objective of nomadology, which involves locating/tracing thought in flight from capitalism's appropriation and management of global resources, including the structuring of desire.

Deleuze had already outlined what he called a nomadic distribution in *Difference and Repetition* (1994). Here he uses the concept as an alternative model for thinking about the unity of Being, to which he opposes a 'distribution which must be called nomadic, a nomad *nomos*, without property, enclosure or measure' (1994: 36). As Deleuze clearly states in the Preface to the English translation, he considers one of the prime aims of this book 'putting into question the traditional image of thought' (1994: xiii). Nomadism enters Deleuze's critical repertoire in just this way.

This idea is carried through into his work with Guattari (Deleuze 1994: xiv). In their chapter on the war machine in *Thousand Plateaus*, Deleuze and Guattari provide a comprehensive outline of their understanding of nomadic thought, space and practices. Here, nomadism serves as a critical figure that allows them to conceptualise modes of thought opposed to the state, with its structuring of civil subjectivity around fixed territory. Over and above this, they use their comments on nomad thought to oppose a philosophy of history that sees state formation as emerging from more primitive social arrangements. In their usage, nomadology becomes a link-concept for bringing together a variety of formal and epistemological oppositions to the capitalist linkages of desire with docile bodies and the earth. Because of this, it should come as no surprise that its usefulness has been tested in the field of postcolonial theory where distinctions between the formal and the epistemological are under scrutiny. While I endorse Eugene Holland's perceptive critique of Christopher Miller, I do not agree that Deleuze and Guattari's concept of nomadism 'has had practically no impact whatsoever on the field of colonial/postcolonial and francophone studies' (Holland 2003: 165). There is a clear line of influence that brings Deleuze and Guattari's discussion of nomadism into the field of postcolonialism, beginning with Edward Said's *Culture and Imperialism* (1993) and Robert Young's *Colonial Desire* (1995). With characteristic insight, Said understood that, with the idea of nomadism, Deleuze and Guattari wanted to speak at a distance from the sociological discourses on nomadism, but at the same time, he wanted a conceptualisation of the conditions that made it possible to speak of such phenomena in philosophical language. After Said, nomadism as a linked philosophical and sociological problem has continued to occupy postcolonialism in a variety of ways.[5]

But even before the postcolonial interrogation of the relationship between docile bodies, the geographical basis of production, and the conceptualisation of desire, Deleuze had, at an early stage, sketched out their interlinkage via his discussions of nomadism, nomadology and imperialism. In his early work he makes it clear that any attempt to theorise nomadology must take this linking into account. In many respects, imperialism was the guiding idea here. It was through Nietzsche that Deleuze and Guattari had first brought nomad thought into line with anti-imperialism. In *A Thousand Plateaus* Deleuze and Guattari are quite clear in their appraisal of Nietzsche as a nomad thinker:

> To place thought in an immediate relation with the outside, with the forces of the outside, in short to make thought a war machine, is a strange undertaking whose precise procedures can be studied in Nietzsche (the aphorism for example, is very different from the maxim, for a maxim, in the republic of letters, is like an organic State act or sovereign judgement, whereas an aphorism always awaits its meaning from a new external force, a final force that must conquer or subjugate it, utilize it). (Deleuze and Guattari 1987: 377)

The proximity of this descriptive imagery to the geography of imperialism is not accidental. Nietzsche's aphorisms were a writing strategy directed against the pact between the signifier and the power that fixes its signification in acts of interpretation; and this writing strategy can be extended to the pact between the conquerors and the narrative that makes sense – makes history – of their conquest. This is apparent if we read the previous quote alongside the passage from the *Genealogy of Morals* quoted in *Anti-Oedipus*:

> They come like fate, without reason, consideration, or pretext; they appear as lightning appears, too terrible, too convincing, too sudden, too different even to be hated . . . Wherever they appear something new arises, a ruling structure that lives, in which parts and functions are delimited and coordinated, in which nothing whatever finds a place that has not first been assigned a 'meaning' in relation to the whole. (Nietzsche 1969: 17)

This passage, which Deleuze and Guattari (1977: 191–2) read as a description of the way the European conqueror appears in the new world, should serve to illustrate the intricate relationship between nomadic and imperialist formations. To be nomadic can be a writing strategy, but it carries with it a positionality, a potentiality that can only be called political. Although Nietzsche is describing the exercise of state power, the terms of his description make it clear that the state, at its fringes, assumes nomadic appearances: the perspective from which the arrival of the conqueror appears like fate is from within a social organisation whose laws and sign systems have no place for the deterritorialising activities they are about to confront.[6] If the capitalist machine works through de- and reterritorialisation, then at its fringes, or in moments of encounter, it presents a deterritorialising face whose name is, in Deleuze and Guattari's writing, nomadic.

The way Nietzsche's writing acquires the status of nomad thought in the context of imperialism was outlined in Deleuze's article 'Nomad Thought' (1985). Here he criticises the modern appropriations of Marx and Freud in the name of reterritorialising our culture's decoded flows – the same de- and recoding activity he and Guattari had, in *Anti-Oedipus*, equated with the mobility of capital in general, and imperialist capital specifically. Nietzsche's task, on the contrary, 'lies elsewhere: beyond all the codes of past, present, and future, to transmit something that does not and will not allow itself to be codified. To transmit it to a new body, to invent a body that can receive it and spill it forth; a body that would be our own, the earth's, or even something written' (Deleuze 1985: 142). Read in the context of the discussion on imperialism in *Anti-Oedipus*, this positioning of Nietzsche places him at the limits of the imperialist project of assigning territory and subjects to the state, making of them codified spaces in which capital can circulate and to which meaning and desire can accrue.

This point is clearly made when Deleuze comments on the above-quoted passage in the *Genealogy of Morals*, which he tells us is specifically about the founders of empires:

> It is true that, at the center, the rural communities are absorbed by the despot's bureaucratic machine, which includes its scribes, its priests, its functionaries. But on the periphery, these communities commence a sort of adventure. They enter into another kind of unit, this time a nomadic association, a nomadic war machine, and they begin to decodify instead of allowing themselves to become overcodified. Whole groups depart; they become nomads. Archaeologists have led us to conceive of this nomadism not as a primary state, but as an adventure suddenly embarked upon by sedentary groups impelled by the attraction of movement, of what lies outside. The nomad and his war machine oppose the despot with his administrative machine: an extrinsic nomadic unit as opposed to an intrinsic despotic unit. And yet, the societies are correlative, interrelated; the despot's purpose will be to integrate, to internalise the nomadic war machine, while that of the nomad will be to invent an administration for the newly conquered empire. They ceaselessly oppose one another – to the point where they become confused with one another'. (Deleuze 1985: 148)

The dynamics of nomadism Deleuze is describing force us to rethink not only what happens in revolutionary philosophy (which is how Deleuze saw Nietzsche in 1973), but also what happens in imperialism. And it allows us to understand revolutionary philosophy and the resistance to imperialism as part of the same dynamics. The problem of postcolonial theory as I outlined it at the beginning of this paper is the problem of nomadology – postcolonialism and nomadology both conceptualise subjectivity in terms of a dynamic (in the sense of an unfolding in time and space) geographical materialism. Representations of subjectivity become the central point of contest, and the material conception of desire comes to hinge on questions of mobility. The task of critical discourse itself is then to theorise the limits of agency in terms of the movements of bodies in the material field of the global economy. The challenge facing critical discourse is one of mapping, of representing the indistinct and changing configurations of human action at the fringes of empire, without reducing them to pre-determined figures of subjectivity. There are three points to be made here, and they provide a transition back to the essential problem of postcolonial theory:

1. Nomadology resists the integration of nomadism into a philosophy of history that sees it as a primitive forerunner to the state. Deleuze mentions archaeology as bearing witness to this process.
2. Consequently, as I have pointed out above, nomadism, nomad thought and nomadology only become meaningful and useful in the sense Deleuze and Guattari employ them if we understand them as material products and by-products of, but also strategies of resistance to the expansion of capital.
3. Understood in this sense, the ceaseless opposition and confusion Deleuze speaks of between nomadism and the state must be taken seriously. Nomadism forces us to reconsider the dualisms that are generally employed to describe the conflicts arising from the expansion of capital, whether these be coloniser/colonised, labour/capital, man/woman, black/white, or any of the other pairs of opposites whose binary opposition have increasingly come under attack in postcolonial theory.

Nietzsche's nomad philosophy is a necessary response to a state system that produces nomadic expansions, thereby unsettling stable economies, only in order to reintegrate them into its own global order. His thought can be regarded as nomad in the sense intended by Deleuze, since it accepts the challenge of modernity's destabilisation of systems (the Death of God), while asking us to draw the full consequences from this process. These consequences involve

> grappling with exterior forces instead of being gathered up in an interior form, operating by relays instead of forming an image; an event-thought, a haecceity, instead of a subject-thought, a problem-thought instead of an essence thought or theorem; a thought that appeals to a people instead of taking itself for a government ministry. (Deleuze and Guattari 1987: 378)

Deleuze's reading of Nietzsche is able to claim Nietzsche's thought as nomad, but not because it follows figurative paths that depart metaphorically from the state's teleologies of power. Nietzsche's thought is nomad because it is produced in the same dynamics that have given rise to nomadic lifestyles, and it does exactly the same thing as these lifestyles. It acts out the impossibility of those boundaries and traditions which capital transgresses and renders obsolete. But unlike capital, Nietzsche's thought refuses to settle on the redrawn boundaries or invented traditions that are so important both in imperialism and in the history of philosophy.

If we believe Deleuze and Guattari, one important dimension of Nietzsche's exteriorisation of thought is that it attempts to mobilise an alternative vision of collectivity, tribe, or race from the one that was current when he was writing. The fact that his comments on the blond beast were so easily incorporated into a racist and fascist ideology is probably what prompts Deleuze and Guattari in their discussion of nomad thought to pose the question: 'What can be done to prevent the theme of race from turning into a racism, a dominant and all-encompassing fascism, or into a sect and a folklore, microfascisms?' (Deleuze and Guattari 1987: 379). This is a question of writing, and it addresses the moment where writing becomes political.

Deleuze and Guattari's use of nomadism as a figure for a certain relationship of critical thought to the activities of the state and the movements of capital found widespread resonance in the 1980s and 1990s, at the very moment when the tenets of postcolonial theory were being set. Its reception was not always in line with the intentions of postcolonialism, but there seems to have emerged at this time a general willingness to consider a geography of mobility in opposition to systemic structures of thought – and a widespread identification of these systemic structures with political oppression, the state and the law. In some cases, this use of the idea of the nomad was evoked in apparent opposition to what Deleuze and Guattari intended. But in spite of the different political uses of the idea, it began to appear as a powerful figure, a constellation of ideas with great political promise.[7]

Nomadism, it seems, can serve to highlight the dualities that have structured our world since the onset of capitalist modernity as produced and not found concepts, since it allows us a way of thinking about the unity that renders these dualities functional. In other words, nomadism can be a useful concept for a historiography that unravels the production of nature, the production of space and their attendant ideologies in capitalism – provided, as Eugene Holland emphasises, we understand it for what it is, a conceptualisation and not a description (Holland 2003: 164). It is this aspect of nomadism that has the greatest potential in the context of postcolonialism, provided Holland's point is foregrounded.

Michael Hardt and Antonio Negri have evoked Deleuze and Guattari's figure of nomadism in order to propose a global response on the part of critical theory to the universalising moves of an international system marked by imperialism. In this system, they argue, the traditional critical response – 'opening the dialectic between inside and outside [of capital]' – is no longer an option (Hardt and Negri 2000: 210). This dialectic was previously enabled by the position of the proletariat both inside and outside of capital, and thus deserving of the title the 'nomads of the capitalist world' (Hardt and Negri 2000: 217). However, the global world order renders this untenable as a basis of theorising resistance. This placelessness of critical theory forces what Hardt and Negri call 'counter-Empire' to look to alternative critical models, such as nomadism. Unlike Said, they are anxious to extend this model in the direction of lifestyle-change, including reconceptualisations of 'the human'. This brings them closer to Deleuze and Guattari's formulation of critique as an all-encompassing attack on unitary subjectivity. The universality of empire requires a universal – or at least a global – response. In Hardt and Negri's adoption of nomadism, this attack on the humanist subject enters into a certain tension with the claim that 'the mobile multitude must achieve a global citizenship' (Hardt and Negri 2000: 361). It is in the latter respect that the nomad ceases to stand in for the breakdown of the unitary subject but, in their words is aligned with 'the postcolonial hero [as] the one who continually transgresses territorial and racial boundaries'. This conception of nomadism sees the 'new nomadic singularity' as 'the most creative force [of the modern state]' – a force ultimately destined to lead to its destruction (Hardt and Negri 2000: 363).

These examples – and there are many more that could be quoted – all show how nomadism comes to function as a critical model in contemporary academic discourse. But what does it mean to adopt the figure of the nomad in this way? How do we take a lifestyle, a socio-economic regime, a mode of production as a model for critical thought? In short, what does it involve to move from nomadism to nomadology? We can only understand this move if we understand that it attempts to follow Nietzsche in bypassing and disabling the pact between signification, subjectivity and the power formations of capital.

This is why, in preparing their discussion of nomadology, Deleuze and Guattari are careful to show that they are not talking in metaphors. Desiring machines are machines. No metaphor. This is one of the founding premises of *Anti-Oedipus*, and it carries through the entire corpus of *Capitalism and Schizophrenia* in important, if not always explicit, ways. Put broadly, the anti-metaphorical direction in their argument is a development of Nietzsche's reaction to idealist philosophy's founding dualism of subject-object, expressed by Kant in terms of reason and understanding, by Schelling as the split between nature and freedom, by Fichte as the positing of the self. Seen in this light, the materialism invoked by Deleuze and Guattari in opposition to idealism is a continuation of the empiricist project of the counter-Enlightenment.

Deleuze and Guattari develop their discussion of subjectivity in capitalism via a political economy and a philosophy of history that are at all times related to a materialism of desire (see Donzelot 1972: 30, 36).

The materialism of desire is one of their principal conceptual tools for dismantling idealist dualisms. Consequently, if we are to appreciate the significance of nomadology within their thought, we will have to grasp it not as a metaphor, but as a materialism – perhaps even a positivism – with specific historical and economic co-ordinates. In other words, it is not good enough to make a distinction between nomadic lifestyles, intellectual migration, the political economy of nomadism and nomadic figures of thought. Nomadology must ask what allows philosophy to take the step from the historical condition and status of nomads in Western culture to the discussions surrounding textual nomadism in the Western academy today. And it must be done in a manner that does not simply take the word nomad as a loose metaphor for crossing conceptual boundaries.

In *A Thousand Plateaus*, Deleuze and Guattari do this by examining both the incorporation of nomadic modes into capitalist production and the nomadic opposition to capitalism. What is important here is that capitalism relies on the production of nomadic lifestyles, just as it relies on the reintegration of these lifestyles into its own modes of production. This is one aspect of what Deleuze and Guattari refer to in *Anti-Oedipus* as capitalism's de- and reterritorialising activity. The way the expansion of capital produces nomadism as a lifestyle both integrative and oppositional to the state is clear if we examine the production of nomadism in colonialism. This in turn allows us to understand the *concept* of nomadism as a product of the expansion of capital. The intimate connection between capitalism's production of nomadism and its production of the concept of nomadism is vital to an understanding of what Deleuze and Guattari see as the potential of nomadology for resistance to ideology. If we take this idea seriously, then nomad thought is indeed dependent on the politics of nomadism. But what can this mean in the late-capitalist world?

When capitalism produced nomadism in the age of empire, it produced it not only as a physical survival strategy, but also as a mode of critical thought. The widespread academic fascination with nomadism that began in the late nineteenth and early twentieth century was indicative of the seduction and provocation that a civilisation in crisis experienced when confronting its limits, and it remains so to this day. The spatial order of capital accumulation that emerged in the Middle Ages was, as Henri Lefebvre has argued, a secularised space that depended for its stability on a 'revival of the Logos and the Cosmos, principles which were able to subordinate the "world" with its underground forces. Along with the Logos and logic, the Law too was re-established' (Lefebvre 1991: 263).

Alongside this ordered, logical space in which capital accumulation was facilitated, there emerged a certain way of conceptualising the spaces and spatial practices that could not be accommodated within the new world order. Lefebvre speaks of 'the dimming of the "world" of shadows', which was 'transformed into "heterotopical" places, places of sorcery and madness, places inhabited by demonic forces – places which were fascinating but tabooed' (Lefebvre 1991: 263). The non-accumulating force of nomadic subsistence which this capitalist restructuring of space produced at the limits of the civilised world was at the same time produced as a world of magic and irrationality. And it was produced as the limit to which philosophy turned time and again to try to conceptualise the structures of thought that might succeed in escaping the logic of capitalism. The secularised network of Logos, Cosmos and Law in the service of capital accumulation thus became responsible for the production of the night side of nature, the dark side of knowledge, whose anti-Enlightenment appeal has been resurrected time and again since the emergence of capitalist space.

To return to the complaint that postcolonial theory is driven by migration of individuals to the first world academy: the move from nomadism to nomadology indeed follows the vicissitudes of intellectual mobility today, and it does so in ways that are important to theory-formation in the academy. To divorce critical theories from this mobility reduces the theoretical figure of nomadism to a metaphor for various interdisciplinary practices and for the reflexive rhetorical strategies these practices need in order to establish shifting subject positions in the critical act. These strategies and practices are certainly worth discussing, but to call them nomadic is misleading, and disregards the materialism intended by Deleuze and Guattari. It assumes that a wilful act of criticism can be divorced from its institutional fixity simply by applying a metaphor of rhetorical or mental mobility. If critical practices are to be described as nomadic, we need to specify where the subjective mobility in such acts lies, how it relates to the institutions in which the practices occur, and how subjective mobility and institutional fixity relate to the mobility of capital.

Nomadology's specificity is given by its relationship to the current configuration of international capital in defining intellectual labour. The nomadism of the academic labour market is of the same order as the brand of nomadism that began to appear in response to the expansion of capital in the age of empire; a strategy in a world where the specific training requirements of multinational corporations and governments render the marketability of university education increasingly insignificant. This is the case not only in the humanities, where it is probably most pronounced, but also in the sciences. And if it is a major source of concern in academic circles in the post-industrial West,[8] then it has reached crisis proportions in the underdeveloped world.

As a consequence, academics need to adopt a high degree of mobility, both within the nations of the West, and (for those fortunate enough to be able to market their skills in this manner) from the third world to the first (and back again, sometimes). This mobility is automatically sedimented in the theoretical models employed in the humanities. Dirlik is right: the story of postcolonial theory is to a large extent the success story of mobile academic careers transformed into a vibrant and highly marketable yet critically reflexive theory.

Given the extreme plight of the victims of forced mobility in our age, it sounds cynical in the extreme to compare the mobility of the international academic job market to what Edward Said calls 'the uncountable masses for whom UN agencies have been created, or refugees without urbanity, with only ration cards and agency numbers' (Said 1984: 50). And yet, we cannot understand the theoretical issues at stake in nomadology unless we recognise that rhetorical figures of mobility and mobile lifestyles in the widest sense are both responses to the same global economic processes. The theoretical vogue for nomadism, like the nomadic fates of refugees, is a lingering consequence of the expansion of capital and the accompanying phenomenon of uneven development. This does not mean that the achievements of the mobile theorists of postcolonialism can be dismissed as the success stories of travellers who have escaped the plight of their own class, resorting to a kind of bad faith in their theorising of a predicament they no longer share (Dirlik's criticism is moving in this direction). On the contrary, in postcolonial theory the difference between thought and experience persists in the integration of mobility into a theoretical apparatus founded on difference – or to put it in other terms, an apparatus that attempts to resist reterritorialisation. To understand postcolonial theory as a nomadological project means to situate it within a specific tradition of critical thought – the Enlightenment critique of the rationality of expanding capital.

The experience of uneven development and the expansion of capital provide current debates in academia with a practicality that underscores the strategic value of theory. And it allows the nomadic lifestyles that capitalism produces to be grasped as strategic responses that would, given the requisite mechanisms of articulation, produce eloquent, complex and valuable theoretical models. The project of postcolonial theory, read through the lens of Deleuze's geographical materialism of desire, emerges as a project in pursuit of and as a supplement to these mechanisms of articulation.

References

Bennington, G. (1994), *Legislations: The Politics of Deconstruction*, New York: Verso.
Benterrak, K., S. Muecke and P. Roe (1984), *Reading the Country: Introduction to Nomadology* Liverpool: Liverpool University Press.
Bignall, S. (2008), 'Postcolonial Agency and Poststructuralist Thought: Deleuze and Foucault on Desire and Power,' *Angelaki* 13 (1): 127–49.
Deleuze, G. (1985), 'Nomad Thought', in D. B. Allison (ed.), *The New Nietzsche: Contemporary Styles of Interpretation*, Cambridge: MIT Press.
Deleuze, G. (1993), *The Deleuze Reader*, ed. C. V. Boundas, New York: Columbia University Press.
Deleuze, G. (1994), *Difference and Repetition*, trans. P. Patton, New York: Columbia University Press.
Deleuze, G. and F. Guattari (1977), *Anti-Oedipus. Capitalism and Schizophrenia*, trans. R. Hurley, M. Seem and H. R. Lane, New York: Viking.
Deleuze G. and F. Guattari (1987), *A Thousand Plateaus: Capitalism and Schizophrenia*, trans. B. Massumi, Minneapolis: University of Minnesota Press.
Deleuze G. and F. Guattari (1994), *What is Philosophy?*, trans. H. Tomlinson, New York: Columbia University Press.
Deleuze G. and C. Parnet (2007), *Dialogues II*, trans. H. Tomlinson and B. Habberjam, New York: Columbia University Press.
Derrida J. (1967), *L'Écriture et la différance*, Paris: Seuil.
Dirlik, A. (1994), 'The Postcolonial Aura: Third World Criticism in the Age of Global Capitalism', *Critical Inquiry* 20: 328–56.
Donzelot, J. (1972), 'An Antisociology', *Semiotext(e)* 2 (3): 27–44.
Engels, F. (1978), 'Letter to Joseph Bloch, 21–2 September 1890', in Robert C. Tucker (ed.), *The Marx-Engels Reader*, New York and London: W. W. Norton, pp. 764–6.
Graff, G. et al. (1997), 'Today, Tomorrow: The Intellectual in the Academy and in Society', *PMLA* 112 (5): 1132–41.
Hall, S. (1996), 'When was "The Post-Colonial"? Thinking at the Limit', in I. Chambers and L. Urti (eds), *The Postcolonial Question: Common Skies, Divided Horizons*, London and New York: Routledge, pp. 242–60.
Hardt M. and A. Negri (2000), *Empire*, Cambridge: Harvard University Press.
Holland, E. W. (2003), 'Representation and Misrepresentation in Postcolonial Literature and Theory', *Research in African Literatures* 34 (1): 159–73.
Howard, J. S. (1998), 'Subjectivity and Space. Deleuze and Guattari's BwO in the New World Order', in E. Kaufman (ed.), *Deleuze & Guattari: New Mappings in Politics, Philosophy, and Culture*, Minneapolis: University of Minnesota Press, pp. 112–26.
Kant, I. (1996), *Critique of Practical Reason* in *Practical Philosophy*, trans. and ed. by Mary J. Gregor, Cambridge: Cambridge University Press.
Kaufman, E. (1998), 'Introduction', in E. Kaufman (ed.) *Deleuze & Guattari: New Mappings in Politics, Philosophy, and Culture*, Minneapolis: University of Minnesota Press.
Lefebvre, H. (1991), *The Production of Space*, trans. D. Nicholson-Smith, London: Blackwood.

Lotringer, S. (1987), 'Forget Baudrillard,' in J. Baudrillard, *Forget Foucault*, trans. Nicole Dufresne, Phil Beitchman, Lee Hildreth and Mark Polizzotti, New York: Semiotext[e], pp. 65–137.
Lowe, L. (1993), 'Literary Nomadics in Francophone Allegories of Postcolonialism: Pham Van Ky and Tahar Ben Jelloun', *Yale French Studies* 82: 43–61.
Marx, K. (1959), *Economic and Philosophic Manuscripts of 1844*, trans. M. Mulligan, Moscow: Progress Publishers.
McClintock, A. (1992), 'The Angel of Progress: Pitfalls of the Term "Post-Colonialism"', *Social Text* 31 (32): 84–98.
Mignolo, W. D. (2000), 'The Role of the Humanities in the Corporate University', *PMLA* 115 (5): 1238–45.
Negri, A. (2008), *Goodbye Mr Socialism*, New York: Seven Stories Press.
Nietzsche, F. (1969), *On the Genealogy of Morals*, vol. 2, New York: Random House.
Noyes, J. K. (2003), 'Hegel and the Fate of the Dialectic After Empire', OPEN SEMIOTICS RESOURCE CENTER Virtual Symposia, Semioticon.com. Viewed at http://www.semioticon.com/virtuals/postcolonialism_2/Noyes%20Hegel.htm
Noyes, J. K. (ed.) (2004), 'Special Issue: Nomadism, Nomadology, Empire', *Interventions* 6 (2).
Parry, B. (1997), 'The Postcolonial: Conceptual Category or Chimera?', *Yearbook of English Studies* 27: 3–21.
Patton, P. (1988), 'Marxism and Beyond: Strategies of Reterritorialization,' in C. Nelson and L. Grossberg (eds), *Marxism and the Interpretation of Culture*, London: Macmillan, pp. 123–38.
Patton, P. (1996), *Deleuze: A Critical Reader*, Oxford: Blackwell.
Patton, P. (2000), *Deleuze and the Political*, London and New York: Routledge.
Said, E. (1984), 'The Mind of Winter: Reflections on Life in Exile', *Harpers Magazine* 161: 49.
Said, E. (1993), *Culture and Imperialism*, London: Chatto and Windus.
Sellars, J. (1999), 'The Point of View of the Cosmos: Deleuze, Romanticism, Stoicism', *Pli* 8: 1–24.
Shohat, E. (1992), 'Notes on the "Post-Colonial"', *Social Text* 31 (32): 99–113.
Spivak, G. C. (1982), 'The Politics of Interpretations', *Critical Inquiry* 9 (1): 259–78.
Spivak, G. C. (1988), 'Can the Subaltern Speak?', in C. Nelson and L. Grossberg (eds), *Marxism and the Interpretation of Culture*, New York: MacMillan, pp. 271–313.
Todorov, T. (1984), *The Conquest of America: The Question of the Other*, trans. R. Howard, New York: Harper and Row.
Wuthnow, J. (2002), 'Deleuze in the Postcolonial: On Nomads and Indigenous Politics', *Feminist Theory* 3 (2): 183–200.
Young, R. (1995), *Colonial Desire: Hybridity in Theory, Culture and Race*, London: Routledge.
Young, R. (2003), *Postcolonialism. A Very Short Introduction*, Oxford: Oxford University Press.

Notes

1. Julie Wuthnow (2002: 183) goes so far as to claim that 'Deleuze's deconstruction of coherent and self-identical subjectivity through this concept disallows the possibility of effective indigenous politics through its lack of accountability to a "politics of location", its implicit reproduction of a universalized western subject, and its delegitimation of "experience" and "local knowledge"'.

2. In this passage, Kant himself is quoting his own formulation in the *Critique of Practical Reason*, which states:

   'Life is the faculty of a being to act in accordance with laws of the faculty of desire. The **faculty of desire** is a being's *faculty to be by means of its representations the cause of the reality of the objects of these representations*. Pleasure is the *representation of the agreement of an object or of an action with the* subjective *conditions of life*, i.e., with the faculty of the *causality of a representation with respect to the reality of its object* (or with respect to the determination of the powers of the subject to action in order to produce the object) (Kant 1996: 144).

   This passage is intended to clear up any misunderstanding concerning the definition of concepts that Kant has, he tells us, borrowed from psychology.
3. Marx sets out his ideas on nature and history in the third manuscript of the *Economic and Philosophic Manuscripts of 1844*. It would also seem that Deleuze derives his concept of the body without organs from a reading of these pages.
4. 'The dialectic claims to discover a specifically philosophical discursiveness, but it can only do this by linking opinions together' (Deleuze and Guattari 1994: 80; see also 147).
5. See for example the multi-faceted work of Paul Patton (e.g. 1996; 2000). See also Krim Benterrak, Stephen Muecke and Paddy Roe, *Reading the Country: Introduction to Nomadology* (1984); and the Special Edition of *Interventions* on 'Nomadism, Nomadology, Empire', edited by John K. Noyes (2004).
6. Tzvetan Todorov makes this argument convincingly with reference to Cortés's conquest of the Inca Empire in *The Conquest of America* (1984)
7. See for example Sylvère Lotringer's comments interviewing Jean Baudrillard (1987); Geoffrey Bennington (1994); Jacques Derrida (1967); Lisa Lowe (1993); and Paul Patton (1988).
8. This has been dealt with extensively in the *Publications of the Modern Languages Association of America (PMLA)*. See for example volume 117 (3) (2002), which addresses the problem that 'there is no longer a consensus on the object of literary studies or on the justifications for pursuing this field as an intellectual object' (401); Walter D. Mignolo (2000); the collected position statements of Gerald Graff, Dominick Lacapra, Bruce Robbins, Joseph O. Aimone, Bryan C. Short, J. Hillis Miller, Ihab Hassan, Walter D. Mignolo (1997); and so on.

Chapter 3
Postcolonial Visibilities: Questions Inspired by Deleuze's Method

Rey Chow

> Foucault is uniquely akin to contemporary film. (Deleuze 1988: 65)

> It is a paradox of contemporary image consumption that exactly at the point when domestic television viewing is moving towards high definition and high resolution, audiences are moving towards arguably the most popular new media phenomenon, YouTube, which presents the lowest definition, lowest resolution images and yet attracts a larger audience among younger age groups because of its user-generated content. It is precisely the 'low-res' look of YouTube clips which allows us to say that the visual is problematised in this sphere, since every subject is abstracted by the rate of compression, and every clip becomes a kind of quotation, either by being sourced from previously existing material and re-presented or, in the case of original material, simply by being uploaded into a stream of pre-existing material. (Grace 2007: 470)

Judging from the regularity with which events of captivity and detention occur on the international political stage, it would hardly be an exaggeration to say that the theme of confinement, a hallmark of Michel Foucault's works from *Madness and Civilisation* (1965, 1967) and *The Birth of the Clinic* (1973) to *Discipline and Punish* (1977), has lost none of its critical relevance at the beginning of the twenty-first century. Indeed, in so many ways, the post 9/11 global scene only seems a fantastical set of demonstrations of Foucault's arguments about the omnipresent and omnipotent reach of technological-cum-ideological surveillance under the guises of our neo-liberal society. Events such as 'Guantánamo' (where potentially innocent men suspected of complicity with terrorist activities are held outside US jurisdiction so as to render unnecessary US citizens' normal access to proper legal representation) and 'Abu Ghraib' (the prison in Baghdad where Iraqi inmates were subjected to physical torture and sexual abuse by US military personnel for purposes of one-upmanship and entertainment), among others, have arguably raised the question of confinement and its implications to an order of significance that goes beyond Foucault's original frames of reference.

Foucault's interest in confinement, we remember, has less to do with the cultural, ethnic and religious conflicts that tend to shape contemporary scenarios like Guantánamo and Abu Ghraib than with his dissection of the historical trajectory by which post-Enlightenment European society organised human social conduct into various generative grids of rationality. Key to this historical trajectory is the close relation established between confinement and visibility, in the sense that the experientially negative phenomenon of being captured and segregated (as in the paradigmatic case of being locked up in prison) was increasingly associated by Foucault not with darkness but rather with the functioning of light – that is, with being turned into a site of institutional and social visibility. Beginning with his massive study of madness (*déraison*; literally, de-reason) – a boundless, excessive, undialectical condition of being, gradually delineated as (and disappearing in) the palpable, reduced state of 'mental disorder', which in turn necessitates collaborative management and control by the network of apparatuses such as clinics, hospitals, psychoanalysis, the police and the prison – Foucault's analyses of confinement and visibility remain most memorable in a work such as *Discipline and Punish*, not least because of its famous reference to Jeremy Bentham's Panopticon as a summary image of the architectural imagination involved in subjugation as a science. Equally thought-provoking is Foucault's emphasis on the discursive linkages between the physically violent acts of arrest and detention, on the one hand, and, on the other, the range of gentle coercions applied on the bodies and souls of prisoners in the form of lenient pedagogy, physical exercise, confession and other types of regulatory, corrective practices.

Foucault's eloquent account of the logistics of confinement and visibility, in other words, is consistent with his theorisation of the way power functions: much more than the prohibitive or censorious features of surveillance and punishment, it is the enabling, generative dimensions of soul making/reformation that turn modern incarceration into such an efficient, cost-effective space/time of social control. In so far as confinement and visibility may be thought of as one of modern society's largest systems of life management, geared toward updating, renovating and improving, rather than simply erasing or annihilating the human being as such in the aftermath of crime, Foucault's work on clinics and prisons is deeply resonant with the logics of his other writings on sexuality, governmentality and biopolitics.

At the same time, this work on clinics and prisons also accentuates the increasingly complex relation between the realms of words and of things, the sayable and the visible.[1] As Foucault demonstrates in works such as *The Archaeology of Knowledge* (1972) and *The Order of Things* (1970), with the progressively widening chasm between words and things, visibility can no longer be treated as the secure opposite of what is hidden or as the simple unveiling of data that can be accessed similarly in (or that share a resemblance with) words. Rather, visibility is now caught up in the shifting relations of political sovereignty and in the discontinuities among different representational orders, which constitute the human sciences and the concept of 'man' that emerges interstitially in their midst. For Foucault, who always emphasised the historical contingency (as opposed to the naturalness) of this state of affairs, visibility is ultimately about the finitude of 'man'.

Deleuze's Foucault

In the context of postcolonial studies, one type of criticism made from time to time of Foucault's work is that it is Eurocentric – namely, that Foucault has paid scant attention to cultures and histories of the formerly colonised, non-European worlds. The point of such criticism can be compelling: if the multifarious social, ideological coercions accompanying Europe's arrival at modern rationalism can be demonstrated by Foucault in such copious detail, is not his relative silence on how such coercions were exercised in Europe's colonies, during exactly the same period when the institutions he studied became consolidated within Europe, indefensible?

The interrogation of Foucault's tendency to focus on Europe proper should obviously not go unheeded, but the criticism of his work on the basis of its subject matter also (if inadvertently) highlights the question of visibility in a specific sense. Translated into the problematic of visibility, the possible complaint about Foucault just mentioned is that he is only allowing institutions inside Europe the privilege of being 'seen' and discussed. Visibility in this case is understood as something to be achieved, like power, hegemony, status and authority. In this politicised but abstract sense, visibility is less a matter of becoming physically visible than a matter of attaining discursive attention and recognition, of which being visible simply serves as a metaphor. The underlying assumption is that visibility is a stand-in for something other than itself, namely, attention and recognition, which everyone wants but few people get. Therefore, it follows, it would be necessary to challenge those who have acquired more 'visibility' than others *and* those who seem to bestow 'visibility' on select parts of the world at the expense of others.

Pursued in these metaphorical terms, visibility has much more to do with the ethical concerns of distributive fairness, equality and justice than with the sensorial event of seeing. In such an alignment, importantly, the visible tends to be considered as still continuous and equitable to, or analogous with, the non-visible – with verbal language, in particular: what you 'see' *is* (or is like) what you speak about.

For Foucault, however, visibility is precisely no longer to be assumed as continuous or equitable with verbal language, but should be understood as a realm that has become irreducible to the order of articulation that is words, statements and the sayable. In Deleuze's reading of Foucault, accordingly, it is this irreducibility of the visible that comes to the fore, though Deleuze does not understand such irreducibility in terms of an innate quality or specificity based on the human sensorium. As Deleuze states it, 'Visibilities are not defined by sight but are complexes of actions and passions, actions and reactions, multisensorial complexes, which emerge into the light of day' (Deleuze 1988: 59). That is to say: the singularity of visibilities needs to be grasped, paradoxically, in the 'multisensorial complexes' that constitute them, and it would be a simplification to attribute to them any clearly demarcated origins or individual agents.

Deleuze takes pains to demonstrate how visibilities are often disjointed from non-visibilities, and that it is such disjunction that Foucault attempted to explore in his writings: 'Between the visible and the articulable a gap or disjunction opens up', Deleuze writes, adding:

> but this disjunction of forms is the place – or 'non-place', as Foucault puts it – where the informal diagram is swallowed up and becomes embodied instead in two different directions that are necessarily divergent and irreducible. The concrete assemblages are therefore opened up by *a crack* that determines how the abstract machine performs. (Deleuze 1988: 38; emphasis added)

Deleuze's difficult language of 'informal diagram' and 'abstract machine' aside, his point is clearly that the discontinuity between the visible and articulable is the crux of the matter here.

Meanwhile, this 'gap', 'disjunction' or 'crack' between the orders of the visible and the sayable is at once a limit and (in our contemporary language) a kind of virtual connectivity that exceeds the readily perceptible, empirical dimension. With characteristically imaginative turns of thinking, Deleuze describes such connectivity in this manner:

> As long as we stick to things and words we can believe that we are speaking of what we see, that we see what we are speaking of, and that the two are

linked: in this way we remain on the level of an empirical exercise. But as soon as we open up words and things, as soon as we discover statements and visibilities, words and sight are raised to a higher exercise that is *a priori*, so that each reaches its own unique limit which separates it from the other, a visible element that can only be seen, an articulable element that can only be spoken. (Deleuze 1988: 65)

By 'a priori' (which is akin to the 'informal diagram' and 'abstract machine' cited immediately above), Deleuze is referring, I believe, to something like an immanent condition of possibility that is both absolute and historical. The last point I'd like to highlight in Deleuze's account of Foucault is, thus:

> [T]*here is a 'there is' of light, a being of light or a light-being*, just as there is a language-being. Each of them is an absolute and yet historical, since each is inseparable from the way in which it falls into a formation or corpus. The one makes visibilities visible or perceptible, just as the other made statements articulable, sayable or readable. This holds true to such an extent that visibilities are neither the acts of a seeing subject nor the data of a visual meaning . . . Just as the visible cannot be reduced to a perceptible thing or quality, so the light-being cannot be reduced to a physical environment . . . *The light-being is a strictly indivisible condition, an a priori that is uniquely able to lay visibilities open to sight, and by the same stroke to the other senses*, each time according to certain combinations which are themselves visible: for example, the tangible is a way in which the visible hides another visible. (Deleuze 1988: 58–9; emphasis added)

Several conceptual moves are discernible in Deleuze's reading: a refusal to be naively empiricist about the visible as something readily accessible; an investment in the disjunction, which is at once the connectivity, between the visible and the verbal; a grappling with the '*a priori*' that enables the visible to become visible and in that way open to the other senses. In particular, Deleuze reiterates the view that visibility is not to be confused with visible objects: '[I]f, in their turn, visibilities are never hidden, they are none the less not immediately seen or visible. They are even invisible so long as we consider only objects, things or perceptible qualities, and not *the conditions which open them up*' (Deleuze 1988: 57; emphasis added). And, again:

> Visibilities are not to be confused with elements that are visible or more generally perceptible, such as qualities, things, objects, compounds of objects. In this respect Foucault constructs a function that is no less original than that of the statement. *We must break things open*. Visibilities are not forms of objects, nor even forms that would show up under light, but rather *forms of luminosity which are created by the light itself and allow a thing*

or object to exist only as a flash, sparkle or shimmer... (Deleuze 1988: 52; emphasis added)

In quoting Deleuze's statements at length, my goal is not necessarily to suggest that his rendition of Foucault should become definitive but rather to ask: why is Deleuze so insistent on reading Foucault this way? What is it in this reading that is, arguably, more Deleuze than Foucault? What I find relevant to think with, especially in the broad context of postcoloniality, is a distinctive method that is oriented toward lines of mutation, mobility, experimentation, emergence and freedom. Instead of simply corroborating instances of blockage and stasis (such as the weighty reality of incarceration), when confronted with such instances Deleuze seeks in them points of departure for an elsewhere, seedlings for a metastasis. Exactly where Foucault's analytics seems to settle starkly on the inescapability of imprisonment as the way to define modern life, Deleuze reconfigures that 'settlement' into a possible transit point, a novel flight path.

To underscore this, let us recall more precisely the way Deleuze delineates visibility as it appears in *Discipline and Punish* (Foucault 1977). Deleuze argues that visibility is what constitutes (or is the *a priori* to) the very architectonics of the event of locking up someone:

> Prison, for its part, is concerned with whatever is visible: not only does it wish to display the crime and the criminal but in itself it constitutes a visibility, *it is a system of light before being a figure of stone*, and is defined by 'Panopticism': by a visual assemblage and a luminous environment (a central tower surrounded by cells) in which the warder can see all the detainees without the detainees being able to see either him or one another. (Deleuze 1988: 32; emphasis added)

This reading is, of course, entirely in concert with Foucault's critical stresses, which in the section on Panopticism bluntly conclude that 'visibility is a trap'.[2] In other words, in tandem with his ongoing investment in the institutionalisation of social relations that takes the forms of asylums, hospitals, schools and the police, Foucault associated the processes of making-visible with an intensifying order of collectively enforced aggression against the human individual. Light – and with it the Enlightenment values of clarity and rationality – is theorised by Foucault not as a medium of emancipation but explicitly as a medium of entrapment: precisely as it enables one to be seen, it also enables one to be caught.

Much as he reads his friend and ally responsively and faithfully, Deleuze also restores a dialectical movement in Foucault's otherwise bleak emphasis. In his rendition, Deleuze first transcends the strictly empirical status of the visible by reinstating the vital mutuality between the visible and the invisible: 'the abstract formula of Panopticism is no longer "to see without being seen" but *to impose a particular conduct on a particular human multiplicity*' (Deleuze 1988: 34, original emphasis).

Then, in an inimitably illuminating stroke, Deleuze goes on to propose that confinement is only one (subordinate) step to a larger set of concerns. From within the tracks of Foucault's preoccupation with the prison, from which there appears little possibility of escape, Deleuze plots an alternative route:

> Foucault has often been treated as above all the thinker of confinement (the general hospital in *Madness and Civilization*, the prison in *Discipline and Punish*). But this is not at all the case, and such a misinterpretation prevents us from grasping his global project . . . In fact, Foucault has always considered confinement as a secondary element derived from a primary function that was very different in each case . . . The imprisonment of madmen was imposed like an 'exile' and took the leper as its model, while the confinement of delinquents was carried out by 'partitioning' and took its model from the plague victim . . . But exiling and partitioning are first of all precisely functions of exteriority which are only afterwards executed, formalized and organized by the mechanisms of confinement . . . As Maurice Blanchot says of Foucault, confinement refers to an outside, and what is confined is precisely the outside . . . It is by excluding or placing outside that the assemblages confine something, and this holds as much for physical interiority as physical confinement. (Deleuze 1988: 42–3)

It is such visionary methodical cracking open of the seemingly secluded or locked-up spaces that leads Deleuze to conclude that 'nothing in Foucault is really closed off' (1988: 43).[3]

For this reason, Deleuze's method can be highly suggestive for postcolonial studies. Returning now to the viable criticism that Foucault has (inadvertently or deliberately) reinforced a certain boundary between the inside and outside of Europe, and thus cut off the study of European institutions of knowledge production from Europe's colonial and imperialist histories, we may say that Deleuze's method shows how this visible foreclosure, this confinement of European history to a presumed interiority, should be taken precisely as the beginning for a divergent engagement. Where Foucault is clearly concentrating on the mechanisms and apparatuses of social control inside Europe is thus also, we might say, a plane of disjunction, where 'Europe proper' has to be grasped in a relation of exclusion, as the illusory interiority produced by a function of exiling and partitioning. Europe's visibility in Foucault's work, in other words, is none other than the visibility of a space of confinement, constituted by an excluded outside. Following Deleuze's lead, it would be eminently logical for scholars to embark on an affirmative postcolonial studies, one that is less anxiously preoccupied with the mechanisms and apparatuses of European exclusion, perhaps, and more substantively engaged with the transformative potential of the ongoing encounters between Europe and the rest of the globe.

Although it constitutes only a small part of his large body of work, therefore, I believe Deleuze's study of Foucault's writings on confinement and visibility stands as an instructive instance of the kind of enabling conceptual engineering he performs (even as certain epistemic predicaments remain unresolved, as they tend to in most thinkers, in ways that are symptomatic of larger issues of our time). Central to such conceptual engineering is Deleuze's manner of wresting even the interiority of a space/time of blockage and social death from what might otherwise be a pessimistically conclusive reading. This turn away from epistemic foreclosure is also traceable to Deleuze's other projects. From the fundamental rejection of Freudian psychoanalysis (with its historically and economically specific ways of perpetuating the patriarchal neuroses of 'Oedipus') and the description of the positivity of schizophrenia, to the creative engagement with the libidinal potentialities of a perversion such as masochism, the sensitive listening for a becoming-minor of language in Kafka's German writing, and the numerous terms he proposes for conceptual experimentation such as becoming, deterritorialisation, assemblages, multiplicities, affects, virtualities, bodies without organs, nomads, the rhizome and so forth,[4] Deleuze's signature utopianism offers infinite inspiration for the postcolonial as a type of liberatory thought.[5]

Battling for the Commodified Media Frame: 'Postcolonial' in Another 'Sense'

Indeed, in the writings of the past several decades by notable thinkers such as Frantz Fanon, Albert Memmi, Edward Said, Gayatri Chakravorty Spivak, Stuart Hall, Homi Bhabha, Paul Gilroy, Robert Young and others, postcolonial theory and criticism have tended to share the emancipatory spirit of anti-colonial political struggles. And while it is true that there are significant differences among these thinkers, some of whom are more old-fashionably humanistic while others are deconstructive in their approaches toward issues of language and identity, it is fair to say that the range of issues that remains central to postcolonial debates, from the racial violence experienced by the wretched of the earth, to the problematics of Orientalism, subaltern representation, and subject formation based on class, gender, ethnic and religious differences, is consistently about resistance. Albeit not always stated, then, the cultural logic at work in postcolonial thought in general is that of repression, understood both in the political and psychoanalytic senses.

Even so, should the term 'postcolonial' continue to be defined exclusively according to this cultural logic? Just as it behooves us, from the perspective of postcolonial consciousness, not to forget the 'outside' that is constitutive of Europe's institutions of knowledge production, so is it salutary to take a closer look at how the postcolonial, as a form of thinking, may exceed the repressive-liberatory terms which have hitherto so powerfully dominated its reasoning. The point here is not simply to attempt to 'trump' postcolonial thinking with the help of Foucault's (1978) critique of the repressive hypothesis (attributed to Freudian psychoanalysis) or Deleuze and Guattari's (1983) critique of the related interpretative hermeneutics encrypted in the Western bourgeois family romance of 'Oedipus' (a legacy also attributed to Freud). Rather, it is to show how, even as it holds on to certain legitimate political aspirations, the term 'postcolonial' as such cannot function in isolation from a web of current discursive articulations in the twenty-first century.

The 1960s, arguably the period that saw the beginnings of many of the postcolonial debates remaining current to this day, was a period marked by populist moral fervour and political activism around the world. But the 1960s also saw the beginnings of a different kind of social struggle. Alongside the demand for an end to Western imperialism and military violence, the demand for national independence among former colonies, the demand for women's equality and liberty, and the demand for civil rights to disenfranchised populations (together with the idealism attached to a non-Western regime such as Mao Zedong's China), large-scale mass demonstrations of that period were increasingly energised by a new type of battle, the battle for what might be called the media frame. In the midst of the political messages about universalisms such as equity, rights and justice was another message – namely, that equity, rights and justice, fought on grounds of class, gender, race, ethnicity and other identity-related particularisms, were themselves thoroughly enmeshed with and indistinguishable from the production and dissemination of media spectacles. Indeed, one may go so far as to say that the 1960s was a period in which the theatre of political activism went through a significant shift in the very concept of struggle – from the plane of physical actions and conflicts, which many continue to want to believe as real, to a political economy of representation and performance, whose actions and conflicts often pre-emptively determine the way we imagine our relation to the real nowadays. In many ways, the media frame has, since the 1960s, become the actual, omnipresent political battleground.

With the emphasis on the media frame, we can see that the multifarious postcolonial insurgencies of the 1960s were, from the outset, confronted with a contradictory set of conditions of possibility as well as urgent political tasks. Such struggles must, on the one hand, discredit and dismantle the agency of some groups while celebrating agency as it was placed with other groups (for example, women instead of men; blacks instead of whites; independent new nations instead of former colonisers). What does this mean in terms of visibilities? If, following the cultural logic of resistance to patriarchal, capitalist and racial repression, the point of such struggles was to take apart the wrongful public images/representations of the groups-to-be-vindicated, it was nonetheless only by actively seizing media attention – and competing for the right to own and manage the visual field, to fabricate the appropriate images and distribute the appropriate stories – that such insurgencies could fulfil their obligation of emancipating the respective groups. Once this process of fighting for the media frame – by acquiring the maximal and optimal visibility – was set in motion, however, postcolonial activists had to face up to the fact that their particular claims are never final or exclusive but always relative, and that still more particular claims, in the name of still other causes, can be advanced, ad infinitum, for media attention.

If media representation is analogised to what Marx described and critiqued as the commodity (that is, a product of labour that receives its stamp of value from a source other than itself, from circulation rather than intrinsic use), what Marx's argument serves to underscore is not only labourers' alienation but also the very process whereby what is hitherto presumed to be mere representation (the commodity), secondary and inferior to the authentic something ('labour', 'the body', 'reality', 'history'), is steadily assuming centre stage as *the* event in the late capitalist social fabric. Rather than simply denouncing the commodity on moral grounds, therefore, the legacy of Marx's observations lies rather in his intimation of a future in which the artificiality and potency of the commodity – precisely in the form of repeatable visibilities – will usurp the significance of the 'original' that is human labour. In this future, even the most precious truths about human life, such as people's identities and histories, and their agency, will need to compete for legitimacy as commodities, as visibilities. (The aforementioned criticism of Foucault's Eurocentrism belongs as well in this competition.)

As a thinker with major works produced during and after the 1960s, Deleuze, though seldom described as postcolonial, shares important affinities with the emancipatory aspirations and objectives of postcolonial thought. At the same time – and this is why he can be so intriguing to think with – he was, of course, explicitly critical of, and distanced himself from, the cultural logic of repression-resistance that genealogically burdens even the most theoretically sophisticated varieties of postcolonial debates. Our present discussion of visibilities is a good case in point: Deleuze's method is poised at the crossroads among multiple visibilities in different *senses* of the postcolonial. From the Foucauldian prison, its system of luminosity, and its '*a priori*', to the spectacles of mass protests and demonstrations for rights, and their imbrications with the commodified media frame (itself oftentimes a kind of trap), the proliferation of visibilities since the 1960s has called forth a new definition of postcoloniality, one that will need to go beyond the conventional, chronological connotations of the term as being the resistance to/aftermath of official colonialism. What must now be recognised as embedded in the postcolonial as such are the thresholds, limits and potentialities of visibilities, of visibilities as the 'multisensorial complexes' of shifting social relations.

In this light, the endeavour, characteristic of postcolonial struggles, to fight for the media frame and contend for the right to be properly imaged, mirrored and represented may be understood anew as a cultural-political practice in an ever-expanding field of visibilities, with the protesting human being herself occupying the status of fetish, rhetorician, artist and performer all at once, while the rebuke of ('incorrect') images must go hand in hand with the massive generation and circulation of more images – be those images about classes, races, nations or persons of different sexual orientations.

The articulation of postcoloniality with visibilities in these conflicting senses, tending both toward liberation from repression *and* toward desire for inclusion in the commodified media frame (which in turn involves ever more occasions for repression), could be one reason Deleuze was invested in a media form like cinema. In cinema, these conflicting, indeed antagonistic, senses of visibilities converge in a collective practice that is as rooted in extra-diegetical commercialism as it is in the transformations internal to film semiotics, which Deleuze addresses in the form of the movement-image and the time-image in his two volumes on film, using the Second World War as a rough dividing timeline (Deleuze 1986; 1989). To isolate what he calls cinematographic concepts, Deleuze at times writes as though he is attempting to aestheticise visibility through familiar avant-garde techniques such as montage, rupture, contrapuntal relations, deframing (wrenching figures and movements from their conventional spaces of representation for a sensation of de-figuration and de-nomination) and the like.[6]

Such aestheticisation of the filmic image should, nevertheless, be seen in the context in which cinema, including art-house cinema, is thoroughly immersed in processes of commodification, the substantial (numerical) scale of which – from production costs to the salaries commanded by movie stars and famed directors, and the profits or losses incurred in worldwide market distribution – could not have been lost on Deleuze. While he accentuates cinematographic concepts that remind us of the avant-garde theorisations of film, therefore, I think he is also accentuating the question of such concepts' ability to survive in the midst of divergent postcolonial visibilities. That is to say, such concepts need to be explored in the form of their limits as well as their linkages to visibilities/discourses of commodification, confinement and freedom, all of which together define our contemporary virtual public sphere. It is in this sense of limit-cum-linkage that we may finally understand Deleuze's description of the relation between the visible and the verbal in Foucault, and of the kinship Foucault, according to him at least, shares with film: 'And yet the unique limit that separates each one is also the common limit that links one to the other, a limit with two irregular faces, a blind word and a mute vision. Foucault is uniquely akin to contemporary film' (Deleuze 1988: 65).

'Capture' in the Age of Shadow Media

Although Deleuze did not write about the more contemporary screen technologies such as cell-phones, palm pilots, videophones, portable cameras, text-messaging, GPSs and so forth, I believe his method also has vast implications for such visibilities, if only because of the paradox of their often minuscule sizes (that is, their extreme individuation and atomisation) and their hyper capacities for connectivity.

Given the steadily diminishing sizes of screens on these portable little machines, have not postcolonial visibilities arrived at yet another conceptual threshold? It might no longer be sufficient to think of visibilities as a system of luminosity (surveillance) in which we are trapped, or even as an ever-commodifiable form of power (such as the media frame) which we all desire to acquire. It has also become necessary to come to terms with visibilities as, literally, objects we can hold in our hands and disseminate widely in a matter of moments. (To pick an egregious example, the scandal of Abu Ghraib came to public attention because the acts of torture and abuse committed by US military personnel were recorded on cell-phones and circulated on the Internet.) What, then, is the import of 'capture' on a tiny screen?

In a study of the emergence of such new visibilities in contemporary Hong Kong (a Special Administrative Region of the People's Republic of China), where citizens have in recent years staged political protests against their government's demolition of historical monuments, the photographer, filmmaker, and new media producer Helen Grace refers to 'a strange new domestication of history' in our 'era of image overproduction' (Grace 2007: 472). Unlike Deleuze's study of film, which approaches the image largely as an aesthetic/semiotic form (as it evolves historically from the movement-image to the time-image in different directors' works), Grace's focus is rather on the affective engagements in moments of expressiveness that lead to the production of images of local significance, on popular sites such as YouTube and Flickr. The important difference, according to Grace, is that instead of becoming a memorial to a past time (as many images, such as photographs, tend to become the instant they are produced), the image seized by the new media technologies serves rather as a way of enacting and performing the present precisely through the small act of capture:

> The ubiquitous image [in contrast to the memorial act of analogue photography] . . . has a much more tenuous link to the present, which it does not necessarily accept as real; rather, it is the act of 'capture' which brings the present into existence, because ubiquitous image-making belongs to a world in which the real *in itself* is so thoroughly mediated that it does not exist without at the same time producing an image of itself – and it is this image which secures the lived reality in which the image-maker is situated. This does not mean that the performative and the memorial are opposed; rather it indicates that memory is also secured via the image and, in its embodied form, is brought forth in action and performance. (Grace 2007: 473; original emphasis)

Insofar as she is interested in the ephemeral coextension of the image and the present, a coextension that is brought forth by the mere click of a button or the pressing of a key, Grace's observations sidestep the large, systemic connotations of visibility-as-confinement that Foucault delineates. Instead, she inserts visibilities into the mundane motions and stoppages of the everyday, replete with the risk (and the certainty) that many of them will remain unnoticed and unseen in the dense strata of online material, except by those with a vested interest in local happenings. Her apparent focus on the local notwithstanding (in this case, the mass political movements in post-1997 Hong Kong), Grace's manner of conceptualising the present as a collective but diffused assemblage of enunciation, one that may be snatched in bits at a time and then plugged into a mutating plenitude of virtualities is, I believe, eminently Deleuzian because of the fluidity and mobility – indeed, the immanent recycle-ability – between images and life that she so provocatively suggests. Likewise is her sense of the blurring of distinctions between heterogeneous categories of knowledge that results from such captured images' incessant flow, crisscrossing and becoming:

> The taking of images amidst everyday action blurs the distinction between significant and insignificant moments, so that every image becomes a variety of family snapshot – from the simple outing to the amateur footage of a train crash, used on the evening news, to the riot, and the overthrow of a regime. Any of these images can be recycled beyond the domestic sphere to become news footage – legitimate records of an event which official news management deems un-newsworthy. (Grace 2007: 472)

Grace describes this contemporary state of visibilities-in-flux, made up of user-generated, often mediocre-quality images, in terms of 'shadow media' (a phrase she borrows from Patricia Spyer): 'the tangential, mobile infrastructure of a counter-discourse to conventional national and international broadcasting' (Grace 2007: 472).[7]

In addition to the post-1960s battling for the media frame, then, the conceptualisation of the postcolonial needs, at this juncture, to address these newly multiplied visibilities and the global/local constituencies formed and unformed in relation to the so-called shadow media. Should the users of these minuscule screens be described as being subjected to the logics of confinement in the Foucauldian sense (in that the atomised screens, in being used, are *de facto* surveillance embodied – by none other than the very persons under surveillance)? How does the existence of channels of communication such as YouTube, together with the entry and exit possibilities they inject into everyday life (from postings of video vigilantism to movie premieres and amateurish performances), complicate and transform the notion of freedom? Or has the dependency on such commodified visibilities replaced freedom's relevance altogether, in an age when human existence seems inconceivable without such media-dependency, which therefore must be recognised as nothing less than a vital force – literally, a life link?

Offshoots from ready-formed shapes of thought, these rhizomic – and schizoid? – questions about visibilities, agglomerating diverse cognitive, gestural, mimetic and perceptive acts across semiotic chains, organisations of power and historical struggles, are clearly some of the potentially fertile contact zones waiting to materialise between Deleuze and postcoloniality. Indeed, we may think of the numerous pathways from Deleuze's work as themselves part of an extensive media network, with the exciting capability of collaborating with a postcolonial studies reconceived against shifting trajectories of global political power and, in particular, against the ambiguities, opacities and uncertainties of postcolonial visibilities.

References

Deleuze, G. [1983] (1986), *Cinema 1: The Movement-Image*, trans. H. Tomlinson and B. Habberjam, London: Athlone.
Deleuze, G. (1988), *Foucault*, trans. S. Hand, foreword by P. A. Bové, Minneapolis and London: University of Minnesota Press.
Deleuze, G. [1985] (1989a), *Cinema 2: The Time-Image*, trans. H. Tomlinson and R. Galeta, London: Athlone.
Deleuze, G. (1989b), *Masochism*, trans. J. McNeil, New York: Zone.
Deleuze, G. and F. Guattari (1983), *Capitalism and Schizophrenia: Anti-Oedipus*, vol. 1, trans. R. Hurley, M. Seem and H. R. Lane, Minneapolis: University of Minnesota Press.
Deleuze G. and F. Guattari (1986), *Kafka: Toward a Minor Literature*, trans. D. Polan, Minneapolis and London: University of Minnesota Press.
Deleuze, G. and F. Guattari (1987), *Capitalism and Schizophrenia: A Thousand Plateaus*, vol. 2, trans. B. Massumi, Minneapolis and London: University of Minnesota Press.
Deleuze, G. and F. Guattari (1994), *What Is Philosophy?*, trans. H. Tomlinson and G. Burchell, New York: Columbia University Press.
Foucault, M. [1965] (1967), *Madness and Civilisation*, trans. R. Howard, New York: Random House; and London: Tavistock.
Foucault, M. (1970), *The Order of Things*, trans. A. Sheridan, London: Tavistock; and New York: Pantheon.
Foucault, M. (1972), *The Archaeology of Knowledge*, trans. A. Sheridan, London: Tavistock; and New York: Pantheon.
Foucault, M. (1973), *The Birth of the Clinic*, trans. A. Sheridan, London: Tavistock; and New York: Pantheon.
Foucault, M. (1977), *Discipline and Punish: The Birth of the Prison*, trans. A. Sheridan, New York: Vintage.
Foucault, M. (1978), *History of Sexuality*, vol. 1, trans. R. Hurley, New York: Pantheon.
Grace, H. (2007), 'Monuments and the Face of Time: Distortions of Scale and Asynchrony in Postcolonial Hong Kong', *Postcolonial Studies* 10 (4): 467–83.
Rancière, J. (2006), 'From One Image to Another? Deleuze and the Ages of Cinema', in *Film Fables*, trans. E. Battista, Oxford and New York: Berg.
Shapiro, G. (2003), *Archaeologies of Vision: Foucault and Nietzsche on Seeing and Saying*, Chicago: University of Chicago Press.

Notes

1. For an important study on this topic, see Gary Shapiro (2003).
2. The statements leading up to this conclusion are:

   The panoptic mechanism arranges spatial unities that make it possible to see constantly and to recognize immediately. In short, it reverses the principle of the dungeon; or rather of its three functions – to enclose, to deprive of light and to hide – it preserves only the first and eliminates the other two. Full lighting and the eye of a supervisor capture better than darkness, which ultimately protected. Visibility is a trap. (Foucault 1977: 200)

3. For an astute analysis of Deleuze's visionary reading of Foucault, see Paul A. Bové, 'Foreword: The Foucault Phenomenon: The Problematics of Style', in Deleuze (1988: vii–xl), in particular the discussion beginning on page xxxii.
4. The works in question include but are not limited to Deleuze and Guattari's volumes on *Capitalism and Schizophrenia* and their work on *Kafka* (1983; 1986; 1987); as well as Deleuze's work on *Masochism* (1989b).
5. As this collection's editors reminded me, Deleuze has expressed reservations about the term 'utopia' because of the mutilated meaning given it by public opinion (see Deleuze and Guattari 1994: 100). However, in so far as he also defines utopia as '*what links* philosophy with its own epoch' and as a word that 'designates *that conjunction of philosophy, or of the concept, with the present milieu*' (1994: 99,100; original emphases), I tend to think it is an apt description of his own work.
6. For a perceptively engaged critique of Deleuze's thesis about cinema, see Jacques Rancière's chapter 'From One Image to Another? Deleuze and the Ages of Cinema', in his book *Film Fables* (2006: 107–23). Rancière's main argument is that the two kinds of images asserted by Deleuze as being distinguished by an external historical event (the Second World War) are not so much opposed as two different points of view on the image (pp. 112–13 and throughout). To cite an example of Rancière's painstaking delineation of the circularity of Deleuze's logic:

   The passage from the infinity of matter-image to the infinity of thought-image is also a history of redemption, of an always thwarted redemption. The filmmaker takes perception to images by snatching them from bodily states and placing them on a plane of pure events; in so doing, the filmmaker gives images an arrangement-in-thought. But this arrangement-in-thought is always also the re-imposition of the logic of the opaque screen, of the central image that arrests the movement in every direction of other images to reorder them from itself. *The gesture of restitution is always also a new gesture of capture.* (p. 116; emphasis added)

   Because my objective in this section is to suggest the affinities between Deleuze's conceptual method and the new media technologies, and also because of obvious space constraints, a full-fledged discussion of Rancière's critique of Deleuze's writings on film will have to wait until another occasion.
7. The work by Patricia Spyer cited by Grace is (2002) 'Shadow Media and Moluccan Muslim VCD's', in B. Abrash and F. Ginsburg (eds), *9/11: A Virtual Case Book*, New York: Centre for Media, Culture, and History, Virtual Case Book [VCB] Series; http://www.nyu/edu/fas/projects/veb/

Chapter 4

Affective Assemblages: Ethics beyond Enjoyment

Simone Bignall

Like some other post-colonial nations, Australia is coming to terms with the knowledge that decades of colonial policy instituting the removal of indigenous children from their families and communities has had a destructive effect on individuals and society, marking a 'blemished chapter in our nation's history' (Rudd 2008). The Stolen Generations describe their lived experiences of post-colonialism in heartrending narratives of personal tragedy, cultural devastation and collective trauma, also evidencing remarkable courage, resilience and stoicism.[1] Such painful accounts call for a just response from settler Australians, so that we might move forward as a national community and begin the task of postcolonial reconciliation. While the symbolic response of a formal apology has finally been offered, the material requirements of a fair rejoinder are complex and as yet undecided.[2] However, no matter what concrete measures of retribution and recompense are finally agreed to be appropriate and accepted by the indigenous peoples of Australia, reconciliation also requires all Australians to materialise the postcolonial modes of sociability and cultural engagement signalled in the Prime Minister's formal apology.[3] While the state's past racist policies of assimilation might ultimately be held responsible for the suffering of the Stolen Generations, these policies were put into practice by countless individuals who, even when they felt uncomfortable in the act of theft, tolerated and participated in the many nefarious practices removing children from parents, siblings, communities, land and culture.

In short, postcolonisation not only calls for measures of formal justice acknowledging and addressing the state's failure to uphold indigenous human rights in the past and guaranteeing such human rights in the future, but also for a less mediated, more intimate kind of ethical assessment and commitment. This might perhaps best be thought of as a kind of care, an attentive quality of comportment one ought to practise in one's social relationships, in order to act in accordance with a postcolonial sensibility. Vitally, the notion of postcolonial care necessarily departs from the colonial discourse of paternalist care, which underscored many of the practices of separation, and continues to inform some contemporary acts of state in relation to indigenous matters (see Altman and Hinkson 2007). In this chapter, I will suggest that aspects of Deleuzian philosophy privilege a certain idea of careful sociability, which expands the realm of practical ethics beyond rights-based and state-mediated discourses of justice, to include unmediated qualities of interpersonal relationship as defining aspects of political and ethical life.

While there is a need for mutual care in postcolonial relationships, this might not necessarily be based on a single philosophy of self-other relations or justice; indigenous and non-indigenous traditions are conceptually diverse, and one need not be privileged over the other when a variety of approaches can combine to reach an agreeable outcome. Accordingly, while indigenous peoples might choose to develop the concepts of self, agency and postcolonial engagement presented here, this chapter is properly addressed to the international body of European settler immigrants who have inherited a colonial legacy of privilege, and must now rethink their histories of colonial-style engagement in order to create better compatibility with others, leading to a postcolonial future. In Australia, the colonial legacy includes the mistreatment of the Stolen Generations, whose scarred testimonies now force conscionable non-indigenous Australians to perform a postcolonial agency of interaction that excludes the shameful possibility of such history repeating. In the first section, I propose that Deleuze's work is part of an alternative tradition of Western thought that offers potentially non-imperial conceptualisations of sociability, motivation and self-comportment. Then, through a consideration of Deleuze's work on assemblage and affective forces in light of his reading of Spinoza, I argue that while this concept of ethical agency is left underdeveloped in Deleuze's own work, it arises from his particular notion of embodiment, which I finally place in relation to a postcolonial ethic of community incorporating a notion of protective justice.

Being Stolen

Ethics regulate social relations and practice. These relations are simultaneously 'concrete' and 'general', encompassing one's engagements with specific others and one's civil relations with society more broadly conceived (Benhabib 1992: 148–77). Furthermore, the ethical quality of one's practice is shaped both by self-concept and by the range of attitudes one adopts towards these others. In the post-Hegelian tradition of communitarian philosophy, the self is never seen to be autonomous and discrete, but always entangled with others: the very possibility of self-concept relies upon the acknowledging reflection of the self by another. Consequently, in this tradition, ethical engagement firstly concerns an ontological struggle for recognition, which negotiates a primarily conflictive social milieu, as part of the process of self-formation and the development of social harmony. For example, Sartre argues that through the act of recognition, the other confers upon me the subjectivity that I desire and lack, but also extracts my Being from me, since the mediating act of recognition objectifies me and distances me from the immediacy of my self. In this way, the other 'steals my Being', and I must seek its recovery in order to achieve my goal to be a self-directing agent, the foundation of my own Being (Sartre 1996: 361ff.).

Slavoj Žižek's influential analysis of the 'theft of enjoyment' resonates with these earlier ideas expressed by Sartre (Žižek 1993). Writing about nascent nationalisms and ethnic conflict in the aftermath of the disintegration of communism in Eastern Europe, Žižek contends that national identity or identification is sustained by a community's belief in its particular 'way of life'. Here, 'way of life' means 'the way a community organises its feasts, its rituals of mating, its initiation ceremonies, in short all the details by which is made visible the unique way a community *organises its enjoyment*' (1993: 201). According to Žižek, then, at stake in ethnic tension is precisely the possession of this common enjoyment: the other is treated with fearful suspicion, as a body that wants to 'steal our enjoyment (by ruining our way of life)' (1993: 203). Satisfaction involves possessive enjoyment of an identifying 'way of life', which is however always perceived to be under threat of being appropriated (or annihilated), and must therefore be jealously guarded and protected from conniving others. However, Žižek insists this 'theft' is only ever an imagined threat, since for the Hegelian subject in a perpetual process of dialectical becoming, the lack of satisfaction or human fulfilment that jeopardises enjoyment of Being is original: '*we never possessed what was allegedly stolen from us*' (1993: 203; emphasis original).

The notion that others can threaten Being and its enjoyment is also central to the liberal tradition of social contract; in this tradition, however, the self is always-already given in full possession of his defining human qualities. The possibility that social participation might undermine these qualities is the underlying basis of human rights, which refer to natural properties understood to be inalienable in human identity.

Rights protect me from the threat posed by others, who might possibly treat me in such a way that they stop me from enjoying aspects of my human Being. Rights thereby affirm that there are certain aspects of my human Being that must not be 'stolen' by others. A failure to recognise someone's human rights involves a failure to respect the inalienable humanity, hence dignity, of a person. Their enjoyment of their human Being is 'thieved', leaving them diminished.

This kind of analysis is particularly instructive in the context of the Stolen Generations of indigenous Australians, removed from their families and their cultural communities by interventionist and racist, post-colonial state policy. The Report of the Human Rights Commission to Government on the subject of the Stolen Generations is overtly presented in terms of human rights:

> To know who you are, where you are from and to whom you belong is a basic human entitlement. It is essential to the realisation of the 'dignity and worth of the human person' which underpins the Universal Declaration of Human Rights (HREOC 1997: 17).

For the Stolen Generations, that which was stolen was, then, exactly the enjoyment of their human Being, as it is experienced in the context of indigenous sociability, or cultural 'belonging'. It is, therefore, unsurprising that responses and recommendations flowing from the *Bringing Them Home* Report revolve around the need to 'restore identity' to indigenous individuals and communities, by renewing and strengthening family bonds, community and culture (HREOC 1997; Cornwall 2002).

While liberalism and communitarianism differ in their basic ontological commitments, they nonetheless share certain underlying values, including an emphasis on Being or identity – either as a given set of defining human qualities, or as a goal to be pursued in common with others. Accordingly, the enjoyment of identity is privileged in both traditions, either as a right or as a benefit flowing from collective goods: in liberalism, individuals have the right to those inalienable qualities that define their human Being; in communitarianism, individuals have a (qualified or mediated) right or 'need' to enjoy the collective practices and goods that sustain both individual and collective forms of identity. A second point of connection between the two positions concerns an underlying ambivalence towards difference or others. In both traditions, benefits flow from the social connections the self forms in community with others, but those others simultaneously threaten one's enjoyment of Being, potentially 'stealing' one's enjoyment of identity either by infringing upon one's inalienable integrity, or by 'stealing', monopolising or withholding the common goods the self requires for the purpose of identity-formation. Thus, in both traditions, an oppositional or annihilating attitude towards difference is evident: the other must either be excluded from potential transgression on the self (liberal), or assimilated and encompassed within an expanding common identity in a process of universal development (communitarian). In either case, the mediating body of the state is the locus of responsibility for this protection and/or construction of identity, which is discursively defined either in cosmopolitan terms of liberal human rights, or communitarian terms of citizenship and nationalism.

The Australian state's past dereliction of responsibility towards indigenous people has recently been acknowledged with an official apology (Rudd 2008). The government now recognises that successive Australian parliaments failed to protect indigenous human Being, by actively instituting policies that authorised the 'stealing' of indigenous enjoyment; not simply in the theft of traditional lands, but also in the destruction of their indigenous identities, their particular humanity as it can only be experienced in an indigenous community of practice. However, the reactions to the National Inquiry into the Stolen Generations at times also indicated that the popular imagination had escaped and exceeded the rhetoric of human rights, justice and formal equality:

> [T]here is something beyond apology. It was found in the quality of concern and genuine sorrow expressed by so many Australians – a kind of grace which moved many of us to feel our potential to make peace with the past and find the basis for a new relationship between the Indigenous and non-Indigenous people of this country. It was experienced, perhaps momentarily, in some Sorry Day events: in parks and local halls; public rallies and small gatherings. It was stimulated by the information provided in *Bringing Them Home*, but it was given substance by the human warmth of those present. The experience of a kind of restorative love, which some Indigenous people felt, is the highest achievement flowing from the Inquiry (HREOC 1997: 14).

In my view, the 'something beyond' referred to here describes a kind of satisfaction not reducible to enjoyment. It is a 'kind of restorative love', an immediate form of communion that corresponds with care and results in a form of satisfaction that is suggestive of Spinozan joy: the experience of a mutually compatible, affirming and empowering affective relation between bodies connected in concrete relations of engagement. This kind of sociability clearly rejects the ambivalent and implicitly suspicious attitude towards difference, which forms the ontological scaffolding for the two dominant traditions of liberalism and communitarianism in Western political philosophy, and which arguably makes these inappropriate as a theoretical basis for a social philosophy of postcolonialism. In the remainder of this chapter, I will explore how aspects of Deleuzian philosophy suggest a more fruitful ontological basis for postcolonial social theory. The following section considers Deleuze's work on affectivity and assemblage as suggestive of an ethics beyond enjoyment, potentially encompassing the sociable principles of 'human warmth', care and joy signalled in the passage above.

Affective Assemblages

For Deleuze and Guattari, a social encounter can only be adequately understood with reference to the complex natures of the bodies involved in the meeting. On their view, a body is not a discrete entity defined by stable boundaries and a set of fixed characteristics; rather, it is an assemblage of components bound into a coherent form, but this bodily consistency is only ever temporary and is always shifting. This is so, because the component parts of a body constantly change as they enter into new relations with other parts encountered by the assemblage in its interactions with its existential milieu. A body is, then, a 'composition of relations between parts' (Deleuze 1990: 218–9), where some of these relations are internal to the body, and some are external relations with other bodies. More precisely, it is a particular mode of expression of the infinite possible expressions of Being, and that which is expressed is a characteristic relation of consistency between parts (Deleuze and Guattari 1987: 254).

Accordingly, a body is best thought of as the collection of relations into which its constituent parts enter. These relations are conceptualised by Deleuze and Guattari in terms of their duration: the speed or slowness with which they form and transform (1987: 258). Fleeting relations describe bodily characteristics that appear only occasionally: a flash of jealousy born from a combination of loss and longing; a twinge of spite spawned by a momentary mixture of anger and envy; a burst of kindness prompted by sympathy and care. These elemental combinations cause the body to be affected, for example with jealousy, spite or kindness. More enduring relations between components define more stable characteristics of a body, expressing its regular ways of being affected. A body is therefore defined not only by shifts in the consistency of its internal relations, but more particularly by the affections these relations produce (Deleuze and Guattari 1987: 258). In fact, however, there are two sorts of bodily affections. Firstly, the body is an extensive entity that is comprised of elemental parts, combined in particular configurations according to the ways in which they affect one another. Secondly, the body itself exists as an elemental part in a multitude of more complex assemblages formed with other bodies in its social milieu. Accordingly, a body forms a characteristic consistency according to the extensive relations involving its internal parts, and also transforms intensively over time as it is affected by its engagements with neighbouring bodies and the complex array of relations into which they enter. This means that:

> depending on their degree of speed or the relation of movement and rest into which they enter, [affects] belong to a given Individual, which may itself be part of another Individual governed by another, more complex relation, and so on to infinity . . . Thus each Individual is an infinite multiplicity. (Deleuze and Guattari 1987: 254)

It remains yet unclear how this complex and abstract notion of the body as an 'infinite multiplicity' defined by its internal and external affective relations might be politically useful in the social context of postcolonialism. How does the nature of this body, which is defined by its affections and determined by its relations with neighbouring bodies, also determine the ways it is affected and the quality of the encounters it experiences? And how might a body actively create postcolonial encounters with other bodies, occasioning care and an affective feeling of joy? While an answer to this last question remains undeveloped in Deleuze's social philosophy, his early work on Spinoza gestures towards an understanding of self-concept, reflexive agency and ethical engagement, which underpins many of the ideas appearing in his later work with Guattari.

Spinoza's theory of the mind as an idea of the body is crucial for understanding how notions of selfhood and subjective agency might arise from Deleuzian philosophy (Gatens 1996; Armstrong 1997; see also Bignall 2007). Because the body is constituted and defined by its relations, the mind necessarily 'thinks the body' in the act of the encounters that define its ways of being affected, and accordingly, in terms of the relations that comprise its existence at a particular time and the transformations that trace shifts in the body over time (Deleuze 1990: 220–1). Deleuze explains that, according to Spinoza, the mind may have either an adequate or inadequate idea of the body. Inadequate ideas are caused by the passive affections a body undergoes when other bodies impact upon it; these ideas are inadequate because they are cognisant only of what the body suffers and remain ignorant of bodily powers of action and active capacity, which describe 'what the body can do'. Conversely, adequate ideas are the mind's awareness of the affections a body causes in itself and to others, when it actively engages with other bodies. Adequate ideas think the full power of a body in terms of the chosen affects it can produce by 'striving to organise its encounters' (Deleuze 1990: 261). In striving to understand bodily composition, the mind 'thinks the body' in terms of its affective relations, and so transforms the body into a self-aware being that is increasingly capable of discerning which relations are compatible and enhance active capacities, thus bringing about joy, and which relations are experienced passively by the body, imposing upon the body and thus occasioning a feeling of sadness.

Here, self-awareness initially involves understanding how one is formed through constitutive relationships, but this initially reflective self-concept develops into a reflexive practice of self formation as the mind develops knowledge of how the body can increasingly engage the kinds of relationships that maximise active affections. In doing so, a body increases its power to experience joyful affections, since the active relations the body chooses are naturally those that increase its existential capacities (the *conatus* of a body entails that it chooses relations that preserve or increase its powers), and hence are experienced as joy. Conversely, passions suffered by the body are the cause of sadness, which the body experiences not only when it is weakened by the impact of another body that imposes upon it in a way that destroys some of its capacities, but also because the experience of a passive affection, even when it is not destructive, does not allow the body to exercise fully its active and joyful creative powers of self assemblage. Spinoza's concepts of sad passions and active joys thus point the way towards an ethics of self conduct. Adequate ideas correspond with actively produced, joyful bodily experiences arising from relations with compatible bodies; to discover adequate ideas, one ought to 'concretely try to become active' (Deleuze 1990: 226), and this involves developing understanding of oneself and others, so that one can organise encounters by seeking out bodies that one can form compatible relations with.

However, a problem concerning postcolonial application is signalled here. What might this ethics of self-conduct augur for the other in my encounters? I ought to seek out compatible others and engage with them in agreeable ways that increase my powers of existence and affectivity because this will increase my experience of joy, but what are my ethical obligations towards the other, for the sake of the other? If a relation is compatible with my powers and enhances them, is it also necessarily compatible with the powers of the other? Is the joy of the other a relevant concern to me, or should I simply attend to maximising my own satisfaction, pleasing myself? In particular, the problem signalled here concerns the nature of joy as the bodily experience of an increased power to be affected. This appears to celebrate the active formation of new relations *per se*, without due regard for their quality and their impact on others, since the combining of elemental bodies evidently produces a common body with increased complexity and a greater power of affection. Thus, 'In any encounter, whether I destroy or be destroyed, there takes place a combining of relations that is, as such, good' (Deleuze 1990: 249).

But how might colonised indigenous peoples interpret this claim? In the case of the colonial meeting of indigenous and non-indigenous Australians, while one body was diminished and largely destroyed by the meeting, the union nonetheless increased the powers of each to be mutually affected, creating a common body with a higher degree of complexity. Deleuze explains that evil 'corresponds to the fact that the relation combined when two bodies meet, are not always those of the bodies themselves' (Deleuze 1990: 251). As was the case in this colonial encounter, the meeting might destroy the internal relation between parts that defines one of the individuals. But for Spinoza, this evil 'amounts to nothing' so long as the meeting produces a new common body with a new set of internal relations that is more complex, more affective, and thus more capable of joy (Deleuze 1990: 251). There is but one case in which evil amounts to something: when the mode of expression of Being 'passes from greater to lesser perfection', when the resulting common body is a diminished power, less capable of actively exacting joy (Deleuze 1990: 251). Accordingly, it appears we do no great wrong when we destroy an encountered body's existing relation, so long as the union creates the conditions of an increased capacity for affection. At face value, this seems like a justification for colonialism.

In fact, Deleuze's interpretation of Spinozan ethics, and the use we might make of this in a postcolonial context, is poorly understood unless Deleuze's quite particular reading of Spinozan embodiment is taken into consideration. This reading details the complex nature of bodily encounters: a body is affected in many different ways and is characterised by the multifarious relations it forms with the great number of neighbouring bodies comprising its contextualising social milieu. Encounters are not simply events describing the meeting of whole bodies as they come into contact, but more precisely involve a multitude of engagements taking place at the many particular sites of the affections that describe a body:

> Existing bodies do not encounter one another *in the order* in which their relations combine . . . Relations combine *according to laws*; but existing bodies, being themselves composed of extensive parts, meet *bit by bit*. So

parts of one of the bodies may be determined to take on a new relation imposed by some law while losing that relation through which they belonged to the body. (Deleuze 1990: 237)

In their later work describing bodies as assemblages, Deleuze and Guattari discuss identity formation as a process of assembly involving the 'piecemeal insertions' of the self into the bodies of social discourse and practice that constitute one's social milieu (1987: 504). From this perspective, my identity is entirely defined by the relations I form with others (both 'concrete' and 'general') in my social world. However, my engagements with other individuals and with communities and bodies of practice involve only certain particular aspects of myself, rather than the whole of my being. For example, during the transition to motherhood brought about by my encounter with a daughter, the ways in which she affected me changed my overall internal composition, adding in new elements and destroying some previous aspects of my identity which had become incompatible with my new configuration as a mother, thus redefining me in significant ways. However, this relationship with my child involves only particular aspects of my identity and affects me in particular ways; other aspects of my being (as it is constituted through my worldly relations) remain unaffected by this particular encounter. In fact, my identity is complex, multiple and shifting according to the social context and the various bodies I engage with at any particular time; the aspects of my identity that are engaged with my friends are different from those that are engaged when I work with colleagues, or with political communities, or with the bodies of ideas I encounter in books. Each of these associations affects me partially and in relatively discrete ways according to the kind of relationship I form with the certain elements in each body that are relevant to me. Furthermore, at any one time I am engaged in many encounters simultaneously, and am at once affected in a great many different ways, which sometimes contradict and conflict within me. Like everyone existing in complex relations with many particular aspects of the world, I can be simultaneously pleased and furious, energetic and hopeless, self-determining and dependent, careful and dispassionate; and as Deleuze notes: 'We may both love and hate the same object, not only by virtue of these relations, but also by virtue of the complexity of the relations of which we are ourselves intrinsically composed' (Deleuze 1990: 243).

In other words, when bodies meet 'bit by bit', only some elements of their complex composition enter into affective relations, while other aspects remain unaffected by the encounter. Sometimes certain elemental parts will enter into new relations with the encountered body, which alters their capacity to remain in the previous relations defining existing bodily configuration, thus transforming the internal composition of the body and changing its expression of consistency as a mode of Being. However, other aspects of bodily configuration will remain untouched and unchanged by the encounter with the other. While one's identity constantly shifts and transforms according to social context and particular constitutive relations, such becomings are only ever partial and incomplete, since one is never affected all at once in one's entirety: some continuity of identity is retained. This is true also of cultural encounters occurring with the colonial collision of communities: each body is transformed by the meeting, and old traditions and concepts shift and change as new connections are formed which alter the internal consistency of each body. However, because encounters proceed by the 'piecemeal insertion' of select elements into new relations with others, some aspects of each culture naturally remain unaffected, relatively stable and intact, allowing it to persevere in some recognisable form. Colonial violence intending the wholesale destruction of a community or a culture is thus a perverse encounter, which disavows the natural partiality of the meeting, where such partiality preserves aspects of bodily integrity despite the transformations compelled by new environmental connections and relations. In the final section of this chapter, I will discuss the need for a (revised) notion of 'rights' to protect a body from the wilful and wholesale destruction of the given relations defining it. However, at this point we are now better placed to observe that no great wrong is done when (some aspects of) an encountered body's existing relation are destroyed in the transformative process of interaction, so long as the union creates the conditions of an increased capacity for affection. In fact, the destruction of established ways of being is natural in the ontological processes of identity formation and cultural transformation, when this occurs through the assembly of shifting and piecemeal affective relations with others.

Furthermore, because encounters take place 'bit by bit' and with a vast number of bodies simultaneously, at any particular time a body is comprised of both passive affections (passions) and active affections (actions). Some of my encounters will be actively chosen by me because I perceive, in the other, a compatibility with aspects of my nature; other relations will eventuate through my chance encounters with others. Because these chance meetings are not deliberately sought out by me, they may impose upon me in ways that are sometimes compatible and beneficial, sometimes harmful and destructive. These chance relations will cause me to endure passive affections, which may be the source of a fortuitous joy, but may equally affect me with sadness. However, the relations I actively seek out on the basis of my understanding of their compatibility with me will always be joyful, since I will always choose those relations that increase my powers of affective existence. By attending to bodily complexity and the affective meeting of bodies 'bit by bit', we can now better understand that the ethical tasks of 'becoming active' and 'organising one's encounters' properly entail that one must not simply strive to unite with bodies that one perceives to be wholly sympathetic and similar, but more precisely with the sympathetic facets of the diverse bodies that comprise one's social milieu, in compatible ways that will agreeably affect relevant aspects of one's body, potentially 'forming a *totality* of compatible relations' and thus a maximal feeling of joy (Deleuze 1990: 262). This ethics is therefore concerned with finding agreement, not by eliminating actual difference and privileging identity, but in the context of the actual diversity of bodies that express Being in infinitely multiple ways. This acknowledgement of a permanent and primary ontological difference is, I suggest, essential in postcolonial thinking about the social.

However, the question remains: what might this ethics of self-conduct augur for the other in my encounters? From a postcolonial perspective, it is imperative that encounters are *mutually* joyful: that each body is able to exercise its active power of existence and affective capacity; that one body is not destroyed or diminished by the other. If the ethics of complex bodies guided by active joy outlined here is to be practically useful in the context of postcolonialism, indigenous and non-indigenous communities must be capable of achieving a sociable quality of agreement and accord at the sites of their affective interactions. This process of seeking agreement and identifying areas of affective compatibility through mutual understanding might be usefully described as the development of Spinozan 'common notions', which Deleuze explains 'internally determine the mind to understand the agreements of things, as well as their differences and oppositions' (1990: 276).

A common notion is an 'idea of a similarity of composition in existing modes' (Deleuze 1990: 275), and so involves reaching an understanding about which aspects of bodies are compatible and can combine in agreeable ways. In this way, 'a common notion is always the idea of something positive'; however the process of finding common notions nonetheless 'begins with bodies very disparate from one another and very opposed to one another' (Deleuze 1990: 285, 281). Indeed, the colonial meeting of indigenous and non-indigenous Australians created a collision of 'very disparate' bodies, which being merely thrown together by geographical and historical circumstance, did not initially actively seek or desire engagement. Each considered the other largely in terms of their opposing ways of being and of doing things. For instance, indigenous Australians were appalled by the way the settlers brutalised and degraded each other according to codes of penal society, and were dismayed by the way they depleted and displaced natural food reserves by clearing land and planting new crops, which the traditional occupiers of the land were then forbidden to harvest and share. Settler Australians were scornful of the apparent absence of (familiar) social, legal and political institutions defining 'civilised' culture, and set about imposing European conventions such as clothing, Christianity and capitalism upon indigenous peoples, who responded with various forms of organised and spontaneous resistance. Inga Clendinnen's (2003: 110–33) insightful account of the punitive spearing of Governor Arthur Philip in 1790 starkly demonstrates how the historical beginnings of the encounter between indigenous and non-indigenous bodies were tragically marked by cultural misunderstanding and mutual incomprehension spawning conflict and disagreement, and it is at this point hard to see where postcolonial compatibility might be forged.

However, over time we have come to understand each other better, and through the 'slow learning of what agrees with our nature, the slow effort of discovering our joys' (Deleuze 1990: 262), we have begun to identify aspects of our respective bodily compositions that share a similarity and so might form the basis of agreement in our relation with each other. For example, we have learned to appreciate that indigenous and non-indigenous children alike benefit from knowing 'who you are, where you are from and to whom you belong', and that wilfully to deprive any child of this knowledge will cause harm. We are beginning to understand that we often now also share a sense of belonging to the land itself (although this sense of belonging might be experienced in culturally different ways), which we have at times recognised in the legislative forms of native and shared title, and in cultural forms of artistic expression. Indeed, dance, music and art have been vital sites of positive interaction since the earliest days of colonial settlement (Clendinnen 2003), often mutually recognised as sites of shared appreciation, mutual understanding and creative joy; we increasingly celebrate emerging hybrid forms of expression such as 'indigenous' country and western music, or the painting of 'traditional' designs and Dreaming stories using oil on canvas.

These instances of joyful encounter occasioning shared understandings of compatible views and practices represent 'common notions'.

While initially arising from passive encounters and inadequate ideas rather than from interactions we have deliberately and actively contrived, common notions represent the point at which a common body becomes capable of an active agency of relation and self-assemblage. When joyful affects are produced in us by fortuitous passive encounters, such as occurred when the British arrivals to Australia danced merrily with indigenous welcoming parties on the sands of Botany Bay and Sydney Cove in 1788 (Clendinnen 2003: 8ff.), 'we can form an idea of what is common to some external body and our own', since 'when we encounter a body that agrees with our own, when we experience a joyful passive affection, we are induced to form the idea of what is common to that body and our own' (Deleuze 1990: 279, 281). From this passive joy, then, emerges an understanding of the way a particular aspect of the other's body combines successfully with ours, which is then the basis for an adequate idea, according to which we can begin to shape our encounters in the future. Since they describe that which participating bodies understand to be 'common' in their union, the joyful experience of common notions is necessarily mutual and shared, and so common notions also describe an ontological agreement that might be thought of as a prerequisite for postcolonialism: 'if it be true that two opposed bodies have something in common, one can never . . . be opposed to the other or bad for the other through what it has in common with it' (Deleuze 1990: 281).

However, most significantly, Deleuze's creative interpretation of Spinoza allows that the development of common notions as the basis for postcolonial sociability does *not* require us to disavow significant differences between bodies and eliminate sites of disagreement, in favour of a smooth and bland social harmony which simply privileges acts of co-identification. Deleuze emphasizes that bodies meet 'bit by bit' and while their meeting should be guided by common notions, these do not describe how bodies are compatible in their entirety, but rather describe an emergent understanding of how disparate bodies can join in partial and selective ways that encourage joyful experiences of the relationship while avoiding conducting the relation in a way that causes sadness to either body. In this way, 'even in the case of a body that does not agree with our own, and affects us with sadness, we can form an idea of what is common to that body and our own' (Deleuze 1990: 286; also Deleuze and Guattari 1987: 258); a body affected by sadness will come to understand that the particular aspect of the union causing the sad affect is incompatible with its nature. Thus, even in disagreement we can find joy, since 'an active joy always follows from what we understand'

(Deleuze 1990: 287). In so far as we understand bodily disagreement to be the cause of sadness, this ceases to be a passion, instead enabling the formation of an adequate idea of our own body and that of the other, and an awareness of how the nature of their respective compositions prohibits their successful combination.

For example, indigenous and non-indigenous peoples have very different understandings about land ownership and use, but these different understandings might be 'combined' via the construction of mediating concepts such as native title, which occupy a space between the two systems of common and indigenous law (Pearson 1997; see also Patton 2000: 128–31). Deleuze and Guattari name this process 'unnatural participation', by which they mean that even when bodies don't by nature agree, the formation of 'common notions' allows a mutual becoming and a unity that 'expresses them both' (1987: 258). However, the indigenous practice of punitive spearing in preference to incarceration (which is perceived by many indigenous people to be inhumane) is arguably incommensurable with non-indigenous views on bodily integrity and criminal justice; likewise, indigenous systems of kinship, social responsibility and collective care for country based on skin-groups and interconnected systems of belonging enshrined in the laws of the Dreaming are arguably incompatible with non-indigenous legal traditions based on notions of individual autonomy and transferable property rights. The two systems embody 'conflicting imaginaries' (Gatens 2008).

In reaching an understanding about the incompatibility of such perspectives and practices, it becomes apparent that their combination or unification can only be achieved by the subordination of one viewpoint to the other and the imposition of one set of bodily features on another, thus destroying the composition defining that other body, and so causing sadness. The alternative to this imposition of a sad relation is to resist the attempt to combine incompatible aspects of bodies, for example by instead enabling both indigenous and non-indigenous systems of justice to exist and be self-determining, comprising separate judicial and punitive forms that apply as necessary and relevant, according to the nature of the crime and the identity of the criminal body involved. The challenge we face is to engage each other in ways that will maximise our mutually joyful affects, and minimise disagreeable combinations that reduce the complexity of our co-existence and affect one or both of us with sadness. Bodies meet 'bit by bit': they might joyfully combine where possible, and might seek to reach agreement through persuasive argumentation, but where agreement is not possible, they should avoid coercing an unhappy fit through assimilation, elimination or subordination. Developing adequate understanding of both agreement and disagreement in the various facets of a relationship allows bodies to relate to one another in ways that find joy and avoid unhappy conflict.

We have now travelled some conceptual distance from the Stolen Generations who populated the start of this chapter. Via his creative reading of Spinozan embodiment, I have described how Deleuzian ontology depicts complex relational embodiment as a process of assemblage, which generates an equally complex notion of selfhood. It is evident how this ontology of relational and affective subjectivity assembled 'bit by bit' through 'piecemeal insertions' into other assemblages, prompting partial transformations and mutual becomings, radically departs from the various ontological assumptions underlying liberalism and communitarianism. In particular, this ontology rests upon a view of difference as primary, positive and creative; engagement with others is the enabling condition of the development of common notions, bringing joy; and a body benefits in exposure to wide and diverse social milieu, maximising scope for compatible engagement. Even disagreement, once understood, can be a source of joy: actively understanding ourselves and others and the ways in which we are compatible and incompatible allows us to direct our meeting in ways that encourage joy and avoid sadness. The concluding section returns to the question of postcolonial care and the continuing need for a more formal notion of justice or 'rights', considered in light of this ontology.

Life Rights

In any new combination of bodies some sadness and some joy will result, as the bodies become affected in novel ways that transform their identities (Deleuze 1990: 222). Joy results from the ways in which the new combination creates new ways of being affected and increases capacity for adequate understanding and active self-assembly. Sadness results from the loss of identity that occurs with the destruction of an existing relation that defines bodily consistency. Arising from common notions, the experience of Spinozan joy is always mutual as both bodies are affected with increased existential power at the sites of their complex union; however, a power relation might alternatively be unequal, occasioning pleasure for the more powerful body (though not *joyful* pleasure, which is necessarily mutual), and sadness for the powerless other. A combination might take place in which one of the bodies suffers a proportionally greater loss of existing identity as the new relationship transforms many of its existing component relations. An exemplary case in point is the devastation caused to indigenous communities decimated in the early period of colonial settlement by exposure to introduced diseases such as smallpox and syphilis. In such cases, the experience of sadness might significantly affect only one of the bodies joined in an encounter, and so the unaffected body might feel no immediate cause to avoid the encounter. As Deleuze explains, while some existential sadness is inevitable as identity naturally shifts and transforms, disproportionate sadness can be debilitating: 'We are defeated if sadness takes us over more and more, in all our component relations, this marking the destruction of our overall relation' (Deleuze 1990: 242–3). Colonial engagements characteristically impose sad relations upon indigenous bodies, increasing the power (and pleasure) of the colonial body and marking the debilitation and sometimes destruction of the overall relation defining indigenous ways of being. For the Stolen Generations, the experience of being removed – of their removal from a way of Being – involved a radical destruction of identity encompassing loss of kinship, and ultimately of communal forms of identification including land, language, philosophy, law and religion. This potential for striking sadness upon those we engage with returns us to the idea of postcolonial care and the need for safeguards against wilful or careless bodily destruction.

I have suggested that postcolonialism depends upon the development of common notions, which are the basis for actively creating complex forms of agreement and union, bringing mutual joy; postcolonisation accordingly involves an 'effort to form an association of men [sic] in relations that can be combined', and also entails that we must strive to join with others in a way that ensures neither will be 'overcome by sadness' (Deleuze 1990: 261, 243). Such effort requires a careful approach that strives towards adequate understanding of ourselves and others and the ways in which we might joyfully combine. This quality of comportment is characteristically attentive to possible agreements and conflicts, is guided by the mutuality of joy, and avoids coercing aspects of relation that knowingly cause sadness. Developing this understanding of the ways in which bodies might meet in a mutually agreeable, and hence potentially postcolonial fashion, requires a careful and caring practice of relationship, in which each listens respectfully to the other in order to learn how the other is affected. As signalled by the passage from *Bringing Them Home* cited earlier, the development of common notions of mutual agreement thus involves a 'kind of grace' demonstrating the careful and conscientious practice of a 'quality of concern' which forms the 'basis for a new kind of relationship'. The outcome of this careful practice is a 'kind of restorative love', which reflects the postcolonial experience of joy.

Unlike one's enjoyment of the entitlement protected by human rights, joy cannot be possessed, nor 'stolen' by others, although it can be transformed, broken or disrupted. Joy properly refers to a felt quality of relationship that is experienced as intensity and complex compatibility, rather than to a property of selfhood that is held or lost. Granted, joy is then a second kind of satisfaction, 'beyond' enjoyment, which arises from a different kind of social practice from the state-mediated politico-juridical observation that results in a person's unimpeded ability to enjoy their given human rights. The nature of this second type of practice involves the immediate and spontaneous association of bodies in concrete relations characterised by their 'human warmth'. Joy arises from a choice made directly by bodies in encountering others, to participate in a caring and attentive kind of association. It describes the satisfaction created by the affirming conjunction of people in a way that mutually enhances them, when they create a complex union that increases their power to understand each other; to empathise and care; to exist well together. In so doing, the experience of the complex union gives something back to each of the participants, in the form of joy. It is perhaps by virtue of their unmediated nature that such joyful encounters are then claimed to be the 'highest achievement flowing from the Inquiry [into the Stolen Generations]'. That is, they involve a spontaneous ethical practice, where participants willingly choose to behave with care for others, rather than the dull observation of socio-ethical duty, regulated by the watchful gaze of the state, where people behave dutifully towards each other primarily because they understand that they legally must.

Unlike the manifestly suspicious and imperial disposition displayed when my attitude towards others is structured by (real or imagined) lack or absence, or fear of theft, and the other is accordingly perceived as threatening or as the object I must appropriate, the kind of desire for association that makes joy possible involves an entirely different attitude towards the other. It involves, at least, a certain openness to joining with the other, an inclusiveness and a mutual effort to listen and understand, a willingness to trust in the other's capacity to behave positively towards me, to refrain from destroying, manipulating or dominating me, and my implicit promise to conduct myself with the same practical care and respect, in my relationship with the other. However, the undeniable fact remains that bodies and Beings are routinely crushed and diminished in daily social life. There will always be a need to safeguard enjoyment, since humans are always capable of colonisation, nastiness and the wilful destruction of Being, even though we are also capable of non-imperial engagements, niceness and the practice of joy. Rights therefore offer a minimum protection we simply can't do without, for as Isaiah Berlin famously points out, there is no guarantee that benevolent and joyful relations of power that exist to secure a communal good will not turn corrupt and become coercive forces of domination and submission in which the very notion of the good becomes a perverted justification for evil (Berlin 1999).

As eternal principles observing fixed and inalienable qualities of human nature and dignity, established notions of human rights clearly do not accord with Deleuzian ontology since, as we have seen, Deleuze conceptualises bodies as 'infinite multiplicities' that are multi-faceted, internally unstable, conflicted and complex assemblages characterised by their mutating affective relations with other bodies. Indeed, Deleuze is notably reticent on the topic of human rights, and neither rights nor the democratic political system that supports them are treated comprehensively as a focus in Deleuze's work.[4] At worse he is scathing: 'human rights' are 'purely abstract, completely empty . . . it's just intellectual discourse, for odious intellectuals at that, for intellectuals who have no ideas . . . those people who are quite satisfied to recall and to recite "the rights of man," they are just dim-witted' (Deleuze and Parnet: 2003).[5] How is it possible to make use of *this* Deleuze in a postcolonial context? Deleuze's remarks seem to support the claims of some who criticise his rejection of political representation, also decrying his lack of concrete prescription concerning political engagement and the institutions of political society and public reason, associated with his unwillingness to take a definitive stand on behalf of powerless subalterns (Hallward 2006; Spivak 1988).

While it remains beyond the scope of this chapter to develop a Deleuzian perspective on rights or political society, it is important to note that his approving comments on jurisprudence as the ongoing creation or modification of legal principles on a case by case basis, 'make it clear that Deleuze is not opposed to rights as such but only to the idea that there exists a definitive set of human rights grounded in some rights-bearing feature of human nature' (Patton 2005a: 405). For Deleuze, 'there are no "rights of man", only "rights of life", and so, life unfolds case by case' (Deleuze and Parnet 2003, video interview). This perspective on rights corresponds to his ontology, which as we have seen, considers bodies to be 'infinite multiplicities' enmeshed in affective relations of power, which are themselves multiple and shift according to changing engagements with other bodies in a social milieu, thus taking form according to the internal composition of a body at a particular time. Because affective relations are variable and contextual, and power is simultaneously a force of composition and of decomposition affecting participating bodies at multiple sites of engagement, the 'rightful' limits to the impact of one body's powers upon another can only be decided according to the context of the situation in which their meeting occurs. In this way, 'Our ability to resist control, or our submission to it, has to be assessed at the level of our every move' (Deleuze 1995: 176).

For Deleuze and Guattari, as well as for Foucault, fluid micropolitical relations act as scaffolding for the emergence of more rigid macropolitical structures and conventions such as rights and political institutions servicing public debate and distributive justice (Deleuze and Guattari 1987: 213–28; Guattari 1984; Foucault 1978: 93; see also Connolly 1999, 2008; Patton 2004, 2005b). According to this logic of 'becoming', 'emergence' or 'actualisation', careful forms of sociability practised at the micropolitical level are conducive to the development of macrostructures that institutionalise and entrench these norms of care within political society as formal guiding principles for just and ethical action. On this view, a right is best seen as a 'political invention [requiring] a whole lot of micropolitical preparation' (Connolly 2008: 234). Rights then act back upon the relations acted out at the micropolitical level, guiding and protecting bodies in their fluid and immediate relations of practice. The complex interplay between micropolitical and macropolitical levels of society constitutes an intricate movement that Deleuze names 'folding', which might be thought to supplement the more common Western political philosophies that maintain a privileged focus on macropolitical justice, often excluding or suppressing the relevance of micropolitical care.[6] However, careful sociability is not guaranteed at the micropolitical level, and bodies frequently find themselves fenced in and immobilised by macropolitical structures that may have emerged from original benevolence; care alone is insufficient as a basis for ethical behaviour and protection from political abuse. Agreed principles of justice are additionally needed to formally regulate micropolitical engagements between bodies; to safeguard participating bodies from wholesale destruction and protect the *mutuality* of their affectivity and becoming. Furthermore, institutions of public reason and deliberation are required for the incremental development of 'common notions' that might define an emergent understanding of 'rights'. In this way, justice and care are different but mutually implicated sensibilities, arising from the fact that one's relations are both particular and general (Benhabib 1992). Indeed, this essay began with the claim that the Stolen Generations compel attention to the complex interplay between concrete and general relations, between abstract principles of justice and the concrete ethics of careful sociability. The historical situation of post-coloniality calls for a particular 'ethos of engagement' that is 'responsive to both the indispensability of justice and the radical insufficiency of justice to itself' (Connolly 1999: 68, cited Patton 2005b).

Of course, indigenous and non-indigenous communities must now find ways to meet in a contemporary situation which is deeply scarred by the history of colonisation. We do not currently meet on equal footing, since one community has emerged from the experience of colonisation diminished, fragmented, curtailed and controlled, while the other enjoys a legacy of historical privilege incorporating a relative freedom to act at will without cultural temperance or due accountability. In assessing the 'rightful limits' to our affective impact upon one another, we must first assess our differing abilities to 'resist control' in light of the history that has brought us to our current state of engagement; we must look at how the scars have been etched over time, and with the benefit of hindsight we may come to appreciate the depth and nature of the injury, and the scope and nature of the redress that is required if indigenous communities are to redevelop a cohesive (though not fixed or essential) sense of self. This primary 'sense of self' is required if we are to affect one another on a more equal basis, properly sharing in the postcolonial production of common notions according to which our bodies are able to actively meet 'bit by bit' in ways that partially transform them both, bringing mutual joy and avoiding debilitating sadness and destruction. Hindsight allows an appreciation of how our historical engagements might have been more careful and more respectful, in turn allowing a vision of how things might alternatively have taken place and form, in turn allowing better understanding of the present in terms of its wounds and its potential for healing, prompting redress for the painful wrongs of the past and shaping postcolonial transformation for the future:

> Inquiry into our confused beginnings suggests that the possibility of a decent co-existence between unlike groups must begin from the critical scrutiny of our own assumptions and values as they come under challenge. We might then be able to make informed decisions as to which uncomfortable differences we are prepared to tolerate and which we are not, rather than to attempt the wholesale reformation of what we identify as the defects of the other. A lasting tolerance builds slowly out of accretions of delicate accommodations made through time; and it comes, if it comes at all, as slow as honey (Clendinnen 2003: 288).

The need to preserve a 'sense of self' that can provide an anchor for the reasoned development of common notions and protect a body from radical debilitation and collapse during its processes of becoming informs a normative dimension to Deleuze's perspective on rights, which is discernible in comments made throughout his work, again stemming from his early reading of Spinoza where he writes: 'All a body can do (its power) is also its "natural right"' (Deleuze 1990: 257). By this he means that any particular body has a 'natural right' actively to form associations that will allow it both to persevere in select aspects of its Being and to enhance its affective power, according to its *conatus*. In so far as the development of common notions is central to this emergent rational activity of self-formation that gradually develops from passive affections, it follows that some core structure or consistency is also rightfully required to persist through the body's transformations, in order for it to be able to form adequate ideas and common notions by coherently 'thinking the body' and the nature of the relations it forms with others. In this respect, Deleuze insists upon the need for both inventiveness and consistency in ontological processes: 'we need both creativity *and* a people' (Deleuze 1995: 176). Accordingly, the nature of the body as an affective assemblage also 'constitutes what can be called *a right to desire*' (Deleuze and Parnet 1987: 147): all bodies have the right to exercise discretion and preference in forming and transforming the situations and associations that constitute their identity, and this activity is normatively guided by the development of adequate ideas of selfhood, common notions of relationship, and the experience of joy. Clearly, the forcible removal of indigenous children from their communities, forbidding their associations with family and territory, with their religious practices and their own languages, demonstrates a comprehensive failure to respect this 'right to desire'.

While a theory of rights remains underdeveloped in Deleuze's work, there is arguably room to develop aspects of his thought towards a more comprehensive notion of rights as agreed 'common notions', which can enable and safeguard the active processes of self-development and joyful practice that are characteristically destroyed by acts of colonisation. Without doubt, Deleuzian philosophy also offers concepts of selfhood and sociability that are useful in the context of creating non-imperial styles of thought and practice. Because his intellectual lineage situates him in a minor philosophical tradition that he incorporates and also creatively transforms in his own *oeuvre*, many of Deleuze's concerns and concepts are not restricted by the dominant emphases and the entrenched terms of debate of much Western political theory. Deleuze's work thus offers Western theory an exit from these habitual terms of reference, which often cause it to remain fettered to problematic notions of identity and difference, and limit its effectiveness in assisting the birth of new forms of postcolonial society. In this chapter I have argued that Deleuze's concept of embodiment as a process of complex affective assemblage enables an understanding of relational selfhood that incorporates a positive and creative role for ontological difference and gives rise to an ethic of joyful sociability based on material practices of self-awareness, listening respect and attentiveness to the other. In this way, Deleuzian philosophy supports an ethics beyond enjoyment, comprising elements of both justice and care, which might now guide us towards the joyful experience promised by a common notion of the postcolonial.

References

Altman, J. and M. Hinkson (2007), *Coercive Reconciliation: Stabilise, Normalise, Exit Aboriginal Australia*, Carlton: Arena Publications.
Armstrong, A. (1997), 'Some Reflections on Deleuze's Spinoza: Composition and Agency', in K. Ansell-Pearson (ed.), *Deleuze and Philosophy: The Difference Engineer*, New York: Routledge, pp. 44–57.
Benhabib, S. (1992), *Situating the Self*, London: Polity Press.
Berlin, I. (1999), 'Two Concepts of Liberty', in G. Sher and B. Brody (eds), *Social and Political Philosophy: Contemporary Readings*, Orlando: Harcourt Brace, pp. 624–36.
Bignall, S. (2007), 'A Superior Empiricism: The Subject and Experimentation', *Pli (Warwick Journal of Philosophy)* 18: 201–17.
Calma, T. (2008), *Speech: Let the Healing Begin*, Members' Hall, Parliament House, Canberra, 13 February. Viewed at: www.humanrights.gov.au/about/media/speeches/social_justice/2008/20080213response_to_gov_to_the_national_apology_to_the_stolen_generations.html
Clendinnen, I. (2003), *Dancing with Strangers*, Melbourne: Text Publishing.
Connolly, W. E. (1999), *Why I Am Not a Secularist*, Minneapolis: University of Minnesota Press.
Connolly, W. E. (2008), 'An Ethos of Engagement', in S. Chambers and T. Carver (eds), *William Connolly: Democracy, Pluralism and Political Theory*, London: Routledge, pp. 231–53.
Cornwall, A. (2002), *Restoring Identity: Final Report of the Moving Forward Consultation Project*, Sydney: Public Interest Advocacy Centre.
Deleuze, G. (1990), *Expressionism in Philosophy: Spinoza*, trans. M. Joughin, New York: Zone Books.
Deleuze, G. (1995), *Negotiations*, trans. M. Joughin, New York: Columbia University Press.
Deleuze, G. and F. Guattari (1987), *A Thousand Plateaus*, trans. B. Massumi, Minneapolis: Minnesota University Press.
Deleuze, G. and C. Parnet (1987) *Dialogues*, trans. H. Tomlinson and B. Habberjam, New York: Columbia University Press.
Deleuze, G. and C. Parnet (2003), *L'Abécédaire de Gilles Deleuze avec Claire Parnet*, CD Rom: Vidéo Editions Montparnasse.
Foucault, M. (1978), *The Will to Knowledge: The History of Sexuality I*, trans. R. Hurley, New York: Random House.
Frazer, E. and N. Lacey (1993), *The Politics of Community*, Hertfordshire: Harvester Wheatsheaf.

Gatens, M. (1996), 'Through a Spinozist Lens: Ethology, Difference, Power', in P. Patton (ed.), *Deleuze: A Critical Reader*, Oxford: Blackwell, pp. 162–88.
Gatens, M. (2008), 'Conflicting Imaginaries in Australian Multiculturalism: Women's Rights, Group Rights and Aboriginal Customary Law', in G. B. Levey (ed.), *Political Theory and Australian Multiculturalism*, New York: Berghahn Books, pp. 151–70.
Gilligan, C. (1982), *In a Different Voice: Psychological Theory and Women's Development*, Cambridge: Harvard University Press.
Guattari, F. (1984), *Molecular Revolution: Psychiatry and Politics*, trans. R. Sheed, New York: Penguin.
Hallward, P. (2006), *Out of This World: Deleuze and the Philosophy of Creation*, London and New York: Verso.
HREOC (1997), *Bringing Them Home: Report on the National Inquiry into the Stolen Generations*, Canberra: Human Rights and Equal Opportunities Commission.
Lefebvre, A. (2005), 'A New Image of Law: Deleuze and Jurisprudence', *Telos* 130: 103–26.
Lefebvre, A. (2008), *The Image of Law: Deleuze, Bergson, Spinoza*, Stanford: Stanford University Press.
Mengue, P. (2003), *Deleuze et la question de la démocratie*, Paris: L'Harmattan.
Patton, P. (2000), *Deleuze and the Political*, London: Routledge.
Patton, P. (2004), 'Power and Right in Nietzsche and Foucault', *International Studies in Philosophy* 36 (3): 43–61.
Patton, P. (2005a), 'Deleuze and Democracy', *Contemporary Political Theory* 4: 400–13.
Patton, P. (2005b), 'Deleuze and Democratic Politics' in L. Tønder and L. Thomassen (eds), *Radical democracy: Politics between Abundance and Lack*, Manchester and New York: Manchester University Press, pp. 50–67.
Pearson, N. (1997), 'The Concept of Native Title at Common Law', in G. Yunupingu (ed.), *Our Land Is Our Life: Land Rights – Past, Present, Future*, St Lucia: Queensland University Press, pp. 150–62.
Rudd, K. (2008), *Speech: Apology to Australia's Indigenous Peoples*, House of Reps, Parliament House, Canberra, 13 February. Viewed at www.pm.gov.au/media/speech/2008/speech_0073.cfm
Sartre, J. P. [1943] (1996), *Being and Nothingness*, trans. H. E. Barnes, London: Routledge.
Spivak, G. C. (1988), 'Can the Subaltern Speak?', in C. Nelson and L. Grossberg (eds), *Marxism and the Interpretation of Culture*, Urbana: University of Illinois Press, pp. 271–313.
Žižek, S. (1993), *Tarrying with the Negative*, Durham: Duke University Press.

Notes

1. See the testimonies recorded in the 1997 Report on the National Inquiry into the Stolen Generations by the Human Rights and Equal Opportunities Commission, titled *Bringing Them Home*.
2. There is no uniform approach to compensation, which has been strongly resisted by the previous Federal Government; however, the Tasmanian Government established a $5 million fund in 2006, and in South Australia in 2007 a Ngarrindjeri elder won a landmark legal struggle to obtain compensation for his 'wrongful removal' as a child.
3. In his response to the *Apology*, Aboriginal and Torres Strait Islander Social Justice Commissioner Tom Calma (2008) notes that the apology lays the foundations 'for

healing to take place and for a reconciled Australia in which everyone belongs. For [the apology] is not just about the Stolen Generations – it is about every Australian.'
4. For a discussion of Deleuze on democracy see work by Paul Patton (2005a; 2005b). These essays respond to the critique presented by Mengue (2003). For discussion of Deleuze and jurisprudence see recent works by Alexandre Lefebvre (2005; 2008).
5. I am grateful to Charles Stivale, via Paul Patton, for assistance with translation of *L'Abécédaire*.
6. The justice/care debate has mainly been taken up by feminist philosophers, who argue that moral perspective is necessarily gendered, and that the abstract principles of Rawlsian liberal justice presuppose a masculine-identified moral perspective defined by an autonomous, rational, self-interested self. The polarisation and privileging of liberalism over communitarianism, and of 'justice' over 'care', is here seen as part of an unacknowledged masculinist political agenda. See Gilligan (1982); Frazer and Lacey (1993).

Chapter 5

The Postcolonial Event: Deleuze, Glissant and the Problem of the Political

Nick Nesbitt

The relation between the philosophy of Deleuze and Guattari and the foremost postcolonial thinker in the francophone world, Édouard Glissant, is long-standing, complex and immensely consequential, both for the work of Glissant himself and for the wider field of Postcolonial Studies in general. Glissant has recently described how he met Guattari in Paris in the 1980s, and the friendship that resulted from the impression the latter made upon him: 'I said to myself, "I'm hearing Socrates." I heard the same wisdom, the same irony, the same bitterness of approach and fundamental kindness' (cited in Dosse 2007: 515). The result of this encounter profoundly influenced Glissant, who is as much an inventor of concepts as Deleuze and Guattari themselves.

Like his predecessors Aimé Césaire and Frantz Fanon, Édouard Glissant has combined a passionate engagement in the politics of decolonisation with a concern to analyse the modes and structures of French colonialism, from its origins to its peculiar perpetuation in the form it has taken since 1946 as the so-called 'Departmentalisation' of the former 'colony' of Martinique (as well as Guadeloupe and French Guiana). In 1959, Glissant was a founding member with Paul Niger and Daniel Boukman of the separatist Front Antillo-Guyanais pour l'Autonomie, and because of his political activity, was barred from leaving metropolitan France for the Overseas Departments from 1961 to 1965 (Calmont 2007: 95). Glissant's nationalist, pro-independence political engagement continued to second his literary and theoretical work throughout the 1970s, culminating in the publication in 1981 of *Le Discours antillais*, the work which stands today, beside Césaire's *Discours sur le colonialisme* (1953) and Fanon's *Peau noire, masques blancs* (1952), as the outstanding critique of French colonialism in the Caribbean.

In the wake of Césaire and Fanon, Glissant is also the most important non-metropolitan French writer in the Anglo-American dominated field of Postcolonial Studies. In its francophone Caribbean variant, Glissant has quite simply defined the entire field of discourse along the lines he set forth in his 1981 theoretical magnum opus *Le Discours antillais*. His thought made a decisive and explicit link with that of Deleuze and Guattari when, in his *Poétique de la relation*, Glissant drew a line from his own pre-existing concept of 'relation' to the concept of the 'rhizome': 'The notion of the rhizome is in principle (*serait au principe*) that of what I call a poetics of Relation, according to which all identity extends outward in a relation to the Other' (1990: 23).[1] Since then, this reference to the philosophy of Deleuze and Guattari has remained a constant for Glissant, continuing to inform his work through to his most recent collection of essays from 2005, *La Cohée du Lamentin* (232).[2]

Beyond this more visible citation of Deleuze and Guattari by Glissant, in what follows I wish to explore a few of the less visible, subterranean conceptual linkages between these thinkers, and in so doing, to trace the complex and often problematic image of the political that emerges at the intersection of the triplet Deleuze–Glissant–postcolonialism. For since the publication of Peter Hallward's groundbreaking *Absolutely Postcolonial* in 2001, it is precisely at the crossroads between these three figures that the field of Postcolonial Studies has found itself the object of an intensive critique of the actual political purchase of so-called 'cultural politics'. If we accept as axiomatic that a principal, indeed *the* principal concern of Postcolonial Studies has been the nature of political change in the colonial world, *Absolutely Postcolonial* has forced postcolonial theorists to question to what degree *any* of these three subjects – Deleuze, Glissant and the postcolonial – are properly to be understood as *political*. While I am sympathetic to the basic distinction Hallward draws, following Alain Badiou, between purely *political* activity (as undivided egalitarianism) and the compromised 'politics' of the worlds they break away from, I will argue that such a wilfully limited (axiomatic) concept of the political impoverishes our resources for addressing systematic injustice in light of the imperative of justice.[3] While I second Hallward's critique of so-called 'postcolonial', 'cultural' and 'identity' politics as a 'disastrous confusion of spheres', (Hallward 2001:47), Hallward's bent for axiomatic, antagonistic analysis of situations leads him into the overarching claim that 'Glissant's work in particular and postcolonial theory in general can *only* [my emphasis] obstruct what is arguably the great political task of our time: the articulation of fully egalitarian political principles which, while *specific* to the particular situation of their declaration, are nevertheless *subtracted* from their cultural environment' (2001: xix, 26). While this may be true to some extent, given among other factors Glissant's long-standing and problematic antagonism to universalism, we must ask whether such a view can adequately account for the enormous critical and specific (in Hallward's sense of the term) insight into the modalities of traditional and late French colonialism of a text such as the *Discours antillais*. To follow Hallward's reasoning, we should, for example, abandon Marx's analysis of political economy in *Das Kapital* as strictly apolitical (a move Badiou has explicitly endorsed, but one which Hallward, in his interest in a 'relational ontology', 'the politics of this world' and 'relations of conflict or solidarity' surely would not [Hallward 2006: 162]). While I fully subscribe to Hallward's egalitarian, universalist understanding of politics, surely 'the great political task of our time' must go beyond merely 'articulating' principles, to engaging concretely (antagonistically, transformatively, relationally) with actually existing situations and worlds and the transcendental logics that structure them.[4]

Similarly, Hallward's wilfully tendential reading of Deleuze (2006), while incisive, suggestive, and original, ends up simply casting aside Deleuze as a thinker of the political in any way, shape or form. Certainly, the image Hallward draws, in the finest Deleuzian tradition, is properly unrecognisable by Deleuzians, yet utterly faithful in its profound engagement with his work. One can only truly betray an author, as Žižek writes of Deleuze, by faithfully repeating his doctrine (2008: 140). And yet, to conclude that 'the political aspect of Deleuze's philosophy amounts to little more than utopian distraction', (Hallward 2006: 162) is surely to ignore, say, the profound symmetry between 'minoritarian' politics and Badiou's subtractive model politics, or the two philosophers' shared (if not identical) philosophies of the event (a symmetry to which I will return in what follows).

Paul Patton, in his book *Deleuze and the Political*, has devoted considerable energy to demonstrating the many political dimensions of Deleuze's work. Deleuzian concepts with strong and explicit political valences include the process of absolute deterritorialisation which extends not only to the actual, but also to a restructuring of the virtual itself (2000: 107), the proto-anarchist critique of (political) representation (2000: 8), the process of counter-actualisation (2000: 28), the concept of becoming (2000: 78), and a Foucauldian ethics of critical freedom that addresses 'the conditions of change or transformation of the subject' via a process of subtraction from the determinations of (social) norms and identity (2000: 83–4). *A Thousand Plateaus* in its totality offers readers, Patton suggests, a new political ontology 'that provides tools to describe transformative, creative, or deterritorializing forces and movements' (2000: 9).

While in his later work Glissant shares Deleuze's concern for non-dialectical, immediate relation, the earlier Glissant's notions of relation and difference were fundamentally dialectical, conceived as a logic of intersubjectivity and the mediation of difference. In drawing this distinction, I am in fact in agreement with Hallward's discussion of the two thinkers (2001: 67, 122); however, unlike Hallward, I will maintain a focus on the earlier Glissant (pre-*Poetics of Relation*) as the only truly *political* Glissant. As both Hallward (2001) and Bongie (2008), as well as myself (2003), have argued in exhaustive detail, Glissant's work since 1990 is of no interest on the plane of global colonial politics (although it may continue to be so in the realm of culture and aesthetics, to which Glissant now exactingly and forthrightly limits his work [cf. Bongie 2008: 341]).[5]

A properly political reading of Glissant would thus need to focus on the concept of the '*nation*' in his work, conceived precisely as the expression of the conscious, general will of the people, a people subtracted from all race, class and gender-based specification. This neo-Jacobin nation, like the Haiti of 1804 that is its model, would be 'made up of all those who, whatever their cultural origin or "way of being," collectively *decide* to assert (or re-assert) the right of self-determination' (Hallward 2001: 127). Beyond the model of the French Revolution Hallward refers to, the Haitian revolution's implementation of a post-racial nation-state more precisely embodies the model of universalist despecification from all identity-based politics that accords with a universalist, neo-Jacobin politics of universal emancipation. This universalist tradition must be, I would argue, the core and foundation of any 'postcolonial' politics. Though vulnerable to various divisive, particularist appropriations, from Human Rights interventionism to wars of empire justified in the name of 'liberty' or 'democracy', the proper response to such perversions of justice is not the retreat into the defence of local particularisms, but to remain faithful to the egalitarian imperative.

We must remain faithful, then, to the founding gesture encapsulated in Aimé Césaire's initial cry in the *Cahier d'un retour au pays natal*: 'Assez de ce scandale!' (1971: 37). While Hallward rightfully critiques the facile and depoliticising conflation of culture and politics in Postcolonial Studies, what remains to be described are those rare moments when a radically subtractive poetics (such as that which Badiou celebrates in Mallarmé) *inhabits* and seconds a political plane of universal emancipation. In distinction to the radical infidelity of Senghorian neocolonial cultural politics, Césaire's was just such a subtractive poetry.[6] This twentieth-century universalism, explicitly modelled on the Haitian example, was for Césaire a process of neo-Jacobin decolonisation founded on the politics of figures such as Toussaint and Schoelcher.[7] As such, in the midst of contemporary colonial scandals such as the destruction of emancipatory politics in Haiti by the forces of global colonialism (in the 2004 coup, the US, Canada and France specifically), a detribalised concept of the nation may indeed offer 'the only really effective vehicle available for these articulations on a broad collective scale' (Hallward 2001: 126).[8] Such a politics, as Hallward has more recently argued, is now, as it has been since 1789, primordially a matter of a general, universalist political will.

Like the later Glissant, Deleuze has always been concerned not with dialectical change, but with what he has called *internal* difference, the self-sufficient transformation of a body in sheer indifference to its surroundings (Nesbitt 2005; Hallward 2006: 162). Moreover, a whole range of other concepts and terms resonate strongly between Deleuze and Guattari and the Glissant of the *Poétique*. To the critiques of identity, territory and Oedipus, along with the celebration of the swarm-like crowd, baroque proliferation, variation, deterritorialisation, quantifiable multiplication and analysis in terms of extension across surfaces as opposed to conceptual depth, all of which Hallward mentions (2001: 359, n.118), must be added a fundamental and all-determining vitalism that has most recently been analysed by Michael Wiedorn (2008). In short, to explore the problem of the political in Glissant, Deleuze and the postcolonial is a task that far exceeds the limitations of this short chapter, and yet it is arguably *the* task confronting, at the very least, my own field of francophone postcolonial studies.[9]

As Chris Bongie has shown, while the *Discours antillais* undoubtedly pursues a multiform exploration of the *relations* inhering (or potentially inhering) between culture and the pursuit of a properly political nationalist autonomy, the project of Glissant's work is not to collapse the two categories into the confused and even meaningless hybrid Hallward decries ('cultural politics'), but rather, rigorously to distinguish the two (Bongie 2008: 345). A useful and less familiar entry point into this Deleuze/Glissant/postcolonial rhizome is perhaps best made via the concept of the event, an arch-political concept explored by both Deleuze and Glissant, as well as by French thinkers from Sartre to Badiou; surely a point of no small interest for contemporary Postcolonial Studies in light of Hallward's critique.

For Deleuze, the event occurs within univocal being (there being no outside to his Spinozist understanding of Being), as a flux or fold that is unpredictable from within the co-ordinates of the world, as a break into a 'revolutionary becoming' (1995: 171). Any revolutionary event, furthermore, is novel in so far only as it is a *repetition*, albeit one with a critical *difference*. And so the Haitian revolution is the *repetition* of all Spartacusian slave revolts of time immemorial (cf. Badiou 2006: 73) as well as of the French Revolution, but precisely with a critical *difference*: it is a revolution as much against those revolutions (as failures, as the white, male, European *perpetuation* of slavery) as against the actually-existing plantocracy in place in St Domingue. The actual failure of 1789 (to end slavery) lived on as a virtual truth, awaiting its actualisation on the periphery of the agrarian capitalist world system (cf. Žižek 2001: 141; see also Foucault 1984).

Deleuze first developed this repetition-based understanding of the event in the 'Twenty-First Series of the Event' in *The Logic of Sense* (1969). There, he famously describes the event as a 'wound' which one bears within one's body 'in its eternal truth as a pure event' (1990: 148). On the political plane, this wound, I would argue, is precisely that of revolutionary failure, of the suffering and failure that the past brings to us – as Benjamin said, as the virtual index of redemption. This virtual event we bear as a wound is an opening onto a political 'will', Deleuze tells us (1990: 148).

In describing the event as wound, the opposition with Alain Badiou could not be more starkly drawn. For Badiou, the suffering of the past and political failure is utterly indifferent, and quite literally does not *count* in his philosophical world. The suffering human is mere base animality, a 'suffering beast' to be kept in prophylactic separation from the 'Immortal' truth of 'Man' (2003b: 26–7). In contrast, Deleuze's Benjaminian understanding of the event and its relation to history retains the two axioms of any Benjaminian 'historical materialism': 'The past carries with it a temporal index by which it is referred to redemption' and 'Nothing that has ever happened should be regarded as lost for history' (Benjamin 1968: 254). The first describes a *historicity* that opposes the mere relativist concatenation of facts ('historicism') with their indexation upon a transcendental (for Badiou) or virtual (for Deleuze) register that Benjamin, in turn, famously figures as 'redemption'. The second, however, tells us that *all* that has happened must count in a materialist understanding of history.[10] Though every detail of the past must be considered and weighed, *all* occurrences remain consubstantial with the elaboration of truths. Egalitarianism is not merely anticipatory, but must cast its gaze over the entire catastrophe of history.

Deleuze's wound of past failures enjoins us to become the 'quasi-cause' of its continued unfolding in time, of 'what is produced within us', that is, autonomously, as an act of will, without waiting for the 'right moment' for political action (1990: 148). It is never the right moment to initiate a political event; we will always carry the wound of past failures as the pain that is the call of redemption. We must, Deleuze tells us, become the 'Operator' of the event. To initiate an event is to produce new surfaces within our place of existence, surfaces that would reflect in their light the remnants of failure, of this wound, of the virtual that has not (yet) been actualised. The event is virtual, 'incorporeal', asubjective, in a word: universal. 'It is a question of becoming a citizen of the world' (1990: 148). If the political logic of the event bears, for Deleuze, a moment of subtraction from the limitations of a world, a will to inhabit a plane of pure, undivided equality, within his positive ontology, the event is ultimately an expansive counter-actualisation of alternative forms of the present.[11] To become minor is not to become a minority, defined by one's race, gender, age, class, or any other limiting identity and distinguishing characteristic, but to move 'beyond . . . the particular, the collective, and the private' (Deleuze 1990: 148). The political logic of the event, for Deleuze as for Hallward and Badiou, is that of universal equality.

This alone, Deleuze concludes, is what we mean by ethics: 'not to be unworthy of what happens to us' (1990: 149). The failures and wounds we inherit are not cause for resentment ('someone else's fault'), even less for Nietzschean *ressentiment*; they are, rather, the reflection of redemption in the past, of an event not simply virtual, but fully actualised. Simply put, this redeemed world would be one in which a body, any body, does all that it is capable of doing. To be worthy of what happens to us, of our inheritance of the past failure that is our wound, is to redeem that failure as the actualisation of our fullest potential. And this is to acknowledge that slaves, say, are in fact bodies capable of expressing themselves fully in a world of undivided freedom from slavery (of whatever kind). What is immoral is any *ressentiment*-based morality that would block us from access to all our body (political) is capable of. Not to be resigned to one's 'fate' (a moral, inhibiting notion if ever there was one), but to discover within the image of the past the light of a (virtual) truth.

To 'will' an event is for Deleuze precisely to 'release its eternal truth' (1990: 149). For Badiou, the eternity of truth lies not in the actual world, but in a radical break with any existing world. In contrast, for Deleuze's vitalist univocity, the event is rather a process of 'release', a release or ignition of expression that opens onto or illuminates 'eternal truth'. The Deleuzian event is not a willing of what *actually* occurs, but to will 'something *in* that which occurs': the promise of the virtual, that it not be extinguished ('the fire on which [the event] is fed') (1990: 149). This event-to-come would be the eventual conformity of the virtual and the actual, 'something yet to come which would be consistent with what occurs, in accordance with the laws of an obscure, humorous conformity: the Event' (1990: 149). Precisely because of this wound that bears within it the promise of the event, action and the will are focused, intervention and militancy are 'actualized on [the event's] most contracted point, on the cutting edge of an operation.' (1990: 149). The event is not 'what occurs' in a world ('an accident'); and yet nor is it, as for Badiou, a break from a world. Instead, for Deleuze, the event 'is rather *inside* what occurs' (1990: 149, emphasis added).

'To will and release the event, to become the offspring of one's own events, and thereby to be reborn': the event is release from determination and the iron cage of identity, more than mere self-refashioning, the event is literally rebirth as another (1990: 149). The event is not the mere redistribution of the elements of a world (more 'equitably'), but rather is the invention of entirely new games and new worlds (1990: 150). This release is an accession to eternity, the eternal truth of the event that awaits its unfolding. 'The divine present is the circle in its entirety, whereas past and future are dimensions relative to a particular segment of the circle' (1990: 150). As the 'actor' of an event (as in 'historical actors') we are subtracted from specification, opened up to the 'impersonal and pre-individual', and we actualise the event not in the depth (of personality, of destiny, of representation) but purely across the 'surface' of time. The event is thus disengaged from the tyranny of specification; it is a 'counter-actualisation'. The truth of the event is actualised on this plane; in the details of its unfolding, there inevitably occur 'many injustices and ignominies' (such as what Deleuze, like Hegel calls the 'terror' of the revolutionary event) (1990: 151). In contrast to this *ressentiment* of the reactive subject, the event 'liberate[s] for each thing [its] . . . *Amor fati*' (1990: 151).

The event is not only the opening onto creative actualisations of the virtual; it is simultaneously the destroyer of all determinate worlds. 'Every event [is] a kind of plague, war, wound' (Deleuze 1990: 151); it is the death of a world, the dissolution of its transcendental structures. The death of the *ancien régime*, of slavery, of colonisation: these events were waged in total warfare against the determining co-ordinates of their world. This destruction is lived as violence from within the immediacy of a world, in 'the present moment of its actualization' (Deleuze 1990: 151). In the moment the event flashes up, it is necessarily '*embodied* in a state of affairs, an individual, or a person' (Deleuze 1990: 151; emphasis added). The event has always gone under a proper name: Spartacus, Toussaint, Haiti, *Libete*. Paul Patton writes:

> Event attributions do not simply describe or report pre-existing events, they help to actualize particular events in the social field. The manner in which a given occurrence is described determines it as a particular kind of event. That is why politics frequently takes the form of struggle over the appropriate description of events. (Patton 2000: 28)

Language is properly political when it withdraws from convention and the attribution of identity. 'All events are incorporeal transformations which are expressed in language' (Patton 2000: 27). The proper name of the event, for Badiou like Deleuze, is the embodiment of its eternity, the exposition and inscription of its eternal truth in the symbolic order (Badiou 2009). From this present moment, the truth of the event radiates out to encompass 'the future and the past' (Deleuze 1990: 151). But from the point of view of eternity, the event 'sidestep[s] each present', it is beyond all 'limitations of a state of affairs' (1990: 151). It is, as Deleuze first argued, in subtraction from any state (of affairs). This subtraction from the determinations and limitations of a present 'must be called the counter-actualisation' of the present state. Finally, in the wake of the event, 'my life' is my own, not another's; it has 'become present'. And yet this 'life' that persists under a proper name slips through our fingers, we can possess of it no more than an 'impersonal instant'. This is the final wound of the event, the death of the self, the 'mortal wound' that is the opening onto the eternity of truth (Deleuze 1990: 151).[12]

Though it may go under a proper name, the event is nonetheless anonymous, neither 'private' nor 'collective' (Deleuze 1990: 152). The event, for Deleuze, is a pure singularity ('everything is singular'), bearing no relation to a world. Although it brings the destruction of worlds, the event is only a wound for the actor who does not merely actualise it (as death, violence, destruction), but counter-actualises the death of a world through the emergence of new ones. Among the names this counter-actualisation took in the twentieth century was 'decolonisation'. Decolonisation was no wound for the colonisers, only an occasion for resentment, an opportunity, to be *re*-actualised under the name of 'neo-colonialism'. It is a wound, on the other hand, for those who lived and continue to live its failure, and the salt we pour in this still open wound is the terrible, derisive adjective 'postcolonial'. Decolonisation is a wound, our wound, a rotting, open sore, still today unhealed, gaping at us.

The event of decolonisation, which shines forth from that wound, in the light of eternity, is the death of *ressentiment*. *Ressentiment* that actualises itself not only in the individual, as Nietzsche expressed, but, Deleuze concludes in one of the most explicitly engaged, political gestures of his entire corpus, 'as the [generalized] power of oppression in society' (1990: 152). *Ressentiment* is at once the mode and the primary affect of domination. 'By spreading *ressentiment* the tyrant forms allies, namely slaves and servants. The revolutionary alone is free from the *ressentiment* by means of which one always participates in, and profits by, an oppressive order' (1990: 152).

For the Glissant of the *Discours antillais*, the event is external to a world. It is 'a fact that manifests itself [*qui s'est produit*] elsewhere' (1981: 100).[13] 'For us', in the situation of late colonialism that is Glissant's Martinique, there are no events. Contemporary Martinique is precisely for Glissant a colonised world, the apex and summation of French colonisation, a world from which all events have been obliterated. For all that, the event reaches us, 'here and in us', but only as an echo [*retentit*]. The event is thus not so much a wound, as for Deleuze, but a *cut*. It is a cut in our world, it 'cuts us from the world'. 'What is done in the world', the way of the world amid colonial alienation, perpetually renews this cut in its every act. We feel this cut, both as isolation, being *cut off* from the world, and as painful desire, longing, for the event: decolonisation.

The name Glissant gives this cut, this alienation, this pain, is 'culture'. Culture is the way of the (colonial) world on the symbolic plane. As it was more explicitly for Deleuze in the *Logic of Sense* (1990: 152), the world of culture is for Glissant the world of the Heideggarian 'they', a world of anonymous lack and disengagement: 'Everyone gives themselves up to it [culture], these days' (Glissant 1981: 100). Culture is the realm of the anti-event, of depoliticisation, of neocolonial 'Departmentalisation'.[14] This is a culture of consumption, underwritten and served up by (French) subsidy. Instead, the only mode or plane (*plan*) in which culture would count, for an unfree community, is in seconding the process of decolonisation and of 'liberation and [the] capacity for the creation' of new worlds (1981: 100).

Glissant's Martinicans are a colonised people, a people unable to 'express' itself in acts that would reveal all that it, as a single body, can do (1981: 100). Instead, he describes 'a mentally enslaved [*asservi*] people', one for whom 'there are no events'. (1981: 100). Instead, these people possess only 'non-history'. This 'non-history', is as much the sanctimonious repetition of dates, events, and names, even the most 'radical' (Delgrès, Ignace), as it is the cloud of ignorance and the perpetual present of colonial alienation. Non-history, the absence of the event, is for Glissant, as for Deleuze, an absence of will: 'the absence of any decision' (1981: 100). It is a perpetual immaturity and subservience, a place where decisions are always made elsewhere (in the Metropole), by others speaking in one's putative 'name' (though this name is never the name of an event, but only the wound of its renewed obliteration).

In fact, culture (whether 'plays or canticles or symphonies or marionettes' writes Glissant derisively) is a matter of pure *indifference* from the perspective of the event and its eternal truth (1981: 100). While distinguishing rigorously between such cultural commodities and true events, Glissant adds to his list the 'political party'. To propose another political party is to deny the the event its autonomy. The political party, for Glissant is merely one more item of alienated consumption to be distinguished rigorously from any properly political (event). Culture is not to be understood as 'cultural politics' (a contradiction in terms). To speak of a cultural 'event' would mean restoring to culture its evental dimension; in this world, culture is first of all the 'cultivation [*culture*] of sugar cane', and a 'cultural' event would precisely be the 're-formation' and reform of the structures of exclusion and alienation therein (sugar cane, the 'scandal of housing') (1981: 100). The Glissantian event is precisely not a punctual, local reform. The actualisation of an event, the conquest of political maturity, refounds a *system*, a world, in its entirety. Its virtual dimension is that of the idea, the articulation of a transcendental that opens onto another world: 'the *whole* system [must be] challenged by a theory that envisages its positive replacement' (Glissant 1981: 100; emphasis original). Anything less would be the continuation of the disease of Antillean consumption, dragging on a mortally wounded system surviving on overseas life-support ('these acts do no more than encourage the persistence of the system' [1981: 100]). The only road to politics leads out of the city: 'All critique within the system reinforces the system' (1981: 100).

This eventless people is a people without a *body*. It is 'cut off from the world', without senses, 'it does not see itself, and does not think itself: that is our most certain calamity'(1981: 101). To constitute this body (politic) is thus the highest exigency in a context of 'depersonalization and cultural genocide' (1981: 101). Culture is not to be confused with 'political action'. And yet the realm of culture, in the light of the event 'is important'. How, Glissant asks, can political action be 'linked' or 'relayed' with 'cultural creation'? In words that Glissant would perhaps have done well to heed in light of his subsequent abandonment and disparaging of the political, he concludes:

Here, we must reject two extremes: 'cultural nationalism' which satisfies itself with its own options and generally misrecognizes the fundamental, socio-economic aspect of the problem; secondly, a priori internationalism, which often ignores the concrete analyses of a given situation and substitutes formulas for analysis [*exposés*]. (1981: 101)

In its condemnation of 'a priori internationalism' (which would soon come to bear the name 'Tout-monde'), the *Discours antillais* still constitutes a compelling (auto-) critique of the apolitical multiculturalist Glissant would soon become (cf. Bongie 2008: 329). In its call to address the 'fundamental, socio-economic' basis of actually-existing colonisation, the Glissant of the *Discours* actually stands closer to a figure like Žižek than to the depoliticised avatar of a transnational aesthetic culturalism rightfully critiqued by Hallward and Bongie. It is Žižek who continues to draw our attention to the necessity, in any properly political procedure, to 'chang[e] the very fundamental structural principle of society' (2000: 93) which Žižek, like the Glissant of the *Discours*, equates with 'the class-and-commodity structure of capitalism . . . the structuring principle that overdetermines the social totality' (2000: 96). Anything less, for both writers, would be to constrain ourselves to 'renounc[ing] any project of a global social transformation, and limit ourselves to partial problems to be solved' (Žižek 2000: 101). Likewise, however, Glissant's militant nationalism is vulnerable to the same sorts of critique Ernesto Laclau has made of Žižek: that his analysis fetishises and reifies a wholly undefined and, finally, unanalysed category (for Glissant, the 'socio-economic'); that there is no privileged standpoint or position from within a system to articulate its global critique; and, linked to the former point, that this critique depends crucially (implicitly for Žižek, quite explicitly for Glissant) on the category of false consciousness and alienation, whose unavowable counterpoint is the reliance on an intellectual vanguard suspiciously similar to the critic himself (Laclau 2000: 201, 203).

The problem of the political is undoubtedly central to any conception of postcolonial studies, and the concerted critiques of multiculturalism and identity politics mounted in recent years by figures such as Žižek, Badiou and Hallward, mean that any conceivable articulation of the field must now address the issues of universalism and relational specificity their work defends. To consider the complex intersection of the work of Gilles Deleuze and Édouard Glissant in the field of Postcolonial Studies offers a concentrated opportunity, as I have tried to show here, to grapple with the problem of the event and its eternal truth, and an opening onto a renewed notion of the '*post*colonial' that would no longer be the mere mockery of the victims of colonialism. Instead, we could sustain the promise of decolonisation to which we must remain faithful, in attending to its scandalous and catastrophic failure, as our intellectual and political inheritance.

References

Badiou, A. (2003a), 'Philosophy and Politics', in *Infinite Thought*, trans. Oliver Feltham and Justin Clemens, London: Continuum, pp. 69–78.
Badiou, A. (2003b), *L'éthique*, Paris: Nous.
Badiou, A. (2006), *Logiques des mondes*, Paris: Seuil.
Badiou, A. (2009), 'On the Idea of Communism', Public Lecture, Birkbeck College, London.
Benjamin, W. (1968), 'Theses on the Philosophy of History', in *Illuminations*, trans. Harry Zohn, New York: Schocken, pp. 253–65.
Bongie, C. (1998), *Islands and Exiles: The Creole Identities of Post/Colonial Literature*, Stanford: Stanford University Press.
Bongie, C. (2008), *Friends and Enemies: The Scribal Politics of Post/Colonial Literature*, Liverpool: University of Liverpool Press.
Britton, C. (1999), *Édouard Glissant and Postcolonial Theory: Strategies of Language and Resistance*, Charlottesville: University of Virginia Press.
Calmont, A. (2007), *Dynamiques migratoires de la Caraïbe*. Paris: Karthala.
Césaire, A. (1955), *Discours sur le colonialisme*, Paris: Présence Africaine.
Césaire, A. (1971), *Cahier d'un retour au pays natal*, Paris: Présence Africaine.
Deleuze, G. [1969] (1990), *The Logic of Sense*, ed. C. Boundas, trans. M. Lester and C. Stivale, New York: Columbia University Press.
Deleuze, G. (1995), *Negotiations, 1972–1990*, trans. M. Joughin, New York: Columbia University Press.
Dosse, F. (2007), *Gilles Deleuze et Félix Guattari: Biographie croisée*. Paris: La Découverte.
Fanon, F. (1952), *Peau noire, masques blancs*, Paris: Seuil.
Foucault, M. (1984), 'What is Enlightenment?', in Paul Rabinow (ed.), *The Foucault Reader*, New York: Pantheon Books, pp. 32–50.
Gay, J. C. (2009), 'Outre-mer à la dérive'. Viewed at http://www.cafe-geo.net/article.php3?id_article=1547
Glissant, E. (1981), *Le Discours antillais*, Paris: Seuil.
Glissant, E. (1990), *Poétique de la relation*, Paris: Gallimard.
Glissant, E. [1969] (1997a), *L'Intention poétique*, Paris, Gallimard.
Glissant, E. [1956] (1997b), *Soleil de la conscience*, Paris: Gallimard.
Glissant, E. (2005), *La Cohée du lamentin*, Paris: Gallimard.
Hallward, P. (2001), *Absolutely Postcolonial: Writing between the Singular and the Specific*, Manchester: Manchester University Press.
Hallward, P. (2006), *Out of this World: Deleuze and the Philosophy of Creation*, London: Verso.
Hallward, P. (2007), *Damming the Flood: Haiti, Aristide and the Politics of Containment*, London: Verso.
Hallward, P. (2008), 'Order and Event: On Badiou's Logics of Worlds', *New Left Review* 53: 97–122.
Laclau, E. (2000), 'Structure, History, and the Political', in J. Butler, E. Laclau and S. Žižek, *Contingency, Hegemony, Universality: Contemporary Dialogues on the Left*, London: Verso, pp. 44–89.

Miller, C. (1998), *Nationalists and Nomads: Essays on Francophone African Literature and Culture*, Chicago: University of Chicago Press.
Nesbitt, N. (2003), *Voicing Memory: History and Subjectivity in French Caribbean Literature*, Charlottesville: University of Virginia Press.
Nesbitt (2005), 'The Explusion of the Negative: Deleuze, Adorno and the Ethics of Internal Difference', SubStance 34 (2) (summer): 75–97.
Nesbitt, N. (2007), 'Departmentalization and the Logic of Decolonization', *L'Esprit créateur* 47 (1) (Spring): 32–43.
Nesbitt, N. (2008), *Universal Emancipation: The Haitian Revolution and the Radical Enlightenment*, Charlottesville: University of Virginia Press.
Nesbitt, N. (2009a), 'La société égalitaire sans état: Gérard Barthélemy et le problème du pouvoir dans la Révolution Haïtienne', *Revue de la Société haïtienne d'histoire et de géographie*, special issue on the writings of Gérard Barthélemy 83 (236) (Janvier–Juin): 131–46.
Nesbitt, N. (2009b), 'On the Political Efficacy of Idealism: Tocqueville, Schoelcher, and the Abolition of Slavery', in A. Craiutu and J. Isaac (eds), *America Through Foreign Eyes: British and French Reflections on the New World From the Eighteenth Century to the Present*, Philadelphia: Pennsylvania State University Press, pp. 91–116.
Patton, P. (2000), *Deleuze and the Political*, London: Routledge.
Wiedorn, M. A. (2008), *Glissant's Deleuze: Vitalism and the Seduction of the Tout-Monde*, PhD Dissertation, Philadelphia: University of Pennsylvania Press.
Žižek, S. (2000), 'Class Struggle or Postmodernism? Yes, Please!', in J. Butler, E. Laclau and S. Žižek, *Contingency, Hegemony, Universality: Contemporary Dialogues on the Left*, London: Verso, pp. 90–135.
Žižek, S. (2001), *Did Somebody Say Totalitarianism? Five Interventions on the (Mis)use of a Notion*, New York, Verso.
Žižek, S. (2008), *In Defence of Lost Causes*, London: Verso.

Notes

1. Unless otherwise noted, all translations are my own.
2. A large literature currently exists on Glissant's explicit appropriation of concepts such as the rhizome and nomadology, and I will thus devote my attention in what follows to other, less visible dimensions of the Glissant/Deleuze/postcolonial constellation. Readers interested in exploring surface articulations of this network will be well served by Britton (1999), Hallward (2001), Bongie (1998; 2008), Wiedorn (2008) and Miller (1998), among others.
3. Indeed, Hallward himself has been consistently critical of Badiou's failure to articulate a relational ontology, in and through his latest *Logics of Worlds (Logiques des mondes)* (2006): 'The task remains' for Badiou, writes Hallward in a review of *Logics*, 'to ensure that [an axiomatic politics of truth not be] weakened by simplification or abstraction. This will require a thoroughly relational ontology' that Badiou, in Hallward's reading, has yet to supply (2008: 121). On the concept of the political as the egalitarian claim for justice in subtraction from any state of affairs, see Badiou (2003a).
4. As Hallward of course fully recognises in works such as his superb study of Haiti and Aristide, *Damming the Flood* (2007), a fully and complexly *relational* study of the multifarious network of political engagements at work in Haiti since 1986, the political *orientation* of which is underwritten by a strictly egalitarian political logic. I have pursued my own archaeology of this egalitarian, subtractive politics in my book *Universal Emancipation: The Haitian Revolution and the Radical Enlightenment* (2008).

5. One task remaining in Glissant studies would be follow Hallward's lead in order to describe the complex articulation of a late-Hegelian dialectical logic in Glissant's work, from the Fanonian-Sartrian dialectics of enlightenment of *Soleil de la conscience* (1956) and *L'Intention poétique* (1969), through the Lukacsian analysis of reification and false- and class-consciousness in *Discours antillais* (1981), and on to the bad infinity and hypostatisation of totality in the late Glissant (cf. Hallward 2001: 72).
6. The figure of the *infidel* is the fourth mode or 'operation', to use the terminology of *Logics of Worlds*, to be added to the 'faithful', 'reactive', and 'obscure' subjects of any event Badiou describes. Without addressing the problem in detail, let me just say here that the infidel (defined by the *Robert* dictionary in perfectly Badiousian terms as a subject 'qui manque à la vérité') is a subject such as Senghor who is immediately involved in the event (of cultural Negritude and political decolonisation) itself (and not merely the legacy of its trace), but one who betrays the event in subjecting it to the tyranny of a transcendent body (what Badiou notes as 'C') (cf. Badiou 2006: 61–8). The infidel is thus a combination of the reactive subject who negates the event (without actively destroying its trace), yet who is nonetheless subject to the ideological tyranny of the transcendent body ('C'), which in Senghor's case went under names such as 'Negritude', 'femme noire', Tradition, Law or even Rhythm. Quite simply, the figure of the 'infidel' is another name for the subject of cultural/identity politics.
7. On this universalist tradition in French anti-colonial politics, see my articles 'On the Political Efficacy of Idealism: Tocqueville, Schoelcher, and the Abolition of Slavery' (2009b) and 'Departmentalization and the Logic of Decolonization' (2007).
8. Though I have argued that we must nonetheless remain attentive to viable social formations that have successfully avoided the formation of alienating representative state structures, at least on a regional scale, such as that of the stateless egalitarianism of the Haitian excluded, or *moun endeyo* (Nesbitt 2008; 2009a). Despite the perhaps limited scope of its applicability, such an example should modulate Hallward's claim that 'institutional alternatives to the national state remain hypothetical at best' (2001: 132). The point of such a social organisation has been for over two centuries systematically and successfully to *prevent* what Hallward rightfully decries as 'the same old problems of institutionalization, representation, bureaucratization [from] re-emerg[ing]' (2001: 131).
9. As witnessed in Chris Bongie's brilliant and original new book, *Friends and Enemies: The Scribal Politics of Post/Colonial Literature* (2008). If Bongie remains uncommitted and ultimately offers readers no image of a true (post/colonial) politics, his work is exemplary in its attempt to extract itself from the abyss of perpetually deferred, Derridean and cultural 'politics' by grappling with the Hallward/Glissant debate that is the contemporary horizon of the field.
10. For Badiou, the suffering of 'the thousands of crucified rebels along the road that leads Crassus the victor to Rome' justifies the Thermidorian abandonment of revolution on the part of the 'reactive' slave, but the author himself remains utterly indifferent, both rhetorically and logically (2006: 64), for the author himself (2006: 64). I would go so far as to say that in his hardened indifference to suffering, Badiou not only reproduces the harshness of capitalist relations themselves, but operates quite literally as an 'obscurantist' subject, for whom suffering is obscured by the blinding light of the Event. In trying to articulate the event as radical *break* with the way of any world, Badiou winds up perversely, blindly, even, reaffirming its mode of operation. Put in Badiou's own formulaic

code, ε=C: the trace of the event is the full body of ideology that blinds us to the materiality of suffering bodies.
11. Thanks to Simone Bignall for this formulation.
12. Badiou's representation of the Deleuzian conception of the event in *Logics of Worlds* tries to portray the event as all-encompassing connection rather than break or disjuncture (between past and future, the synthesis of the One of all becomings, intensification of a body): 'The event [for Deleuze] is not identical to the bodies it effects, but neither is it transcendent to what happens to them or what they do. Such that one cannot say that it is (ontologically) different from bodies' (2006: 405). While Deleuze's philosophy of pure immanence clearly bears some affinity to this image of the event as vitalist and empiricist continuity (2006: 410), a close reading of *Logic of Sense* clearly reveals the high degree of resemblance between the two philosophers' conceptions of the event as break or 'coupure' (2006: 406). This resemblance appears most obviously in their shared reference to the problem of truth, which Badiou would like to claim, quite problematically, as a thoroughly unDeleuzian category (2006: 408). The most convincing element of this tendential portrayal is, perhaps, Badiou's insistence that a body is the result, and not the cause, of an eventful break (2006: 407).
13. The following is a close reading of the chapter 'Événement' from *Discours antillais*.
14. Though since 1946, the former colonies of Martinique, Guyana and Guadeloupe have been juridically integrated into France, it was not until 1996 that they gained full legal equality of rights with France, while colonial processes of exploitation and inequity continue today unabated, as exposed in the general strikes that paralysed the Overseas Departments in the winter and spring of 2008–9 (Gay 2009).

Chapter 6
Postcolonial Haecceities

Réda Bensmaïa
Translated by Paul Gibbard

> If philosophy of the future exists, it must be born outside of Europe or equally born in consequence of meetings and impacts between Europe and non-Europe. (Foucault 1999: 113)
>
> It is impossible to understand how they have got as far as the capital: however, they are there, and every morning their numbers seem to grow. (Kafka, from a draft of *The Great Wall of China*)[1]

Arnaud Bouaniche has recently drawn attention to the curious way in which Gilles Deleuze opens his *Spinoza: Practical Philosophy* (1988) with a dialogue excerpted from Bernard Malamud's novel *The Fixer* (1966), a dialogue which Bouaniche (2006: 131) describes as 'a perfect *mise en abyme* of the change in perspective' that, in his opinion, occurred in Deleuze's work after May 1968, and which points to the position that Spinoza occupied in Deleuze's thought. What Bouaniche emphasises, and what is of particular interest for us as we try to understand the nature of the relations between Deleuze and his 'mediators', is that when one character in the dialogue is ordered by the other, a judge, to explain what brought him to read Spinoza and what meaning he took from this encounter, the character in question

> emphasises *not the speculative content or the theoretical propositions in Spinoza's thought, but the* PRACTICAL EFFECTS *that they have had* not only on him as a reader and an individual ('After that I wasn't the same man'), but also on their author ('[Spinoza] was out to make a free man of himself'), having decided, in the words of the judge, to approach the problem 'through the man rather than the work'. (Bouaniche 2006: 131; emphasis added)

For those of us who wish to gain a better understanding of the popularity that Deleuze has attained among postcolonial writers, what is interesting about this story is that it gives a first hint of the direction we must take in order to approach the question correctly. Spinoza was, as we all know, an important point of reference for Deleuze in the area of philosophical theory, but also in the area of 'encounters' between philosophers and non-philosophers, between professional theorists and the 'general public'. This 'pedagogical' concern can be found in the major texts, but also in more 'spontaneous' ones, letters, interviews, and so on: a concern that philosophy should be produced – enjoyed and understood – *by all* and not just by the 'professionals'. This point appears clearly in a reply that Deleuze sent to me when I was editing a collection of articles about his work for the German journal *Lendemains*. I asked him whether he thought his work was 'accessible' to the general public, and what place he allotted to philosophical discourse. This is how Deleuze answered, again making reference to Spinoza:

> The paradox in Spinoza is that he's the most philosophical of philosophers, the purest in some sense, but also the one who more than any other addresses non-philosophers and calls forth the most intense non-philosophical understanding. That is why absolutely anyone can read Spinoza, and be very moved, or see things quite differently afterward, even if they can hardly understand Spinoza's concepts (Deleuze 1995).

Deleuze adopts the same position when discussing the status of philosophy in 'How Philosophy is Useful to Mathematicians and Musicians': 'What directly orients the teaching of philosophy', Deleuze tells us,

> is the question of how useful it is to mathematicians, or to musicians, etc., even and especially if this philosophy does not discuss mathematics or music. *This kind of teaching has nothing to do with general culture; it is practical and experimental*, always outside itself, precisely because the students are led to participate *in terms of their own needs and competences*. (Deleuze: 2007; emphasis added).

One inference we can draw from these two statements, made many years apart, is that postcolonial writers, activists and intellectuals encounter Deleuze not so much through the *speculative* content of his thought but through the 'practical effects' that his work has for each one of them. In what follows I shall try to bring out the critical and theoretical elements which have made the encounter between Deleuze and the postcolony possible. As we shall see, this assumes that we *start* by considering the multiple 'avatars' of Deleuzean thought, and that we are able to determine *which* 'Deleuze' we are dealing with when his 'name' is linked to different strands of postcolonial theory.

On Deleuze's Names

Few exponents of postcolonial and subaltern theories now dispute the influence that Deleuze's work exerted on the intellectuals and theorists who developed those theories. Some cite his political stances (on Algeria, Palestine and colonialism, as well as on prisons and societies of control) as the reason why he became one of the chief inspirations for postcolonial theory, while others point to particular concepts he forged with Félix Guattari. What is problematic about this sort of theoretical appropriation is its tendency to assume too lightly and uncritically what logically ought to be the object of preliminary analysis. The current postcolonial orthodoxy, particularly in the United States, holds that Deleuze's writings from the 1970s onward *unquestionably* form part of what is called 'postcolonial theory'. But what 'theory' is being referred to here? Should such specialised and complex work as Deleuze's be assimilated, without any kind of qualification, into a theory of this sort which has its own particular framework as well as a strong tendency to resist any form of ideological annexation or appropriation? By taking as given something that ought to be the object of initial enquiry, is there not a danger of blurring boundaries and losing sight of what is genuinely important in the 'encounter' between the work of Deleuze and the movement of postcolonialist thought? We are obliged to make a careful assessment and show that it is indeed 'Deleuze' that we are dealing with when we refer (only) to the texts he wrote with Guattari; and the same applies when we proceed *as though* what Deleuze wrote *before* his collaboration with Guattari 'amounted to the same thing'. Isn't it a misrepresentation of his thought simply to assume that the Deleuze we are dealing with in *A Thousand Plateaus* is the same Deleuze of *The Logic of Sense*?

There are other questions of this kind that must be raised. Have the promoters of a generalised Deleuzeanism taken care to check whether the borrowings they have made from such specialised work as his do him justice? Have they considered the distortions that can occur when concepts arising in Deleuzean philosophical practice are applied or borrowed non-problematically? And lastly, where is the 'crossroads' of their meeting? Where exactly does the encounter take place between a philosophy supposed to be 'untimely' and which rejected the idea of the philosopher as leader or guru, and a theory which had as one its chief goals direct action on current circumstances and the transformation of the social and political forms of a world inheriting decolonisation?

One of my contentions in this essay is that postcolonial and subaltern theorists have engaged with Deleuzean thought in ways which have perhaps produced a long series of misunderstandings for which Deleuze himself is not responsible. Nevertheless, it is important for us to consider how Deleuze's work has come to play such a crucial role in the development of postcolonial theories and to understand, as François

Cusset says in *French Theory* (2008: 10, 11), 'how such trenchant texts, often quite difficult to access, could come to be woven so deeply into the American cultural and intellectual fabric', as well as into the intricate weft of what would emerge as 'a new global discourse on micropolitical resistance and subalternity'. The best critical strategy for approaching this, it seems to me, is not to review the obvious cases in which the Deleuzean 'graft' has taken, but to reveal the 'elements' which enable us to understand – if I may be allowed to employ a Derridean concept here – the 'dissemination' of Deleuze's 'names' across the broad field of postcolonial theory. What I hope to show in the following pages is that the encounter between Deleuze and the postcolonial movement can only be understood through the idea of a 'field', we could even call it a 'transcendental' field, in which Deleuze and his postcolonial followers find themselves captured.

As numerous commentators have noted, in comparison with that of other philosophers Deleuze's work was slow in gaining recognition for the important influence it had on the major intellectual debates of the 1970s and 1980s. If the work he published on Hume, Kant, Bergson, Nietzsche and Spinoza won him recognition among professional philosophers, it was only with the publication of *The Logic of Sense* and, especially, *Difference and Repetition*, that the 'name' of Deleuze began to emerge as a genuine intellectual 'event' for those who had realised that his early books were something more than the straightforward work of a historian of philosophy. And while these readers were beginning to suspect that he was doing more than simply accepting the torch from the great historians of philosophy (Guéroult, Hyppolite, Delbos and so on), there was nothing yet to indicate that his work was on its way to becoming (along with that of Jacques Derrida, Jean-François Lyotard and Michel Foucault) an essential point of reference in what would first be called 'French Theory' and soon afterwards 'postcolonial theory'. Deleuze's innovative style and the difficulties in his texts created barriers to the quick adoption of his ideas and made it hard (notwithstanding his study of Sacher Masoch) for others to 'adapt' them to the debates of the time, whether these were concerned with questions about the status of language, the subject, power, gender theory, the theory of sexuality and perhaps, most problematically, postcolonial theory.[2] It would be necessary to wait until the 1990s before it was definitively recognised that any understanding, not just of essentially European philosophy, but of philosophy on a global stage, was impossible without taking into account the 'Deleuzean project' (as Alain de Beaulieu [2005: 10] very aptly calls it).

Moreover, since Deleuze's death, the influence and impact of his work has continued to grow. In 2002 and 2003, in addition to the publication of *Desert Islands and Other Texts* and *Two Regimes of Madness*, the 'Gilles Deleuze documentary archive' was established at Saulchoir in France, and the lectures that Deleuze gave at Vincennes were published online. What we should also add, concerning the reception of Deleuze's work, is how, as Arnaud Bouaniche (2006: 294) puts it, '[E]ven before his influence became apparent in the conscious or deliberate use that was made of his themes and analyses, it could be seen in the enriching and stimulating effects it had on all those involved in intellectual and artistic matters.'[3] It is through these effects that many figures who might at first be thought to have little in common are able to come together and unite around Deleuze's work: the historian of science Isabelle Stengers, the composer Pierre Boulez, the philosopher Dionys Mascolo, as well as the Portuguese film-director Manoël de Oliveira, who wrote to Deleuze saying how much he had been moved by a talk Deleuze gave on cinema at the French national film school FÉMIS, and that Deleuze's comments about the creative process had dazzled him. Oliveira's response is particularly interesting as it gets to the heart of what many artists will say about their 'encounter' with Deleuze's writings on film, music, painting or literature, and does so in very clear terms. All speak of the 'curious disquiet' they experience as they read one or other of Deleuze's texts, and of the 'secret' affinities they uncover between what they have tried to do in their work and the way Deleuze describes his own experience of the creative process. 'Themes' change and questions vary, but all whom Deleuze's work has touched share the feeling that he has revealed something of great importance to them. It is as though, they say, Deleuze's work makes them suddenly aware of a dimension of their own work which, until then, they had sensed but had not been able to define conceptually. Examples abound of artists and thinkers who have testified to the profound significance an 'encounter' with Deleuze's work has held for them and the 'joy' it engendered in them.

The poet Jean-Philippe Cazier, for example, recounts in an interview with Stéfan Leclerq: 'As I read Deleuze more closely, my work took new directions, *related to developments in Deleuze's thought and his idea of minor literature*. My "encounter" with a very bold style and very intense movements of thought all generated poetry in me' (see de Beaulieu 2005: 164; emphasis added). For his part, the painter Ange-Henri Pieraggi is quick to attribute a broadening in the scope of his work and the discovery of new creative directions to a similar sort of 'encounter': 'Reading *The Movement-Image* was very important for me. The way it demonstrates that a face in close-up loses its connections in space and time, and so loses any capacity for individuation, socialisation and communication, raising itself to the level of another entity expressing the affect . . . *gave me great intellectual pleasure*' (de Beaulieu 2005: 160; emphasis added). What a great many other 'encounters' with Deleuze show, as Bouaniche observes, is that the perception that Deleuze has something of the 'oracle' or 'seer' about him 'stems not so much from the difficulty of identifying something like a monologic main thread in what he says or writes, and even less from the way he marshals his conceptual arsenal', but, more commonly, from a 'listening' or 'understanding through percepts and affects' which in some way resonates directly with a concept that 'hits home' and connects with something important. In these types of 'encounter' there is an experience of the same order as that described by Roland Barthes when he speaks of a relationship with a text 'according to pleasure' rather than according to a 'tactical aim', a 'social usage' or even an 'image-reservoir' (Bouaniche 2007: 295): 'I cannot,' writes Barthes, 'apportion, imagine that the text is perfectible, ready to enter into a play of normative predicates: it is too much this, not enough that; the text (the same is true of the singing voice) can wring from me only this judgement, in no way adjectival: that's it! And further still: that's it for me!' And Barthes goes on to specify, in a Deleuzean vein: 'This "for me" is neither subjective nor existential, but Nietzschean' (Barthes 1975: 13).

As we shall attempt to show, the writers and critics who will serve here as 'mediators' testify to exactly this type of experience in relation to Deleuze's work: work which wrings from them a *That's it! that's exactly it for me!* coming from an elsewhere which they are not always able to locate or even name, but which they experience neither as simply 'subjective' nor uniformly 'existential', but . . . Deleuzean! There are thinkers, and Deleuze is one, whose work provides the occasion for such 'intuitive transition'. This is why, as Jean-Hugues Barthélémy (2005: 151) says of Gilbert Simondon, in words which could apply equally well to Deleuze, his work 'enthrals' and is often 'used' by many 'without being deployed or even explained in detail and for itself absolutely'. From one text to another, from one concept to another, the same type of experience is intensely encountered and shot through with extremely strong affects: the individual undergoing the experience has just recognised a 'scene of language' which delights her, and has just encountered a 'conceptual persona' which cleaves her in two and causes her to enter in an unprecedented way into a 'bloc of becoming', an 'a-parallel evolution' (Deleuze and Parnet 2006: 5).

Having said that, it is not the case that all 'encounters' with Deleuze's work occur under the same auspices. While we have discussed the 'pythic' or 'psychopompal' Deleuze, the Deleuze who inspires creators and whom they consider to be the thinker who has best explored certain of their concerns, the situation becomes much more complex if we decide to look at all the texts whose relations to the work of Deleuze – and in particular to the texts he wrote with Guattari – appear without the same degree of transparency:[4] texts which show that the Deleuze of artists and creators is not always the same as the Deleuze of professional philosophers, for example, or postcolonial theorists. Foucault was perhaps referring to this Promethean quality when he declared that 'one day, perhaps, the century will be Deleuzean' (Foucault 1997: 343)[5] – a 'quip' which, in my view, did not imply that Deleuze's ideas would one day come to dominate the global intellectual scene, with Deleuze acknowledged as its ruling figure and the century's greatest thinker, but rather alluded to something much more profound, which we shall call 'Deleuze's "names"'. Wasn't it Deleuze 'himself' who said that 'individuals find a truly proper name for themselves . . . only through the harshest exercise in depersonalisation, by opening themselves up to the multiplicities everywhere within them' (Deleuze 1995: 6).[6] What Foucault sensed and very quickly understood is that a thinker who 'complicates' the idea of a radical univocity of being with a theory of multiplicities and pre-individual identities can never be 'reduced' to a (single) name; the century would be 'Deleuzean', above all, because of this *dispersion of names*, and consequently, of the *problematics* that it draws in its wake. The century would be Deleuzean because it would 'perhaps' find in his work a resonance chamber for its own great tumult, for its waves of thought, for its movements of ideas and events – whose intense energies could only be seized by an individual who was prepared to *surf* on them.[7] The century would be Deleuzean due to the apparatuses [*dispositifs*] that he set up: he ended up transforming himself into a 'mediator', and by doing so enabled 'a new light, new enunciations, new forms of subjectivation' to emerge. But doubtless Foucault did not insert that 'perhaps' inadvertently or as a manner of speaking: in the context in which it was uttered, Foucault's 'quip' was perhaps alluding to a danger that Deleuzean thought – that true 'nomadic war machine' – might be transformed into a 'toolbox' (another of Deleuze's terms, of course), which would owe nothing to the initial radicality of the task that Deleuze undertook in his writings. Foucault understood that the 'Deleuze effect' along with the apparatuses [*dispositifs*] that mediated it could go just as easily towards bringing about a revolution in 'images of thought' and 'morals' as they could go in the opposite direction: molar 'stasis', the hardening of identity, communitarianism . . . This ought to be clear to us from the warning that Deleuze (and, in this case, Guattari) repeatedly issued to their readers: that a rhizome can always hide roots, and a line of flight can always hide strata, segmentarities and even a repressive apparatus of the state: 'Sometimes,' write Deleuze and Guattari,

> *one overdoes it*, puts too much in, works with a jumble of lines and sounds; then instead of producing a cosmic machine [for music and painting!] capable of 'rendering sonorous,' *one lapses back to a machine of reproduction* that ends up reproducing nothing but a scribble effacing all lines, a scramble effacing all sounds . . . All one has left is a resonance chamber well on the way to becoming a black hole. (Deleuze and Guattari 1987: 343–4; emphasis added).[8]

What these 'examples' show is that many different 'names' try concurrently to attach themselves to the avatars of a Deleuze who is a historian of philosophy, all arriving with the same (false) supporting evidence. In this way, a *poststructuralist Deleuze* belonging to 'French theory' is hastily hitched to a multitude of different strands of thought (aesthetic theory, literary theory, queer studies, feminist theory, 'artistic practices' and so on).[9] We come across, for example, a Deleuze who is a *pop philosopher*, who gathers artists around him (painters, musicians, poets and so on); we also come across a *schizo-analyst Deleuze* – that is to say, a Deleuze who now writes his books 'using four hands', with Guattari, and who has radically distanced himself from his work as a historian or as a poststructuralist 'pure and simple' in order to embark on a more directly political programme. And at this point, as will be seen, he is hitched to other strands of thought: altermondialism, anarchism, neofascism, postcolonialism, subalternism, identity politics and so on. Now, it is precisely this proliferation of names (Deleuze's names) which led us to delay the moment at which Deleuze became enlisted without further ado in the postcolonial movement.

While it is always possible to adduce (Deleuze's) texts to justify or defend any of these interpretations of Deleuze's oeuvre – doesn't Spinoza say that no heresy has difficulty or trouble finding a text that justifies it? – it remains the case that firstly the names to which these texts refer are not always consistent at a theoretical level:[10] the pop philosopher Deleuze can exist alongside the schizo-analyst Deleuze, but nobody can claim that the two display the same outlook on things, or that she is dealing with the 'true' or the 'real' Deleuze because she has managed to reconcile the two 'currents' of thought; and secondly as such, no one and/or other of these 'hypotheses' is able to *define* what conditioned the setting up of the 'Deleuze-postcolony' apparatus [*dispositif*] and to specify the name under which Gilles Deleuze makes his theoretical 'entry' into it. This question seems all the more legitimate to us because for so long Deleuze was viewed as a difficult writer, and seemed incapable of being linked with any particular current of thought. As one very acute commentator, Alain Badiou, has perceived, Deleuze remained 'at a slant to all blocks of philosophical opinion' and was neither 'a phenomenologist, nor a structuralist, nor a Heideggerian, nor an importer of Anglo-Saxon analytical "philosophy", nor a neo-humanist liberal' (Badiou 1997: 141)[11] and we could add, no more was he a subaltern or postcolonial theorist in the works he wrote *in his own name*. His favourite (or even 'fetish') authors were not Kateb Yacine, Édouard Glissant, Aimé Césaire, Albert Memmi or Frantz Fanon, but rather Kafka, Melville, Beckett and . . . Proust, and it is in this sense that it can indeed be said that 'in perfect harmony with the aristocratism of his thought . . . Deleuze [created] *a polarity all his own*' (Badiou 1997: 141; original emphasis). How can we, from this point of view, account for the fact that he is considered, along with Derrida, Foucault and Lyotard, to be one of the inspirations for postcolonial or subaltern theory? How do we explain the fact that so many theorists and critics of these two currents of thought do not hesitate to insert him into the movement of their work when he in fact superbly ignored all of their *fetish authors*. What apparatus do we look to in trying to understand the way in which Deleuze has been adopted as a 'mediator' of postcolonial thinkers? We can also think about this question by reflecting on the *name* and the conditions under which Deleuze enters the 'postcolonial theory' apparatus [*dispositif*], and by asking what, then, are its characteristics?

What seems to us to have conditioned the actualisation of this singular apparatus [*dispositif*] is an insistence on the 'appeal', that can be found in practically all the texts that *Deleuze wrote with Guattari*, to the production of subjectivities capable of resisting the different forms of control that colonisation imposed on the colonised. Deleuze was not perhaps *directly* interested in the leading figures of postcolonial theory (Fanon, Memmi, Gramsci or even Edward Said, Homi K. Bhabha, Gayatri C. Spivak, Ranajit Guha, Gyan Prakash, Dipesh Chakrabarty, Valentin Mudimbe and Achille Mbembe), but he always took careful account of the *political* consequences of the ideas he advanced in his work. In any case this is one of the reasons which led him to engage in the genuine 'conversion' that he carried out in the work he did with Guattari, but also with Carmelo Bene, Dyonis Mascolo and many others. This, anyway, is how I understand the place he gave to the idea of the 'encounter' in his work, and the 'pathos' he attached to it: 'When you work,' he argues, *in a book written with Claire Parnet,*

> you are necessarily in absolute solitude. *You cannot have disciples, or be part of a school.* The only work is moonlighting and is clandestine. But it is an extremely populous solitude. Populated not with dreams, phantasms or plans, but with encounters. *An encounter is perhaps the same thing as a becoming, or nuptials.* It is from the depth of this solitude that you can make any encounters whatsoever. You encounter people (*and sometimes without knowing them or ever having seen them*) but also movements, ideas, events, entities. (Deleuze and Parnet 2006: 5; emphasis added)

Deleuze was also fond of saying that 'philosophers aren't reflective, they are creative' (Deleuze 1995: 122, trans. modified), by which he meant he was not interested in 'thinking on'[12] (cinema, politics and so on) or 'speaking for' (the public, minorities and so on), but rather he was interested in 'setting things in motion', in creating concepts which do not remain simply at the level of words or sentences – or 'phrase-making' – but rise to the level of utterances: 'thought as archive' (Deleuze 1995: 95)! And, from this, we arrive at the hypothesis that postcolonial theories were developing *at the same time* (that is, in the same *epistemic frame*) as Deleuze's thought was taking shape, in an a-parallel evolution: once again, the wasp and the orchid!

We recall that in his short text about 'mediators' Deleuze discusses the factors that condition the relations between radically different practices: 'How is it possible – *in their completely different lines of development,* with quite different rhythms and movements of production – *how is it possible for a concept, an aggregate, and a function to interact?*' (Deleuze 1995: 123–4; emphasis added). In this text we also come across the 'elements' – in the Kantian sense of *Elementarelhere* – which enable us to understand how the most demanding philosophical practice can resonate with practices that seem completely alien to it. 'Creating concepts,' writes Deleuze,

> is no less difficult than creating new visual or aural combinations, or creating scientific functions. What we *have* to recognise is that the *interplay between the different lines* isn't a matter of one monitoring or reflecting another. A discipline that set out to follow a creative movement *coming from outside* would itself relinquish any creative role. You'll get nowhere by latching onto some parallel movement, you have to make a move yourself. If nobody makes a move, nobody gets anywhere. *Nor is interplay an exchange: it all turns on giving or taking.* (Deleuze 1995: 125; emphasis added)

All the same, it is not entirely by chance that many of the 'examples' which Deleuze offers in this text by way of 'illustrating' the manner in

Postcolonial Haecceities   129

which 'mediations' function relate to questions linked to colonisation and the necessity of escaping the discourse of the 'master': 'Perrault thinks,' writes Deleuze,

> that if he speaks on his own, even in a fictional framework, *he's bound to come out with an intellectual's discourse, he won't get away from a 'master's or colonist's discourse*,' an established discourse ... So, to the established fictions that are *always rooted in a colonist's discourse*, we oppose a minority discourse, *with mediators*. (Deleuze 1995: 125–6; emphasis added).[13]

At this point in our analysis, we might be tempted to 'close the circle' and defend the argument that it is precisely *as a mediator* that Deleuze *comes into play* in the postcolonial debate – or ritornello. To achieve this, all we would have to do, as many commentators have done, is allude to the multitude of works, familiar to both scholars and the general public, which profess a direct 'debt' to the work of Deleuze, or which boldly declare their allegiance to Deleuze.[14] We could support this argument by, for example, citing the concepts that nowadays define what might be called the 'Deleuzean postcolonial orthodoxy'. And indeed can any text claiming to belong to the postcolonial or subaltern movement ignore the concepts of 'minor literature', 'multitude', 'nomadic war machine', 'becoming' (-minor, -animal, -woman, -intense), 'rhizome', 'ritornello' or 'faciality'? Can any critic ignore the adaptation (to postcolonial problematics) of concepts that Deleuze and Guattari introduced in *Anti-Oedipus*, *A Thousand Plateaus* and *What is Philosophy*? Can anyone neglect the schizo-analytic concepts of 'desiring-machine', 'body-without-organs', 'anomalous' and many other 'Deleuzo-Guattarian' concepts without feeling she has missed a 'plateau' or an important 'encounter'? But we might ask: what's left of Deleuze in all this? Which Deleuze is being spoken of when we observe that most of the concepts that have 'passed' into postcolonial theory are drawn from works that Deleuze wrote *with* Guattari? Which of Deleuze's *names* is being referred to in this case? Which Deleuze is being referred to when postcolonial theory engages with one or other of the concepts listed above without concerning itself with the ruptures (in style or theme) which have marked the development of Deleuzean thought over the years? Doesn't one run the risk of *instrumentalising* his thought by ignoring the transformations that have marked the evolution of his thought and the progression from the work he did alone to that done with Guattari? Is it not a great oversimplification to integrate the *pre*-Guattarian Deleuze with the *post*-Guattarian Deleuze without any qualification whatsoever?[15] These, in any case, are the types of questions which have led us from the outset to enquire into Deleuze's 'names' – an enquiry which, it should now be clearer, is less concerned with casting doubt on Deleuze's theoretical involvement in the postcolonial movement than with mapping certain *critical* aspects of the question.

These types of questions also lead us on to another problem, one which is concerned, paradoxically, with the idea of 'mediation' itself. We have seen that the concepts and the theoretical and political problematics with which Deleuze and Guattari engaged in the books they wrote together enabled a 'connection' to be made between their work and the 'spin-offs' that their work produced for postcolonial theory. Deleuze and Guattari perhaps never engaged in direct 'dialogue' with their postcolonial colleagues, but all the texts they published in tandem or individually reveal that they were perfectly aware of the implications that their ideas might have for the global theoretical field. We have only to reread that 'concept accelerator', *A Thousand Plateaus*, from this point of view to realise it could never have been written without its authors' possessing the sharpest sensitivity to the great global questions of the moment. Isn't it from chapters such as 'November 20, 1923: Postulates of Linguistics', '1933: Micropolitics and Segmentarity', '1227: Treatise on Nomadology: – the War Machine' and '7000 BC: Apparatus of Capture' that the leading theorists of postcolonialism draw certain of their key concepts on the status of language 'in a dominated country' (see Chamoiseau 1997), on questions of space, territory and borders, but also on questions relating to the 'formation of subjectivity' and identity, of *socius* and state, and finally to the relations between Power and Knowledge? When, in September 1999, Didier Eribon asked Deleuze, in relation to *What is Philosophy?*, that is, a text which doesn't at first sight appear to make any trenchant political attacks, whether this book of 'geophilosophy', co-authored with Guattari, didn't amount to a 'political manifesto', Deleuze gave an unexpected response:

> The current political situation is very muddled. People tend to confuse the quest for freedom with the embrace of capitalism. *It seems doubtful that the joys of capitalism are enough to liberate a people.* The bloody failure of socialism is on everybody's lips, but no one sees capitalist globalisation as a failure, *in spite of the bloody inequalities that condition the market, and the populations who are excluded from it.* (Deleuze 2007: 383; emphasis added)

As other texts reveal, everything concerned with globalisation held great importance for Deleuze and Guattari – particularly France's postcolonial situation, and the neocolonialist aspirations of the United States. All the 'ingredients' of encounter and mediation are there, and yet the original paradox remains: at no time did our authors, and in particular Deleuze, engage in direct dialogue with the representatives of postcolonial theory or join in the debate (or 'conversation', as some commentators call it) which raged elsewhere: across India, Latin America and Algeria, as well as across Italy, Spain and before long, the whole world.[16] And how consequently do we overcome this problem and escape from this apparent impasse? How do we interpret the *gap* that exists between the 'influence' of Deleuze and Guattari's work on theorists of the postcolony and the absence we have already referred to of any direct relation between them? It is through the notion of the 'mediator' that we can find a 'way out'. What exactly, we must then ask, does Deleuze mean by mediator? What characterises a mediator for him?

'Mediators are fundamental,' writes Deleuze. '*Creation's all about mediators. Without them nothing happens.* They can be people – for a philosopher, artists or scientists; for a scientist, philosophers or artists – but things too, even plants or animals, as in Castaneda.' So much for the generic definition. But Deleuze immediately goes on to specify:

> Whether they're real or imaginary, animate or inanimate, you have to *form* your mediators. *It's a series. If you're not in some series, even a completely imaginary one, you're lost.* I need my mediators to express myself, *and they'd never express themselves without me*: you're always working in a group, even when you seem to be on your own. And still more when it's apparent: Félix Guattari and I are one another's mediators. (Deleuze 1995: 125; emphasis added)

It is impossible to read this passage without recalling what Deleuze said when pursuing a different line of thought in *The Logic of Sense*, one relating to the idea of structure. It is interesting to note the parallels that can be established between the two definitions, along with the importance allotted to the idea of 'series' for both mediator and structure. Deleuze describes the minimal conditions for a 'structure in general' as follows:

> 1) There must be *at least two* heterogeneous series, one of which shall be determined as 'signifying' and the other as 'signified' (a single series never suffices to form a structure). 2) Each of these series is constituted by *terms which exist only through the relations they maintain with one another* . . . 3) The two heterogeneous series converge toward a *paradoxical element*, which is their 'differentiator'. This is the principle of the emission of singularities. (Deleuze 2004a: 60; emphasis added)

What is striking in both cases is of course the reference to heterogeneous series. But, for those of us trying to arrive at a better understanding of the composition of this structure and the place that the *series* occupies in its functioning, a new element makes its appearance – one which was not present in the text concerning mediators, but which will acquire here an extremely important status and play a fundamental role: we are referring to the 'paradoxical element' that Deleuze mentions, the 'differentiator', which, as we know, can assume a *multitude of names*, but which can never be 'pinned down', never reduced to a single name. It is of this atopic element, this element always in movement, that Deleuze will say: '[I]t *does not belong to any series*, or rather [it] belongs to both at once, and never ceases moving through them' (Deleuze 2004a: 60; emphasis added). Our attention is inevitably drawn to other characteristics attributed to this element, which is gradually endowed with greater and greater powers, and with a capacity for metamorphosis all the more extraordinary: always 'displaced in relation to itself', always 'lacking its own place', 'its own identity', 'its own resemblance and its own equilibrium', it is constantly 'becoming'.

I do not believe that I am giving way to interpretative delirium in saying that Deleuze defines his philosophical practice on the model of this 'element': the philosopher as 'differentiator' who never ceases moving between series, between discourses; the philosopher-*Stalker* (Bensmaïa 1989a; 1989b) always displaced in relation to himself, lacking his own place and his own identity and who, by this fact, can never be bound to ideologies or doctrines that are 'fixed' and closed upon themselves. It is this characteristic, in our view, that has conditioned the different types of relations that can be entered into with regard to Deleuze's work and which enables us to understand the multiplicity of 'names' that he has been able to 'embody' for a 'public' more and more numerous and heterogeneous. It is from this position (of 'differentiator') that Deleuze will tackle all the questions that characterise his philosophical practice: a position which dispenses with the 'subject', as it appears in transcendental philosophy and metaphysics, in favour of a 'free, anonymous, and nomadic singularity which traverses men as well as plants and animals independently of the matter of their individuation and the forms of their personality' (Deleuze 2004a: 123). Just like Nietzsche (of whom Deleuze was a remarkable interpreter, and who was the 'mediator' *par excellence* of all Deleuze's work), in his discovery of impersonal and pre-individual singularities, Deleuze also saw a 'new way of exploring the depth, of bringing a distinct eye to bear upon it, *of discerning in it a thousand voices, of making all of these voices speak* – being prepared

Postcolonial Haecceities 133

to be snapped up by this depth which he interpreted and populated as it had never been before' (Deleuze 2004a: 123). Moreover, it is all these 'actualisations', along with this 'atopicality' and the constantly changing nature of a 'subject' that is always other than what it 'founds'[17] that ensure that (the name of) Deleuze is capable of being associated with the diversity of 'encounters' to which his work gives rise. It will always be necessary, in this sense, to recognise that there is a *virtual and/or undifferentiated* (name of) Deleuze which remains always to be discovered *despite all its actualisations*, and that his readers reinvent him, just as 'himself' but always 'other', each time that an affect or a percept drawn from one of the concepts of his work speaks to them.

It is, in our view, just such an apparatus [*dispositif*] that conditions the *different natures* of the 'encounters' to which Deleuze's work gives rise to in its readers. And so, for example, it is with full awareness of the obstacles he must overcome and the theoretical precautions he must take that a philosopher like Žižek writes his book 'on' Deleuze. He immediately warns us that

> a Lacanian book on Deleuze cannot ignore *all these facts* [*that is, the debate between Lacan and Badiou on the relationship between psychoanalysis and philosophy*]. Consequently, *Organs without Bodies* is not a 'dialogue' between these two theories [those of Badiou and Lacan via Deleuze?] but something quite different: an attempt to trace the contours of an encounter between two incompatible fields.

And Žižek then adds an observation which is close in nature to the questions we raised about Deleuze's concept of 'encounter': 'An encounter cannot be reduced to symbolic exchange: what resonates in it, over and above the symbolic exchange, is *the echo of a traumatic impact*. While dialogues are commonplace, encounters are rare' (Žižek 2004: xi; emphasis added). 'So, be it!' But what is remarkable in this case is the sensitivity Žižek displays regarding the nature of the type of 'encounter' that one can have when one is dealing with philosophical work of the calibre of Deleuze's. Žižek 'understands' that the encounter cannot be reduced or related to a simple 'symbolic exchange' and doesn't hesitate to evoke the idea of 'a traumatic impact' because he realises that in writing a book 'on' Deleuze, *arising out of his own disagreement with Badiou and Lacan*, he must marshal 'all the facts', that is, get to the bottom of things and settle his account with Badiou and Lacan through the mediation of Deleuze. And, this being the case, it is perhaps not entirely by chance that the concept of 'Bodies without Organs' ('BwO') is used as the catalyst between series and the release mechanism for the 'encounter': 'the limit of deterritorialisation of the schizo body and created in concert with the fragmented body and bad partial objects' (Sasso and Villani 2003: 62), converted into OwB (Organs Without Bodies) in the title of the book, it is transformed into the 'dark precursor' of the critical ambitions that Žižek will develop in his book and functions as a connector between the questions that will be treated in it. But by saying that he must marshal 'all the facts', Žižek is also indicating that one of the aims of his book is to 'track down' the Deleuze who threads his way between the ideas expressed in his own books or those written with Guattari. For Žižek, it is less a question of *providing a better explanation* of Deleuze's thought than of testing out his own hypotheses and concepts through a systematic reading of Deleuze's work. To undertake such a venture, it is first of all necessary to know *who* you are dealing with. You may *know*, but what is the nature of your knowledge? Taking Deleuze as a 'mediator', Žižek seeks to test his thought and the problematics it is based on at the same time that he once more works through the reading he has done *via Deleuze* of Lacan, Foucault, Derrida, Badiou and Butler, using this reading to serve his own system. The 'encounter' has a 'traumatic' dimension because *in this particular case* it runs the risk at every moment of giving up what it has for an uncertain alternative, taking *for Deleuze (or Deleuze's thought)* what may yet reveal itself to be only one of his avatars. This is why, in our view, having set out in search of the 'true' Deleuze, Žižek finds himself having to peel away and discard what he sees as certain of Deleuze's names (or *false* names): 'So, why Deleuze?' he asks at the very start of his book.

> In the past decade, Deleuze emerged as *the central reference of contemporary philosophy*: notions like 'resisting multitude', 'nomadic subjectivity', the 'anti-Oedipal' critique of psychoanalysis, and so on are the common currency of today's academia – not to mention the fact that *Deleuze more and more serves as the theoretical foundation of today's anti-globalist Left and its resistance to capitalism.* (Žižek 2004: xi; emphasis added)

In less than two sentences, Žižek has already confronted two of Deleuze's 'names' that have 'emerged' over the years, but in which he does not recognise his 'own' Deleuze or, to put it another way, the most 'authentic' Deleuze (who has been 'hidden' behind his other incarnations). Several lines later, an apparently even more 'traumatic' encounter takes place with another of Deleuze's 'ghosts', the Deleuze who is 'much closer' to psychoanalysis and Hegel:

> *Organs without Bodies* here goes 'against the current': its starting premise is that, *beneath this Deleuze* (the popular image of Deleuze based on the reading of the books he co-authored with Félix Guattari), *there is another*

Deleuze, much closer to psychoanalysis and Hegel, a Deleuze whose consequences are much more shattering. (Žižek 2004: xi; emphasis added)[18]

Other philosophers, including some of the subtlest interpreters of Deleuze's thought, have had to confront the same problem, which relates to 'capturing' Deleuze, enclosing him within a system and *giving him a name*. Alain Badiou is a case in point: his book is intended as a homage to Deleuze but is unable to resist the temptation of reducing Deleuze's thought to a single dominant strand, or to a particular 'taste' even, all in the name of the univocity of being (see Badiou 1997). The idea of mediation takes on its full meaning in this work, and Badiou presents to us a Deleuze with whom he feels great affinity and with whom – in what makes him the perfect 'mediator' – he has the most profound philosophical and theoretical disagreements. Deleuze's names inundate the text: he is described as the 'philosophical inspiration for the *anarcho-désirants*' during the Vincennes years; at the same time, no less, he is presented as 'an enemy [who was] all the more dangerous because he was inside the [leftist] movement'. Later in the same text, Badiou recounts how once he didn't hesitate to 'label as "fascist" the defence [which Deleuze made] of spontaneous movement, his theory of "spaces of freedom," his hatred of dialectics, [and] in summary: his philosophy of life and of natural all-One' (Badiou 1997: 9). Elsewhere, in the same text, Badiou dismisses Deleuze's thought as being nothing more (or less) than 'reworked Platonism'. Badiou concludes that Deleuze and he ended up forming a 'paradoxical duo', based on 'active divergence'. And, having criticised the 'dubious role of the disciples' who tended to rally round their master for 'the wrong reasons' and ended up betraying him, Badiou himself arrives at the same conclusion: *there is an equivocity between the different names of the Master, an equivocity which bears the name 'Deleuzeanism'*. Badiou explains: 'There exists in fact a *cynical Deleuzeanism* which is the diametric opposite of the sobriety and asceticism of the Master' (Badiou 2000: 96). And what if the notion of the 'Master' itself is flawed? What if it is simply the 'spin-off', both fortuitous and necessary, of the 'logic' which underlies the proliferation of Deleuze's names within the field of philosophy *as well as outside it*? And what if, to put it another way, 'Deleuzeanism' (as philosophers call it) were only a 'machine' (a *'machine-désirante'* even!) with multiple fissures and 'spin-offs'? And what if finally the 'Deleuze' that philosophers have tried so hard to pigeonhole was only ever the 'dark precursor' of the 'differentiator' that Deleuze discusses in *Difference and Repetition*, and of which he says: '[I]t has no place other than that from which it is "missing", no identity other than that which it lacks: it is precisely the object = x, the one which is "lacking in its place" as it lacks its own identity'? (Deleuze 2004b: 146).[19] In this particular case, it is not 'Deleuze' who should be asked to explain certain (conceptual, affective or perceptive) 'spin-offs' produced by the dark precursor's 'coupling' of divergent series – rather it is his readers. To criticise Deleuze for 'deviating' from certain norms or transcendental principles, and to attribute to him, without any qualification, an identity at the end of one or other of the series that he has caused to resonate – Bergson-duration-cinema, Nietzsche-Spinoza, Virtual-Actual, time-truth, chance-eternal return, fold-outside and so on – is to ignore the multiple warnings that Deleuze gives about the nature of the relationship that the differentiator maintains with what it conditions in any intensive system. Deleuze specified very clearly:

> If difference is related *to its differentiator, and if we refrain from attributing to the differentiator an identity that it cannot and does not have*, then the difference will be small or large according to its possibilities of fractionation – that is, *according to the displacements and disguise* of the differentiator. In no case will it be possible to claim that a small difference testifies to a strict condition of resemblance, any more than a large difference testifies to the persistence of a resemblance which is simply relaxed. Resemblance is in any case an effect, a functional product, an external result – an illusion which appears *once the agent arrogates to itself an identity that it lacked*. (Deleuze 2004a: 147; emphasis added)

If in *Difference and Repetition* and *The Logic of Sense* the theory of the subject and the event is explained within the (post)structural(ist) framework of the 'differentiator' which causes heterogeneous series to resonate, in *Dialogues* Deleuze approaches the question in a completely different way and opens it out into a radically new dimension. We remember that in Chapter 3 of his dialogues with Claire Parnet, Deleuze (2006: 68) indicates that one must distinguish between 'two types of planes': a plane which is 'as much as one wishes, structural *and* genetic', which he calls 'one of *organisation*', and which essentially concerns 'the development of forms and the formation of subjects' (Deleuze and Parnet 2006: 91; emphasis added)[20] and a 'completely different plane' which he calls the '*plane of consistency*', whose distinctive characteristic is that it 'knows only relations of movement and rest, of speed and slowness, between unformed, or relatively unformed, elements, molecules or particles borne away by fluxes', and which, moreover, 'knows nothing of subjects, but rather what are called "haecceities"'. We learn indeed, in the same text, that on the one hand, 'no individuation takes place in the manner of a subject or even of a thing. An hour, a day, a season, a climate, one or several years – a degree of heat, an intensity, very different intensities which combine – have a perfect individuality which should not be confused with that of a thing or of a formed subject'; and, on the other hand, that 'it is not the *moment*, and it is not *brevity*, which distinguishes this type of individuation', and that '*a haecceity can last as long as, and even longer than, the time required for the development of a form and the evolution of a subject*'. When we appreciate that haecceities are not concerned with *the same type of time* but with 'floating times' (Deleuze and Parnet 2006: 92; emphasis added) as distinct from Chronos, we are perhaps beginning to assemble the elements which will enable us to understand better how this mysterious entity, the haecceity, is linked with the problematics of the multiplicity of Deleuze's names, which we have discussed above. Because it serves to 'determine an impersonal and pre-individual transcendental field . . . which nevertheless is not confused with an undifferentiated depth [and] cannot be determined as that of a consciousness', and refers to 'what is neither individual nor personal' (Deleuze 2004a: 118), the concept of haecceity is revealed to be what, from now on, *presides over* the genesis of individuals and people as emitters of singularities:

> It is haecceities that are being expressed in *indefinite, but not indeterminate,* articles and pronouns; in proper names which do not designate people *but mark events, in verbs in the infinitive which are not undifferentiated but constitute becomings or processes.* (Deleuze and Parnet 2006: 92; emphasis added).

The one explains the other: haecceities allow the naming of the singularities which characterise 'forces, events, movements and moving objects, winds and typhoons', but equally the naming of a period of time, even of a century: what a terrible five o'clock in the afternoon! what a terrible twentieth century!

What do Deleuze (and Guattari) undertake in *Anti-Oedipus* if not to locate and give a name to all the waves of force which formed the century, as well as to those which silently approach – still 'indefinite, but not indeterminate'? Deleuze knew that we belonged to the apparatuses [*dispositifs*] corresponding, between other becomings or processes in formation, to the haecceities which we shall call *postcolonial*[21] and which have the names: 'movements of national liberation', decolonisation, emigration, crisis in the struggle of the working class, 'crisis in the republican model', 'post-history', 'diasporisation of knowledge', 'postmodernism', 'conflicts between civilisations', 'racialisation of social conflicts', 'whiteness', 'death of the grand narrative', 'third world,' 'fourth world', 'AIDS' . . .

Deleuze and Guattari did not *invent* these haecceities but, by reviving the concept of haecceity, they allowed new light to be thrown on the way the present could be tackled, while being quite aware, as Deleuze aptly observed, that 'the present [*actuel*] is not what we are but rather what we become, what *we are in the process of becoming, in other words the Other, our becoming-other*' (Deleuze 2007: 350, emphasis added, trans. modified). In our view, it is this 'process of becoming . . . Other', and the haecceities to which it relates, that Deleuze (and Guattari) were pursuing when they created the concepts they have left to posterity. Concepts which they hoped would allow us to map out better new modes of subjectivation and socialisation: 'What new modes of subjectivation do we see appearing *today* that are certainly *not Greek or Christian?*' Deleuze asked, in a text devoted to Foucault (Deleuze 2007: 352; emphasis added). So many questions which, understandably, in light of the way they 'overflowed' a strictly European frame, appealed to and even enthralled postcolonial writers, thinkers and researchers. *Appealing* because, even if they were not always addressed directly to them, they touched on what was unfolding in the world and shared in this according to the principle which, in this case, holds that: HAECCEITIES = WHAT CENTURY ARE WE IN? WHAT WAVE IS SWEEPING US ALONG? WHAT HISTORY? WHAT NEW VISIBILITIES ARE POSSIBLE AFTER THE POSTCOLONY? and so on *Enthralling* because, even if the encounter did not always take place on a speculative level, there was always a concept that could come and *cleave* in two, postcolonial poets, musicians and filmmakers who went to encounter Deleuze's work and who discovered themselves to be 'Deleuzean' not 'without realising it' but through 'something that seems to have been brought about by him alone' (Deleuze 1988: 129). We nowadays know that this 'something = x' which carries the philosopher and the non-philosopher onwards comes from the multiplicity of Deleuze's names and the rich concepts he created in order to give an account of the haecceities that fascinated him so much and which turned out to be the very haecceities which writers such as (confining ourselves just to postcolonial writers of the Maghreb) Kateb Yacine, Abdelwahab Meddeb, Abdelkébir Khatibi, Rachid Boudjedra and Nabile Farès explore in their work.

'To 'illustrate' the ideas I have put forward, I invited the Algerian writer Nabile Farès to respond to the following request: to give his reaction to the text I wrote about his 'encounter' with Deleuze and to decribe

Farès and 'The Fig Tree's Malaise'

> It should not be thought that a haecceity consists simply of a decor or backdrop that situates subjects, or of appendages that hold things and people to the ground. *It is the entire assemblage in its individuated aggregate that is a haecceity*; it is this assemblage that is defined by a longitude and a latitude, by speeds and affects, independently of forms and subjects, which belong to another plane. (Deleuze and Guattari 1987: 262; emphasis added)

What characterises the encounter between Farès and Deleuze is that they tackle the same problems– even if in radically different ways – of minority, marginality and ethnic, religious and sexual difference, yet they avoid getting trapped by the deceptive simplicity and transparency of the responses to the political and ideological difficulties that these notions raise.

Indeed at first glance the problem of minorities seems remarkably simple to define: there would be on the one hand a majority or majorities made up of the greatest number of people in a given community who would represent dominant values, standards and so on; and on the other, a minority or minorities that could be distinguished by number (in this case, a smaller number), race, language, culture or all these elements at once.

What strikes me in Farès' work – and this too leads to the comparison between his work and Deleuze's – is that neither he nor Deleuze rehashes any elements of the *doxa* regarding minorities. Let us consider, for example, the question of number, or rather of numerical quantity as Deleuze and Guattari define it in *A Thousand Plateaus*:

> When we say majority, we are referring not to a greater relative quantity but to the determination of a state or standard in relation to which larger quantities, as well as the smallest, can be said to be minoritarian: white-man, adult-male, etc. (1987: 291)

Thus, to be able to speak of both the majority and the minority, we need a state or a standard that goes beyond both of them and to which we can compare them both.[22] This is what Farès identified as 'The Fig-tree's Malaise' in *Un Passager de l'occident (A Passenger from the West)* (1971):

> It's what we call the fig tree's malaise ... the song says that 'our fig tree has always been infested with fungus' and 'the coming of the people from the

> plains rotted our orchard' and 'if the fig tree doesn't speak to us any more, it's because his friend, his friend, the hedgehog, was stolen from him'. The theft of the hedgehog is for us, living on the peninsula, a completely narcissistic malaise, comparable to a malaise of naming. for, if you say, outside the peninsula, to an Algerian you meet, 'I am a Kabyle', what do you think he will answer? . . . he will say 'that's wrong, you are Algerian before you are Kabyle', which for us is historically unthinkable. Algeria came after Kabylie. that's a fact . . . (Farès 1971: 31–2)

There are additional important characteristics related to the question of minority/majority: first, the majority takes for granted a state of (political or cultural) dominance, and not the opposite; second, the majority also takes 'as pregiven the right and the power of man' (Deleuze and Guattari 1987: 291), that is, what for the minoritarian will be experienced as what I shall call the 'civilised white man' *hypostasis*. Farès sees this hypostasis as reaching its apogee in the supremacy of the Algerian patriarchy and bureaucracy.[23] And third, another meeting point between Deleuze and Guattari and Farès is the distinction they make between the minoritarian as a becoming or process, and the minority as an already constituted aggregate or state: a climate, a wind, a fog . . . a 'malaise'!

> It is important not to confuse 'minoritarian', as a becoming or a process, with a 'minority', as an aggregate or a state. Jews, Gypsies, etc. [and we could add Algerians, and all Maghrebis in general] may constitute minorities under certain conditions, *but that in itself does not make them becomings*. One reterritorializes, or allows oneself to become reterritorialized, on a minority or a state; *but in a becoming, one is deterritorialized*. (Deleuze and Guattari 1987: 291; emphasis added)

From this point of view, *Un Passager de l'occident* may be considered as the perfect instrument for this becoming-minoritarian and for this deterritorialisation as becoming, since it results from the double movement of deterritorialisation that characterises its mechanism as

> one by which a term (the subject) is withdrawn from the majority, and another by which a term (the medium or agent) *rises up from the minority*. There is an asymmetrical and indissociable *block of becoming*, a block of alliance. (Deleuze and Guattari 1987: 291; emphasis added)

Both Farèses – the Algerian and the non-Algerian – enter into a becoming-Kabyle. And in reality, things are even more complex with Farès, since there are always at the same time other becomings that destabilise the national majoritarian good conscience and *all* majoritarian good conscience in general.

As Deleuze and Guattari write: 'There is no subject of the becoming except as a deterritorialized variable of the majority; there is no medium of becoming except as a deterritorialized variable of a minority' (1987: 292). In *Un passager de l'occident*, Farès makes himself into this medium and becomes this deterritorialised and deterritorialising subject. He is a *deterritorialising subject* in relation to his own *Algerian majority*, whose transparency and historical grounding he questions when he reinvents himself as Brandy-Fax or Ali-Saïd; he is a *deterritorialised subject* in relation to the *Kabyle minority* when he appeals to James Baldwin in order to deterritorialise his own belonging to the Kabyle minority, linking it to a becoming-black that destabilises and renews it. In so doing, however, he clearly shows that becoming minoritarian is not merely an individual or psychological question but essentially a political one as well: 'Becoming-minoritarian is a political affair and necessitates a labour of power [*puissance*], an active micropolitics' (Deleuze and Guattari 1987: 292). Thus, to this *molar-becoming*, we must now oppose an active micropolitics of a *molecular* becoming that involves a line of becoming that passes through points – stases, states, communities – and comes up through the middle. Crab-grass! (Deleuze and Guattari 1987: 292, 7). In other words, in Farès' work the boundary no longer falls between history and individual memory but rather between punctual systems (history/memory) and multilinear or diagonal organisations that no longer refer to the eternal, or even to the historical – to a 'cathartic' history, as Farès calls it[24] – but to a becoming of both history and memory. This is what Farès calls a 'total history' of Algeria, an 'authentic' history of Algeria. After all, Algeria was not always colonised or Muslim, it *became* colonised, became Muslim. So Farès prefers 'Paganism' – 'the very old belief, despite all opposition' (1971: 73) – to the *basso continuo* of 'Algerian', 'Islam', 'Kabyle', 'Arab' which is supposed to 'say'[25] eternal 'Algeria: "This belief is pagan, for it would never occur to anyone to deny that Algeria was an important center of paganism before becoming the stomping grounds for the edifying discourses of Christianity or Islam' (1971: 73). This, in any case, is the mission he assigns to poetry and to artistic work in general, work that no longer refers to the history of Algeria but to the sketch of what it is becoming – *a becoming that it intuits through the haecceity of paganism*. But it is what Farès *knows*, with a knowledge that he derives above all from his work as a writer and from the percepts it enables him to bring to up to date – that 'history is the archive, the drawing of what we are and what we cease to be, *while the present is the sketch of what we are becoming*' (Deleuze 2007: 350; emphasis added trans. mod.). Farès knows that the '*I* of history and of utterance did not know what had marked it after the staging of "this other scene" that

Freud speaks of, the site of the Other' (see Farès' letter, below). This, in any case, explains why, in relation to political censorship and dictates, 'only an artistic discovery, or a life that is LIVED ARTISTICALLY can make sense of, or bear witness to a meaning other than political servitude' (1971: 74–5; Farès' capitalisation).

Farès catches *contemporary* Algerian history in another *double movement*: a movement of deterritorialisation that wrests it from its present history by bringing it back to its *prehistory* (paganism), and a movement of reterritorialisation that, by confronting Algeria's present history with a cosmic history – 'Dialogues between Earth and Twilight' – summons us to find quickly a way to get our feet back on the ground and rediscover the country:

> A country where you can simply live, go to the cafés, have a drink, flirt with girls, study, go out dancing at night, and work 15 hours a day, a cigarette in your mouth. In short, a country where the citizens could build bonfires, find shelter from the oil wells, and eat their couscous and meat flavoured with orange flower or olive oil whenever they wanted. A country, in short, on a par with its political reality. A country, in short, really political. (1971: 77)

Thus, as I intimated, the 'Dialogues between Earth and Twilight' that close the book were not concocted to relativise things, or to show their arbitrary nature. For Farès, neither colonisation nor Islam is 'arbitrary'. Rather, it seems to me that, above all, he wants to make things undergo an eternal return that would reveal their fundamental *contingency*. And in this sense, Farès echoes Mallarmé's wonderful phrase, '*Un coup de dés jamais n'abolira le hasard!*' That which brought Islam can once again bring paganism! Islam was imposed by the repression of ancestral paganism. But this paganism is perhaps the only true *basso continuo*, the only fundamental movement that will resist historically and perhaps return. Everything became on a foundation of paganism. Once again, it hardly matters whether its return is possible or not, utopian or realist. The task of the writer lies elsewhere. The only thing that matters is the minor variable, the minor mode. Yet we need to understand that for Farès, this minor mode must also be made to move, made dynamic by the fact that in all becoming the terms are not interchangeable: never, in this sense, will the authentic minoritarian become majoritarian. Both are caught in an asymmetrical block where the one must not change any less than the other. Thus the Kabyle's becoming-black American (or Sahraoui) must correspond to the Algerian's becoming-Kabyle. This does not mean that concessions to either block must be made. On the contrary, both blocks must undergo a movement of translation or deportation through which the majoritarian block will see the movement of deterritorialisation that carries it toward a becoming-minority accelerate, and the minoritarian island will transcend its marginality, its regional localisation through the acceleration or intensification of the movement of deterritorialisation that carries it along and that will result in 'changes of all *states*'. This in any case explains how Farès can create a dialogue between Twilight and the Earth as two singularities in becoming, in other words two haecceities the conditions of whose visibility must be – *poetically* –reunited.

> (Words of dusk): 'Beautiful woman of the Earth, are you unaware of the change; the change? not the change from one state to another; but *the change of all states*. This long wound that you know, and that goes through me through you, what else is it? a change of state? or a change of place? of all places?' (1971: 151)[26]

Such were Farès' ideas on the *states* (of the Maghreb) and of their *becoming* in Un Passager de l'occident (1971). In *L'État perdu: Discours pratique de l'émigré* (1982) it seems to me that Farès has moved to a more advanced and at the same time more complex phase. It is as if it were no longer a question of elaborating a theory of becoming-Kabyle, but rather of resolutely moving on to *practice*. He no longer seems to be dealing with an economy of *ideas* about a state or a stasis but rather with the *book* that corresponds to them. With *L'État perdu*, Farès seems to put forward the idea that one cannot change attitudes or habits regarding things or the world without changing the nature of the (static/statist?) relations that exist between the book and the world, the book and ideas, and, finally, the book and subject.[27] For Farès, there were too many books in the Maghreb that were still merely the palest reproductions of social, political and aesthetic reality that we view as already given, that is, as carbon copies or tracings (*calques*). Even when they dealt with realities that were always already destructured and/or in formation, too many Maghrebi writers continued to write *as if* the eternal task of the book were to represent an organic beautiful totality as a signifying and subjective interiority, or as an imitation and reproduction of the world. What Farès seems to be suggesting, rather, is that this epoch of the book as the reflection of the One and the transparency of the world has come to an end. From now on, what must guide us is not what a book (or an author) wants to say or means, but how the book functions, or, better yet, how it is connected to the world, how it adjusts to the world in order to be in direct contact with it. In such a context, as Deleuze and Guattari (1987: 4) say:

> [W]e will never ask what a book means, as signifier or signified; we will not look for anything to understand in it. We will ask what it functions with, in

connection with what other things it does or does not transmit intensities, in which other multiplicities its own are inserted and metamorphosed, and with what bodies without organs it makes its own converge.

This is the kind of rhizomatic book that Farès wanted to promote by writing *L'État perdu*. It is a rhizome-book because, unlike books that draw their inspiration from models of the tree or of the root, it does not hesitate to connect 'any point to any other' and to bring into play 'very different regimes of signs, and even nonsign states' (Deleuze and Guattari 1987: 21). Like the rhizome-book according to Deleuze and Guattari, it

> is reducible neither to the One nor to the multiple. It is not the One that becomes Two or even directly three, four, five, etc. . . . It is composed not of units but of dimensions, or rather directions in motion. It has neither beginning nor end, but always a middle course [*milieu*] from which it grows and which it overspills. (Deleuze and Guattari 1987: 21)

Unlike the narrative-representative book that proceeds by mimesis and reproduction, *L'État perdu* is made up of only lines (and sometimes literally even lines): '[L]ines of segmentarity and stratification as its dimensions, and the line of flight or deterritorialization as the maximum dimension after which the multiplicity undergoes metamorphosis, changes in nature' (Deleuze and Guattari 1987: 21). What strikes us here is that each *trait* no longer necessarily nor always refers to a linguistic sign: semiotic links of all kinds are connected to very different modes of encoding: biological, political, economic and so on, that bring into play not only different regimes of signs but also the *statuses of the state of things*. The book is no longer content merely to re-present the world or reality, it is no longer a copy or a photograph or even a simple drawing, but a map 'that must be produced, constructed, a map that is always detachable, connectable, reversible, modifiable, and has multiple entryways and exits and its own lines of flight' (Deleuze and Guattari 1987: 21).

In fact, how does *L'État perdu* begin? 'The cover illustration is an Attic borrowing in which the various elements of Berber and Mediterranean symbolic still in use today are combined' (Farès 1982: note, first unnumbered page – see illustration opposite)

Thus, from the outset, a drawing or design short-circuits or emphasises the hegemonic nature of the linguistic sign. Indeed there is an emphasis, but more in the sense of the Hegelian *Aufhebung*: for if there is in fact both a going beyond and a retaining of the sign, this retaining (of the Berber sign) is also a going beyond, a subversion, a transformation, of

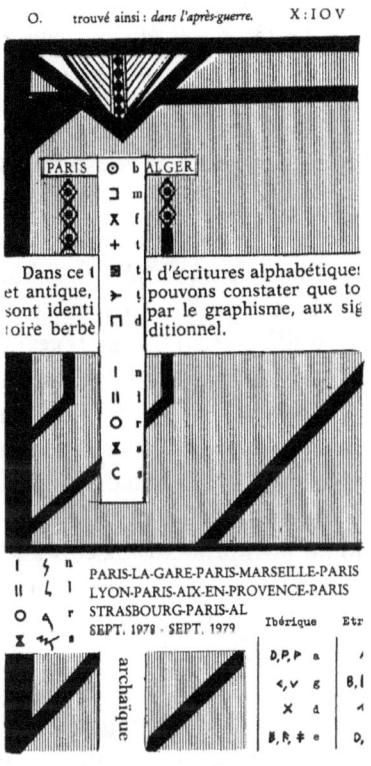

... *écrit dans l'Après-Guerre.*

Une poésie qui redresserait l'arbre de sa chute ; le jour de son éclipse ; la terre de sa déchéance ; une poésie qui ouvrirait le monde comme un regard aimé étendu beau sur le regard visible des terres et des plantes ; une poésie qui réconcilierait la présence, la liberté, l'être, et, la vie ; qui détournerait la mort, le vide, l'esclavage ; une poésie que la main dessine, tandis que le corps devient opéra où se joue la plus simple joie du monde ; une poésie...

Août 1981.

Figure 1 An 'Attic borrowing' in the work of Farès.

what, in another context, would fall completely flat by referring such a word back to a fixed signifier. If in *L'État perdu* the drawing intervenes in the work, it is no longer to illustrate or decorate it, no longer to create a kind of local colour, but rather the drawing is there to mobilise those signs that, because they are charged with affects, allow the text to be transformed into a veritable map of haecceities which cross the field of the Algerian imagination. Farès is not content to attach (Berber or Arab) signs arbitrarily to the text. By multiplying the signs of the most heterogeneous languages and pictorial systems which he brings into resonance by means of the drawings and motifs of Kabyle carpets and Arab or Tiffinagh words, he presents the text as a cryptogram of haecceities which *speak* this 'non-place of being and time' that Algeria is and which Farès forcefully calls the 'un-birth' of the subject who tries to understand what postcolonial Algeria is becoming beneath the iron rule of military power:

Non-place of being and time, he says what in himself is in a state of agony: the *un-birth* in which *his body of letters and worlds* was already caught in ancient times. He speaks in order to know and make known what is occurring in the state discourses born of fundamentalism: he names the conquered space, always possible, of the difficult existence of oneself and others, of those who, like him, in space and time, are subject to expulsion. (1982: 11; emphasis original)

In Farèsian semiotics, then, the sign – whether drawing, pictogram or other – no longer signifies only as a signifier that refers to a signified, but as a mark, a tattoo or a wound charged with affect. In this sense, the sign is transformed into a scarification, becoming like a gash on the text, or better yet, like a *stigmata*. The sign is like the *symptom* of the repression of a language or a more ancient, more archaic system of signs, rather than like the signifier of a signified. In fact, from the moment it is inscribed in an arrangement where it is no longer emphasised or co-opted like in a book of images, stories or linguistics, the sign undoubtedly contaminates the entire field of thought with its emotional (symptomatological) and historical charge, finding itself directly connected to an unprecedented reality. By integrating as he does the Lybic, Berber or Tiffinagh signs in a text where they no longer figure as illustrations of a theory, Farès transforms them into the practical inscription of cultural difference. Because they are inscribed in a system that is 'a-centered, non-hierarchical, and non-signifying, without a General, without an organizing memory or a central automaton . . . *defined only by a circulation of states*' (Deleuze and Guattari 1987: 21; emphasis added), these signs from now on refer to a (potential or virtual) reality that until then had no right to exist. The sign no longer (only) presents itself as a linguistic-representative sign, but as a numeral, a kind of registration number profoundly marked both emotionally and historically:[28]

> The registration numbers found throughout this book (numbers that are ciphers in the sense of codes and decipherings) are numbers of chapters as well as numbers imposed by the registration or inscription of a name and a language that, always according to the same history, were *borrowed*. Journeys to the heart of the signs-therefore-where the serpent represented xxxxxxxx manifests the meaning of a *reality* (Farès 1982: first page, original emphasis).

One appropriation leads to another: First we are told that the borrowings are from Berber, and now we discover that French itself is a 'borrowed' language. What, then, is the true language? Or could it be that all languages are borrowed? In fact, once it is assimilated to a politics of numbers and numbering – and thus to a politics of identification –

language, and here French in particular, becomes the object of a coded trajectory (*parcours*) that allows it to be assigned a status it did not have prior to the *deciphering* it undergoes in this book. Because it has been subjected to operations of grafting and cutting, the borrowed language – French – reveals (itself) and is transformed into an emitter of flux and intensities which were until then imperceptible to the writer subjected to the economy of the one Book. That is, it reveals itself to be a language that constantly overcodes 'indigenous' languages: Arab, Kabyle and Tiffinagh. By *deciphering* myself in a borrowed language, I can only find myself in a *registered* identity: a reified or monadised state, (sociological) fact or condition. Finding itself thus attached to a regime of signs that is profoundly heterogeneous to it, French reveals itself to be *one code among others* – and, for the Maghrebi, an *arbitrary* code at that; or, in Farès' words, 'the sequestered form of the word that cannot pronounce the tune of its nomination' (1982: 20).

Thus, far from finding himself alienated from the French language – that is acculturated, Farès inscribes this language – the signs of the French language – in a *process* where it can finally appear in its historical function, that is, as a language that has covered over and even debarred another.[29] Practically speaking, Farès could only make this aspect of things apparent in an active – practical! – way by an assemblage of heterogeneous signs and semiotic links that go on to connect yet other regimes of signs, organisations of power, and occurrences that refer to the arts, history, the sciences, and to social struggles as well.

It is in this sense that the title of the book – *Lost State* – is important. What is lost is any state that does not take into consideration the multiplicity of language, races, cultures and mores that exist in a given country. What is also lost is the state of a language that has become monologised, or monolingualised. To the degree that identity – a certain type of psychological and national identity – is linked to a state (stasis) of language, by questioning the stability of language, Farès simultaneously questions the identity of the subject that it registers and the reasoning behind the different modalities (linguistic, cultural, ethnic and national) of registration. For Farès also, each time language is considered – used – as a code that *pre-exists* the forces, affects and precepts it is supposed to transcribe, it becomes an instrument of the reduction of the multiplicities at work in the slightest thought and transforms itself into an instrument of state repression.

In this book as in many others by Farès, there are numerous passages that could be quoted, summoned to support this thesis. Here is one of the most eloquent:

> The compass card [*rose des vents*] indicates that the movements of stars and countries are mixed in a diverse, corporeal work, even if – once again – *there exists the fear of touching a word, of taking it exploded, as a personal Rose of sand or Blood: fear of being, in the closed book*. 'But where on earth did you find this illusion of signs?' The permanence of the important gaze that exile from the earth fixes in the days. (1982: 25; emphasis added).

Deleuze liked to say that there are animal-becomings in writing, which do not consist in talking of one's dog or cat, but which are 'rather an encounter between two reigns, a short-circuit, the picking-up of a code where each is deterritorialised' (Deleuze and Parnet 2006: 44). Now this is exactly what occurs in the way that Farès writes. Like many postcolonial writers, he too wishes through his writing above all to give 'writing to those who do not have it' – hence the subtitle of his book-poem *Lost State*: 'The Emigrant's Practical Discourse', while being aware that those to whom writing is addressed 'give writing a becoming without which it would not exist, without which it would be a pure redundancy in the service of the powers that be' (Deleuze and Parnet 2006: 44).

We could point to many passages in *Lost State* that accord with these assertions, but we should not give in too quickly to the temptation of seeing them as the book's sole aim. To restrict ourselves to this level of interpretation would be to miss one of the essential dimensions of Farès' approach in the book. Once again, what Farès aims at are not the great signifying ruptures (the political, ideological and artistic), but at the 'contamination' of these formations by *cutting*, *graft* and asymmetrical *assemblage* of the heterogeneous signs which constitute 'being Algerian'. So, for Farès, what must be put in place in order to provoke a (poetic/political) event are not signifying or 'rational' cuts, but 'irrational' cuts.[30] To write, consequently, begins to look like deambulation, like a migration across the most heterogeneous signs. It is a question then of writing like a nomad and producing books that will be true war machines against the (ideological) apparatuses [*appareils*] of the state and the registration cards that they impose. As Farès says in his letter (see below):

> [T]he psychological can be tackled in its epistemological and schematic, rather than clinical, representations, only through line or drawing or written forms, all being lines which define a space, or more precisely, space, contours, proximities, vicinities, territorialities, topoi which are semantically undetachable from places.

These 'vicinities', these 'territorialities' and these 'contours' refer of course to places that are quite real – a city, a quarter, a shanty town, a transit camp – but also to those quasi-cities (*outrevilles*), the shifting cities of telecoms, airports, railway stations and ports. Farès did not need to read Deleuze or Virilio to join with them in tracing out the haecceities that characterise modern nomadism – that is to say, a nomadism where 'trajectography'[31] has little by little replaced geography. In short, a period in which the *moving*, and no longer the *stationary*, is what is now inhabitable, a period in which the good old 'place of one's own choosing' of yesteryear, the city and the nation, have become 'places of dejection'. But it is as well to leave the final word to Farès (1982 39–40):

Ils
Racontaient
Ou fabulaient
Sur nous: que nous
N'étions nés
Nu L II
    E part
Que nous étions
  Soupçonnés
  D'être nourris
  De la mort-de-
  L'étranger
  Et que
  Sans coutumes
  Sans-bras
  Sans-pieds
  Sans-cartes
  Ni pays;
Nous ne pouvions être garantis
d'une ou quelconque
nationalité ou.
    INSCRIPTION PERSONNELLE
    D'IDENTITÉ: À CAUSE DE CETTE
    RIGUEUR
    DES CHIFFRES
    QUI COMPOSAIENT (SANS DOUTE)
    LE DÉLIRE D'UNE IMMATRICULATION CALCULÉE
      ARRACHÉE
      ÉCRITE
They
Related
Or made up stories
About us; that we
Were born

No
 Where
That we were
 Suspected
 Of having being fed
 On the death-of-
 The-foreigner
 And that
 Without customs
 Without-arms
 Without-feet
 Without-cards
 Or country;
 We couldn't be certain of having
 Any nationality at all.
 REGISTRATION OF PERSONAL
 IDENTITY: DUE TO THE
 RIGOUR
 OF THE NUMBERS
 WHICH UNDOUBTEDLY MADE UP
 THE DELIRIUM OF A REGISTRATION CALCULATED
    TORN OUT
    WRITTEN

Appendix: Letter from Nabile Farès

By email
Paris, 15 October 2008
Dear Réda,

Ahead of the new elections which have spurred me to travel to the United States for the first time . . . Yes, *A Passenger from the West* is, if I may say so, a book ahead of its time – in that it anticipates the linking of psychoanalysis, literature and political criticism of the so-called social state. We live in a time of political formulations of the social state: that is, a time of politics which claims to look after the totality, but for which individuals, especially those who wish to belong to this social state, must stump up the cost of a ticket, the symbolic price of admission – that is, they must accept what politics says about where the social state is today, a form connected with globalisation.

But let's get back to what you so elegantly called your 'request' [*requête*] . . . You begin with *A Passenger from the West*, which is a good choice because this text reintroduces the political dimension of fracture and the way out from 'catastrophe', the colonial holocaust, through poem and dream. The final text of 'Cavales frontalières' ['Secret border crossing'] being an alternative reading of utterances, rhymes, and territories already travelled over and evoked; so, *Deleuze, Guattari, yes, on the condition that that they are once again situated in the field discovered by Freud which is, as Deleuze and Guattari put it, a territorialisation other than the psychological and historical*; psychoanalysis being, in singularity, 'fundamental', and, if I may be allowed this paradox, 'a-territorial'. But, by way of perfect contradiction, *the psychological can be tackled in its epistemological and schematic, rather than clinical, representations, only through line or drawing or written forms, all being lines which define a space, or more precisely, space, contours, proximities, vicinities, territorialities, topoi which are semantically undetachable from places*, as if words and places were, in their upheavals, marked symbolically, or were, to put it better, symbolic geographies. So, if you like, my texts, my books, in different ways and the same, *reveal different symbolic territories, networks, geographies inscribed on surfaces that are at once visible and invisible, visible and exterior, invisible and interior in their inscriptions*; these texts work by revealing symbolic geographies, both collective and singular, which weave together, more so than they delineate (a *feature that distinguishes me from Glissant*) beings, dead or alive, spaces of inscription in which a society, or societies, and historical periods, move, collide, assemble [*s'agencent*], in Deleuze and Guattari's expression, are named, transformed, deployed – I could describe this as involving territorialised subjectivities symbolically written and spoken, at certain times, into their pre-history and their present:

A-territoriality is that Damascene moment, a-territoriality which allows the seizing of that moment in which unknowing (to use one of Lacan's apt, well-chosen terms) begins to appear; the *I* of history and of utterance did not know what had marked it after the staging of 'this other scene' that Freud speaks of, the site of the Other, of both *the big and little other*, as Lacan would say:

What triggered a new kind of fiction writing and company was the *Anti-Oedipus* or the broadening of the question posed by the fiction of Oedipus and desire, that is, other *desire*, not desire for the other, which passes through the other, Other and Other, but other desire: the true sense of the Oedipus, in short: to escape the unconscious wish and the realisation of death, murder, crime, psychological death and real death; *this is how the 'revolt' of Deleuze and Guattari responds to this tension of exiting outside of closure, outside the programmed determinants of a historical subject hypnotised into unknowing by the language of repetition.*

This is why we have such interest in those mobile creations of language, those words introduced into the vocabulary of language, philosophy and psychoanalysis, such as *folds, assemblages, plateaus, picturalities, nodes, threads, corners, angles . . . creations of another space, of another fictionalisation of visible space*, and, as Freud says, endopsychic: a space of myth and dream, of wish, of the suspension of death and of the . . . impossible word which means *après-coup*, as Brechet put it, history is written 'after the disasters' – I'm quoting from *A Passenger from the West*; an essential idea, that of rupture with entelechies and imaginary generalisations, fantasmic-screens of the ontological which, in Derrida, were advanced as 'deconstruction'; it seems that *Deleuze and Guattari have gone one step further by refusing to remain in a hermeneutic ontology, not of being, but of philosophy as practice* – I'm speculating widely and ask for your opinion of these ideas, knowing as I do how

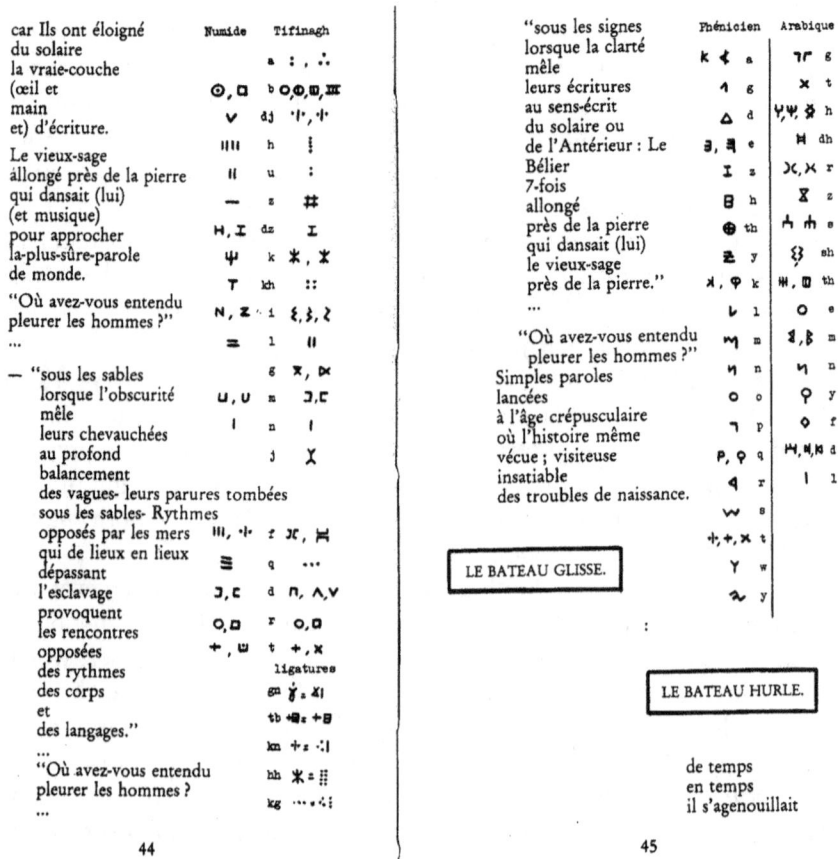

Figure 2 An excerpt from Nabile Farès' book, *L'État perdu*.

keenly you appreciate these sorts of distinctions. And this allows me to say that you in the United States are working in the ways and caesuras between historical periods and forms of creation – Jean-Luc Nancy, Philippe Lacoue-Labarthe; hence the even greater rupture made by Lacan and his writing of the real-impossible: the hole, the incision, the division . . .

It would be very interesting to look into this differentiation between types of writing, the abandonment of ontological hermeneutics in this *après-coup* of history; this was my preoccupation in that text which is now impossible to find anywhere and which across the distance of the years would be the counterpart of an 'I insist upon the "a"' ['*j'insiste sur le "un"*'], amongst others, *A Passenger from the West* and *The Lost State, an Immigrant's Practical Discourse* in which the deterritorialisation of identity goes as far as the pinning down and spelling of different phonemes of languages as skeletons of the differentiated transliterations and the enduring samenesses [*mêmetés*] of civilisations and histories

I have just reread a few pages of Hannah Arendt which are concerned precisely with this *après-coup* that defines, for those who would take pleasure in the spectral omnipotence of a political power destructive of swathes of human beings considered superfluous, a disgust [*dégout*], in short a sewer [*égout*] – so easy are all these things, riches, power and destruction, and so well they go together;

which, fortunately, in a way, cannot not be infinitely perceived[32]
this, my dear Réda, is how your elegant request has inspired me
with my regards and warm wishes
I look forward to hearing from you soon
Nabile.

References

Alliez, E. (1991), *Les Temps capitaux: Récits de la conquête du temps*, vol. 1, Paris: Éditions du Cerf.
Alliez, E. (1993), *La Signature du monde ou qu'est-ce que la philosophie de Deleuze et Guattari?*, Paris: Éditions du Cerf.
Ansell-Pearson, K. (ed) (1997), *Deleuze and Philosophy: the Difference Engineer*, London: Routledge.
Antonioli, M. (1999), *Deleuze et l'histoire de la philosophie, ou de la philosophie comme science-*fiction, Paris: Kimé.
Badiou, A. (1997), *Deleuze: La clameur de l'être*, Paris: Hachette.
Badiou, A. (2000), *The Clamour of Being*, trans. L. Burchill, Minneapolis: University of Minnesota Press.
Barthélémy, J.-H. (2005), *Simondon ou l'encyclopédisme génétique*, Paris: PUF.

Barthes, R. (1975), *The Pleasure of the Text*, trans. R. Miller, New York: Hill and Wang.
Beaulieu, A. de (2005), *Gilles Deleuze, héritage philosophique*, Paris: PUF.
Bensmaïa, R. (1989a), 'Gilles Deleuze ou comment devenir un *Stalker* en philosophie', *Lendemains, Études comparées sur la France 53*, Special Issue on Gilles Deleuze edited by Réda Bensmaïa: 7–8.
Bensmaïa, R. (1989b), 'L'effet-Kafka' *Lendemains, Études comparées sur la France 53*, Special Issue on Gilles Deleuze edited by Réda Bensmaïa: 63–72.
Bogue, R. (2003), *Deleuze on Literature*, London: Routledge.
Bouaniche, A. (2007), *Gilles Deleuze, une introduction*, Paris: Pocket.
Chamoiseau, P. (1997), *Écrire en pays dominé*, Paris: Gallimard.
Cusset, F. (2008), *French Theory: How Foucault, Derrida, Deleuze & Co. Transformed the Intellectual Life of the United States*, trans. J. Fort with J. Berganza and M. Jones, Minneapolis: University of Minnesota Press.
David-Ménard, M. (2005), *Deleuze et la psychanalyse*, Paris: PUF.
Deleuze, G. [1981] (1988), *Spinoza, Practical Philosophy*, trans. R. Hurley, San Franciso: City Light Books.
Deleuze, G. [1985] (1989), *Cinema 2: The Time-Image*, trans. H. Tomlinson and R. Galeta, London: Athlone.
Deleuze, G. (1995), *Negotiations, 1972–1990*, trans. M. Joughin, New York: Columbia University Press.
Deleuze, G. (1998), 'Gilles Deleuze, immanence et vie', *Rue Descartes* 20, Collège International de Philosophie.
Deleuze, G. [1969] (2004a), *The Logic of Sense*, ed. C. V. Boundas, trans. M. Lester with C. Stivale, London: Continuum.
Deleuze, G. (2004b), *Difference and Repetition*, trans. P. Patton, London: Continuum.
Deleuze, G. (2007), *Two Regimes of Madness: Texts and Interviews, 1975–1995*, ed. D. Lapoujade, trans. A. Hodges and M. Taormina, New York: Semiotext(e).
Deleuze, G. (2008), 'Gilles Deleuze, l'intempestif', *Rue Descartes* 53, Collège International de Philosophie.
Deleuze, G. and F. Guattari (1987), *A Thousand Plateaus*, trans. B. Massumi, Minneapolis: University of Minnesota Press.
Deleuze, G. and C. Parnet (2006), *Dialogues II*, new edn, trans. H. Tomlinson, B. Habberjam and E. R. Albert, London: Continuum.
Dumoncel, J. C. (1999), *Le Pendule du Docteur Deleuze: une introduction à L'Anti-Œdipe*, Paris: Cahiers de l'Unebévue.
Farès, N. (1982), *L'État perdu: Discours pratique de l'émigré*, Le Paradou: Actes Sud.
Farès, N. (1971), *Un Passager de l'occident*, Paris: Éditions du Seuil.
Fiat, C. (2002), *La Ritournelle: une anti-théorie*, Paris: L. Scheer.
Flaxman, G. (ed.) (2000), *The Brain is the Screen: Deleuze and the Philosophy of Cinema*, Minneapolis: University of Minnesota Press.
Foucault M. (1997), 'Theatrum Philosophicum', in P. Rabinow (ed.), *Essential Works of Foucault 1954–1984*, trans. R. Hurley et al., vol. 1, New York: New Press, pp. 343–68.
Foucault, M. (1999), 'Michel Foucault and Zen: A Stay in a Zen Temple', in J. R. Carrette (ed.), *Religion and Culture*, Manchester: Manchester University Press, pp. 110–15.
Gualandi, A. (1998), *Deleuze*, Paris: Les Belles Lettres.
Hardt M. and A. Negri (2000), *Empire*, Cambridge: Harvard University Press.
Hême de Lacotte, S. (2001), *Deleuze, philosophie et cinéma: le passage de l'image-mouvement à l'image-temps*, Paris: L'Harmattan.

Holland, E. W. (1999), *Deleuze and Guattari's Anti-Oedipus: Introduction to Schizoanalysis*, London: Routledge.
Jaglé, C. (2005), *Portrait oratoire de Gilles Deleuze aux yeux jaunes*, Paris: PUF.
Leclercq, S. (2001), *Gilles Deleuze, immanence, univocité et transcendantal*, Mons: Éditions Sils Maria.
Levinas, E. (1974), *Autrement qu'être ou Au-delà de l'essence*, The Hague: Nijhoff.
Mbembe, A. (2001), *On the Postcolony*, Berkeley: University of California Press.
Patton, P. (ed.) (1996), *Deleuze: A Critical Reader*, Oxford: Blackwell.
Patton, P. (2000), *Deleuze and the Political*, London: Routledge.
Patton, P. (2006), 'The Event of Colonisation', in I. Buchanan and A. Parr (eds), *Deleuze and the Contemporary World*, Edinburgh: Edinburgh University Press, pp. 108–24.
Petrosino, S. and J. Rolland (1984), 'La vérité nomade: introduction à Emmanuel Lévinas', *La Découverte* 45: 45–6.
Rajchman, R. (2000), *The Deleuze Connections*, Boston: MIT Press.
Rodowick, D. N. (1997), *Gilles Deleuze's Time Machine*, Durham: Duke University Press.
Sasso, R. and A. Villani (eds) (2003), *Le Vocabulaire de Deleuze*, *Les Cahiers de Noesis* 3 (Spring): 172–3.
Virilio, P. (2008), 'Les Damnés de l'exode', *Le Nouvel Observateur* 2299: 16–17.
Žižek, S. (2004), *Organs without Bodies: Deleuze and Consequences*, New York: Routledge.
Zourabichvili, F. (2003), *Le Vocabulaire de Deleuze*, Paris: Ellipses.

Notes

1. Quoted by Claire Parnet in *Dialogues II* (Deleuze and Parnet 2006: 31, trans. modified). Translator's note: *The Great Wall of China* was pieced together from Kafka's manuscripts after his death. The quotation in question was translated into English as part of a fragment of 'The Great Wall', under the title 'An Old Manuscript', in Nahum N. Glazer (ed.) (1983), *The Complete Stories*, New York: Schocken, p. 416: 'They come like fate, without reason, consideration, or pretext . . . In some way that is incomprehensible they have pushed right into the capital. At any rate, here they are; it seems that every morning there are more of them.' See also 'A Leaf from an Old Manuscript', in Franz Kafka (1992), *The Metamorphosis and Other Stories*, trans. Malcolm Pasley, Harmondsworth: Penguin, p. 163: 'By some means that is incomprehensible to me, they have penetrated as far as the capital, although this is a very long way from the frontier. At all events, there they are; it seems that every morning there are more of them.'
2. See Patton (2006). Patton opens his article with the observation that 'Colonisation was not a topic that figured largely in Deleuze's work' (p. 109). Other critics and commentators also note this.
3. See de Beaulieu (2005) and Bouaniche (2006, particularly p. 294 and following). I am only summarising here the examples which these two commentators provide of the impact made by Deleuze's work on artists, scientists and critics.
4. The following is only a partial list of the works to which I am alluding. French-language books: Badiou (1997); Gualandi (1998); Antonioli (1999); de Beaulieu (2005); Zourabichvili (2003); Hême de Lacotte (2001); Jaglé (2005); David-Ménard (2005); Dumoncel (1999); Leclercq (2001); Fiat (2002); Alliez (1993); Deleuze (1998); Deleuze (2008). English-language books: Rajchman (2000); Holland (1999); Bogue (2003); Patton (1996; 2000); Flaxman (2000); Rodowick (1997); Ansell-Pearson (1997).

5. Deleuze (1995: 88): 'I don't know what Foucault meant, I never asked him. He was a terrible joker. He may perhaps have meant that I was the most naive philosopher of our generation. In all of us you find themes like multiplicity, difference, repetition. But I put forward almost raw concepts of these, while others work with more mediations.'
6. Deleuze (1995: 6). To show that the question of names does not appear by chance in Deleuze's work, we could cite many other instances where this 'theme' is broached. See, for example, the way he explores it in *Dialogues II*, (Deleuze and Parnet 2006: 6):

   You *encounter* people (and sometimes without knowing them or ever having seen them) but also movements, ideas, events, entities. All these things have proper names, *but the proper name does not designate a person or a subject*. It designates an effect, a zigzag, something which passes or happens between two as though under a potential difference: the 'Compton effect', the 'Kelvin effect'. (emphasis added)

7. This is how Deleuze characterises the nature of 'movement' in the modern world:

   nowadays we see movement defined less and less in relation to a point of leverage. All the new sports – surfing, windsurfing, hang-gliding – take the form of entering into an existing wave. There's no longer an origin as starting point, but a sort of putting-into-orbit. The key thing is how to get taken up in the motion of a big wave, a column of rising air, to 'get into something' instead of being the origin of an effort. (Deleuze 1995: 121)

8. I have in mind here the warnings that Deleuze and Guattari give their readers every time an experiment (relayed by a concept) presents the risk of the disintegration of the subject or a danger to its survival. One 'example' among hundreds of others in *A Thousand Plateaus* is: 'A mistake in speed, rhythm, or harmony would be catastrophic because it would bring back the forces of chaos, destroying both creator and creation' (1987: 343). On this point, it is interesting to note the frequency with which Deleuze (and Guattari) use the (imperative? prescriptive? descriptive? preventive?) expression '*il faut*' ('it is necessary'/'one must'). This subreption of the phrase '*il faut*' could (erroneously, in my opinion) be interpreted as an example of 'voluntarism' on the part of the authors. In my view we *must* rather interpret their use of this expression as a term of warning, of the following sort: 'If you wish to avoid the danger that is represented by a becoming-animal or a BwO, you *must* avoid [*il faut éviter*] . . . ' In this sense, the '*il faut*' is less of the order of a command than a warning sign or signal that serves either as an alarm ('wrong move', 'no trespassing' and so on) or as a kind of 'user's manual'. Here are some 'examples' drawn from the first chapter of *A Thousand Plateaus*: 'The problem of writing: in order to designate something exactly, anexact expressions are utterly unavoidable' ('. . . *il faut absolument des expressions anexactes* . . .'), p. 22; 'The multiple must be made, not by always adding a higher dimension, but rather in the simplest of ways' ('*Le multiple, il faut le faire* . . .'), p. 7; 'the tracing should always be put back on the map' ('*il faut toujours reporter le calque sur la carte*'), p. 14; 'To attain the multiple, one must have a method that effectively constructs it' ('*Pour le multiple, il faut une méthode* . . .'), p. 24; and for the 'user's manual' type of usage: 'Go first to your old plant and watch carefully the watercourse made by the rain', p. 12; 'Make rhizomes, not roots, never plant! Don't sow, grow offshoots! Don't be one or multiple, be multiplicities!', p. 27. There is no better way of saying that we are essentially dealing with a practical philosophy (or philosophy of practice). Deleuze himself said: 'Truth is producing existence. It's not something in your head but something existing. Writers generate real bodies' (1995: 134).

9. See Cusset's superb book *French Theory*, in particular, the chapter entitled 'The Politics of Identity' (2008: 131–65), in which he has no difficulty tracing the links that would be forged between French theoretical imports and postcolonial theory. Nevertheless, he struggles to force Deleuze's work into the 'crusher' of postcolonial, subalternist or 'identity' theory: 'The reception given to Deleuze and Guattari was more complex [than that given to Derrida], marked in this arena by twenty years of misunderstandings'! (2008: 150). On the other hand, when Cusset is discussing the Deleuzean 'theoretical machinations' of innovators and experimenters on the internet and in film – such as the DJ Paul Miller (DJ Spooky), the Lords of Chaos, the Legion of Doom, or the Wachovski brothers – he doesn't hesitate to add: 'These French authors are presented, one after another, as prophets of the Internet – *with Deleuze and Guattari as the key voices*, because their botanical notion of the rhizome, an underground and non-hierarchical network of laterally linked stems, appears to be a precise foreshadowing of the Web' (2005: 251–2, emphasis added).
10. As we shall see, many critics and commentators identify enormous contradictions between the Deleuze of *The Logic of Sense* and *Difference and Repetition*, for example, and the Deleuze who instigates a new theoretical advance in the works written with Guattari. For them, there is not simply a discontinuity between one of Deleuze's 'avatars' and another, but a radical theoretical rupture. I'm thinking here of the way in which theorists such as Slavoj Žižek, Alain Badiou, Jean-Loup Amselle and Christopher L. Miller tackle these questions in their books on Deleuze or specific aspects of his work.
11. Does Badiou not show a keen awareness of the problem we are trying to tease out here – that of a certain 'equivocity' of Deleuze's 'names' – when he gives the title 'Which Deleuze?' to one of the first chapters in his book, and when he remarks: '*We can scarcely . . . expect that this philosophy*, in which the One is sovereign, in which the hierarchy of power is ascetic, and in which death symbolises thought, *should be, as is commonly thought, devoted to the inexhaustible variety of the concrete*' (my emphasis). Rare indeed are the postcolonial theorists who take up the challenge thrown down by Deleuze at any attempt to 'dialectise' the relationship between being and the simulacra which are the different modes of its actualisation. It is perhaps only in the works of Achille Mbembe that the sovereign One and death, theoretically at least, come into play. See the chapter 'Out of the World', in Mbembe, A. (2001: 173 ff.).
12. 'Whenever it is in a fallow period, philosophy takes refuge in reflecting "on",' Deleuze declared in *L'Autre Journal*. 'If it creates nothing itself, what else can it do but reflect "on"? Then it reflects on the eternal, or on the historical, but it does not manage itself to set things in motion' (Deleuze 1995: 122). Deleuze gives the same reaction in 'Portrait of the Philosopher as a Movie-goer'. To the question of how he made the leap from painting to film, he replies: 'I didn't make a leap from painting to film. I don't think of philosophy as a reflection on one thing or another – painting or film. Philosophy is about concepts, it creates them' (Deleuze 2007: 213).
13. He later raises questions linked to the problems in New Caledonia: 'On the Caledonian problem we're told that from a certain point onward the territory was regarded as a settler colony, so the Kanaks became a minority in their own territory. When did this start? How did it develop? Who was responsible? The Right refuses these questions' (1995: 127).
14. I'm thinking less here of the studies, monographs and critical readers 'on' Deleuze, which have appeared all around the world, than of works such as Hardt and Negri (2000) or Alliez (1993), and studies whose goals are not so much to 'explain' some aspect of Deleuze's thought than to put into practice certain

theoretical or political 'expectations' which run through it. The scope of this chapter does not allow me to analyse such relations as they appear in the work of leading postcolonial thinkers like Homi K. Bhabha, Gayatri C. Spivak, Edward Said and so on. It is sufficient for our purposes here to have shown what has conditioned the 'dissemination' of Deleuze's names.

15. Failure to pose such questions entails serious consequences, of course, since it inevitably tends to invalidate the 'logic' of the mediation as Deleuze formulates it. What if, at the very moment he embarked on this new form of collaborative writing, Deleuze had continued to pursue a philosophical perspective that was *his alone*? And what if, in his encounter with Guattari, Deleuze was continuing to pursue and probe more deeply problematics he felt he had not 'finished' in the texts that he wrote without Guattari. Last but not least, by considering only the texts that Deleuze wrote with Guattari, are we in a position then to understand how far Deleuze's contribution goes, or the point from which it proceeds, in the Deleuzo-Guattarian 'project'? The assumption that clearly underlies all these questions is that there is a Deleuzean agenda which is not analytically inscribed in the work he produces with Guattari. What is the contribution that the wasp makes to the orchid?

16. However, it should be borne in mind that, as Cusset has clearly demonstrated, the epicentre of this 'conversation' is located in the United States, even for problems relating to postcolonial questions. It's true that this 'conversation' has never really taken off in France. Cusset's rather pessimistic observation, outlined in a chapter bearing the revealing title 'Meanwhile, Back in France . . .':

> 'France; or the World Inverted.' Following the developments in the United States, Lacanian-Derridean and *Foucauldian-Deleuzean* [sic] perspectives gradually began to occupy *the intellectual field in many countries*. But not only did these discourses gradually subside in France, the very possibility of discussing theory was virtually banished from the scene. As the authors passed away (Barthes in 1980, Lacan in 1981, Foucault in 1984, Guattari in 1992, Deleuze in 1995, Lyotard in 1995), their presence in the public sphere gradually shrank into obituaries and intellectual nostalgia, and their legacy became the monopoly of a few isolated heirs and the official rights holders of their publications. (Cusset 2008: 309; emphasis added)

It should be pointed out that Cusset makes this observation in a long chapter in which he tries to show how strong a hold postcolonial theory has gained in American universities. It is revealing to compare what Cusset says here and what he says at the start of the chapter entitled 'The Politics of Identity'. The description he gives of what is occurring in American universities contrasts starkly with what is happening *at the same time* in French universities:

> *Following the investigation into cultural studies*, we must consider what lies at the heart of the new community-centred discourses in American universities: ethnic and postcolonial studies. It is here that the old concept of identity is called into question, or at the very least combined into two main components: first, the role of cratology is considered, where identity plays a central role in determining international relationships of power, revealing complex layers of historical battles; second, pluralisation is examined, along with the increasing complexity of identity that it entails, with so many composite narratives and interwoven journeys, and large numbers of diaspora identities and migrant descendants. (2008: 138; emphasis added)

And Cusset adds the following, which shouldn't greatly surprise us:

> This combination can be said to have sprung from a *Foucauldian* line of thought – where the subject is constructed first through subjugation by institutions of control and their dominant discourse, and from the Deleuzean motif of a subject that has been de-composed over the course of passages of nomadic flight. (2008: 138)

Here also the reference to Deleuze as one of the leading theoretical figures of postcolonial theory, in one or other of his manifestations, is presented as self-evident. It is as though one of the conditions of the possibility of his emergence was inseparable from this 'reference'.

17. See also Deleuze (2004a: 130):

    > Only when something is identified between divergent series or between incompossible worlds, an object = x appears *transcending individuated worlds, and the Ego which thinks it transcends worldly individuals*, giving thereby to the world a new value *in view of the new value of the subject which is being established*. (emphasis added)

    This text, dating from 1969, highlights the enduring nature and the importance of the problematics of divergent series and of their 'encounter' due to the (esoteric and atopic) object = x. It is the problematic of the philosopher as 'dark precursor' of the protocols to come that is outlined in this 'informal' or 'modal' definition of the subject (of the utterance).
18. Žižek cites many other metamorphoses of Deleuze's incarnations and reincarnations which all tend to show that Deleuze has 'misread' or 'misunderstood' Hegel, whom he apparently parrots, clumsily and partially, without being aware of it. A detailed study could be undertaken to show how ignorance of the 'logic' of the Snark, brought into play by Deleuze, can create a great deal of critical harm. It should be conceded, though, that Žižek claims to attack Deleuzeanism rather than Deleuze. Our theory about the multiplication of Deleuze's names finds confirmation later in the same text, in a chapter entitled 'A Yuppie Reading of Deleuze': 'There are, effectively,' writes Žižek, 'features that justify *calling Deleuze the ideologist of late capitalism*' (2004: 183; emphasis added).
19. The fact that Deleuze once again uses in almost the same terms the 'logic' of 'esoteric words' in his definition of the 'dark precursor' and its efficacy in intensive systems says much about the continuity of his thinking on this point. This 'insistance' shows just how important Deleuze considered the vicariousness of the 'subject' in the system of differences.
20. Deleuze and Parnet (2006: 92). He adds: 'One such plane is that of the Law, in so far as it *organises and develops forms, genres, themes, motifs, and assigns and causes the evolution of subjects, persons, characteristic features and feelings: harmony of forms, education of subjects*' (emphasis added).
21. Not because they relate exclusively to questions concerning the postcolony, but in as much as they refer to questions which took shape only after the end of the process of decolonisation. But they can be called 'haecceities' in that they widely 'overflow' any determination of nation, race, culture or even history.
22. Think, for example, of the recent events in South Africa where one can see how the white majority – in fact an actual (numerical) minority – is in the process of *becoming* a minority. Thus the desperate attempts of the reactionary, conservative wing to halt the events by means of violence; they are, in psychoanalytic terms, *acting out*. It seems, however, that the white progressive 'minority' is, on the contrary, experiencing a *becoming minoritarian* worth paying attention to.
23. Farès does not state that the 'civilised white man' hypostasis is the cause of this bureaucracy or patriarchal regime which was going to be established in Algeria

after independence, but it most certainly is for him one of the *transcendental conditions of possibility of its hegemony*. Without this 'great bass' (Ezra Pound), it would be impossible to establish a patriarchal and bureaucratic regime. We can easily imagine that, for Farès, the supremacy of the integrationist Islamic Salvation Front (IFS) draws from the same source. The whole 'Paganism' theme in Farès' work may be/must be read as an attempt to extract Algeria – even if it is by poetic, and thus *virtual*, means – from the usurpation of all (the) power by this 'false' majority, that is, a usurped majority that was arbitrarily imposed on Algeria. 'The renewal of ancient Paganism in a belief in life without obstacles is the route by which an Algerian artistic consciousness will be defined. Any other determination on the cultural level will be nothing other than a false and dull ideological reconstruction. It is the idea that must be made apparent, and not giving an idea to a rotten appearance.' And Farès adds, unambiguously: 'The true homeland of Algeria is its most ancient past, and the most ancient past of Algeria, AESTHETICALLY SPEAKING, is Paganism. When revolutionary expression meets pagan expression, the life-moment the country is going through will increase in political fervor' (1971: 74ff.; Farès' capitalisation).

24. Farès (1971: 74–5):

> The cultural history of contemporary Algeria is still a 'cathartic' history. The recognition of an internal dialectic in Algerian society as such has not yet occurred . . . After the French decolonisation of Algeria will come the Islamic decolonisation of Algeria. For whatever our Islamic brothers think and want us 'to think', the Islamisation of Algeria is not a divine phenomenon, but like all phenomena, it is a historical one. And given this, only a pagan belief can endure the wait for Algeria to precipitate out of Islam. For, just as the revolutionary geography of Algeria in its time shattered the yoke of colonialism, so the assertion of a glorious, ancient way of life will break the patriarchal spine of Algeria. Thought of a murder whose necessity will signal to the sons the way upward.

It is perhaps worth remembering that these lines appear in a book written and published in 1971!

25. I am thinking of course of the distinction that Emmanuel Levinas (1974) makes between the 'said' [*le dit*] and 'saying' [*dire*]. Silvano Petrosino and Jacques Rolland (1984: 45) define the difference between these two types of saying: 'Saying is not the Said in which meaning is constituted, in which Being [*être*] is thematised and beings [*étant*] objectivised. If the origin is that of meaning in the Said, the Saying must be thought of . . . as pre-original or even *an-archic* – before *arche*, without *arche* but coming to disrupt it'.

26. The double – or, even better, the *crossed* (*croisée*) – deterritorialisation allows us to identify a deterritorialising and a deterritorialised force, even if it is the same force that moves from one value to the other according to the 'moment' or the aspect under consideration; furthermore, the least deterritorialised element or force always precipitates the deterritorialisation of the most deterritorialising, which affects it even more. During the war of liberation, Algeria (as a national entity with a majoritarian vocation?) was the most deterritorialising force; but as soon as the war ended and independence was gained, this force changed valence. We can't in any case read these passages without thinking of what Deleuze (2004a: 169) says of the relation between 'events' and the 'wound':

> We are sometimes hesitant to call Stoic a concrete or poetic way of life, as if the name of a doctrine were too bookish or abstract to designate the most personal relation with a wound. But where do doctrines come from, if not

Postcolonial Haecceities 161

from wounds and vital aphorisms which, with their charge of exemplary provocation, are so many speculative anecdotes? . . . To the extent that events are actualised in us, they wait for us and invite us in. They signal us: 'My wound existed before me, I was born to embody it'.

27. We find here in Farès the same logic that governed the demultiplication of the subjects of utterance in Deleuze. We saw that it was under the name of Brandy Fax that Farès deterritorialised as a 'Kabyle' subject; but, when he reincarnated himself as Ali Saïd, it was his 'Algerianity' that he bent to a becoming that radically called into question the transparency it was supposed to have in the dominant discourse. Therefore at least three proper names are required in order to give an adequate idea of the assemblages that currently determine the new formation of subjectivity. In *L'État perdu*, Farès will have recourse to many other names to unleash the forces of liberty and creation which are 'contained' by the postcolonial state: 'No. I have invented nothing in all that, even if a name which speaks to me and recognises me is still lacking, I have invented nothing in all that: neither my loss, nor my illusion' (1982: 12).
28. As registration numbers, the drawings as well as the words are symptoms, especially if we think of the affects attached to the registration cards of the Maghrebi immigrants, and on an even deeper level, of all the connotations attached to this lexeme: car registration, the registration of Jews in Nazi concentration camps and so on. And let's not forget that registration's goal is always to *identify* individuals.
29. Things are in fact a bit more complicated than that. The same kind of operation is at work here as the one that, according to Deleuze and Guattari, links the wasp and the orchid. The orchid becomes deterritorialised by forming an image or a copy of the wasp; but the wasp in turn reterritorialises itself on this image while simultaneously reterritorialising itself by becoming a pawn in the reproduction apparatus of the orchid, that is, in a new organisation. Yet the wasp also reterritorialises the orchid by carrying its pollen. This process can easily be adapted to the question of languages that are at stake in *L'État perdu*. French (the language, the signs of this language) is deterritorialised by forming an image, a copy of Arabic or Kabyle; but Arabic and Kabyle are in turn reterritorialised on this 'image': '3. (4 in Arabic)' (1982: 66). Yet by moving to a regime of signs that is foreign to them, both Arabic and Kabyle are themselves deterritorialised by becoming pawns (one signifier among others) in the apparatus of production and reproduction of meaning in French. Yet they are not themselves metamorphosed as graphic systems, without deterritorialising French, by carrying, not pollen this time, but the materiality of their signifiers that will come to fertilise the French language with their poetic power (the power of their *gesture*, rhythm, written forms). Thus French, Arabic, Kabyle, Lybic make up a rhizome, but remain heterogeneous. Just as the orchid is said to imitate the wasp whose image it reproduces in a meaningful way, so French begins to 'imitate' Arabic, Kabyle and so on, the images of which it reproduces in a meaningful way. But this too is merely another relatively simple view of things for, in fact, on another level, something else entirely is happening. It is not only a matter of imitation, but of a veritable capturing of the code that opens onto a plus value, an increase of valence that provokes a series of becomings: the becoming-Arabic or Kabyle of French (see for example *L'État perdu*: 65), the becoming-French of Kabyle and of Arabic. Each one of these becomings ensures the deterritorialisation of one of the terms and the reterritorialisation of the other; the two becomings, the two semiotic systems connecting, joining each other according to a circulation of intensities that pushes the deterritorialisation of the languages mobilised ever further: '[M]ixing signs

– enough to move the sun in its "course" to make one admit that the influence of the moon has not ended at all' (1982: 21–2). In fact, it would be necessary to quote entire pages and reproduce here signs from the Berber symbolic system which run though them in order to show what we intend. You should go and look for yourself! Cf. Deleuze and Guattari 1987: 256ff.

30. I'm borrowing here for my purposes the distinction that Deleuze introduces in his book on cinema between what he calls 'rational' and 'irrational' cuts in what makes up the 'power of continuity'. See the chapter 'Thought and Cinema':

> [C]uts and breaks, in cinema, have always formed the power of the continuous. But, in cinema as in mathematics, sometimes the so called *rational* cut forms part of the two sets that it separates (being the end of one and the beginning of the other). This is the case with 'classic' cinema. Sometimes, as in modern cinema, the cut becomes the interstice, *it is irrational and does not form part of either set, the first set no more having an ending than the second has a beginning*: false continuity is just such an irrational cut. (Deleuze 1989, 181; emphasis original; trans. modified.)

31. I have borrowed from Paul Virilio (2008) the concepts of *outreville* as a shifting city and 'trajectography' as the permanent traceability of individuals through mobile phones, iPods, computers, GPS and so on.
32. Translator's Note: Nabile Farès here plays on the Lacanian 'small a' in 'a-perçu'.

Chapter 7

'Another Perspective on the World': Shame and Subtraction in Louis Malle's *L'Inde fantôme*

Timothy Bewes

What is the source of the shame with which writers of the 'West' so frequently seem to approach their interactions with the 'non-West'? What is its ethical significance? What is its relation with its supposed contrary, the shame of the colonised subject? Is there any political potential to postcolonial shame, other than as something that we need to 'get over'? Can we envisage a form of writing that would be free of the shame of the post-colonial epoch, a truly postcolonial literature?

Such questions seem as urgent and intractable as they have ever been. This chapter will try to navigate them by suspending the inclination to see shame as a problem requiring a solution, or as implicated in a relation of cause and effect, for any such relation would suggest the possibility of a simple reversal, a narrative of exculpation or exemption from shame. Likewise, it is necessary to resist the temptation to extract ourselves, ethically or methodologically, from the situation of a 'postcolonial shame', or even to approach shame as a theorisable term, since in the postcolonial situation we cannot guarantee that such a project of 'theorisation' would itself be free of implication in shame. This essay will consider, rather, what happens if we understand shame not in 'ethical' terms but 'ontological' ones – not as an entity that may be removed from the present, but one from which the present, including any questions that we might direct towards the present, is inseparable. It seems impossible even to assume that the shame of the postcolonial present arises from the colonial past, and that it will disappear once colonial structures of power have been eradicated. We would have more justification in arguing the contrary: that a primary or fundamental shame, rooted in our definition as embodied, intersubjective beings, is at the origin of the history of colonial domination. 'Shame and immodesty,' writes Merleau-Ponty, take their place in a dialectic of the self and the other which is that of master and slave: insofar as I have a body, I may be reduced to the status of an object beneath the gaze of another person, and no longer count as a person for him, or else I may become his master and, in my turn, look at *him*. . . . Saying that I have a body is thus a way of saying that I can be seen as an object and that I try to be seen as a subject, that another can be my master or my slave, so that shame and shamelessness express the dialectic of the plurality of consciousness, and have a metaphysical significance. (2002: 193)

J. M. Coetzee has depicted the colonial encounter in such terms. In his work *Dusklands*, the 'savage' appears to the eighteenth-century settler as a representative of

that out there which my eye once enfolded and ingested and which now promises to enfold, ingest, and project me through itself as a speck on a field which we may call annihilation or alternatively history. He threatens to have a history in which I shall be a term. Such is the material basis of the malady of the master's soul. (2004: 81)

In such passages, shame is so profoundly implicated in the colonial enterprise as to be ontologically continuous with it. Colonialism is shameful, then, not primarily in an 'ethical' sense – as an event that demands or elicits our shame – but in an 'ontological' one. Shame and colonialism share a certain organising presupposition: the conceptual opposition of identity and difference. This structure is apparent in the most influential philosophical conceptualisation of shame, the dialectic between 'self' and 'other' put forward by phenomenology. Jean-Paul Sartre famously defines shame as 'a unitary apprehension with three dimensions: "*I* am ashamed of *myself* before the *Other*." If any one of these dimensions disappears, the shame disappears as well' (1989: 289–90). Yet Sartre's approach to shame, theorising it as such – as if shame could be separated from the structure of perception that enables it to be theorised at all – cannot solve the 'problem' of shame, since the supposedly universal categories of *I*, *myself* and *other* are presupposed in this theorisation. Shame for Sartre is an effect of the conditions of human perception. A theory of shame that begins from those same conditions must end there too; such a theory cannot gain any purchase on its object. The theory that will be adequate to the formation of 'postcolonial shame', then, will be less a theory of shame than a theory of being, of ontology; it will seek neither to reiterate nor to correct existing modes of perception, but instead to grasp the inseparability of shame from perception in order to decentre, even vacate both. To free ourselves of this most intimate residue of the colonial enterprise it is necessary to overcome the models of thought and perception that made colonialism possible in the first place.

Such an approach, I will argue here, may be derived from a reading of the work of Gilles Deleuze. However, the most crucial insights do not appear in Deleuze's scattered remarks on shame, invaluable and fascinating as these are. Ian Buchanan has suggested that if there is an 'ethical' dimension to Deleuze's thought it 'stems from a conviction that man is shameful' (Buchanan 2000: 196). We may recall Deleuze's rhetorical question at the beginning of *Essays Critical and Clinical*: 'The shame of being a man – is there any better reason to write?' (Deleuze 1998: 1). Yet the shamefulness of 'man' is a complex proposition. 'Man' in Deleuze is associated with a certain logic, rather than a particular identity formation. Man, we read in *A Thousand Plateaus*, is 'majoritarian par excellence, whereas becomings are minoritarian'; man constitutes 'a standard in the universe in relation to which men necessarily (analytically) form a majority' – where 'analytically' is opposed to 'quantitatively' (Deleuze and Guattari 1987: 291). It is not quite accurate, then, to say that for Deleuze 'man *is* shameful'. What is shameful is not 'man', but the logic of the 'is', the 'standard', which is inseparable from 'man' but not attributable to any particular man or men. For Deleuze, the subject of a becoming is necessarily 'man' and, as such, is ensnared in a shame that is simultaneously achieved and evacuated. 'What's so shameful is that we've no sure way of maintaining becomings, or still more of arousing them, even within ourselves' (Deleuze 1995: 173). Consequently, shame itself is never elaborated as a concept in Deleuze's work, for the simple reason that shame is the substance and materiality of Deleuze's philosophy. Shame, we read in *What is Philosophy?* is 'one of philosophy's most powerful motifs. And there is no way to escape the ignoble but to play the part of the animal (to growl, burrow, snigger, distort ourselves): thought itself is sometimes closer to an animal that dies than to a living, even democratic, human being [*homme*]' (Deleuze and Guattari 1994: 108). Shame has no positive ontology, and can be subject to no process of theorisation. Insofar as it *appears*, shame is an interruption of its own becoming, the emblem of a longing to escape the logic of subjectivation that is itself framed in subjective terms; as such, it remains within that logic. Yet shame is not only a manifest presence in Deleuze's work; it has also a hidden, unnamed existence, operating below the surface of everything that Deleuze writes, and as the principle, or event, of its own *untheorisability*. This second shame is as central to Deleuze's thought as, say, *desire* or *difference*; and it may be found almost anywhere in Deleuze, especially in those places where no mention of the word is made.

In the pages that follow, this 'event' of shame will be pursued in Deleuze's two books on cinema – this despite the fact that Deleuze does not use the word there. If we read those volumes closely, I will argue, we can find in them, and in cinema itself, nothing less than a model for a postcolonial literature able, in the words of Frantz Fanon, 'to touch the other, to feel the other, to explain the other to myself' (Fanon 1986: 231).

The problem of shame may be illustrated with a text by the French ethnologist and autobiographer Michel Leiris, produced during the ethnographic Dakar-Djibouti mission from 1931 to 1933, in which Leiris held the position of secretary-archivist. The journal Leiris kept on the trip was published in 1934 as *L'Afrique fantôme*. This unconventional text documents Leiris' complex and shifting relation to Africa; in particular, his disillusion with the possibility of travel in Africa as a means of personal liberation from the disgust that he felt for European civilisation. On 23 July 1932, in Gondar, Ethiopia, he begins an entry with the following words: 'Intense work, to which I give myself with a certain assiduousness, but without an ounce of passion. I would rather be possessed than study possessed people, would rather have carnal knowledge of a "zarine" than scientific knowledge of her ins and outs [*ses tenants et aboutissants*]' (Leiris 1996: 560). A month later, attesting his growing frustration with the project and discomfort with the premises of ethnographic research in general, he begins another entry as follows: 'Bitterness. Resentment against ethnography which makes you take so inhuman a position as that of an observer, in circumstances where it would be better to let go [*s'abandonner*]' (Leiris 1996: 599).

The problem of shame revealed by this text is the problem of mediation. What causes Leiris' shame is the condition of mediatedness to which he feels condemned – by his profession (ethnography), his origins (Europe) and his medium (writing). Ethnography is shameful because it participates in a structure of perception that is inseparable from a certain logic of self-authorisation. Ethnography presupposes a centred or, to use Merleau-Ponty's term, 'anchored' consciousness (2002: 78) that situates the self in relation to the world and to its objects of study. Ethnography shares this presupposition with colonialism, but also with writing. How can we distinguish, then, between the mediation that causes Leiris' shame, relegating him to the position of 'observer' rather than 'participant', and the mediation that enables him to tell us about it, or to conceptualise it? How do we separate his Parisian 'intellectualism' (Leiris 1996: 270), the tormenting actuality of which drove him to Africa in the first place, from the fact that it is only as an intellectual that he is able to formulate it as a problem?

Ruth Larson makes the following observation about the Dakar-Djibouti mission: 'By the end of the trip, [Leiris] had become sadly aware of the iterative relation between objects and subjects, difference and identity. Neither ethnography nor travel offered any resistance to the resilience of Western identity; both were, on the contrary, an integral part of its expansion' (Larson 1997: 237). With the word 'iterative', Larson brings writing into the equation. It appears that the most hated, shameful fact of Leiris' existence is that of being a writer; in any case, there is no possibility of extracting that fact from the disgust he feels at being a European and an ethnographer. What Deleuze says about T. E. Lawrence applies equally to Leiris: his real 'mission' is not ethnographic but a mission of 'depersonalisation', a quest to destroy or escape from the self, which is rarely, if ever, successful. For Leiris' project of becoming-other, becoming-Dogon, runs up perpetually against his inability 'to let myself go' [*m'abandonner*] (Leiris 1996: 616). Indeed, in the rest of Leiris' work, continuing through another five decades, no escape will ever be possible except paradoxically, by way of a thorough immersion in language and in his own interiority.[1]

Thirty-five years after the Dakar-Djibouti mission, the French film director Louis Malle made *L'Inde fantôme*, the record of a journey through India undertaken over a period of several months, and broadcast on French television in seven 52-minute episodes (Malle 1993: 73). On his own account at least, Malle finds a way of achieving what Leiris found impossible: a sensuous connection with the 'other'. In the fourth episode, filmed in Kerala some twelve weeks into his trip, Malle finds himself in a village without access to newspapers or post, far from Europe in every sense. Over a sequence showing a group of women walking along a dusty road carrying baskets and water vessels on their heads, Malle offers the following commentary:

> We went where the winds of chance blew us, sleeping anywhere, our only goal to lose ourselves in the infinity of Indian villages . . . . Freed from my habitual anxiety and dissatisfaction, I lived in the present moment. We may not understand these people, but we're instinctively connected to them, sharing their link with nature. Letting ourselves go in their presence, we feel as if we've rediscovered something we'd lost. (V)[2]

How is Malle seemingly able to achieve what Leiris is not? Is Malle's comment anything other than an idealising sentiment? How does his talk of 'we' on one hand and 'these people' on the other avoid reproducing the phenomenological structure of ethnography, with all its shameful consequences? The case to be put forward here is that the apparent absence of shame from Malle's project, as compared to Leiris', has less to do with the factors that might be foregrounded in a commentary (differences of personality, differences in the culture under observation, chronological discrepancy between the two projects, issues specific to the process of decolonisation in India) and more to do with the form and technology of the work. With the camera, Malle escapes both the condition of perception to which Leiris is riveted and the territorialising force of language itself. The possibilities for a shame-free world contained in Malle's images, then, would seem to have little to do with the words that he appends to them. Yet, if this is the case, what hope do we have for the emergence of a postcolonial literature, one that genuinely merits the term 'postcolonial' (or the term 'literature')? Before going any further, we need to clarify the link between shame and visual perception.

Shame and Perception

The origins of shame in perception were established with the publication of Jean-Paul Sartre's *Being and Nothingness* in 1943. For Sartre, shame occurs with the experience, or rather, the possibility of being looked at. 'By the mere appearance of the Other, I am put in the position of passing judgment on myself as on an object,' he writes, 'for it is as an object that I appear to the Other' (1989: 222). Sartre's account is remarkable for its interruption of the subjective illusion of shame: the notion that the explanation for shame should be sought primarily in the ethical or 'reflective' sphere, in the individual's thoughts or behaviour. Shame, according to Sartre, is generated not by the revelation of oneself 'as one is', but by the self's attainment to being with the look of the other. Shame does not hang on the nature of the self, but simply on its production *as* a self. The 'distortion' of the self that is experienced in shame is not a violation of being, but constitutive of it; the relation of shame to guilt is therefore purely incidental, an association produced by the newly individuated subject out of the structures of social, psychological and ethical interpellation. 'Shame,' says Sartre, 'is the feeling of an *original fall*, not because of the fact that I may have committed this or that particular fault but simply that I have "fallen" into the world in the midst of things and that I need the mediation of the Other in order to be what I am' (Sartre 1989: 288–9).

Nearly twenty years later, in Sartre's 1961 Preface to Frantz Fanon's *The Wretched of the Earth*, and after he had been rebuked by Fanon in *Black Skin, White Masks* for ignoring differences in the bodily shame experienced by blacks and whites (Fanon 1986: 138), Sartre introduced a new visual aspect to shame: the experience of *not* being looked at. This, it turns out, is a specifically European shame, the post-colonial shame of the coloniser: 'Europeans,' he addresses his readers:

> you must open this book [*The Wretched of the Earth*] and enter into it. After a few steps in the darkness you will see strangers gathered around a fire . . . They will see you, perhaps, but they will go on talking among themselves, without even lowering their voices. This indifference strikes home: their fathers, shadowy creatures, *your* creatures, were but dead souls; you it was who allowed them glimpses of light, to you only did they dare speak, and you did not bother to reply to such zombies. Their sons ignore you; a fire warms them and sheds light around them, and you have not lit it. Now, at a respectful distance, it is you who will feel furtive, nightbound and perished with cold. Turn and turn about; in these shadows from whence a new dawn will break, it is you who are the zombies. (Sartre 1990: 11–12)

The experience of reading Fanon's book, says Sartre – a book that 'is not written for us' – 'will make you ashamed, and shame, as Marx, said, is a revolutionary sentiment. You see, I, too,' he goes on, 'am incapable of ridding myself of subjective illusions; I, too, say to you: "All is lost, unless . . ." As a European, I steal the enemy's book, and out of it I fashion a remedy for Europe' (1990: 12). In this text, Sartre seems to be invoking the very ontology of self and other, of 'us' and 'them' that, according to *Being and Nothingness*, results in shame. To cling to 'subjective illusions' would seem to be at odds not only with that earlier work, but with Fanon's thinking also. It is unclear, for example, how Sartre's relentless interpellation of his reader as a European resistant to decolonisation escapes the charge of ascribing an 'absolute density' to 'European consciousness' (and, by implication, to 'black consciousness' also), off-loading a 'historical' meaning upon it in precisely the way that Fanon saw Sartre doing in *Orphée noir* (1948).

This tendency also affects Sartre's understanding of the role of literature. In *What is Literature?* (1948), a collection of essays produced immediately after *Being and Nothingness* (1943), we find a conception of the writer's relation to her material and readership that is organised around those same foundational categories. This is glaringly illustrated in a discussion of the African-American author Richard Wright. For Wright, says Sartre, 'Negro readers represent the subjective. The same childhood, the same difficulties, the same complexes: a mere hint is enough for them; they understand with their hearts' (2001: 60). When it comes to Wright's white readers, the role is entirely different: for 'they represent the *Other*': 'It is only from without that he conceives their proud security and that tranquil certainty, common to all white Aryans, that the world is white and that they own it . . . When he speaks to them . . . it is a matter of implicating them and making them take stock of their responsibilities. He must make them indignant and ashamed' (Sartre 2001: 60). This is the Sartre whom Fanon holds responsible for replicating a certain phenomenological (and racial) structure which ensnares him – Fanon – in corporeal shame; the Sartre who attributes an 'absolute density' to black consciousness, reducing it to 'a term in the dialectic' (Fanon 1986: 134, 132). The basis of Sartre's analysis is consciousness – specifically, the fundamental distinction between consciousness and its object. The purest embodiment of the free consciousness, for Sartre, is the figure of the writer; thus Sartre's ontology is inseparable from the implicit sovereignty that he reserves for the writer, and that finds its logical expression in the notion of the writer as society's 'guilty conscience' (Sartre 2001: 61).

Sartre's conception of the importance of shame to the human subject, together with the notion of the writer as the 'conscience' of society, seems to be as far from Deleuze's philosophy as can be imagined. In Deleuze's 'Letter to a Harsh Critic' – one of very few texts in which he refers to himself in the first person – Deleuze remarks: 'The idea of feeling guilty is, for me, just as repugnant as being someone else's guilty conscience' (1995: 4–5). In Deleuze's writing, however, there is another more profound shame that he calls (using a phrase of Primo Levi's) the 'shame of being a man' (*la honte d'être un homme*) (Deleuze 1998: 1; Deleuze and Guattari 1994: 107; Levi 1989: 109). This is a shame redoubled upon itself, *taken to the power of* itself; a shame so encompassing that it includes within its circuit the very category of shame; a shame that subjects itself to its own power. This 'profound' shame is not at all a shame that can be referred to a subject; on the contrary, shame is for Deleuze precisely a shame *of* the subject, and of everything that emerges from it. It is a shame that annihilates the subject – annihilates, that is to say, the principle of a shame that relates solely *to* the subject. Annihilation does not mean self-destruction, for nothing demonstrates the fruitlessness of the category of the subject more conclusively than suicide, the most egoistic gesture. In Deleuze, shame implies the suspension of the subjective principle, even as the thematic *instantiation* of shame (as in, say, T. E. Lawrence's *Seven Pillars of Wisdom* [1935]) frequently takes the form of a strafing of the self (Deleuze 1998).[3] This 'more profound' shame is not an 'affect' in any straightforward sense; it is not a 'concept' either, since it is not treated to the degree of elaboration that, say, 'deterritorialisation' and 'becoming' are accorded in Deleuze's writing. Rather, Deleuze's shame is an 'event' – inexpressible and unnameable, a shame that is discontinuous with its naming and conceptualisation.

In his most sustained discussion of shame, an essay on Lawrence entitled 'The Shame and the Glory' (1998), Deleuze notes this incommensurability between the event of shame and its named presence in the work. Shame of one sort or another is acknowledged and indeed advertised on almost every page of *Seven Pillars of Wisdom*: 'I assured [the Arabs] that England kept her word in letter and spirit. In this comfort they performed their fine things: but, of course, instead of being proud of what we did together, I was continually and bitterly ashamed' (Lawrence 1935: 276). Yet shame is also a principle of the work. In Lawrence, according to Deleuze, 'shame enlarges the man', even at moments when Lawrence seems on the point of disappearing into a vortex of self-reflection (Deleuze 1998: 121). This paradox reaches a climax in the 'grandiose' Chapter 103, every page of which has the word 'Myself' as a running head; the chapter largely follows (or anticipates) a Sartrean logic of shame 'before the Other' (meaning, in Lawrence's case, both the Arabs and his fellow British soldiers and officers). 'The hearing other people praised made me despair jealously of myself,' writes Lawrence, 'for I took it at its face value; whereas, had they spoken ten times as well of me, I would have discounted it to nothing . . . The self, knowing the detriment, was forced into depreciation by other's uncritical praise' (Lawrence 1935: 565–6). Such moments do not distract Deleuze from his insistence that Lawrence's shame is an 'experimental' motif, an occasion for the construction of an apparatus of thought, a 'machine' that enables him to write. For Deleuze's most profound engagement with shame, however – the shame that, as he says at the end of 'The Shame and the Glory', is 'cosubstantial with being' (Deleuze 1998: 125) – we need to turn to moments in Deleuze's work at which the shame is not repeated, or annulled, by the circumstance of being named as such.

Subtraction

In the fourth chapter of *The Movement-Image*, Deleuze poses the following question: 'How can we rid ourselves [*nous défaire*] of ourselves, and demolish [*défaire*] ourselves?' (Deleuze 1986: 66). The question is irresolvable, as Deleuze realises, for how is it possible to 'demolish oneself', or even disparage oneself, without thereby positing, asserting oneself? To name or conceive of this principle as 'shame' would interrupt the operation by subjectivising it; consequently in the cinema books Deleuze does not use the word at all.

A usable name for this principle will be one that can do justice to its technical rather than moral or affective quality. Such a term is found in the work of Henri Bergson, Deleuze's most important resource for the challenge to the phenomenological model of consciousness. Deleuze describes Bergson's theory of perception as follows:

> In perception . . . there is never anything else or anything more than there is in the thing: on the contrary, there is 'less'. We perceive the thing, minus that which does not interest us as a function of our needs . . . The first material moment of subjectivity . . . is subtractive. It subtracts from the thing whatever does not interest it. (Deleuze 1986: 63)

The audacity of Bergson's theory of consciousness, as outlined in the first chapter of *Matter and Memory*, is to take as the basis of his enquiry not real, concrete, human perception, but what he calls a 'pure' perception:

> a perception which exists in theory rather than in fact and would be possessed by a being placed where I am, living as I live, but absorbed in the present and capable, by giving up every form of memory, of obtaining a vision of matter both immediate and instantaneous. (Bergson 2002: 97)

Against this 'pure' perception, our merely subjective consciousness is an interruption, a blockage, or a subtraction. Deleuze writes (quoting Bergson): 'As for *our* consciousness of fact, it will merely be the opacity without which light "is always propagated without its source ever having been revealed"' (Deleuze 1986: 61). For Deleuze, this account of perception impacts upon everything; not only the presupposition, associated with phenomenology, that consciousness is fundamentally a positive entity which 'is directed towards the thing and gains significance in the world' (Deleuze 1988: 108), but also the tradition of European philosophy 'which placed light on the side of spirit and made consciousness a beam of light which drew things out of their native darkness' (Deleuze 1986: 60). More radically still, Bergson's theory of consciousness dismantles any idea of a positive quality to human activity and its effects in the world. The subject is not a centre of 'determination' – that is to say, of action or perception – but rather of 'indetermination' – the interruption of action and the blockage of perception. Thus – from the perspective of 'pure perception' – in so far as we speak, write, act or paint, in so far as we express ourselves in any form whatsoever, we do not add to knowledge of the world but detract from it. 'Shame' would be a quality of any speech or writing in which an intimation of this fact – in however tentative a form, and whether acknowledged or not – is expressed in subjective terms. Even in this intimation, however, shame is a further departure from the immediacy and instantaneity of 'pure perception'. Shame is an example of a particular kind of image that 'surges' in the centre of indetermination (the subject) 'between a perception which is troubling in certain respects and a hesitant action' (Deleuze 1986: 65). Deleuze calls these 'affection-images'; they represent the way that the subject appears to itself, 'from the inside'. Affection (and shame is here merely exemplary – the same might be said of 'joy', or 'frustration') measures and bridges the distance between perception and the 'delayed reaction' that constitutes the 'activity' of a centre of indetermination. In shame, therefore, as in all affections, subject and object coincide. Affection 're-establishes the relation' between perception and action; it obscures their incommensurability. Affection, the self-image of the subject, is thus 'a third absolutely necessary given' of what Deleuze calls the 'perception-action system' (Deleuze 1986: 65).

'Subtraction', then, is the name of the principle according to which we can develop a non-subjective understanding of shame, a notion of shame that is not susceptible to what Sartre called 'subjective illusions' (1990: 12). Subtraction divides shame against itself: into a nameable shame on one hand, which refers to a centre of indetermination, and an unnamed, 'profound' or 'redoubled' shame that cannot be referred to the subject, a shame from which all merely 'subjective' qualities have been removed. The theory of subtraction, in other words, is the best answer that one might offer to the question, 'How can we rid ourselves of ourselves, and demolish ourselves?'

The argument put forward in Deleuze's cinema books is that cinema, by virtue of its material actuality, brings into effect a historical dismantling of the regime of immobile sections, of categorical thinking, the ontology of subject and object, of 'us' and 'them'. The essence of cinema is an 'eye' free of the factors that interrupt pure perception: not merely 'ideology', but 'personality, identity, subjectivity, consciousness, signification' (Hallward 2006: 91). As Bazin notes of photography, 'All the arts are based on the presence of man, only photography derives an advantage from his absence' (Bazin 1967: 13). Deleuze extends this observation to cinema, the form in which the idealist separation of image and movement (that is to say, consciousness and thing, subject and object) is overcome – in 'fact', not simply in theory. Cinema expounds a world in which, for the first time, *image = movement* (1986: 58). The movement that is actualised in cinema, says Deleuze in *The Time-Image*, 'no longer depends on a moving body or an object which realises it, nor on a spirit which reconstitutes it. It is the image which itself moves in itself' (1989: 156). The cinematographic image 'makes' movement, thereby 'mak[ing] what the other arts are restricted to demanding (or to saying)'. In so doing, cinema 'converts into potential what was only possibility' (1989: 156).

This is where cinema has such importance for the 'subtractive' theory of consciousness, predicated upon a theoretical liberation from the limits of the human. If Bergson used cinema to demonstrate the partial, 'subtractive' quality of human individual consciousness, for Deleuze cinema demands to be regarded not in such derivative terms – as subordinate to the model of human perception – but in its specificity, as the realisation of the 'pure perception' spoken of in a hypothetical mode by Bergson. 'The model cannot be natural perception,' says Deleuze; 'the model would be rather a state of things which would constantly change, a flowing matter in which no point of anchorage nor centre of reference would be assignable' (1986: 57). It is cinema that, *pace* Bergson, 'lacks a centre of anchorage and of horizon' (1986: 58). Cinema offers us, not occasionally but perpetually, by its mere existence, what Bergson is only able to conceptualise: a perception that is 'absorbed in the present', 'a vision of matter both immediate and instantaneous' (Bergson 2002: 97); and it does so irrespective of what we, with our conscious, subtractive perception, may think it is offering us.

Louis Malle's *L'Inde fantôme*

Towards the end of the first episode of *L'Inde fantôme*, during a sequence showing a number of fishermen hauling in their catch on a beach on the Madras coast, Louis Malle offers the following commentary:

> Tuesday February 27. I awoke very early. The light is still undecided, very soft and sad, as it often is in the tropics. I'm suddenly projected 15 years into the past, to early mornings in the Seychelles, on beaches like this. I was 20, shooting my first film. The tropics enchanted me, the entire world one big promise of happiness [*promesse de bonheur*]. Suddenly, the fishermen in front of me are replaced by others. Once again memory fills the foreground. Once again, I'm incapable of living in the present, of feeling it, of touching it. Even in the Seychelles, reality escaped me, that elusive harmony between men, light and landscape. I had to reinvent it, modify it, project onto it my dreams and memories. I had to destroy it. Westerner, filmmaker, time's tamer, time's slave. (I)

It is obvious, however, that the images of the fishermen onscreen do not correspond to this memory-filled commentary. Malle's voiceover registers a discrepancy that exists throughout the film between words and images. This tension is registered so frequently by Malle that, even when it is not thematised explicitly, it is part of the fabric of the film. Words, of course, are the only means of *noting* the discrepancy; one of the principal uses that Malle makes of words through all seven episodes of the film is precisely to inform us of their inadequacy.

The first episode opens with a montage of highly educated, English speaking Indians addressing Malle behind the camera. Only 2 per cent of Indians speak English, Malle tells us, but that minority talks a great deal, in the name of the rest. 'I immediately sensed that the real questions were not being addressed.' *L'Inde fantôme* promises to tell – in 'images gathered without a script, or preconceived concept' – a story that is truer than any that could be told in the former colonial language. It will be 'a film of our chance encounters'. When Malle films a father and son performing a 'Tiger dance' in Mysore during the Muslim festival of Muhurram, he comments: 'Words are useless between us. The image is our only connection. They dance and I film them. That's all.' Over the image of several brick-makers at work, who, we are told, earn one rupee for every 150 bricks, Malle says: 'We film them as they are, the hypnotic repetition of their movements. There's some sort of truth to be found there at least. To tell how they work 10–12 hours a day, live in huts, come from neighbouring villages, have no land – would all that add anything to what the images already reveal?'(I)

This investment in 'images', however, opens up another question related to the people who are subject to the attention of Malle's camera. The many shots in *L'Inde fantôme* of peasant women picking crops, for example, might be thought to invite a critical analysis in terms of the Western, scopophilic 'male gaze'. Indeed, despite his repeated appeal to the discrepancy between words and images, Malle is aware of problems posed to his project by the presence of the camera; in the first episode he describes himself and his crew as 'Westerners with a camera; Westerners twice over'. On the first day of shooting (19 January 1968) they come across a pair of women picking clumps of grass from a barren piece of land outside Delhi. As soon as they arrive, one of the women gets up and leaves, cursing them. 'She doesn't want to be filmed. It's evil, a spell we cast upon her. Being filmed will steal from her everything she is' (I). Malle is sympathetic, even as he continues to film the woman who remains:

> The camera's fundamental brazenness is something I've constantly experienced, even in Paris, even with actors, even on film sets. Here, it's worse. These women have absolutely nothing. They spend the morning on their knees to glean a handful of fodder and I steal a bit more from them. To them . . . our camera is a weapon, and they're afraid of us.

In another scene featuring a line of evidently exploited labourers, Malle attributes the subtractive quality of his images not to the human element in the project, but to the camera: 'In this scene, rich ground for political analysis, I notice the camera's chosen only one aspect. It keeps returning to this young woman, because we're drawn to her beauty, her graceful modesty, her laugh. Because she dazzles us. Because that's what it was like that morning' (I). Malle, it seems, needs words in order to instantiate, to formalise, the importance of images to his project, as well as to acknowledge the ethical foundations and implications of the project itself.

The tension between words and images is never resolved in Malle's film. The quest for immediacy – for 'that elusive harmony between men, light and landscape' – remains an aspiration for Malle; indeed, how could it be realised as long as it is articulated in subjective terms? Yet the discrepancy is also a necessary element in the film, in so far as it dramatises the more fundamental distinction between human perception and the 'pure perception' that Bergson ascribes to the hypothetical sphere, the sphere of 'theory' – a perception that would be conditional upon the subtraction of all merely human perception, all memory, all consciousness in general. When Malle offers his commentary alongside the images of the fishermen on the beach, a distance is established between his own perception – subtractive by definition, haunted by memory and by his own subjectivity – and that of the camera. This distance will become a principle of the work; indeed, it is on those same grounds, pertaining to cinema in general, that the hypothesis of the 'male gaze' of the camera is rejected by Deleuze.

Like phenomenology, the 'male gaze' hypothesis analogises cinema to 'natural' perception, albeit in a critique of that perception. 'Cinematic codes create a gaze, a world, and an object, thereby producing an illusion cut to the measure of desire,' writes Laura Mulvey. 'The conscious aim [is] always to eliminate intrusive camera presence and prevent a distancing awareness in the audience.' For Mulvey, resisting or disrupting these codes is a critical procedure: 'The first blow against the monolithic accumulation of traditional film conventions . . . is to free the look of the camera into its materiality in time and space and the look of the audience into dialectics, passionate detachment' (Mulvey 1999: 843–4). For Deleuze, however, cinema is the form in which the male gaze, or the 'Western' gaze, is *deposed*; this is not a matter of intentionality or volition, and it is not a 'critical' or 'political' project. Cinema – 'the in-itself of the image', Deleuze calls it (1986: 81) – is not analogical to a human eye, for the simple reason that the camera is not an immobile centre; or it is so only if is regarded 'from the point of view of the human eye' (1986: 81). Deleuze reminds us of the Bergsonian formulation: in subjective (subtractive) perception 'the images vary in relation to a central and privileged image', while an objective perception is one where 'all the images vary in relation to one another, on all their facets and in all their parts' (1986: 76). As soon as we have the principle of montage we have a camera that is separate from the privileged centre, a camera capable of giving us 'the pure vision of a non-human eye, of an eye which would be in things' (1986: 81).

Thus, if there is a resolution to the discrepancy between words and images in Malle's film, it is found in the mere presence of the camera, which elevates the discrepancy into a formal principle. Malle himself is not necessarily aware of this as a solution. Indeed, since the voiceover constitutes one term in the discrepancy, we should not look for the truth of the film in Malle's words. Nor are the images alone sufficient; attention should be paid, rather, precisely to the discrepancy between them. Three exemplary moments from *L'Inde fantôme* illustrate the way in which this discrepancy functions as a principle of the work, establishing a centre of consciousness that is outside the human subject – what Deleuze calls a 'spiritual automaton', or Pier Paolo Pasolini a 'free, indirect subjective' (Deleuze 1989: 156, 148).

One of the most striking and defining sequences comes near the beginning of the first episode, as Malle and his crew notice that the people they are filming are staring back at the camera. With his frame filled with faces, Malle says: 'We came to see them, but they're the ones looking at us. So we preferred to film them that way, their sea of enormous eyes turned on us, on the camera's single eye. We decided to film all these looks, to make them the leitmotif of our journey' (I). In the sequence that immediately follows, the crew comes upon a wedding celebration; again they find themselves the object of scrutiny as all activity at the wedding temporarily halts. 'The roles are reversed. We've become the show, and they're the audience.' Slowly, however, the participants in the wedding 'seem to forget about us. The ceremony continues, with its precise ritual, unchanged for centuries' (I).

The effect on Malle of being excluded from the ritual may be contrasted to the 'shame' that Sartre offloads on Fanon's European readers by the circumstance that the book they are reading is not 'intended' for them. For Malle the effect is quite the reverse; he feels not shamed, but liberated by having been obliterated from the scene. 'This eternity erases us,' says Malle, 'like an unimportant spot in the crowd' (I). Yet perhaps it is not the eternity of the 'ritual' that erases them, but an 'eternity' that is brought into manifestation by the presence of the camera. Pure (non-human) perception, pure (non-human) memory, implies also pure (non-human) temporality: what Bazin calls 'objectivity in time'. 'Now, for the first time,' says Bazin, 'the image of things is likewise the image of their duration, change mummified as it were' (Bazin 1967: 14–15). Deleuze takes this a step further when he talks of cinema's 'de-actualisation' of the present. In direct time-images – pure optical or sound situations – the present is 'separated from its own actual quality' (Deleuze 1989: 100). The 'peaks' of the present are brought into continuity with the 'present of the past' and the 'present of the future' (that is to say, recollection-images and anticipations of recollection); all three are 'rolled up in the event', in a 'simultaneity of . . . three implicated presents' (1989: 100). It is this quality of duration, not the encounter with a history or ritual that is 'older than we are', that deposes the self. A quality of temporality is achieved in *L'Inde fantôme* that is incommensurable with the human propensity to divide time into sections of successive 'presents', or to remove eternity to a sphere outside the here and now.

This effect is even clearer in a scene from the beginning of the fourth episode of *L'Inde fantôme*. Over the image of a caravan slowly moving towards the camera, Malle apostrophises the figures on the carts and on the road, as follows: 'You peasants, met at dawn on a remote road in southern India. Your life flows imperceptibly, to a rhythm different from ours, from the minutes and seconds we consider so valuable. At this point in our journey we've almost found your rhythm' (IV). Just as it seems impossible to distinguish Leiris' shame from the fact of his writing, so it seems impossible to distinguish the absence of shame in Malle's film, exemplified in such apparently euphoric moments, from its actuality as a film. Malle, we learn from a 1990 interview, spent an intense year 'in the cutting room' after returning to Paris from India, working with his footage.

> It was as if I was still in India. It was the continuation of my trip. Just looking at my images and remembering what happened, I discovered certain contradictions that I had not even noticed . . . I was deepening my experience of India by just watching what I had shot, and trying to make sense of it. (Malle 1993: 74)

Malle is not merely experiencing India *as if* it were a film; in his voiceover it is the film – or rather, the inseparability of the film from the object – that is experienced. The movement, the temporality he is lyricising belongs not to the peasants, but to the image. The 'rhythm' he has found, or 'almost' found, is sensuously present as a 'crystal' of pure time; it is reducible neither to the moment of the filming, nor to that of the editing, nor to that of the viewing. The crystal displaces the object; and not only the object but the very situation of the object's contemplation by a subject. In fact, the entirety of Malle's film follows the principle of the time-image; every shot is a pure optical situation – whether what we are seeing is a hundred vultures dismantling the carcass of a buffalo (I), innumerable bats hanging from the trees in twilight at Trivandrum (IV), laundry workers at a river outside Madras (V), or a prostitute sticking out her tongue at the camera from a window in Bombay (VII). Every image is detached from its 'motor extension' – from any direct narrative purpose (Deleuze 1989: 126). 'When I was shooting I was never thinking, "Well where is it going to come, how does it relate to something I did yesterday?" No, we were just shooting at random' (Malle 1993: 71). Yet Malle's commentary, in all its subtractive limitation, is as necessary for the production of the crystal as the images, for the commentary brings together those several 'presents' (filming, editing, viewing) that, in their respective incommensurability, constitute the fabric of the film, its plane of consistency.

Consider another scene, in which we see two purely optical situations in immediate succession: a man ploughing a field with a hoe, and another man spreading grain over a mat with his feet. 'Nothing shocked me anymore,' says Malle,

> for I'd accepted another perspective on the world. It's not about explaining or dominating the world, but being a part of it, fitting into it. Watching them perform simple gestures as if they were rituals, strange ideas come to mind. If happiness is defined as a sense of balance and bliss, being in harmony with one's surroundings, interior peace, then these Indian peasants are happier than us, who've destroyed nature, and do battle with time in the absurd pursuit of material well-being, in the end sharing only our loneliness. (IV)

What is the 'other perspective' talked of by Malle? Does it belong to India, or to Indians? What is the 'world' that Malle feels himself becoming 'a part of', 'fitting into'? Is it that of Indian society? No: the 'other perspective' discovered by Malle in *L'Inde fantôme* is one that is given substance by the cinematic apparatus. The world of immediacy and intimacy that beckons to Malle is that of the cinema itself, the plane of immanence in which the shameful condition of being stapled to a fixed point of consciousness, a 'centre of indetermination', is overcome. Where is the 'happiness' that Malle finds so appealing and so moving? Is it really located in the peasants, the objects of his 'Western' gaze? How could it be? The 'vision of matter both immediate and instantaneous' (Bergson 2002: 97) that has been his quest all along is discovered not in India but in the cinematic image. That which Bazin called 'the impassive lens' (1967: 15) is the means by which Malle escapes (although it is not exactly he who escapes) the 'Western' gaze. Is his 'loneliness' that of the Western consciousness? No again, except in so far as the 'West' names a structure of domination predicated upon the separation of identity and difference, the principle of self-expression and a regime of 'organic' description that assumes the independence of the object from its perception. The 'freedom from shame' achieved by Malle in *L'Inde fantôme*, then, does not belong to him any more than it is attributable to the presence of the Indians in his film. If the film, or filming, enables him to transcend his ('our') loneliness, what is transcended is not so much 'loneliness' as the logic of *his, their, our*.

If for Sartre the purest embodiment of the free consciousness is the writer, for Deleuze the 'free consciousness' is not found in the writer at all, but in the machine, the camera. If a truly postcolonial writing is to evolve, a writing unburdened by the shame of its partiality and inadequacy, the lessons of Malle's *L'Inde fantôme*, and of Deleuze's works on cinema, are that it will take the form of a 'machinic' writing, a form that is perhaps already in development; indeed, such a form is crystallised whenever an instance or a detail of writing cannot be explained in terms of the perception of an object by a subject. The postcolonial writing to come will be a writing liberated, like cinema, from the subtractive consciousness of a being who writes.

References

Bazin, A. (1967), 'The Ontology of the Photographic Image', in *What is Cinema?*, vol. 1, trans. H. Gray, Berkeley: University of California Press, pp. 9–16.
Bergson, H. (2002), *Key Writings*, ed. K. Ansell-Pearson and J. Mullarkey, New York and London: Continuum.
Buchanan, I. (2000), *Deleuzism: A Metacommentary*, Durham: Duke University Press.
Coetzee, J. M. (2004), *Dusklands*, New York: Vintage.
Deleuze, G. (1983), *Cinéma 1: L'Image-mouvement*, Paris: Minuit.
Deleuze, G. [1983] (1986), *Cinema 1: The Movement-Image*, trans. H. Tomlinson and B. Habberjam, London: Athlone.
Deleuze, G. (1988), *Foucault*, trans. S. Hand, Minneapolis and London: University of Minnesota Press.
Deleuze, G. [1985] (1989), *Cinema 2: The Time-Image*, trans. H. Tomlinson and R. Galeta, London: Athlone.
Deleuze, G. (1995), *Negotiations 1972–1990*, trans. M. Joughin, New York: Columbia University Press.
Deleuze, G. (1998), 'The Shame and the Glory: T. E. Lawrence', in *Essays Critical and Clinical*, trans. D. W. Smith and M. A. Greco, London: Verso pp. 115–25.
Deleuze, G. and F. Guattari (1987), *A Thousand Plateaus: Capitalism and Schizophrenia*, trans. B. Massumi, Minneapolis: University of Minnesota Press.
Deleuze, G. and F. Guattari (1991), *Qu'est-ce que la philosophie?* Paris: Minuit.
Deleuze, G. and F. Guattari (1994), *What is Philosophy?* trans. H. Tomlinson and G. Burchell, New York: Columbia University Press.

Fanon, F. [1952] (1986), *Black Skin, White Masks*, trans. C. L. Markmann, London: Pluto.
Hallward, P. (2006), *Out of this World: Deleuze and the Philosophy of Creation*, London and New York: Verso.
Larson, R. (1997), 'Ethnography, Thievery, and Cultural Identity: A Rereading of Michel Leiris's *L'Afrique fantôme*, *PMLA* (*Publications of the Modern Language Association of America*) 112 (2): 229–42.
Lawrence, T. E. (1935), *Seven Pillars of Wisdom: A Triumph*, New York: Doubleday, Dorian and Co.
Leiris, M. (1948), *La Règle du jeu I: Biffures*, Paris: Gallimard.
Leiris, M. (1955), *La Règle du jeu II: Fourbis*, Paris: Gallimard.
Leiris, M. (1966), *La Règle du jeu III: Fibrilles*, Paris: Gallimard.
Leiris, M. (1976), *La Règle du jeu IV: Frêle bruit*, Paris: Gallimard.
Leiris, M. [1946] (1984), *Manhood: A Journey from Childhood into the Fierce Order of Virility*, trans. R. Howard, San Francisco: North Point Press.
Leiris, M. [1934] (1996), *L'Afrique fantôme*, in *Miroir de l'Afrique*, Paris: Éditions Gallimard.
Levi, P. (1989), 'Translating Kafka', in *The Mirror Maker*, trans. Raymond Rosenthal, New York: Schocken, pp. 106–9.
Malle, L. (1993), *Malle on Malle*, ed. Philip French, London: Faber and Faber.
Merleau-Ponty, M. (2002), *Phenomenology of Perception*, trans. C. Smith, London and New York: Routledge.
Mulvey, L. (1999), 'Visual Pleasure and Narrative Cinema', in L. Braudy and M. Cohen (eds), *Film Theory and Criticism: Introductory Readings*, New York: Oxford University Press, pp. 833–44.
Sartre, J. P. [1948] (1976), *Black Orpheus*, trans. S. W. Allen, Paris: Présence africaine.
Sartre, J. P. [1943] (1989), *Being and Nothingness: An Essay on Phenomenological Ontology*, trans. H. Barnes, London: Routledge.
Sartre, J. P. [1961] (1990), 'Preface', in F. Fanon, *The Wretched of the Earth*, trans. C. Farrington, Harmondsworth: Penguin.
Sartre, J. P. [1948] (2001), *What is Literature?*, trans. B. Frechtman, London and New York: Routledge.

Filmography

L'Inde fantôme: Reflexions sur un voyage (1969), film, directed by Louis Malle, France: Nouvelles Éditions de Films.
The Documentaries of Louis Malle (2007), DVD, USA: Criterion.

Notes

1. See Leiris' *Manhood* (1984) and the four volumes of *La Règle du jeu* (1948, 1955, 1966, 1976).
2. All quotations from Malle's voiceover are translated by Lynn Massey, and taken from the English subtitles provided on the 2007 Criterion DVD release of *L'Inde fantôme* as part of the DVD boxed set *The Documentaries of Louis Malle*. I have indicated the relevant episode (I–VII) in brackets after each passage quoted.
3. During the period covered by the narrative of Lawrence's *Seven Pillars of Wisdom*, Lawrence was participating in what might be regarded, and not only from our 'postcolonial' perspective, as a profoundly 'shameful' enterprise: the

attempt by the British military during the First World War to foment a nationalist Arab revolt against the Turks, so as to distract Turkey, a German ally, from the war in Europe. The events narrated in Lawrence's book led directly to the foundation of the state of Iraq, initially as a mandate under the administrative control of the British, a situation that lasted until Iraq's independence in 1932.

Chapter 8

Becoming-Nomad: Territorialisation and Resistance in J. M. Coetzee's *Waiting for the Barbarians*

Grant Hamilton

It is certain that geography holds a special place within J. M. Coetzee's early novel, *Waiting for the Barbarians* (1980). Indeed, in this novel Coetzee exposes two combative conceptualisations of the earth that seem to characterise the colonial encounter. On the one hand is a State conceptualisation of the world that devours the essential quality of the earth, using it merely as a foundation to impose a reflection of its striated thought. It is a thought that thrives on the practice of limitation, organisation and compartmentalisation, which can only produce an always already falsified knowledge of the rich and various earth, but nevertheless continues to pass for truth. On the other hand is what we might think of as a smooth conceptualisation of the world – a world without limitation and organisation, a world that is not conceived as different from or apart from those that walk within it. This chapter discusses the way in which Coetzee uses the dynamic that develops between these two conceptualisations of the earth in the colonial encounter to describe the complex ontological character of the key figure of the unnamed Magistrate. Turning away from a State conceived and perceived organisation of physical and psychological space, the Magistrate enters into a process of 'becoming-nomad' that ultimately casts him in opposition to the colonial power that he serves. Such movement, according to both Coetzee and Gilles Deleuze, cannot be tolerated by the State, which must begin a process of capture that will seek once again to bring the Magistrate under its control – into its territory. However, inextricably linked to the onset of the State's attempts to reterritorialise those factions it finds outside of its immediate control is an internal destabilising force that threatens to corrupt the whole State apparatus. As such, the figure of the Magistrate in his becoming-nomad stages a very powerful kind of resistance to colonial practice – a deterritorialisation of the Self that instructs the self-destructive drive of the State apparatus.

The reader is introduced to the Magistrate as a man who is quietly but conscientiously serving out his days in a lazy frontier town, waiting to retire. Recalling his usual duties, he explains:

> I collect the tithes and taxes, administer the communal lands, see that the garrison is provided for, supervise the junior officers who are the only officers we have here, keep an eye on trade, preside over the law-court twice a week. For the rest I watch the sun rise and set, eat and sleep and am content (Coetzee 1980: 8).

It is a languid programme that suitably reflects the intentionally unhurried life of the Magistrate. However, his quiet and predictable life is soon to be shattered by his love for a girl from beyond the town's borders – a 'barbarian girl'. In this intense relationship, the Magistrate opens himself up to a perception of the world that is *other to* the Empire's totalised representation of reality. As such, the Magistrate finds himself undergoing a profound transformation. It is a transformation that is marked by his turning away from the doctrines and truths of a conditioning State-thought, towards a new and ultimately revolutionary kind of thought – a nomad-thought.

Deleuze tells us that State-thought proceeds in much the same manner as an archaeology. Starting at the surface of an object and slowly working downwards to reveal the object's 'essential quality' (Deleuze 1998: 63), the nature of State-thought is characterised by the act of prising apart, breaking and eventually penetrating the expressive layers of an object. Of course, this is precisely the way in which the Empire's special interrogator Colonel Joll thinks of his task of extracting the 'truth' from his barbarian prisoners. Explaining his interrogation technique to the Magistrate, he says, 'I am speaking of a situation in which I am probing for the truth, in which I have to exert pressure to find it' (Coetzee 1980: 5). Such a need to probe for the truth is nothing unusual to the Magistrate, who similarly 'hunts back and forth' across the body of the barbarian girl he is falling in love with, in the hope of 'seeking entry' (Coetzee 1980: 46) to her essential otherness. Indeed, the Magistrate is not blind to the comparison between his actions and those of her interrogators – 'Is this how her torturers felt hunting their secret, whatever they thought it was?' The Magistrate, then, is just as skilled in the practices of State-thought as the insidious figure of Colonel Joll.

But there comes a moment when, unlike Colonel Joll, the Magistrate realises that such attempts to break the surface of the incomprehensible other are predestined to failure. He continues, 'For the first time I feel a dry pity for them: how natural a mistake to believe that you could burn or tear or hack your way into the secret body of the other!' (Coetzee 1980: 46). Importantly, this moment of 'dry pity' expresses the Magistrate's dawning realisation that there are other ways of perceiving and understanding the world. For the Magistrate who is slowly becoming aware of the naturalised 'mistakes' of a State-thought that had previously conditioned his own thinking, the direction of interrogation is no longer the top-down method of a striated State-thought, but rather the bottom-up vector associated with intensities, thresholds, qualities and affects. In short, it is no longer a question of objects and origins, but rather of becomings and intensities. As the Magistrate recognises, it is the moment in which the desire for penetration is replaced by the necessity of affection:

> In the snowbound warmth of the tent I make love to her again. She is passive, accommodating herself to me. When we begin I am sure that the time is right; I embrace her in the most intensive pleasure and pride of life; but halfway through I seem to lose touch with her, and the act peters out vacantly. My intuitions are clearly fallible. Still, my heart continues its affectionate glow towards this girl who so briskly falls asleep in the crook of my arm. There will be another time, and if not, I do not think I mind. (Coetzee 1980: 71–2)

In this moment that sees the Magistrate replace the act of penetration with a subtle reawakening of his ethical bond to others, the Magistrate truly begins to feel the force of his turning away from the doctrines and practices of the Empire. It is the moment in which his State-conditioned relationship with the earth is finally severed (deterritorialised) and replaced with a fundamentally different perception, which challenges him to see the morally and ethically intolerable condition of the Empire's relationship with its others. On the barbarians with whom the frontier town trades, the Magistrate comments:

> In the past I have encouraged commerce but forbidden payment in money. I have also tried to keep taverns closed to them . . . It always pained me in the old days to see these people fall victim to the guile of shopkeepers, exchanging their goods for trinkets, lying drunk in the gutter, and confirming thereby the settlers' litany of prejudice . . . Where civilization entailed the corruption of barbarian virtues and the creation of a dependent people, I decided, I was opposed to civilization. (Coetzee 1980: 41)

It is the same kind of antagonistic thinking towards Empire and its products that leads the Magistrate finally to announce to himself that 'I must assert my distance from Colonel Joll! I will not suffer for his crimes!' (Coetzee 1980: 48). In this call to assert distance between himself and the Empire, the Magistrate cements his turn away from State-thought towards nomad-thought. Through his developing relationship with the barbarian girl, the Magistrate undergoes a metamorphosis that slowly allows him access to this fundamentally different way of perceiving and understanding the world. This is a world in which the chaotic forces of the earth are to be embraced rather than subjugated or organised; it is a world of unlimited movement that stands in strong opposition to the efforts of the State to impose structural gravity, inhibition and, thereby, limitation; and, it is a world, finally, in which the composition and instruction of territory is an intolerable imposition on the earth. Indeed, as the Magistrate realises, his metamorphosis allows an appreciation of the world that is beyond the totalising gaze of Empire, and therefore pulls those inside the Empire to its (impossible) outside. The Magistrate conceptualises this dramatic movement in terms of his relationship with the barbarian girl:

> From the very first she knew me for a false seducer . . . If only she had found the words to tell me! 'That is not how you do it,' she should have said, stopping me in the act. 'If you want to learn how to do it, ask your friend with the black eyes.' Then she should have continued, so as not to leave me without hope: 'But if you want to love me you will have to turn your back on him and learn your lesson elsewhere'. (Coetzee 1980: 148)

The charge the Magistrate makes for himself, via the barbarian girl, is to find an 'elsewhere', a place that is beyond the ideological and physical spaces territorialised by the State. Indeed, it is for this reason that he must accompany the girl back to the nomads who are beyond the sight and the reach of the Empire. The Magistrate is forced into a condition of movement, into a deterritorialisation, which will see him leave behind not only the territory of the State but every territorial assemblage known to him – those created by himself and those created by others. It is not even that the Magistrate must exchange one territory for another, State territory for the territory of the nomad. He must negate all such organised, territorialised forces of the world in favour of 'the liberated or regained forces of a deterritorialized Cosmos' (Deleuze and Guattari 1999: 326). However, this is not to suggest that the Magistrate must create a space of pure abstraction. Just as the scars inflicted on the body of the barbarian girl during one of Colonel Joll's interrogation sessions lose none of their particularity when they open out onto the other more 'cosmic' scars caused by the universal epistemological violence implicit in the imperial project to determine the world, so the Magistrate must organise a trajectory for his deterritorialisation that is both particular and absolute. His movement is, therefore, twofold: the physical journey towards the mountains and the waiting barbarians, which constitutes his particular trajectory (the specific); and the accompanying mental journey, the movement of a psychological deterritorialisation from the State, which assumes an absolute trajectory (the singular).

Experiencing this continuing deterritorialisation from the State, the Magistrate witnesses the territorialising sounds of Empire, the tones produced by the bugle-calls from the ramparts, the language of the frontier people, both being consumed by their own elemental condition. 'Then all at once,' he writes, 'the wind rises to a scream . . . I shout. My words are nothing but a whisper, I cannot hear them myself' (Coetzee 1980: 72). He also imagines the stones that construct the borders of the Empire returning to a deterritorialised state, 'as though not one spadeful of earth had been turned or one brick laid upon another' (Coetzee 1980: 55). Ultimately, the Magistrate looks through everything that is terrestrial, everything that can be territorialised, to see the forces of a deterritorialised cosmos. So, in describing the early days of his incarceration, he writes:

> I stare all day at the empty walls, unable to believe that the imprint of all the pain and degradation they have enclosed will not materialize under an intent enough gaze; or shut my eyes, trying to attune my hearing to that infinitely faint level at which the cries of all who suffered here must still beat from wall to wall. I pray for the day when these walls will be levelled and the unquiet echoes can finally take wing . . . (Coetzee 1980: 87)

The Magistrate's reflection on his incarceration clearly reveals the deterritorialised forces of the cosmos. Such manifestations of pain and suffering simultaneously belong to no*body* and every*body*, and, like caged birds, seek escape from the manufactured confinement of the cell. Thus, the Magistrate can no longer conceptualise the world, the earth, only in terms of a chaos to be subjugated or organised at the hands of a territory. Through his state of deterritorialisation, he returns to a conceptualisation of the earth as a literal support for the foot, as a support for movement rather than as a support for any kind of colonisation. It is the attainment of this state that he relentlessly pursues. 'I look forward with craving to exercise times,' he relates, 'when I can feel the wind on my face and the earth under my soles' (Coetzee 1980: 87). His is a desire to commune with the deterritorialised forces of the earth itself.

However, the force of the Magistrate's deterritorialisation is not realised until he returns to the frontier town after escorting the barbarian girl back to 'her own people' (Coetzee 1980: 148). Finding himself stripped of his magistracy and thrown into prison for releasing the barbarian girl without the permission of Colonel Joll, the Magistrate *chooses* to work against the State – to render visible the non-visible forces implicit in the power exercised by the State and thereby expose the covert operation of the State to its territorialised people. It is clear that such a project has the potential to serve as a catalyst for revolution. In the words of Paul Virilio, the Magistrate must 'dwell as a poet' (Virilio 1975: 49), encouraging private thought to exceed State-thought and in so doing sow the seeds for a 'new' people to demand autonomy from State control. It is a potential force that Colonel Joll both recognises and wishes to dissipate. During interrogation, Joll says to the Magistrate:

> 'When I arrived back a few days ago, I had decided that all I wanted from you was a clear answer to a simple question, after which you could have returned to your concubines a free man . . . However, you seem to have a new ambition . . . You seem to want to make a name for yourself as the One Just Man, the man who is prepared to sacrifice his freedom to his principles.' (Coetzee 1980: 124)

That Joll links the stance of the Magistrate to the concept of the 'One Just Man', and later to the concept of the 'martyr', reveals both the potential route and potential product of the Magistrate's refusal to conform to State thinking. Clearly, the possibility of the Magistrate's private thought connecting to the collective consciousness of the wider populace is intolerable to the State authority since it would blur the veracity of all State created information and future State articulations. This is why Joll leads with a seemingly innocuous offer that promises to dissipate the static energy building behind the Magistrate's position. But the offer is nothing other than an attempt to get the Magistrate to adopt and, importantly, express the preconceived truth of the State. As such, the offer stands as little more than a repetition of Joll's interrogation technique that he relates to the Magistrate earlier in the novel, 'First I get lies . . . then pressure, then more lies, then more pressure, then the break, then more pressure, then the truth. That is how you get to the truth' (Coetzee 1980: 5). Yet, such manoeuvres only double the resolve of the Magistrate. In declining Colonel Joll's offer, the Magistrate reasserts his state of deterritorialisation, a deterritorialisation that allows him to proclaim on the return from his journey, 'my alliance with the guardians of the Empire is over, I have set myself in opposition, the bond is broken, I am a free man' (Coetzee 1980: 85).

Nonetheless, the State opposes the 'deterritorialised forces of the Cosmos' drawn together by the Magistrate, with a refrain of methodical and total territorialisation. The State seeks to territorialise everything, to make everything known through a process of limitation that results in the absolute inhibition of possibility. For Deleuze, this process describes the progressive closure of all territorial assemblages and results in an 'ever wider and deeper black hole' (Deleuze and Guattari 1999: 345). Ultimately, this 'black hole' of inhibition finds its clearest expression in the literal black hole of the Magistrate's prison cell:

> brushing my hand mindlessly over my face, I realize how tiny I have allowed them to make my world, how I daily become more like a beast or a simple machine . . . Then I respond with movements of vertiginous terror in which I rush around the cell jerking my arms about, pulling my beard, stamping my feet, doing anything to surprise myself, to remind myself of a world beyond that is various and rich. (Coetzee 1980: 93)

In the form of the prison cell, one can perhaps recognise the most visible effort of the State to limit the proliferation of competing representations of itself. The prison cell stands as the product of the State's excessive territorialisation of the forces of the earth. Indeed, it is the product of an absolute territorialisation that aims to reassert State powers through the capture, control and eventual annihilation of the cosmic forces of deterritorialisation embodied by the Magistrate. So, while the Magistrate continues to threaten the release of destabilising forces, the State reacts through the well-recognised strategy of disconnection. Through this, the prison cell promises not only physically to disconnect the Magistrate from the population, but also to disconnect his private thoughts from the collective consciousness of the frontier town. In its fullest extension, the prison cell is intended to be experienced as a 'tiny world', a tiny world that functions as a metonym of the actual world. In this tiny world, it is beyond doubt that the State holds absolute domination, and it is precisely this exactitude that the State hopes the prisoner will internalise and therefore transfer into the actual world upon release. Therefore, the Magistrate, if he is to remain in opposition to the State, must offer resistance to the tiny world created by his prison cell. He must remind himself of the world beyond that is various and rich, and the only way he can do this is to reclaim the very possibility of movement that is denied to him by his confinement. Put simply, the Magistrate must jerk his arms, pull his beard and stamp his feet, both as a reaffirmation of his deterritorialisation and as a reaffirmation of possibility itself.

However, in the State's attempt to territorialise everything in order to draw everything inside its totalising stance, it inevitably creates marginal and minority groups that, in their very being, 'affirm the rights of segmentary societies in opposition to the organs of State power' (Deleuze and Guattari 1999: 360). Therefore, the constitution of the State as an absolute structure is punctuated with crystals of antagonism, minor communities that constantly seek to destabilise the absolute claim to the real that the State makes. Because of this, the 'barbarian problem' that frames the Magistrate's narrative in Coetzee's novel must be seen as a result of the State's own processes of control. Importantly, it is the State's inability to control its own fabricated myth of the barbarian that causes it to endure a forced deterritorialisation. While the myth is useful in determining the qualities of the State, left unchecked it quickly spirals into a force that questions the integrity of the State. That is to say, it becomes a force of deterritorialisation.

Deleuze writes that the State begins to experience this forced deterritorialisation through the metamorphoses of its own industrial and technological innovations, and the interruption of its commercial circuits. It is a metamorphosis that motions towards the exteriority of State apparatuses, an outside which 'presents itself as a diffuse and polymorphous war machine' (Deleuze and Guattari 1999: 360). Following a suspected barbarian offensive against the frontier town, where part of an embankment had been cut away in order to flood planted fields, the Magistrate writes:

> I can see that weeks of hard work await the farmers. And at any moment their work can be brought to nothing by a few men armed with spades! How can we win such a war? What is the use of textbook military operations, sweeps and punitive raids into the enemy's heartland, when we can be bled to death at home? (Coetzee 1980: 109–10)

Importantly, while the commercial value of the frontier town's farmland is clearly compromised by this act to disrupt striated space, the manner in which the act is conducted proves also to be worthy of State concern. That the weapon of this act is the tool of the agriculturalist reflects the kind of metamorphosis indicative of a forced deterritorialisation. The tool, the essential factor in any civilisation, is turned into a weapon that makes violence 'durable, even unlimited' (Deleuze and Guattari 1999: 396). As such, the very technology that supports the State's conquest of physical space is transformed into the means by which such endeavours are interrupted, and the State, in the words of the Magistrate, 'bleeds to death at home'.

Such metamorphoses are not, however, limited only to the innovations or commercial circuits of the State apparatus. The segmentary societies in opposition to the organs of State power have the potential to reconstitute the equivalent of this metamorphosis in the collective bodies of the State. As the State is induced into a forced deterritorialisation through its inability satisfactorily to condition every component of its interiority, certain elements of its collective bodies experience a kind of metamorphosis. Through claiming a certain privilege of autonomy from the State, such collective bodies 'open onto something that exceeds them, a short revolutionary instant, an experimental surge' (Deleuze and Guattari 1999: 366–7). So, the Magistrate claims a certain privilege through his association with the barbarian girl and 'opens onto' a revolutionary instant through an experimental surge. The Magistrate's close affiliation with a member of a segmentary society merely doubles the privilege associated with his high-ranking official position in the State apparatus. It results in his perceived privilege to keep personal matters private, even under the pressure of a State that insists that such matters intersect with public security. In claiming this privilege the Magistrate knowingly enters into a becoming-nomad, symbolised most overtly by the caterpillar scar he shares with the barbarian girl,[1] which can do no other than act as a revolutionary force of deterritorialisation on the State apparatus.

Clearly, the becoming-nomad of the Magistrate conditions his project to destabilise the established powers of the State, for it is certain that he wishes to turn the self-constituting exterior gaze of the Empire upon itself. 'We have no enemies,' the Magistrate says under interrogation, 'unless I make a mistake . . . Unless we are the enemy' (Coetzee 1980: 85). It is certain that the Magistrate's particular deterritorialisation does not assume a stance that is directly oppositional to the State. Rather, it is one that aims at corrupting the certainty of State-thought without formalising itself as a competitor. Demonstrating the architecture of State-thought, the Magistrate tries to discern the meaning of some enigmatic wooden slips recovered from the ruins of an ancient buried civilisation:

> There were two hundred and fifty-six slips in the bag. Is it by chance that the number is perfect? After I had first counted them and made this discovery I cleared the floor of my office and laid them out, first in one great square, then in sixteen smaller squares, then in other combinations . . . (Coetzee 1980: 16–17)

Such efforts of arrangement reveal an architecture of thought built on the processes of homogenisation, stratification and identification, which plays itself out through the modality of striation. It is a return to the belief that every component of the world is coded by intrinsic properties that, if revealed, can ultimately describe their internal 'nature'. However, it is certain from the Magistrate's failed attempts to read the slips that the world will not always succumb to such logical translation. Even so, he finds it impossible to break the linear condition of State thinking: 'I have even found myself reading the slips in a mirror, or tracing one on top of another, or conflating half of one with half of another' (Coetzee 1980: 17). It is because of his inability to think outside of State-thought that the reciprocity between such thoughts and the State apparatus becomes apparent. While State-thought clearly borrows its architecture from the model of the State apparatus, the State apparatus profits from the immutability of State-thought since it functions to generate a consensus of opinion throughout its consenting population. The charge at hand is that if the operation of the *cogitatio universalis* of State-thought cannot discern a meaning then there is no meaning to discern; and this becomes the consensus of rational opinion. Such power to condition rational opinion on all matters is significant since it is only this power, Deleuze writes, which 'is capable of inventing the fiction of a State that is universal by right, of elevating the State to the level of *de jure* universality' (Deleuze and Guattari 1999: 375; italics added). And it is only after the elevation of the State to the universal that it can claim to span the whole world, and thereby claim the right to be the defining principle by which rebel subjects can be separated from consenting subjects (Deleuze and Guattari 1999: 375).

Therefore, the force of the Magistrate's becoming-nomad, his condition of constant variation, has the potential not only to corrupt the linearity of State-thought, but also to destroy the fictitious gravity appropriated by the State apparatus from the consensus bred by State-thought. This is why the State will first try to dismantle the properties of the Magistrate's deterritorialised condition. In an effort to reterritorialise him, to make him subscribe once again to the State's position, they will place him into the confinement of the prison cell, an environment over which the State has absolute control, and then attempt to overhaul his perception of himself. To this end, Colonel Joll interrogates the Magistrate, endeavouring to train his self-image by repeating the assertoric speech acts bound to the *imperium* of State truth:

> 'Believe me, to people in this town you are not the One Just Man, you are simply a clown, a madman. You are dirty, you stink, they can smell you a mile away. You look like an old beggar-man, a refuse scavenger. They do not want you back in any capacity. You have no future here . . . You are living in a world of the past. You think we are dealing with small groups of peaceful nomads. In fact we are dealing with a well organized enemy. If you had travelled with the expeditionary force you would have seen that for yourself.'(Coetzee 1980: 124–5)

Colonel Joll's diatribe is a clear effort to make the Magistrate internalise the accusations and denunciations of State opinion. It is a process of saturation that reflects, once again, State thinking – to know solely through an internalisation of the local. The Magistrate is perhaps too quick in the rebuttal of the claims made against him, since he merely reverses the role of the accuser and repeats the operation of State thinking: '*You* are the enemy, Colonel . . . *You* are the enemy, *you* have made the war, and *you* have given them all the martyrs they need' (Coetzee 1980: 125). While the Magistrate's reversal may carry a certain currency on the personal level, it cannot be a sustainable position of resistance to the State apparatus because it is a position that relies on the very ground that is problematised by his becoming-nomad. Indeed, before the anger, before the impassioned defence of his character, the Magistrate produces a far more damaging assault on the State. In the exchange between the Magistrate and Colonel Joll concerning the meaning of the ancient wooden slips, the Magistrate offers a counter-thought to State thinking. It is an epistemologically aggressive act that offers an image, through the figure of the barbarian, which does not assume a stance of direct opposition but rather one that simply threatens the destruction of the model of State-thought. That is to say, the counter-image that the Magistrate produces problematises the very possibility of the State endeavour to subordinate thought to a model of 'the True, the Just, or the Right' (Deleuze and Guattari 1999: 377):

> 'Now let us see what the next one says. See, there is only a single character. It is the barbarian *war*, but it has other senses too. It can stand for *vengeance*, and, if you turn it upside down like this, it can be made to read *justice*. There is no knowing which sense is intended.' (Coetzee 1980: 122)

Although the Magistrate remains ignorant of the 'true' meaning of the characters, the readings he produces expose the ideological impetus of the history written by the unitary State apparatus. The Magistrate's reading of history acknowledges dynamic layers, multiple narratives sitting on top of each other, narratives that penetrate, reflect and deflect the force of other narratives according to whether they reveal convergent or divergent directions of sense. As such, the sedentary and singular quality given to State history is exposed as an artificial construction of a State that seeks only to control the complexity of the multiple through limitation. In reclaiming control through limitation, the State is exposed in its project to collapse history, which is implicitly the domain of collective assemblages of enunciation, into a unitary enunciation. The Magistrate's history cannot, and does not even attempt to, reconcile the ambivalence that is inherent in the historical text. Moreover, the indeterminacy of the literal meanings of the characters on the wooden slips results in 'other troublesome political implications' (Moses 1993: 122). As Michael Moses writes, such indeterminacy means that:

> The history of the progressive establishment of justice is inseparable from, is in fact merely another name for, the history of war, of vengeance. The liberal attempt to overcome barbarism thus turns back upon itself, until the very concept of the just regime ceases to have a stable meaning that merits respect (Moses 1993: 122–3).

The Magistrate manifests the most disruptive product of his deterritorialisation – his 'outside thought' (Deleuze and Guattari 1999: 376), which necessarily enters into combat with State thought. It is as if the Magistrate's counter-thought joins together with forces of the outside to make what Deleuze terms 'a war machine';[2] a war machine that does not encounter the State in any other space than its interior, even though it has repercussions that span the length of its spatio-geographic extension. It is a war machine that functions by bringing something incomprehensible into the State apparatus. For the Magistrate, the war machine of counter-thought opens up the projections and enunciations of the Empire that, once unveiled, can never again be ignored:

> I know somewhat too much; and from this knowledge, once one has been infected, there seems to be no recovering. I ought never to have taken my lantern to see what was going on in the hut by the granary. On the other hand, there was no way, once I had picked up the lantern, for me to put it down again. The knot loops in upon itself; I cannot find the end. (Coetzee 1980: 22–3)

His knowledge has the potential to combat the State by influencing the consensus of opinion that had previously been the sole preserve of State thinking. All the potential force of the Magistrate's private thought needs in order to become revolutionary is the 'new' people that such thought will make manifest. So, while the State forces the Magistrate into the solitude of his prison cell, it is an extremely populous solitude. It is, as Deleuze postulates, 'a solitude already intertwined with a people to come, one that invokes and awaits that people, existing only through it, though it is not yet here' (Deleuze and Guattari 1999: 377). The enigmatic marks in the Magistrate's prison cell bind him to the apparitions of all subjugated people; and it will be all such subjugated people that will lend their ears to the Magistrate to allow him to hear the incomprehensible.

Nevertheless, the State continues to try to apprehend the deterritorialised forces that the Magistrate and the myth of the barbarians have let loose, the very forces that encourage the population of the frontier town to leave in fear of their lives. The Magistrate explains:

> Every week there is a convoy of the prudent leaving town, going east, ten or twelve families travelling together 'to visit relatives', as the euphemism has it . . . They leave, leading pack-trains, pushing handcarts, carrying packs on their backs, their very children laden like beasts. (Coetzee 1980: 142–3)

Faced with these kinds of deterritorialised movements, the State suffers a significant disruption to the gravity of its relationship with control. That is to say, in losing its affinity with the restrictive apparatus of control, the State striation of space is demonstrated to be a wholly temporary practice. Clearly, such a situation is intolerable to a State that claims a stable, global character. In this context, the State attempts to counter the surge of deterritorialisation by gradually assuming the stance of a war machine. Retaining belief in the strength of the genetic elements of striation, the State responds first by promoting the visibility of the military form. Indeed, the Magistrate comments that 'officials of the Third Bureau of the Civil Guard were seen for the first time on the frontier, guardians of the State, specialists in the obscurer motions of sedition, devotees of truth, doctors of interrogation' (Coetzee 1980: 9). However, it is important to note that the salience of this promotion of visibility rests solely on its association with number. Deleuze writes, 'Tens, hundreds, thousands, myriads: all armies retain these decimal groupings, to the point that each time they are encountered it is safe to assume the presence of a military organization' (Deleuze and Guattari 1999: 387). This, we should note, is a procedure of organisation that is enabled by the practice of striation. The State endeavour is to arrange a strong association between visibility and number, intentionally to produce and display a knowable, because countable, military force that can be measured by the opposition in direct relation to their own forces.

Yet it is certain that only similarly organised forces can conduct such measurements. While the State ensures that number retains the principle of measurement in striated space, for Coetzee's barbarians number is the principle of smooth space itself. The number of nomad-space is the substantive multiple (Deleuze and Guattari 1999: 389). In nomad-space number is never a question of metric organisation but rather the principle of direction. Given the ability of the nomad seemingly to manifest and recede instantaneously, number proves to be the principle by which '*the* everywhere' and '*the* simultaneous' affirm a non-abstracted character, and attest to the potential of the nomad to form a discernible force of opposition from 'nowhere'. Thus, narrating his first vague sighting of the nomads, the Magistrate notes:

> As the pinks and mauves of the sunrise begin to turn golden, the specks materialize again on the blank face of the plain, not three of them but eight,

nine, ten, perhaps twelve . . . Then as I watch the figures begin to move. They group in a file and like ants climb the rise. On the crest they halt. A swirl of dust obscures them, then they reappear: twelve mounted men on the skyline . . . Though I keep my eye on the crest, I fail to catch the moment at which they vanish. (Coetzee 1980: 75)

Without number but numerous, without distinction but individual, without substance but concrete, the nomad owns the rhizomic character of the forgotten pack through his ramified extension in every direction;[3] an extension that is only possible when number assumes the unlimited condition of the substantive multiple. Given such a context, the nomad/barbarian *hordes* cannot be thought of in terms of a numbered or structured organisation, even if separate nomad tribes threaten to unite (Coetzee 1980: 9). It is the association between nomad and pack, between nomad and unlimited extension, which insists that the State's combative organisation of visibility and number is predestined to fail in its attempt to assuage the processes of deterritorialisation, since the nomad cannot be measured by the number of his force against the number of the State's military force.

Like the rat and the cockroach, the nomad possesses a speed that is drawn from the substantive multiple described by the rhizome. Number becomes a principle of direction rather than measurement, a principle of intension rather than extension, which places the nomad, rat and cockroach 'nowhere' and 'everywhere', simultaneously. So, while the Magistrate talks to Colonel Joll 'about rats and ways of controlling their numbers' (Coetzee 1980: 2), he demonstrates a State-conditioned way of thinking that can just as easily talk about nomads and the ways of controlling their numbers, since the terms of the respective problems are identical.[4] Certainly, one ought to be cautious in drawing similarities between the nomad and such creatures because of the negative connotations that are invested in the names of the rat and the cockroach. That is, until one realises that such negative connotations only arise because of the rhizomic nature and operation of such creatures. Rather than the creatures themselves, it is the rhizome that is always already detested by State thought. Necessarily uncountable, unknowable and indestructible, the rhizome is a force of deterritorialisation that crosses all the limits and limitations erected by the State. Since the State cannot counter the force of the rhizome directly, it imbues creatures which exhibit rhizomic actions and interactions with negative connotations. In a return to the State process of image training, the population is encouraged to equate the properties and characteristics of such creatures with horror. In this way, it is hoped that the resulting disgust of the creatures will be transferred to the operation of the rhizome itself, to the extent that its deterritorialising impetus will be dissipated. As such, the Magistrate's reflection on the cockroach while he is incarcerated is extremely significant:

> At night when everything is still the cockroaches come out to explore. I hear, or perhaps imagine, the horny clicking of their wings, the scurry of their feet across the paved floor . . . One night I am awoken by the featherlight tread of one crossing my throat. Thereafter I often jerk awake during the night, twitching, brushing myself off, feeling the phantom probings of their antennae at my lips, my eyes. From such beginnings grow obsessions: I am warned. (Coetzee 1980: 87)

The Magistrate convincingly captures the horror that is caused by the speed, phantom presence and invasiveness of the cockroach – all characteristics that are necessarily shared by the rhizome and thereby the nomad. It is certain that the Magistrate recognises this association, since the 'obsession' that is bred by these qualities describes the State's obsession with the nomad as much as his own with the cockroach. It is an obsession born of the inability to apprehend the capacity of an ultimately phantom entity to become invasive – an obsession that always already tends towards paranoia and, correspondingly, a self-destructive drive.

As such, the failure of the combative organisation of visibility and number, coupled with a growing paranoia about the activities of the nomad, leads to the second movement of the State in its drive towards assuming the stance of a war machine. The State relinquishes authority, and passes it into the hands of its military form, as Colonel Joll reminds the Magistrate during interrogation: '"For the duration of the emergency, as you know . . . the administration of justice is out of the hands of civilians and in the hands of the Bureau"' (Coetzee 1980: 124). However, while the State controls its people through the implementation of juridical forces of capture, perhaps most easily recognised in the form of the police, the machinery to which Joll belongs seems to work outside the sovereignty of the State and 'prior to its law' (Deleuze and Guattari 1999: 352). In claiming the power of final authority, and therefore being outside of State control, the war machine itself begins to destabilise the State. It is as if the State does not so much adopt the stance of a war machine as create a war machine that must always already challenge the integrity of the very State it is intended to defend. Thus, the war machine problematises the sovereignty of the State in several ways: firstly, it instructs a furore against the State, so the soldiery are invested with a capacity not only to protect a town but also to tyrannise it, as the Magistrate describes – 'After the meeting the soldiers led a procession through the streets. Doors were kicked in, windows broken, a house set on fire' (Coetzee 1980: 143); secondly, it displays a swiftness that is more akin to the modality of the rhizome than the gravity claimed by striation, as Joll demonstrates – 'I should not want to commit myself to a course beforehand. But, broadly speaking, we will locate the encampment of these nomads of yours and then proceed further as the situation dictates' (Coetzee 1980: 12); and, lastly, it employs secrecy rather than courts publicity. So, the Magistrate asks Colonel Joll:

> 'And can you tell us whether we have anything to fear? Can we rest securely at night?' The corner of his mouth crinkles in a little smile. Then he stands up, bows, turns, and leaves. Early next morning he departs accompanied by his small escort . . . My first action is to visit the prisoners. I unlock the barracks hall which has been their jail, my senses already revolting at the sickly smell of sweat and ordure, and throw the doors wide open. 'Get them out of here!' I shout at the half-dressed soldiers . . . I last saw them five days ago . . . What they have undergone in these five days I do not know. (Coetzee 1980: 25–6)

Here, the exteriority of the State induced war machine is without question. And it is this position of exteriority that French ethnographer Pierre Clastres claims ensures that war is the surest mechanism of warding off the formation of the State (Clastres 1977). Indeed, just as the State must ward off war to ensure its stability, so the war machine endeavours to ward off the State in order to complete its function. While the State attempts to conserve itself through the continued management of exchange (of populations, commerce, capital and so on), the State's formation of the war machine cannot be considered as merely another exchange. As Deleuze explains, '[F]ar from deriving from exchange, even as a sanction for its failure, war is what limits exchanges, maintains them in the framework of "alliances"; it is what prevents them from becoming a State factor, from fusing groups' (Deleuze and Guattari 1999: 357–8). That is to say, the war machine initiates a programme by which it aims to maintain the disparity and segmentarity of marginal local groups through limiting the possibility of exchange between them. In this process of internal division and marginalisation, the State war machine is revealed to be a mechanism of partition that ultimately becomes the State's own black hole of inhibition – its own dark chamber that withholds the power associated with the State's project of striation.

So, the true force of the Magistrate's becoming-nomad is revealed. For the State to combat the war machine initiated by the nomad-poet it must invoke the war machine of the 'assassin' (Virilio 1975: 49). Hence, while the Magistrate threatens to destabilise the State apparatus through invoking a new revolutionary people who open onto the 'deterritorialised forces of the Cosmos' by way of his 'outside thought', the State manifests people like Colonel Joll who bombard the existing people with limitations and inhibitions that have the effect of closing off all exchange and thereby also the very possibility of the creation of a new revolutionary people to come. Yet, in this project of absolute territorialisation, Colonel Joll can make no distinction between consenting and rebelling subjects. The assassin inhibits the State apparatus as much as any other assemblage, even to the extent that it is forced to undergo a deterritorialisation of its own, since the constellation of exchange upon which the State is founded is necessarily collapsed. Ultimately, in attempting to combat the force of deterritorialisation wielded by the Magistrate and the nomad, the State deterritorialises itself, and the nomad war machine is shown to possess an irresistible force.

References

Clastres, P. (1977), *Society against the State*, trans. Robert Hurley, New York: Urizen.
Coetzee, J. M. [1980] (1997), *Waiting for the Barbarians*, London: Minerva.
Deleuze, G. (1998), *Essays Critical and Clinical*, trans. D. W. Smith and M. Greco, London: Verso.
Deleuze, G. and F. Guattari (1999), *A Thousand Plateaus: Capitalism and Schizophrenia*, trans. B. Massumi, London: Athlone Press.
Moses, M. V. (1993), 'The Mark of Empire: Writing, History, and Torture in Coetzee's *Waiting for the Barbarians*', *The Kenyon Review* 15 (1): 115–27.
Virilio, P. (1975), *L'insécurité du territoire*, Paris: Stock.

Notes

1. Compare, for example, the Magistrate's description of the barbarian girl's facial scar: 'I notice in the corner of one eye a greyish puckering as though a caterpillar lay there with its head under her eyelid, grazing' (Coetzee 1980: 33) with his own, 'the wound on my cheek, never washed or dressed, is swollen and inflamed. A crust like a fat caterpillar has formed on it' (Coetzee 1980: 125).
2. It is worth noting that Deleuze makes the distinction between the machinery by which war is waged and the mechanisms by which the possibility of combat can occur. The term 'war machine' refers strictly to the latter, and is the sense in which I employ it here. See Deleuze and Guattari's *A Thousand Plateaus* (1999: 351–423).
3. Deleuze argues that Sigmund Freud ceaselessly worked to crack multiplicity apart in order to ascertain a singular understanding of the unconscious. In this respect, Deleuze notes that where a subject demonstrated a neurotic or psychotic association with a multiplicity, Freud always sought to reduce the association to a singular object. So, for example, it was never a question of a subject's association to

a pack of wolves for Freud, but rather always a question of the subject's association to the wolf. In this sense, the 'pack' is always 'forgotten'. See Deleuze and Guattari's *A Thousand Plateaus* (1999: 26–38).
4. Of course, this kind of enunciation is also reminiscent of the Nazi rhetoric concerning Jews. Indeed, it seems less than surprising that the following discussion of the State's response to its abhorrence of the immediacy of the rhizome is also telling of the Nazis' response to the Jews whom they abhor.

Chapter 9

Violence and Laughter: Paradoxes of Nomadic Thought in Postcolonial Cinema

Patricia Pisters

> Art is never an end in itself. It is only an instrument for tracing lines of lives, that is to say, all these real becomings that are not simply produced *in* art, all these active flights that do not consist in fleeing *into* art . . . but rather sweep it away with them towards the realms of the asignifying, the asubjective.
> (Deleuze and Guattari 1988: 187)[1]

In *Chronicle of a Disappearance* (1996) and *Divine Intervention* (2002), director Elia Suleiman features as one of the main characters. He did not cast himself; rather he was casted by the script that drew him into the film, as he points out in a DVD-interview (A-Film 2003). Although both films are set in his native village, Nazareth, they are not autobiographical in a classic way, representing events in the life of the director when he returns to Palestine. Rather, the films depict an invented self-portrait that is carefully constructed by the director's selection of images, actions and situations and simultaneously completely undetermined by his personal subjectivity. Suleiman's approach can be characterised as a 'politics of the impersonal' that is of central importance in Deleuzian philosophy. In this chapter I will address the objections raised against Deleuze by postcolonial and political theory, by focusing on this 'politics of the impersonal' and other Deleuzian concepts, such as the nomad, that have stirred many discussions. Through a concrete reading of Suleiman's films I will argue that in order to understand the political accountability of Deleuzian philosophy it is necessary to grasp the paradoxical implications of nomadic thought and immanent philosophy.

Postcolonial Charges against Deleuze

Since Gayatri Spivak's rigorous dismissal of Deleuze in her seminal article 'Can the Subaltern Speak?' the significance of Deleuzian philosophy for postcolonial studies has been heavily contested.[2] Postcolonial critics have argued that Deleuzian philosophy cannot take account of the political. In general terms, two basic charges are held against Deleuze (and Guattari). First, Deleuze's critique of representation and his emphasis on desire, lines of flight and the virtual are seen to prohibit any contact with concrete postcolonial and political reality. Secondly, Deleuze and Guattari's philosophy arguably leaves no room for the specific voices of (third world) others. The political concepts they provide, such as the nomad and becoming-minoritarian, are problematic from a postcolonial point of view.

Spivak formulates her critique with respect to Deleuze's rejection of representation. For Spivak, both political representation (speaking for, *Vertretung*) and re-presentation as in art and philosophy (*Darstellung*), make representation the most important concept for understanding the ideological nature of reality, and hence for speaking about reality itself (Spivak 1994: 74). Accordingly, Deleuze's critique of representation is seen by Spivak as a refusal to deal with the ideological nature of 'reality'. Also Deleuze's claim that 'we never desire against our interests, because interest always follows and finds itself where desire has placed it' is unacceptable to Spivak because it downplays ideology (Spivak 1994: 68). In a similar critique, Christopher Miller reproaches Deleuzian thought as a mystification of the virtual which leaves reality in a 'now-you-see-it-now-you-don't limbo'. According to Miller this imprecise 'limbo' means that only 'certified Deleuzians' would be able to say whether reality and representation is left behind or whether there is still contact with (represented) reality (Miller 2003: 5).

According to Spivak, Deleuze also ignores the epistemic violence of colonial and imperial conceptions of the other. The real (local) voice of experience of the colonial or postcolonial subject remains absent, in favour of a so-called universal, but in the final analysis Eurocentric, theory. Miller also argues against the 'postidentitarian' predicaments faced by Deleuze and Guattari, and points to the problematic abstraction of 'the other' in nomadic thinking: 'Colonial and postcolonial studies have taught us, perhaps above all else, that "the other" cannot be so quickly and permanently dissolved in abstraction' (Miller 2003: 5). In this respect, Deleuzian concepts such as the nomad and becoming-minoritarian are considered to be particularly problematic. These concepts are often considered as part of a 'politics of disappearance of local or indigenous knowledge systems' (Wuthnow 2002: 184). The general fear is that 'becoming-minoritarian' might lead to a literal becoming-imperceptible, a condition too familiar for minorities of all sorts, and something they would like overcome rather than strive for. The nomad is often seen to romanticise mobility and fragmentation at the margins. This coincidentally perpetuates the terms of colonial discourse by holding on to a universalised and unmarked Western norm (Wuthnow 2002: 189).

Most recently, Peter Hallward goes even further, arguing that Deleuze's ultimate aim is to reach escape velocity and disappear into an impersonal cosmic vitalism. According to Hallward, Deleuze's philosophy 'inhibits any consequential engagement with the constraints of our actual world' (Hallward 2006: 161). He, too, argues that Deleuze has no concept of the other: 'Deleuze writes a philosophy of (virtual) difference without (actual) others'. Concrete historical time or actuality cannot, according to Hallward, be taken into account, and Deleuze's emphasis on the loss of the subject is considered here as a 'politicide'.[3] In the conclusion of his book, Hallward explicitly advises those who 'still seek to change the world and to empower its inhabitants' to look elsewhere. A more devastating 'philocide' is hard to imagine. Many have already commented elaborately on the one-sidedness of Hallward's reading of Deleuze (Shaviro 2007; Seigworth 2007). But Hallward's reading of Deleuzian philosophy of creation does bring together the main postcolonial critiques concerning the lack of political accountability of Deleuzian philosophy, and clearly indicates that abstract notions such as 'the virtual' and 'the impersonal' are problematically situated 'out of this world'.

Politics in Schizoanalysis and the Virtual

It is striking how consistently all the references to the complexity and the multiple layers of social and political reality in Deleuze and Guattari's work are downplayed in these various charges against Deleuze. In fact, it is quite obvious that politics is present on almost every page of Deleuze and Guattari's philosophy, especially in their work on capitalism and schizophrenia. The very notion of schizoanalysis describes a sociopolitical investment. As Deleuze points out in his essay 'Schizophrenia and Society', the delirium of the schizo is 'overflowing with history' and it is 'composed of politics and economics' (Deleuze 2007: 26). And in answer to the criticism that schizoanalysis entails escape from concrete socio-political reality, Deleuze and Guattari state: 'To those who say escaping is not courageous, we answer: what is not escape *and social investment at the same time?*' (Deleuze and Guattari 1984: 341; original emphasis). Furthermore, there are several instances in which Deleuze and Guattari have expressed themselves explicitly about political issues, such as the public debates around the Palestinian situation (Deleuze 2007).[4] I will return to this connection to concrete politics in reference to the films of Suleiman.

Another problem that immediately should be cleared in response to the postcolonial critiques is the conception of the virtual as something 'out of this world' and as 'not related to actual reality'. This is simply a classic misunderstanding of virtuality, in which the virtual is considered to be opposed to the actual. In fact, the virtual is always connected to the actual, but in a far more intimate way than by opposition. In a posthumously published text, 'The Virtual and the Actual', Deleuze argues that 'every actual is surrounded by a mist of virtual images', just like every 'virtual reacts on the actual' (Deleuze 1996: 179–180; my translation). The Bergsonian movements of the present that passes (actual) and the past that preserves itself (virtual) are tightly interwoven (in 'actualisations' and 'crystallisations'); this is particularly relevant in contemporary image culture where all images (actual and virtual) refer to other images (actual and virtual). In a Deleuzian system of thought it is wrong to see the virtual as 'out of this world' – the virtual is an immanent force that has to be taken into account in *this* world. The consequence of this circulation between the virtual and the actual is that the virtual is also real (albeit on a more invisible level – in our minds, in memories, in fantasy/ imagination, in the invisible layers of images and culture). The important and political point in Deleuze's philosophy is precisely that he proposes a different conception of the relationship between 'reality' (actual) and 'imagination' (virtual) than has previously been posited through the concepts of representation and ideology. How to conceive this relation between the virtual, actual and reality in a politically accountable way is a critical question that postcolonialism asks, and which I will concretely engage with by referring to Suleiman's *Divine Intervention*.

Violence of the Burlesque: The Laughter-Emotion Circuit

In both *Chronicle of a Disappearance* (1996) and *Divine Intervention* (2002), Elia Suleiman returns to his native village, Nazareth in Palestine, which he presents in fragmented, sometimes *tableaux vivants*-like scenes. In both films he is the speechless protagonist who acts as a silent mediator looking at the world, receiving images from the world and giving them back to us filtered through his consciousness.[5]

Both films have been described in relation to the passive energy of the protagonist/director, which he appears incapable of extending into action. *Chronicle of a Disappearance* 'measures the gradual disappearance, following the Oslo Agreement, of Palestinian identity and agency in Israel . . . the main sense of the film is of passivity, infighting (reflecting the corruption of the newly established Palestinian Authority), and paralysis' (Marks 2000: 60). In *Divine Intervention* there is also 'no progression, development or resolution . . . Progression has no currency here, there is only action and reversal, an endless dialectic of aggression and response . . . there is no narrative structure to perform a revelation of "truth" that suggest an appeal to justice. There is simply repetition, accumulation of acts and no "greater" meaning' (Harbord 2007: 157–8).

This dimension of inertia and passivity in the performance of the director/protagonist can alternatively be seen more actively, as a performative style that creates a distance from his own subjectivity, which turns his 'absent' and silent acting into a 'politics of the impersonal' that is also at the heart of Deleuzian philosophy (see also Schérer 1998). In his last text, 'Immanence: A Life', Deleuze pays homage to the impersonal qualities of a life:

> The life of the individual gives way to an impersonal and yet singular life that releases a pure event freed from the accidents of internal and external life, that is, from the subjectivity and objectivity of what happens: a 'Homo Tantum' with whom everyone empathizes and who attains a sort of beatitude (Deleuze 2001: 28).

Now, this impersonal dimension of the immanence of life could indeed be taken for an 'abstraction from reality' or 'cosmic vitalism out of this world' that postcolonial critics find problematic in Deleuze. So let's have a closer and more concrete look at *Divine Intervention* to see how Suleiman addresses concrete political reality while going beyond representation and beyond any notion of the subject and signification.

Suleiman's style could be described as a 'small form' (ASA') of the action-image as described by Deleuze in *The Movement-Image* (Deleuze 1986: 160–77).[6] His unspeaking face resembles Buster Keaton, but in the way he performs and films, Suleiman is an heir of Charlie Chaplin. As Deleuze argues, the genius of Chaplin is that

> because he knows how to invent the minimum difference between two well-chosen actions, he is also able to create the maximum distance between the corresponding situations, the one achieving emotion, the other reaching pure comedy. It is a laughter-emotion circuit, in which the one refers to the slight difference, the other to great distance, without the one obliterating or diminishing the other, but both interchanging with one another, triggering each other off again. (Deleuze 1986: 171)

Likewise every scene in *Divine Intervention* is set up to play with several associations or double meanings of the visual scene that creates, with a minimum of difference, a maximum of effect. The first time we see the protagonist in *Divine Intervention* (at the beginning of the second part of the film) he is driving in his car, eating an apricot. We see him in profile, filmed close from the interior of the car. When he has finished the apricot, he throws the stone out of the window. It's a very simple and ordinary gesture. The image then cuts to a position outside the car. From a distance we see the car driving and we hear the stone of the apricot hitting something hard. A giant tanker on the side of the road is briefly visible. At the sound of the apricot stone hitting it, it suddenly explodes. The image becomes a giant sea of fire. The protagonist does not notice the effect of his small gesture. He only chucked out the stone of his fruit. He continues to drive. The contradiction between the small gesture and the enormous effect it has creates a Chaplinesque effect. We enter a laughter-emotion circuit, or more precisely a laughter-violence circuit, that is as comic as it is shocking.

Here we have an 'impersonal performance'; the director embodying his character as a man eating an apricot has nothing to do with his own subjective self, while at the same time he traces lines of life and lines of resistance that have everything to do with a life in Palestine. In this burlesque political style, the question of the film's reference to reality is not irrelevant. But it is delegated to the spectator to decide how many layers of reality she wants to see. Of course, the sudden appearance of a tanker on a deserted road is significant, and its explosion is as well. Paradoxically the blowing up of a tanker can be seen as a pacifist gesture. The scene can be read as a figure of thought as well (the stone of the apricot symbolises stones of the intifada; the tanker can be read as a symbol for Israeli occupying forces). In itself, the whole scene is hilariously absurd, which could be read allegorically as the absurdity of the whole political situation. These readings are not necessary for the viewer to enjoy the scene, but the possible layers of significance add to the 'pleasure and pains' of watching the film. It is not a matter of reality being in a limbo, but a matter of the virtuality surrounding the actual images that make them ever more powerful and infuse the images with socio-political and historical layers. This is the immanence of the virtual at work. And it is very political.

Many other instances can be identified to show the various ways in which Suleiman plays with ambiguities and multiple meanings in the images that make the film work in the mind of the spectator. Just before the apricot scene, we have seen three men in a garden violently hitting something on the ground with sticks. The camera is at a distance and the garden is fenced, so we don't know exactly what they are beating. 'Knock out the vermin,' we hear one of them say. Watching this scene, infamous video-images of Israeli soldiers hitting Palestinians start resonating in our brains. Then a fourth man arrives with a gun and shoots at the 'vermin' on the ground. More images of beating and killings that circulate on YouTube pop up from our virtual/mental storage rooms. Then we see how one of the men takes two sticks and picks up the poisonous snake they just killed . . . The difference of the actual image from all the virtual images that had crossed our minds is small, but the difference in the actual situation is enormous. Again Suleiman has played with the 'mist of virtual images' that surrounds the actual images he is showing.

A final example from *Divine Intervention* occurs at the end of the film, where the protagonist stops at a traffic light. On one side of the road he looks at a giant billboard that invites Israelis (over the image of a woman covered in a Palestinian Arafat shawl) to 'come and shoot when they are ready'. On the other side, next to him, a man wearing a kippah stops in his car, the Israeli flag waving on the roof top. Our protagonist opens the window, puts on a music cassette, and looks (dark sunglasses shading his eyes) at the man in the car next to him. While Natasha Atlas sings her Arabic trance version of 'I put a spell on you', they keep on staring at each other, traffic lights turning green and then red again, until the cars behind them start to hoot. It's a fight without words, without violence, a fight of pure image and sound, an exchange of blank looks and music. The scene immediately following this one shows two forcefully gripping hands in extreme close-up. This is easily taken as a metaphoric commentary on the fight between the two men we just saw, or even the two countries. But just when we allow that reading of the image sequence, the frame shifts and it now appears to be the protagonist helping his sick father get out of bed in the hospital where he is being treated after a heart attack. And then this image of the 'wrestling/helping hands' starts to resonate with a scene from *Chronicle of a Disappearance* where we see Suleiman's (real and still healthy) father's hand wrestling with his friend's, and (almost) always winning. Whereas in other scenes, the images that seem to be private or ordinary turn out to be (virtually) political, here an image that seems to be very political turns out to be a very private affair. The actual image of the father's hand as he is being helped out of bed is reminiscent of the strong hands he used to have. At the end of the film the father dies. The virtual brings in the notion of generational time.

All these scenes indicate the ways in which Suleiman reaches the impersonal dimension of immanent life by stepping back from both himself and from the political situation, as he constantly shifts between events in his personal life and observations that have collective and political resonances. He creates images that enter into circuits of the virtual and the actual and therefore are 'swept towards the asubjective' (Deleuze and Guattari 1988: 187). He does this on the one hand by employing a burlesque composition of the image typical for the small form of the action-image. Suleiman's inert performance and the images that open up to so many virtual dimensions could perhaps be considered as the 'burlesque of the time-image'. On the other hand his films can also be considered as a modern political cinema of the time-image.

Political Cinema: Fabulation and Double-Becoming

In *The Time-Image* Deleuze refers to modern political cinema, especially films that address contemporary political issues such as decolonisation, migration and globalisation (Deleuze 1989: 215–24). Consistent with Deleuze's conception of cinema as movement-images and time-images that have an immanent power independent of representation, this modern political cinema does not represent reality, but instead operates as a performative speech act that plays a part in constructing reality (Pisters 2006: 175–93). In a postcolonial world that is characterised by fragmentation, migration, transnational movements and intercultural encounters, some postcolonial scholars including Stuart Hall have suggested that representation in the classic sense is no longer possible or even desirable, instead commonly constituting a 'burden of representation' (Hall 1996: 441–9). The political accountability of these images is necessarily situated on the level of their power to do something (if only to affect us and cause debate) *to* reality, rather than on the level of accurate representation *in or as* reality. For the filmmaker, this implies that he should not try to *represent* a people, but his 'fabulating' films can contribute to the *creation* of a people. Fabulations are forms of story-telling that are 'neither impersonal myth but neither personal fiction' (Deleuze 1989: 222). The relation between the filmmaker and his characters is one of becoming: '[T]he author takes one step towards his characters, but the characters take one step towards the author: double-becoming' (Deleuze 1989: 222).

In his films, Elia Suleiman is both director and character, and in that sense this double-becoming takes place in his own performance where he becomes his character. *Chronicle of a Disappearance* and *Divine*

Intervention are modern political films that create fabulations between the personal and the collective, between the objective and subjective, between fiction and reality, expressing and addressing *both* the actual *and* the virtual as part of reality. In an interview, Suleiman discusses his way of working and the way in which he wants to renew the story of Palestine with his films. He explicitly addresses the question of fiction and reality, arguing that a film is real (it exists), and also that dreaming and the imagination is part of reality:

> What I'm trying to do is bring the imagination down and put the supposed reality up so that they are moving on the same, let's say, strata. There is no rupture between one and the other, but they are blurred territory. The spectator imagines and decides him or herself what's real and what is not real. This is always an open question, we can never know for sure. (A-Film 2003)

Suleiman's reference to the 'strata' and (at another moment in the interview) the layers (that is, the virtual, memories, associations) in his images, corresponds to Deleuze's argument that time-images can link up in an infinite number of ways and therefore become 'stratigraphic':

> In this sense, the archaeological, or stratigraphic, image is *read* at the same time as it is seen . . . Not in the sense that it used to be said; to perceive *is* to know, is to imagine, is to recall, but in the sense that reading is a function of the eye, a perception of perception, a perception which does not grasp perception without also grasping its reverse, imagination, memory, or knowledge. (Deleuze 1989: 243)

Deleuze here calls for a new analytic of the image, reading the stratigraphic condition of the image in all its richness and virtuality. This implies a different relation to the political than has traditionally been sought through representation.

As Deleuze has argued, the modern political film is based on the condition that 'the people are what is missing' (Deleuze 1989: 215). Nowhere is this political fact of a 'missing people' more explicitly acknowledged in Deleuze's work than in the case of the Palestinian people. In a short article titled 'Stones', Deleuze writes:

> Europe owes its Jews an infinite debt that Europe has not even begun to pay. Instead, an innocent people is being made to pay – the Palestinians . . . We are to believe that the State of Israel has been established in an empty land which has been awaiting the return of ancient Hebrews for centuries. The ghosts of a few Arabs that are around, keeping watch over the sleepy stones, came from somewhere else. The Palestinians – tossed aside, forgotten – have been called on to recognize the right of Israel to exist, while

the Israelis have continued to deny the fact of the existence of a Palestine people. (Deleuze 2007: 338)

Suleiman's films are modern political films in that they contribute to the 'invention' of a missing people, by 'renewing its story' in a non-representational and impersonal, stratigraphic way that allows a free play between reality and imagination, memory and knowledge, with often humorous and empowering effects. A most powerful symbol of that empowerment through imagination is a pink balloon that the protagonist in *Divine Intervention* inflates in his car at a checkpoint in Ramallah where he meets his female (Israeli) lover from across the checkpoint. As the balloon grows bigger, the face of Arafat becomes visible and grows bigger.[7] Then the rooftop of the car opens and the balloon escapes, crossing the checkpoint. Leaving the Israeli soldiers baffled and waiting for orders to act on a balloon crossing the border unauthorised, the balloon travels over Jerusalem to land softly on top of the golden mosque.

Besides the burlesque strategy that puts us in a politically engaged circuit of laughter-emotions, the stratigraphic conflation of imagination and reality is another way in which the political is taken into account in a virtual/actual circuit. One does not need to be a Deleuzian to 'disentangle' these layers. It's precisely that they cannot be disentangled and that they are always mixed that makes the film so powerful, both aesthetically and politically. It's just that Deleuze provides useful concepts, such as the paradoxical combination of the laughter-emotion circuit, the impersonal fabulating powers of political cinema and the stratigraphic layering of (political) images, that makes his work very useful for understanding the complex interweaving of the virtual and the actual in contemporary media culture.

Nomadic Thinking: Mixing Codes, Outside/Intensity, Humour

Arguably, it is Deleuze's concept of the nomad that has most stirred postcolonial debates about the politics of his philosophy. The idea of nomadic thought and nomadic subjectivity 'have led to a plethora of work within poststructuralist theorizing that strongly privileges notions of mobility, movement and becoming over conceptions of being, essence or stable subjectivity' (Wuthnow 2002: 184). As previously indicated, a general concern with this poststructuralist conception of the 'nomad' is that it becomes yet another unmarked universalised Western subject that does not acknowledge the voice and experience of the (indigenous or minoritarian) other: it marginalises local knowledges and experiences and poses another abstract binary opposition between state and nomadic 'war machines'.[8] Taking these objections seriously, let's look again at Deleuze's essay 'Nomadic Thought', in which he describes the basic principles of this concept, in order to discern whether and how these principles are translated in *Divine Intervention*.[9] Here, I think it is important to emphasise that I am not 'applying' a theory to a work of art. Rather, what I'm trying to do is to see how philosophy and non-philosophy, art and non-art, understand each other, as was called for in *What is Philosophy?* (Deleuze and Guattari 1994: 218).

'Nomadic Thought' was published in 1973 and is developed around the question of the importance of Nietzsche for the contemporary world. Deleuze points out that Nietzsche's first concern is to address cultural codes (family codes, state codes) in a new way, for the purpose of 'getting something through in every past, present, and future code, something which does not and will not let itself be recoded. Getting it through on a new body, inventing a body on which it can pass and flow' (Deleuze 2004: 253). This process can be developed by 'mixing up all the codes', an activity which is especially noticeable in an artistic style (a style of writing, a style of filming). Deleuze argues that this mixing up of codes into something new and uncodeable, is 'what style as politics means' (Deleuze 2004: 254). This is what he calls 'the beginning of the nomadic adventure' (2004: 260). Accordingly, it is important to see how Deleuze defines nomadic thought as an artistic experimentation in style that nevertheless has political relevance, precisely because of its escaping of codes.

In this sense, *Divine Intervention* is a nomadic adventure, not because it represents a 'nomadic' ('fragmented, multiplied, in flux') people, but because it mixes several codes. If the dominant code in cinema is Hollywood, this film plays with the cinematographic codes and escapes them by seeking to 'Breson-ianise *The Matrix*. I wanted to break away from the ghettoisation between the *auteur* film and commercial cinema . . . You can entertain aesthetically, politically, authorially. Entertainment is not necessarily superficial or ephemeral' (A-film 2003). The scenes previously discussed demonstrate the ways in which Suleiman mixes expected codes to create something new by bringing the actual and the virtual, private and public, and violence and laughter together in challenging mixed circuits.

The scene that most clearly mixes the stylistic codes of the *auteur* film, the political film and Hollywood, and also the codes of religion, politics and pop culture, is the much discussed scene at the end of the film where Israeli soldiers are training to shoot, firing at targets which depict the image of a Palestinian woman – previously seen on the billboard – dressed in a long black 'Matrix' coat and covered in a Palestinian shawl. This image on the billboard observed by Suleiman when driving in Israel is described as a 'sparkle from reality', which he took 'up' into the realm of the imagination by making the movements of the soldiers more like choreographed dances and the image of the woman come alive and enter into a martial arts combat scene. As Janet Harbord describes:

> [T]he action sequence of a human figure rising magically into aerial combat recalls the martial arts set pieces of recent transnational films, the potency of the body matched with special effects, a particular configuration of technology and the body from popular film. This is mixed with the symbols of a Palestinian national state, and the Christian reference as a reminder of the history of this space as a 'Holy land'. In the moment of magical breakthrough, the thick effects of space-time are in condensed form, as though the past and present appear together, hovering over this site as a visionary, out-of-time apprehension. (Harbord 2007: 159)

A second principle of nomadism that Deleuze distinguishes in 'Nomadic Thought' is its relation to 'the outside'. This principle does not refer to a state of being or of thinking that is 'out of this world'. On the contrary, it refers to the ways in which a work of art shares something with experiences 'outside' of its apparent frame of reference: the principle of the outside is therefore related to the opening up of a philosophical text, a work of art or a film to the forces of life outside the text. Deleuze evokes the psychoanalyst Winnicot who realises at a certain point that he is no longer translating, interpreting fantasies into signifiers and signified, but he has put himself in the patient's shoes. In the same way philosopher and artist do not simply represent reality, but share in the experiences they present:

> We are in the same boat: a sort of lifeboat, bombs falling on every side, the lifeboat drifts toward subterranean rivers of ice, or toward rivers of fire, the Orinoco, the Amazon, everyone is pulling an oar, and we're not even supposed to like one another, we fight, we eat each other. Everyone pulling an oar is sharing, sharing something, beyond any law, any contract, any institution. Drifting, a drifting movement or 'deterritorialization'. (Deleuze 2004: 255)

As Deleuze points out, we find something beautiful when it relates to something beyond 'its frame':

> What is this: a beautiful painting or a beautiful drawing? There is a frame. An aphorism has a frame, too. But whatever is in the frame, at what point

does it become beautiful? At the moment one knows and feels that the movement, that the line which is framed comes from elsewhere, that it does not begin within the limits of the frame. It began above, or next to the frame . . . Far from being the limitation of the pictorial surface, the frame is almost the opposite, putting it into immediate relation with the outside. (Deleuze 2004: 255)

The outside opens up the interiority of the text or the image, relating it to the invisible because virtual, but very real, forces in the world. At other instances in Deleuze's thought these virtual forces are related to a universal consciousness of becoming-minoritarian, and also to the external forces of the body without organs (BwO), that can however only be experienced as forces of intensity acting upon a body. Intensity is thus a third principle of nomadism, closely related to the outside:

> The lived experience is not subjective, or not necessarily. It is not of the individual. It is flow and the interruption of flow, since each intensity is necessarily in relation to another intensity. In such a way that something gets through. This is what is underneath the codes, what escapes them, and what the codes want to translate, convert, cash in. But what Nietzsche is trying to tell us by this writing of intensities is: don't exchange the intensity for representation. (Deleuze 2004: 257)

In this nomadic way, the images and the performing body of the filmmaker in *Divine Intervention* open up to the intensive forces of love and pain outside the frame of the film. Love for the land, love for the father, love for a woman, pain for the land, pain for the violence and frustrations in the Israeli–Palestine conflict, pain for a lost love. Asked about the meaning of the title of his film, Suleiman's answer in the DVD interview is nomadic, in that it indicates a poetic licence to mix codes. 'Divine intervention' does not so much refer to something holy, 'but to something close to that', namely imagination, that allows one to cross borders and checkpoints. When the protagonist loses both his father and his lover, the lover returns as an imaginary heroine. Whereas earlier in the film she has crossed the checkpoint just by walking past the soldiers in a sexy pink dress and high heels (which makes the watchtower collapse), in the 'ninja' scene at the end of the film she returns as comic and aestheticised violence that carves out a new story, a fabulated story, for the Palestinian people.

The subtitle of the film relates to Suleiman's previous film. Where *Chronicle of a Disappearance* clearly addresses the disappearance of Palestine (the final image of Suleiman's old parents having fallen asleep in front of the television set where the Israeli flag marks the end of a broadcasting day was the subject of much political comment), the subtitle of

Divine Intervention is *Chronicle of Love and Pain*. 'It grounds the film's imagination,' as Suleiman says, precisely by addressing lived experiences outside the frames of the image. Once more we see how the Divine and the Outside do not refer to an abstract virtual realm out of this world, but on the contrary, to an interpenetration of the world, the outside and intensity, within the text, the work of art and cinema.

In his seminal essay on nomadic thought, Deleuze indicates that humour is another characteristic of nomadism:

> Call it the 'comedy of the superhuman' or the 'clowning of God'. There is always an indescribable joy that springs from great books, even when they speak of ugly, desperate, or terrifying things . . . You cannot help but laugh when you mix up the codes. If you put thought in relation to the outside, Dionysian moments of laughter will erupt, and this is thinking in the clear air . . . Laughter in Nietzsche always harks back to the external movement of humours and ironies, and this is the movement of intensities. (Deleuze 2004: 258)

This playing with the codes and with spectators' coded expectations is clearly part of the joy of *Divine Intervention*, making it such a wonderful nomadic experience. Clearly, this experience does not literally take us on a journey, nor is it about a diasporic moving around of people. Even if the journey goes nowhere and takes place in a single space (the 'Holy land'), *Divine Intervention* infuses our perceptions and thoughts with its visionary nomadic and impersonal wanderings/wonderings. Its laughter is laughter in the midst of the intolerable, in the midst of violence, and hence is laughter that is necessarily and vitally related to the world.

The Splendour of the Impersonal: Violence and Laughter

I hope to have demonstrated that much of the postcolonial criticism of Deleuze is based on a misunderstanding of the Deleuzian concepts of the virtual and the impersonal as abstract notions that are opposed to concrete reality and figuratively expressed in terms of a conception of the nomad as a romanticised wanderer in constant flux without any roots. Granted, many of the concepts that Deleuze proposes are indeed slippery and multilayered, and their definitions and meanings change and develop in the course of his work, so such misinterpretations are likely to happen. Deleuze's concepts are indeed hard to accommodate within the usual postcolonial framework of political representation and the critique of ideology, since they operate within a wholly different philosophical framework of virtual becoming and actual being, rather than that of reality and ideology. But that does not mean that his work is apolitical. As I hope to have made clear by referring to a concrete 'nomadic' work of art, Deleuze's concepts have nothing to do with abstractions or escape from the world, but are related to fundamentally mixed states of the world and the mixed state of our perception and consciousness that is always layered with multiplicities, visions, memories, knowledge: in short, with virtualities. To clarify the difference between a representational framework and a nomadic framework of thinking and artistic practice, I would like to conclude by looking once more at the 'politics of the impersonal', by comparing the violence in *Divine Intervention* to the violence in a recent French television film, *Pour l'Amour de dieu* (Bouchaala and Tari 2006), that in a very different way, calls for some 'divine intervention'.

In an essay on Deleuze's impersonal politics, René Schérer explains that the impersonal power of Deleuze's philosophy of immanence implies a paradoxical logic. First of all the impersonal of 'a life' reveals itself most explicitly in a confrontation with death (Schérer 1998: 33).[10] Think here of the Dickens example, given by Deleuze in 'Immanence, A Life', of doctors trying to save the life of a rogue: 'Between his life and his death, there is a moment that is only that of *a* life playing with death' (Deleuze 2001: 28). A second paradox lies in the implication that the most original and authentic expression of 'self' can only be expressed by the impersonal, where 'I' has no longer a subjective significance. To illustrate such 'splendour of the impersonal', Schérer refers to the use of the impersonal pronoun '*on*' ('one') in a poem by Arthur Rimbaud: 'On n'est pas serieux quand on a dix-sept ans' ('One is not serious at seventeen'). This 'One' is not an 'I' nor a 'We', but the impersonal of 'anyone' that Rimbaud speaks of; it addresses anyone young and in love, an 'anyone' that is nobody in particular, and yet exists as any body (Schérer 1999: 36). This paradox of the impersonal sets the stage for many other paradoxes implied in nomadic thought, and is not easy to grasp from within a representational image of thought (Deleuze 1994).

The telefilm *Pour l'Amour de dieu* takes this poem by Rimbaud as its framing device. At the beginning of the film the poem is read in a classroom, and the teacher explains that when one is young one doesn't yet understand all the dimensions of love, life and the future. *Pour l'Amour de dieu* is a film that fits easily into a representational logic. It is the story of seventeen-year-olds Kevin and Meriem, both born in France of Algerian parents, thus representing second generation migrant youngsters. Kevin is attracted to Meriem because she practises the religion from which he is completely alienated. He feels lost in post-colonial French society and looks for certitude, pureness and pride, which he finds with his Islamist brothers who give him strict rules to which to adhere. He cannot see counter-messages from the Koran, instructing values such as tolerance, simplicity and freedom of religious choice. When Meriem returns from a visit to Algeria where she has seen her grandmother for the first time, Kevin, who now calls himself Mohammed, asks her to marry him. Referring to Rimbaud's poem again, she reminds him that they are too young, not only to marry but also to be able to decide upon more political issues such as whether or not to wear the headscarf (Meriem in fact decides to stop wearing a headscarf until she has developed a full understanding of all the dimensions entailed by such an act). Pushed by his friends, Kevin/Mohammed then kills Meriem, whom they consider unfaithful. In desperation, Kevin/Mohammed turns on the gas in the kitchen of the Islamist meeting point. When he reconsiders this act of violence and wants to call his friends to warn them, his eye catches a passage from the Koran that he could never see when Meriem quoted it: 'If God had wanted it, everybody would believe.' Kevin/Mohamed breaks down, imprisoned in a phone box that frames him in his failed attempt to create a stable self.

Pour l'Amour de dieu relates in a much more identifiable way to contemporary political reality, where terrorist fundamentalism is a serious challenge to society.[11] The film addresses these problems, and oppositional religious and political positions register a simple representation of contemporary postcolonial problems. Not understanding the impersonal 'one' of Rimbaud's poem, and replacing it with a destructive identity quest, he can only find a 'way out' when he breaks down, leaving a trail of violence without any laughter.

In his essay on violence, Fanon showed that violence was necessarily part of national decolonisation processes, as 'the naked truth of decolonization that evoked the searing bullets and bloodstained knives which emanate from it' (Fanon 1963: 3). In an ideological representational framework, this violence has turned into a postcolonial religious violence, where God is called upon as a higher authority to justify human judgemental and avenging violence. Here we have a call for some divine power 'out of this world', which does not seem to bring anything good, or any change of perception, or a restoration of a positive belief in this world. In his essay on violence, Fanon acknowledges that in the end violence makes life, any life, impossible, and that it is necessary to reintroduce mankind into the world. Fanon explicitly addresses European peoples to help in this project: 'To achieve this, the European people must first decide to wake up and shake themselves, use their brains, and stop playing the stupid game of Sleeping Beauty' (Fanon 1963: 106). It is for that reason that nomadic thought and nomadic political art is of extreme importance. By affecting us on an impersonal level, the universal level of 'one', anyone can be reached by the paradoxical pleasures and pains of violence and laughter, and as such, change established visions of the actual world, restoring our belief in a 'divine intervention' that belongs to this world, though is not the property of any one in particular, and yet, paradoxically, helps to create a people that are missing.

References

Ashcroft, B., G. Griffiths and H. Tiffin (1998), *Post-Colonial Studies: The Key Concepts*, London and New York: Routledge.
Bhabha, H. (1994), *The Location of Culture*, London and New York: Routledge.
Bogue, R. (2004), 'Apology for Nomadology', *Interventions* 6 (2): 169–79.
Braidotti, R. (1994), *Nomadic Subjects: Embodiment and Sexual Difference in Contemporary Feminist Theory*, New York: Columbia University Press.
Deleuze, G. (1986), *Cinema 1: The Movement-Image*, trans. H. Tomlinson and B. Habberjam, London: Athlone.
Deleuze, G. (1989), *Cinema 2: The Time-Image*, trans. H. Tomlinson and R. Galeta, London: Athlone.
Deleuze, G. (1994), *Difference and Repetition*, trans. P. Patton, London: Athlone.
Deleuze, G. (1996), 'L'Actuel et le Virtuel', in G. Deleuze and C. Parnet, *Dialogues*, Paris: Flammarion, pp. 180–1.
Deleuze, G. (1998), *Essays Critical and Clinical*, trans. D. Smith and M. Greco, London and New York: Verso.
Deleuze, G. (2001), *Pure Immanence: Essays on a Life*, trans. A. Boyman, New York: Zone Books.
Deleuze, G. (2004), *Desert Islands and Other Texts 1953–1974*, trans. M. Taormina, New York and Los Angeles: Semiotext(e).
Deleuze, G. (2007), *Two Regimes of Madness. Texts and Interviews 1975–1995*, trans. M. Taormina, New York and Los Angeles: Semiotext(e).
Deleuze, G. and F. Guattari (1984), *Anti-Oedipus: Capitalism and Schizophrenia*, trans. R. Hurley, M. Seem and H. R. Lane, London: Athlone.
Deleuze, G. and F. Guattari (1988), *A Thousand Plateaus: Capitalism and Schizophrenia*, trans. B. Massumi, London: Athlone.
Deleuze, G. and F. Guattari (1994), *What is Philosophy?*, trans. G. Burchell and H. Tomlinson, London and New York: Verso.
Fanon, F. (1963), *The Wretched of the Earth*, trans. C. Farrington, New York: Grove Press.
Hall, S. (1996), 'New Ethnicities', in D. Morley and K. Chen (eds), *Critical Dialogues in Cultural Studies*, London: Routledge, pp. 441–9.
Hallward, P. (2001), *Absolutely Postcolonial: Writing between the Singular and the Specific*, Manchester: Manchester University Press.
Hallward, P. (2006), *Out of this World: Deleuze and the Philosophy of Creation*, London and New York: Verso.
Harbord, J. (2007), *The Evolution of Film: Rethinking Film Studies*, Cambridge and Malden: Polity Press.
Marks, L. (2000), *The Skin of Film: Intercultural Cinema, Embodiment, and the Senses*, Durham and London: Duke University Press.
Middelaar, L. van (1999), *Politicide: De Moord op de Politiek in de Franse Filosofie*, Amsterdam: Van Gennep.

Miller, C. (1993), 'The Postidentitarian Predicament in the Footnotes of *A Thousand Plateaus*: Nomadology, Anthropology, and Authority', *Diacritics* 23 (3): 6–35.
Miller, C. (2003), 'We shouldn't Judge Deleuze and Guattari: A Response to Eugene Holland', *Research in African Literature* 34 (3): 129–41.
Patton, P. (2000), *Deleuze and the Political*, London and New York: Routledge.
Pisters, P. (2006), 'Arresting the Flux of Images and Sounds: Free Indirect Discourse and the Dialectics of Political Cinema', in I. Buchanan and A. Parr (eds), *Deleuze and the Contemporary World*, Edinburgh: Edinburgh University Press, pp. 175–94.
Said, E. (1978), *Orientalism*, New York and Toronto: Random House.
Schérer, R. (1998), '*Homo tantum* – L'impersonnel: une politique', in E. Alliez (ed.), *Gilles Deleuze, une vie philosophique*, Paris: Institut Synthélabo, pp. 25–42.
Seigworth, G. (2007), 'Little Affect: Hallward's Deleuze'. Viewed at http://rime.tees.ac.uk/cmach/Reviews/rev65.htm
Shaviro, S. (2007), 'Hallward on Deleuze'. Viewed at http://www.shaviro.com/Blog/?p=567
Spivak, G. (1983), 'Displacement and the Discourse of Woman', in Mark Krupnik (ed.), *Displacement, Derrida and After*, Bloomington: Indiana University Press: pp. 169–95.
Spivak, G. (1994), 'Can the Subaltern Speak?', in P. Williams and L. Chrisman (eds), *Colonial Discourse and Post-Colonial Theory. A Reader*, New York: Columbia University Press, pp. 66–112.
Young, R. (1995), *Colonial Desire: Hybridity in Theory, Culture and Race*, London and New York: Routledge.
Wuthnow, J. (2002), 'Deleuze in the Postcolonial: On Nomads and Indigenous Politics', *Feminist Theory* 3: 183–99.

Filmography

Chronicle of a Disappearance (Palestine/Israel/Germany/France, 1996)
Dir./Writ. Elia Suleiman; Cam. Marc-Andre Batigne; Ed. Anna Ruiz; Prod. Asaf Amir/Elia Suleiman; Cast: Elia Suleiman, Nazira Suleiman, Fuad Suleiman, Jamel Daher a.o.
http://www.imdb.com/title/tt0115895/
http://en.wikipedia.org/wiki/Chronicle_of_a_Disappearance
DVD-distribution A-Film (www.A-Film.nl)
Divine Intervention. Chronicle of Love and Pain (France /Morocco/Germany/Palestine, 2003)
Dir./Writ. Elia Suleiman; Cam. Marc-Andre Batigne; Ed. Veronique Lange; Prod. Humbert Balsan/Elia Suleiman; Cast: Elia Suleiman, Manal Kadher, a.o.
http://www.imdb.com/title/tt0274428/
http://en.wikipedia.org/wiki/Divine_Intervention_(film)
DVD-distribution A-Film (www.A-Film.nl)
Pour l'amour de dieu (France, 2006)
Dir./Writ. Ahmed Bouchaala and Zakia Thari; Cam. Laurent Brunet; Ed. Julien Leloup; Prod. David Kodsi ; Cast Rachid Hami, Leila Bekhti a.o.
http://www.imdb.com/title/tt0765838/

Notes

1. Modified translation quoted from Daniel Smith's introduction to Deleuze's *Essays Critical and Clinical* (1998: iii).

2. While Foucault has been an important influence on Edward Said's seminal starting point of (post)colonial theory *Orientalism* (1978), postcolonial studies have been profoundly influenced by Derrida's philosophy of deconstruction (Spivak 1983, 1994; Bhabha 1994). Deleuze and Guattari have not consistently been taken up in a postcolonial context, with the exception of Peter Hallward's recent work (2001; 2006); the concept of desire in the work of Robert Young on colonial desire (1995); and the concept of the rhizome in relation to the organisation of imperial power (Ashcroft et al. 1998). In most cases whenever Deleuze is referred to within the context of postcolonial studies, it is in a very negative way.
3. Dutch philosopher Luuk van Middelaar argues in his book *Politicide* that Deleuze's desiring machines would create 5 billion Crusoes, each tyrant on his own sand plate (van Middelaar 1999). According to Van Middelaar all twentieth-century philosophy is politically useless.
4. 'The Indians of Palestine' was published in *Libération* (1982); 'The Importance of Being Arafat' in *Revue d'Études Palestiniennes* (1984); and 'Stones' in *Al-Karmel* (1988). See Deleuze 2007: 194–200; 241–5; 338–9).
5. In the episode *Homage by Assassination* (1992) from *The Gulf War ... What's Next?* Suleiman is also the silent protagonist. He is currently working on his film *The Time that Remains*.
6. Deleuze distinguishes two forms of the action-image in *The Movement-Image*:

> The large form – SAS' – moved from the situation to the action which modified the situation. But there is another form, which, on the contrary, moves from the action to the situation, towards a new action: ASA'. This time it is the action which discloses the situation, a fragment of an aspect of the situation, which triggers a new action. The action advances blindly and the situation is disclosed in darkness, or in ambiguity. From action to action, the situation gradually emerges, varies, and finally either becomes clear or retains its mystery. (1986: 160)

7. In 'The Importance of Being Arafat' Deleuze discusses the importance of the PLO and the symbolic function of its leader. Here he emphasises the Palestinian desire to be 'a people like any other people, that's all we want to be' as opposed to the Israeli claim to be 'a people not like any other' (Deleuze 2007: 244).
8. In her essay, Julie Wuthnow specifically takes issue with the conceptions of the nomad in the work of Rosi Braidotti (1994) and Paul Patton (2000).
9. Ronald Bogue has taken up this criticism by looking into the *de jure* and *de facto* principles and definitions of 'the nomad' (Bogue 2004).
10. 'Et ces deux puissances impliquent une logique paradoxale: la première est la révélation *d'une vie* par la mort; la seconde est que la plus originale et authentique expression de "soi", la plus singulière, ne se conquiert que par l'impersonnel' (Schérer 1998: 33)
11. In his article on Arafat and the PLO, Deleuze in the 1980s argued that the 'disappearance' of the Palestinians as a people will give in to a double terrorism, a state and a religious terrorism 'which will make any chance of a peaceful settlement with Israel impossible' (Deleuze 2007: 245). Seen the important symbolic function of the Palestinian people for the Arabic and Islamic world, the rise of religious terrorism in the twenty-first century can (at least partly) be connected to the missing of the Palestinian people.

Chapter 10

The Production of *Terra Nullius* and the Zionist-Palestinian Conflict

Marcelo Svirsky

On the evening of 30 May 2007, the municipality of the city of Acre – one of the few mixed Jewish-Arab cities in Israel – removed metallic Arabic letters spelling *Akka*, the city's name in Arabic, from the official sign at the east entrance to the city. These had been inlaid the previous day by leftist activists in response to the municipality's omission of the Arabic inscription on the official sign. A week after the event, the activists returned and placed another sign, at the same site, with the caption, '*Acre For All Its Inhabitants*', in Hebrew and Arabic, as well as the Arabic letters for *Akka*. This, too, was immediately removed by local police – but a few days later the municipality finally inscribed the name *Akka* in Arabic, as well as an English transliteration of the Hebrew name, *Akko*. A small victory was achieved in the struggle for recognition of the Arab presence in Israel. But why did the municipality of Acre not prepare a signpost that respected all the city's inhabitants in the first place?

At first glance this episode is about deliberate and blatant disregard of Arab sensibilities, but closer inspection reveals the fundamental drives that produce these characteristic practices of symbolic disregard. I believe the Acre municipality did not deliberately set out to ignore the Arab-Palestinian inhabitants of the city, and moreover, the municipality does not assume Arab-Palestinians in Acre are undeserving of symbolic representation as part of the city. More importantly, what underlies this episode of lack of recognition is a hegemonic collective state of mind – unconsciously constructed over time and through experience – that directs flows of alienation towards the Arab-Palestinian residents of Acre. How can we expect the Palestinian to be conceived as an integral part of the welcome signpost to the city when the majority of residents are like blind, marching bodies, with no room in their hearts or minds for the other?

The important point is that the lack of recognition of the Arab presence in Acre is but one of many recurring incidents of wilful disregard that have characterised Zionist practices for a hundred years or so. My aim is to explain how these diverse incidents, though varied in nature, have an underlying family resemblance and how they are symptomatic of a certain *sense* that goes beyond the consciousness of people. I will argue that Zionism as a practice, and more specifically the practice of sovereign Zionism since the birth of the State of Israel, habitually conjoins the deterritorialised resources of the former Mandatory Palestine with those of the Palestinian community, and appropriates the surplus arising from monopolistic reterritorialisations (Holland 1999: 19–20) for the exclusive use of the Jewish citizenry. At the overt political level, this subjugation of life through a set of ethnically-based axioms is evident in social arrangements that produce a systematic fusion of extensive and intensive discrimination against the Arab-Palestinian citizens.[1] Together with a spatial logic of ethnic segmentation, this has given rise to a governmentality of ethnic exclusion that is present in every area of life (Lustick 1980; Shafir 1989; Kretzmer 1990; Falah 1991; Peled and Shafir 2002; Davis 2003; Yiftachel 2006). This set of conditions, it will be argued, derives from the particular way in which the Zionist fabric has developed and articulated the Palestinian entity through specific assemblages of a collective desire, which actively produces the *effective incremental disappearance of the other*. This mode of social-political functioning can be understood by examining the colonial concept of *terra nullius*.

In revisiting the concept of *terra nullius*, I draw on Deleuze and Guattari's understanding of philosophy as the creation of concepts enabling better comprehension of the operations in our lives (Deleuze and Guattari 1994). The aim is to recreate and transform this concept to offer alternative perspectives for considering hitherto unevaluated aspects of this particular post-colonial conflict. The original meaning of the concept of *terra nullius* is derived from its interconnections with the family of concepts relating to the European colonial event; but its history changes as different incarnations of colonialism created new becomings of the concept – it 'zigzags, though it passes, if need be, through other problems or onto different planes' (Deleuze and Guattari 1994: 18, 79). In the context of the present study, *terra nullius* is linked specifically to the problem of the *disappearance of the other*, interpreted here as the continuing social production of collective displacement-and-replacement within a particular form of settler-colonialism – Zionism. From its legalistic discursive functions within the history of colonial theory, *terra nullius* is transformed within this colonial context, replacing its previous contents and function in order to become a productive social machine.

My intention is to observe the genealogical orientation of the Zionism-bearing forces as both a socio-historical phenomenon and an immanent event. The aim is not to offer another theoretical representation of Zionism through modelling (for example, Jewish-and-democratic, ethnocracy, ethnic democracy, bi-national state, and so forth) or to evaluate its ideological dimensions vis-à-vis reality, but rather to decipher the *sense*, the course or 'directive power' (Patton 2000: 45) of the phenomenon of Zionism as a specific form of modern colonial politics. In Deleuzian terms, this *sense* bespeaks the event of colonial Zionism and explains action and speech within Zionist practice. It will be argued that the *sense* of the Zionist event is manifest – to the extent of its relationship to the Palestinian entity – in the operations of *terra nullius* as an assemblage, a concrete arrangement of things that execute movements both of deterritorialisation – transforming the nature of things and their inner relationship – and of reterritorialisation, 'which tend[s] to fix and stabilise its elements' (Patton 2000: 44), both corporeal and discursive. The unconscious and collective operation of Zionist desire, as perceived through the abstract machines of *terra nullius*, continues to capture a given historical tract of civilised *terra* as the object for human and cultural nullification – for the purpose of making it into another kind of civilised *terra*.

Methodologically, the genealogical picture is based on a historical examination of the ways in which Zionist practices were implemented and morphed at different periods – from the first waves of Jewish immigration to Palestine in the late nineteenth century onwards – in order to evaluate how these practices formed the infrastructure, the collective desires that still make up the Israeli-Jewish society. To understand the nature of the Zionist body and the ways in which it evolved as a socio-political *corpus-separatum* in relation to the Palestinian society and to the British Mandatory administration, 'the investigation must push beyond the interpretative realm, into the functional or machinic realm' (Buchanan 2008: 121), to describe the constructive forces Zionism has deployed since its historical breakthrough. This description evaluates the machinic forces by symptomatically tracing what this particular body did and does. As Buchanan explains, this move constitutes the first positive task of schizoanalysis; 'understanding how and why those reterritorialisations were constructed in the first place' (Buchanan 2008: 121), so as to discern the nature of the Zionist desiring-machines. To some extent the processes and effects of subjectivation are scrutinised, to observe how practices of ethical relation and desire intertwine, constituting and structuring the attitude of the archetypal Zionist settler towards the Arab-Palestinian as the other. Seen through these lenses, the concept of *terra nullius* is situated within the framework of Zionist-Palestinian historical relationships.[2]

Deleuze and Guattari's philosophy of desire as the 'quality of social relation that is actualised in collective production' (Goodchild 1996: 196) will help to explain the functioning of the Zionist *terra nullius* machines operating from the unconscious, producing real fruits in the social realm. Deleuze and Guattari's important achievement is to offer a philosophy and a politics that acknowledges how 'desire is implicated in all social and political processes' (Patton 2000: 68). According to their factory model of 'desiring-production', desire invests the social landscape within which we deploy our forces of construction and change. Desire is diagrammatic of the unconscious, while the real is the end-product and incorporates desire, and for this reason desiring-production is social production: '[T]here is only desire and the social, and nothing else' (Deleuze and Guattari 1983: 28–9).[3] Desire issues goals, interests, ends and needs, 'even though they appear (in consciousness) to guide it, but submitting desire to pre-conceived goals would make it reactive rather than productive and creative' (Holland 1999: 101). In Deleuze and Guattari's constructivist approach, the machines operating as desire are not figurative but real, and 'everywhere *it* is machines . . . machines driving other machines, machines being driven by other machines, with all the necessary coupling and connections' (Deleuze and Guattari 1983: 1). The formation of the embryonic Zionist-Jewish society in Palestine may best be understood in terms of the multiple connections, productions and relations from which the Zionist-Palestine structure emerged. Therefore, at least part of the answer for explaining the formation of collective Zionist political practices towards the Palestinians must be sought at the level of the workings of desire.

Palestine: Becoming *Terra Nullius*

Terra nullius is a colonialist legal concept that perceives the land as formally unoccupied when the colonisers arrive. Generally speaking, the doctrine of *terra nullius* has served European colonisation around the world by justifying the forced removal of indigenous populations from their lands, the occupation and appropriation of the land and its resources, and the implementation of means of exploitation. In the strict sense, as Patton explains, the term historically refers to a doctrine under eighteenth-century international law that acknowledged sovereignty over a given territory upon conquest, cession or settlement. However, European colonists all too often regarded natives as 'backward peoples', claiming 'that the indigenous inhabitants were not sufficiently settled or had not tilled the land in a manner that made them rightful owners' (Patton 2000: 119), thus widening the scope of the doctrine and opening the way to impose English law and claim sovereignty upon settled land (Patton 1996: 4). The absence of fixed institutions and Western agricultural practices in the nomadic lifestyles of the native peoples of North America and Oceania legally justified the land's physical capture (Patton 2000: 120).

In Australia, the convention of *terra nullius* historically implemented by the white settlers was partially retracted in 1992 by the Australian High Court in the famous *Mabo* case, leading to a comparative recognition of Aboriginal land titles (Mercer 1993; Patton 1996). Commentators agree that since *Mabo*, an important deterritorialisation in the public sphere has been under way, where a new politics of minorities has flourished and a broad public debate regarding colonialism and reconciliation in Australian society has commenced.

In this article, the concept used to explain Zionist practice is indeed *terra nullius*, but this differs from the conventional use of the term in European colonialism. In the first instance, applications of *terra nullius* during the earlier phases of Zionist colonisation must be distinguished from those of contemporary schemes. Nonetheless, in both instances, and unlike the Australian condition, in the Zionist-Palestinian scenario there has never been a legal conflict between *terra nullius* and its dialectical counterpart – the claim of native title. In Zionist politics, dispossession and appropriation of land is justified by unabashed and plainspoken ethno-national arguments. In fact, the very concept of *terra nullius* itself is almost absent in the colonial discourse of the 'founding fathers' of Zionism, including both ideologists and activist figures. Instead, we find utterances invoking analogous notions of a land empty of native inhabitants – notions that have become cornerstones of Zionist-Israeli mythology: 'making the desert bloom' (in Hebrew, *hafrahat hashmama*); the 'conquest of the land' (*kibush ha ha'adama*); and 'land redemption' (*ge'ulat ha-karka*). In the first myth, the term 'desert' has a double meaning: as an arid environment with no systematic cultivation, and a wilderness devoid of any deep-rooted human presence. This fiction was clearly expressed in the writings of the Zionist leader Israel Zangwill, an Anglo-Jewish writer and a Zionist spokesman, who in 1920 acknowledged the existence of the

Palestinians – but not as a people. Indeed, one of his famous pronouncements was that the Zionist enterprise was about 'a people without a land returning to a land without a people' (Kimmerling 1983: 9); and further: '[T]here is no Arab people living in intimate fusion with the country, utilizing its resources and stamping it with a characteristic impress: there is at best an Arab encampment' (Masalha 1992: 6). The second and third myths deliver a belligerent message tying in with the idea that rehabilitating the land – that is both sacred and 'contaminated' by the other – can be achieved only through conquest and devastation. In this way, mythical concepts are recruited in Zionism, as cultural representations and disciplinary devices aimed at rallying the population behind the cause of a historical enterprise.

In contemporary schemes, scholars of Zionism (Yacobi 2001; Dalsheim 2004; Peteet 2005; Yiftachel 1995, 2006) argue that the term of *terra nullius* encapsulates a fantasy, a product of a nationalist imagination, a way of thinking that fundamentally gives rise to 'a longing to be rid of those who were never fully known' (Dalsheim 2004: 152). This is epitomised by a well-known story about David Ben-Gurion, Israel's first Prime Minister. Whilst being driven around Galilee in the North of the country in the early years of the state's existence, he often closed his eyes. In response to his driver's question as to why he did so, Ben-Gurion replied that he could barely stand the sight of the Arab villages on both sides of the road – an attitude that was typical of the man (Masalha 1992: xi–xii). We can imagine him, eyes closed, mumbling and praying for a reality in which, on opening his eyes, he would enjoy a landscape that had magically swallowed up those villages. But, I will suggest, this wish is not at its heart a longing, yearning or hope to be rid of the other, but a crude historically constructed and productive assemblage of desire, a mechanism potentially alleviating collective moral pains. In this respect, Dalsheim conceives *terra nullius* in Zionism as a construction that illustrates 'how Israeli Jews represent themselves to themselves today, re-inscribing a settler imagination' concerning the alleged or wished absence of Palestinians, a representation that erases and reconstructs the past and memory, and also fits the way in which Israeli Jews see themselves as a nation with high moral standards (Dalsheim 2004: 154, 156). Here, denial and associated memoricide are ingredients of the Zionist practice of *terra nullius*. Memoricide is a displacement or disturbance in the process of recollection occurring at the last movement or aspect of the actualisation of the past in the present (Deleuze 1988: 70–1). Zionist memoricide may usefully be analysed in terms of Elster's political psychology, which elaborates how mental acts of self-deception lead to a collective belief involving the obliteration of objects that are unpleasant and incongruent with the way the Zionist project is discursively implemented. According to Elster, self-deception involves a dual commitment to incompatible or contradictory beliefs: the one that one holds, and that which one believes is grounded in evidence (Elster 1983: 149–50). Elster deconstructs the operation of self-deception through 'a four-step process: (1) arriving at the well-grounded belief; (2) deciding that it is unpalatable; (3) suppressing it and only then; (4) adhering to another and more tolerable belief' (Elster 1983: 152).

Self-deception is problematic: '[H]ow does one manage to *forget intentionally* what one 'really' (somehow, somewhere) believes?', and '[H]ow does one achieve that of *believing at will* what one also believes that there are no adequate grounds for believing?' (Elster 1983: 149). However, as Elster shows, although the notion of self-deception may seem incoherent, the phenomenon is present in everyday life. In particular, the mechanism within Zionism that distorts the memory associated with the products of *terra nullius* is defined by Elster as a 'joint production': 'I come to believe something at a later time, if I can also and simultaneously bring about forgetfulness of the process itself' (Elster 1983: 150). Once the belief is achieved, unfolding the unconscious into the present (Deleuze 1988: 71), it is rationalised by attributing plain intention to what seems to be a more obscure process. However, distortion occurs, and in the end the existence of the belief depends on the obliteration of the process from memory. The decision to forget involves the effort to erase a specific product of the unconscious. In the case of Zionism, the unpalatable object of collective memory that warrants erasure is the ethnic cleansing of 1948. This memoricide of the *Nakbeh* (Pappe 2006: 225–40) allows Zionists to bypass what is politically unsustainable.[4] Another example, which illustrates Zionist fantasies and denial concerning the *Nakbeh*, again involves Ben-Gurion: in one of his final interviews to Israeli state television in 1972, he was asked about the prospects for peace with the Palestinians. Still affected by the euphoria of the 1967 war, he evaded most questions, but when asked about the Palestinian refugees he replied: 'Those who fled from the country, who told them to flee? . . . Where do these million and two hundred thousand refugees come from? They were never in our territory. This whole business is a sham.'[5] For Ben-Gurion, the Palestinians in the refugee camps fall simultaneously into two contradictory categories: on the one hand, he says, they fled from the country of their own accord; on the other hand, he asks '*Where do they come from?*' and says '*They never were in our territory.*' The issue of expulsion is altogether absent. For

Ben-Gurion, the equation is simple: they never were in the specific territory; therefore, they were not expelled. Which brings us, indeed, to the questions of where they came from and why? The fact that Ben-Gurion could see 'this whole business' as a sham is indicative of his denial. Scholars resolve these impossible contradictions in Ben-Gurion's words by applying the concept of *terra nullius* to express an act of imagination 'that fantasises a removal of the local population, often without force, but somehow magically' (Dalsheim 2004: 153).

In view of this scholarship, two important remarks should be made. Firstly, willing an object's disappearance 'also lends it a mental presence, *qua* object of the negating attitude', since, 'by wanting the non-existence of the object, one confers existence on it' (Elster 1983: 49). In other words, the attempt to make the physical subjects and the memory of the ethnic cleansing of Palestine disappear is enough to ensure the presence of that memory – since, as Elster suggests, 'the decision to forget has the paradoxical feature that the harder you try to carry it out, the less likely it is to succeed' (Elster 1983: 149). In this respect, the memoricide itself serves as the mechanism that helps historical injustice to survive on the political agenda. The internal negation of a certain state (form of thought, knowledge or consciousness, or certain reality) cannot bring about the external negation of that state, because of the reality principle. That is to say, the evidence of the expulsion of Palestinians from the land during all periods, and the manifest disregard of Palestinian rights, interests and needs, has been and is always present. Oppression-repression is produced not by a small, secret group of individuals, but is the official policy of the state and is supported and implemented by the vast majority of Israeli Jews. No matter how much effort is invested in expunging the objects of memoricide from the Israeli collective memory and from the political agenda, they nevertheless obstinately accumulate as present registers. Secondly, the negating agent depends on the object of negation for its own being: the other is a constitutive and vital element in the formation of the actual identity of the one. Therefore, 'the anti-believer may be the only one to keep the belief alive, and in the struggle against his own past may only be affirming his identity over time' (Elster 1983: 50). This notion is particularly striking in the context of this discussion, given that the Zionist subject was formed through a violent process that is itself denied.

Lastly, self-deception in the Zionist attitude is adopted mainly for reasons of 'affective pressure' (Elster 1983: 156–7), since Zionists find it hard to reconcile the historical dispossession, expulsion and oppression-repression of Palestinians with the emancipatory discourses that Zionist ideology promotes. Therefore, the unpleasant awareness of what has been done (and is still being done) is consciously rejected and another belief that may reconcile practice and discourse is instead adopted. The mechanism of self-deception has certain political, social and cultural benefits for the believers. First and foremost, it helps Israel earn moral self-relief, and to market its sense of morality to its own citizenry and abroad. However, in contrast to Elster's suggestion, it is important to keep in mind that interests alone cannot explain those benefits and the deceptive belief itself. It is rather the desire structuring Israeli subjectivity that produces the reality, which in turn calls for relief. The unconscious production of Palestinian absence, invested by desire, generates the need for a psychological mechanism like *terra nullius*, which can ameliorate the wrong.

There are, however, changes afoot in the political culture of the conflict, and recently the Israeli-Jewish public has transitioned from a mindset of denial to shamelessness. The Zionist appetite for ethnic cleansing is no longer morally repressed, which was perhaps the only positive side-effect of denial. This is particularly apparent with regard to 'the demographic problem': the racist discourse expressing the Israeli fear of losing demographic control which, as Pappe has pointed out, plagues almost every political party in Israel's parliament, as well as apparently leftist extraparliamentary groups that promote peace initiatives. Moreover, 'by now most mainstream journalists, academics and politicians in Israel have liberated themselves from their earlier inhibitions . . . On the domestic scene, no one feels the need any more to explain what is at the heart of it and whom it affects' (Pappe 2006: 251). Paradoxically, this racist discourse is counter-productive to the psychological mechanism of *terra nullius*, since its widespread popularity helps tear off the mask from the historical-material appetite of the Zionist colonialist machine.

All in all, the representative accounts of the concept of *terra nullius* overlook important aspects that may assist in our understanding of the Zionist-Palestinian structure. It is not that *terra nullius* has no fantastical facet that allows *post factum* explanation and justification of Zionist practices, but that it falls far short of exhausting the latent potential of the concept of *terra nullius* in the context of Zionist practice. We are not looking for a meta-explanation of the conflict, nor for a reductionism that may oversimplify its causes and reasons and explain its continuation. Beyond ideological representations of reality, the concept of *terra nullius* is suited to explaining a specific historical production of libidinal forces embracing tangible implementations of human and cultural displacement and nullification. Indeed, *terra nullius* is here understood as a plane of immanent productive forces that have evolved into a collective desire, redefining the relationship with earth. As we see it, *terra nullius* is not an *ex post facto* explicative and static device, but a virtual *ex ante facto* active desire. It does not primarily represent a state of affairs but rather helps to bring about a state of affairs. The Zionist masses are not ideologically deceived by political leadership or by history to vote for the ethnic displacement of the other (Deleuze and Guattari 1983: 29, 257); rather, they deceive themselves regarding the products, the existence and the implementation of their very desire. They immanently impose *terra nullius* upon Palestine.

Colonial Constructions

The problem of the cross-cultural encounter may appear in several modes or guises – ranging from 'outright domination over a number of intermediary stages, to benign or empowering forms of self-other relations' (Dallmayr 1996: 3). Colonialism is one solution to the question of the encounter, or, as Patton states more precisely in Deleuzian terms, the recurrent encounter between European nations and aboriginal peoples is characteristically resolved by 'different forms of political and legal capture' (Patton 1997: 4).

As a particular solution to the question raised by the encounter, Patton perceives colonisation as a pure event, an incorporeal and open-ended entity irreducible to its material enactment in diverse sets of colonial conditions. Distinct forms of colonisation, such as Zionism, may be linked with other applications in a single common series, from which a symptom or a sense of the pure event may be extracted, allowing its explanation and its awareness in lived experience (Patton 1997: 1). This symptom derives from the immanent relations that compose the social formation. The phenomenon of colonialism is a pure event of this kind, as its different flows of energy and matter over various temporal and spatial actualisations have reached a level of consistency and sense, imposing an emergent order upon virtual chaos (Deleuze 1994: 156). In the event of colonisation, the coloniser views the encounter from a standpoint of self-attributed global permissibility, which in turn sanctions a *carte blanche* prerogative to act according to her discretion in a certain part of the world. This unconditional and self-vindicating authority is what motivates the journey beyond the encounter, retroactively explaining its consequences. In European history, this privileged status was generally supported by an ideology of cultural supremacy; in Zionism, it was accompanied by a redemptive nationalism.

From the outset, Zionist colonial settler society did not define itself as a classic form of civilising colonialism embarking upon an exploration of strategically important, far-flung corners of the globe, installing a capitalist infrastructure based on local exploitation and treating 'the natives as a vast pool of cheap labour' (Smith 1993: 735). Rather, Zionism's colonial impetus arose as a specific response to the 'Jewish Question': Palestine was never as attractive for immigrants as North America, and 'cheap labour' was not an opportunity for exploitation but a problematic constraint destined to usher in new solutions. In Palestine, the colonialists did not encounter nomads but a settled, agricultural society of peasants, and they were not protected within military cocoons, as were European settlers in other parts of the world (Shafir 1989). In contrast to the 'Freeland' state of territory conceived by European colonialists in Oceania, America and Africa, the Jewish immigrant-settlers in Palestine had to grapple with a nascent land-market based on a traditional land ownership (Kimmerling 1983: 31).[6] The main divergence from classic European colonialism lay in the relationship to native culture: instead of attempting 'to graft onto it a colonial superstructure that would allow the convenience of indirect rule, freezing the original indigenous culture by turning it into an object of academic analysis, while imposing the mould of a new imperial culture' (Young 1995: 174), Zionism's main goal was incrementally to drain the land of all existing human and cultural materials and fill it with new ones.[7] This may be defined as a synthetic process of *displacement-replacement*.

The Zionist project is largely depicted as a developing colonialist fabric[8] woven by a growing Jewish settler-nationalist society in Palestine, starting between 1882 and 1903 with the First Zionist *Aliyah* (wave of immigration).[9] The waves of Jewish immigration that convulsed Palestine at the beginning of the twentieth century were crucial in constituting the growing colony (Khalidi 1992).[10] From the third decade, Zionist leadership of the Jewish *Yishuv*[11] initiated 'the institution of borders and the constitution of a milieu of interiority' (Patton 2000: 990) and activated a state-machine long before Israel became a formal state in 1948. A 'state within a state' is the term that best fits the development of the Zionist enterprise in Palestine, at least from the end of the 1930s, including 'a military organisation and political, social, economic, and financial institutions separate from those of the indigenous population as well as from the British Mandatory Administration' (Smith 1993: 3). Moreover Zionist institutions leased the land they purchased to Jewish settlers with special incentives that 'were analogous to similar incentives . . . provided by colonial governments in allocating free or generously cheap

Crown lands to European settlers' (Metzer 1998: 202). The involuntary dispossession of the Arab tenant-farmers when their land was sold was also 'qualitatively similar to (though quantitatively much smaller than) the consequences of various "land alienation" schemes for natives who lost their . . . grazing rights and other rural possessions in settlement colonies' (Metzer 1998: 202).

Patton maintains that the event of colonisation involves 'a particular form of capture of both earth or geographical surface and the people or their productive activity' (Patton 2000: 122), but the Zionist colonisation of Palestine was more complex, since free activity on earth-surface was not simply transformed into labour and land. The rigid feudal system that characterised Ottoman rule began to crumble during the second half of the nineteenth century, allowing the infrastructure of capitalism to grow in its stead (Ben-Porath 1995).[12] At the time of the first waves of Zionist immigration, Palestine was mainly an agrarian society based on a quasi-feudal regime of land and labour with no unclaimed land: rent and common tenure were the main apparatus of land capture. By the time Zionism started to deploy its machines, Palestine was not a homogeneous territory of nomads, nor was the Palestinian society comprised of 'free action and smooth space that have no use for a work-factor' (Deleuze and Guattari 1987: 491), a situation which, according to Patton, allowed colonialists to look upon indigenous peoples in their conquered lands as not labouring at all, 'much less [working] the land in a way that afforded them rights over it' (Patton 2000: 123). Nevertheless, there was no 'money for land' in feudal Palestine until the early days of the British Mandate. Therefore, the confrontation between the Jewish immigrant-settlers and the native Palestinians did not concern the imposition of an external system of capitalist surplus labour in which the former exploits the latter, or the capture of a 'free action' territory. Instead, the Zionist phenomenon brought about a succession of new exploitations of the same landed territory: land remained land and labour remained profitable, but with a newly installed assemblage governing the three basic elements of land, labour and people.

We cannot sufficiently clarify the historical process of colonisation by looking exclusively at the effects that emerged from such connections, just as 'we cannot tell from the mere taste of wheat who grew it; the product gives us no hint as to the system and the relations of production' (Deleuze and Guattari 1983: 24). Since the product of the real depends on the process of production, a genealogical symptomatic inspection is needed. This traces the developing regularities of flows and connections between bodies and elements caused by the operations of desire, into associations which reach relatively stable points over time, creating territories, relations, subjects and consumptions. We must ask: what kinds of desiring-machines act, produce and motivate molar aggregates within the realm of the Zionist-Palestinian structure, that cause the past to be actualised in specific flows of violence? Bergson provides an ontological reply to the theoretical aspect of this question through his *'attention to life'*, which refers to the 'the utilization of the past in terms of the present' (Deleuze 1991: 70). These unfoldings are sensitive to the real, since 'desire always remains in close touch with the conditions of objective existence; it embraces them and follows them, shifts when they shift, and does not outlive them' (Deleuze and Guattari 1983: 27). The dynamic and transformative contact occurs between the macroscopic or molar entities (the Real) and the microscopic or molecular entities (desiring-machines) which engineer them (Buchanan 2008: 91). Thus, genealogy helps to trace the cultivation of the Real through desire, in which we may discern the nature of the Zionist desiring-machines that emerged over time and transformed Palestinian reality by their effectuations. This is in fact the task of schizoanalysis, 'to demonstrate the existence of an unconscious libidinal investment of socio-historical production, distinct from the conscious investments coexisting with it' (Deleuze and Guattari 1983: 98).

A good starting point for the schizoanalysis of Zionism may be to put the ideological dimension in perspective. Shafir's criticism of teleological theories that overstate ideology is relevant in this respect. According to him, both orthodox Zionist theoreticians and certain critics of Zionism such as Edward Said (1979) have attributed to Zionism's initial aims an extra focus that 'removes the actual events from history, replacing them with an "inexorable logic" that recognises only a direct path of evolution leading from the presuppositions to the aims of Zionist history' (Shafir 1989: 212). From a neo-Marxist point of view, however, Ben-Porath explains the Zionist enterprise as reliant upon a 'realm of opportunities' (Ben-Porath 1995) – neither settlers' ideology, nor historians' ideology lies at the heart of the *explanans*, which must instead attend to the settlers' material responses to conditions on the ground and to the given constraints. According to Ben-Porath, political ideas and aims indeed classified Zionism as a settlement enterprise, but their impact was limited and regulated by historical circumstances. Instead, what particularly marked the Zionist phenomenon was its timing: the transformation of Palestinian feudalism into capitalism produced economic conditions that allowed a breakthrough for the Zionist settlement project, since it gave birth to a land-market that had hitherto been nonexistent (Ben-Porath 1995: 287).[13] Social structures are not formed by ideology; they are produced by desire and 'take desires – or those connections which enhance life – in order to produce interests, coded, regular, collective and organised forms of desire' (Colebrook 2002: 91). By over-stressing 'the actual influence of the voluntary dimension of ideas in creating outcomes', historians have over-emphasised the intentions of the Jewish immigrant-settlers, ignored material constraints on infrastructure, and attributed to Zionism abstract forces irrespective of real investments, to the point that 'it could do whatever it wished' (Shafir 1989: 213). For this reason, instead of emphasising the presupposition that the negation of the Palestinians is a transcendental and leading Zionist political *telos*, the transformation of the concept of *terra nullius* from a discursive to a libidinal plane heightens the importance of the desiring-machines that produce specific socio-historical realities, consuming us as part-elements; as fixed and separated ethnic subjects of the Zionist-Palestinian structure. These machines create specific concrete connections and consumptions of bodies and objects, producing the image of the Zionist reality that interests us, also enabling understanding of the way in which Zionism has historically composed its generalities out of singular political investments (Colebrook 2002: 93). As Buchanan explains, this is the highlight of Deleuze and Guattari's strategy for socio-political analysis: '[T]hey reject as imprecise political praxis built on the notion of ideology and in its place offer the three syntheses of connection, disjunction and conjunction as a more efficient means' (Buchanan 2008: 72). The desiring-machines of *terra nullius* are as real as their products, which include the separatist logic, the ongoing ethnic cleansing, the military and legal apparatuses that implement the national accumulation of land, the discrimination and so forth.

Shafir's main thesis is that Jewish settlement in Palestine characteristically developed in response to given conflicts in the labour market. Specifically, struggles began in the small settler-plantation colonies when the First *Aliyah*'s landowners had to decide whether to hire Palestinian workers from the areas surrounding the Jewish settlements, or the landless Jewish immigrants who arrived during the First *Aliyah*: 'The planters opted for the cheaper and more pliant Palestinians' (Shafir 1989: 52–4). This tendency attracted severe criticism by the workers of the Second *Aliyah*, who 'demanded a re-evaluation of the preference for Arab workers' (Shafir 1989: 55), but ultimately Jewish workers were forced to forge alternative appeals for employment. Even reducing their wage demands to equal those of the Arab workers failed as a competitive strategy (Shafir 1989: 58–9). Since the immigrants lacked their own land on which to settle, and failed to create the proper conditions for securing employment in the labour market, they opted for an alternative strategy designed to monopolise the labour market under the slogan of 'Conquest of Labour' (*kibush ha-avodah*). As Shafir explains, this expression carries at least three meanings: self-conquest (inverting the Jewish occupational structure in Europe to acquire agricultural work habits); class conflict (between the planters and landowners over working conditions); and struggle for exclusion, which implied the ethnic conquest of labour by displacing Arab workers in the labour market (Shafir 1989: 60). Although the conflict in the labour market was principally between Jewish workers and Jewish employers and was over wages, in the course of this conflict the Palestinian workers became an ethno-national target of the Jewish workers' struggle, 'even if ultimately it was not national differences that were the formative causes of their conflict' (Shafir 1989: 58). At this point, the impetus to 'replace' was starting to emerge. Rapidly, this strategy gained the support of the World Zionist Organisation, and was politically coded as 'a necessary condition for the realisation of Zionism' (Shafir 1989: 60). This molecular change imparted a new ethno-national character to the conflict between the communities. The strategy of replacement was initially maintained only by subsidies (through Jewish external funds) and later also by monopolising skills to gain Jewish permanence in more and more agricultural work areas (Shafir 1989: 66). In this exclusionist strategy of accumulated replacement by ethnicised bodies, we find the embryonic material actions leading to the bifurcation of the labour market and the economy in Palestine in the first decades of the twentieth century, transforming it over time into the social-machine of segregation that in due course would pervade the entire time-space. At this point, consciousness gave way to the construction of a new collective unconscious that repeatedly surfaced in the form of desire suffusing everything and tying 'into molecular levels . . . already shaping postures, attitudes, perceptions, expectations, semiotic systems, etc.' (Deleuze and Guattari 1987: 35, 215).

The forces that gathered and constructed the Arab-Palestinian as other and as an object of replacement in the labour market, in turn produced new assemblages of desire, related to the ones already in place and directed at enlarging the Jewish presence, thus establishing the appetite of the Zionist machine for demographic expansion. Territory was the next plane to be engaged. Indeed, the Jewish colonisation of Palestine had an important organisational metamorphosis in the sphere of housing and settlement from 1910 onwards: the creation of the co-operative settlement, the *kibbutz*.[14] At this point, practical considerations in the struggle for defending the livelihood of the Jewish immigrants (in order for them to become immigrant-settlers) led Jewish labour and settlement to be fused into a single separatist-exclusionist experiment. The Zionist colonial strategy intensified its ambitions beyond attempts at monopolising the labour market, towards the conjoint monopolisation of land, settlement and labour through the collective experimentation of the *kibbutz;* national-collectivism was recruited to compete in the Palestinian economy. As with many other social-machines, the *kibbutz* was built statistically following the law of large numbers, as the aggregation of microscopic desiring-machines and their contingent dynamism and syntheses (Buchanan 2008: 88–90). This was a 'decisive organisational innovation which provided the infrastructure of effective Jewish colonisation, that is, the method of Israeli state formation' (Shafir 1989: 146). The advent of the *kibbutz* brought to an end the ethnic plantation-type settlement promoted by the Jewish plantation owners of the First *Aliyah*, transforming settlement according to a logic of purely ethnic colonisation.[15] At the heart of this colonial type, demography and agricultural work were interwoven to assure ethno-national control of the land (Shafir 1989: 154). The co-operative model of settlement ensured permanent employment and a national foothold on the land, becoming entrenched after the First World War so that 'the kibbutz would be viewed as a fundamental and typical form of colonisation of Palestine by all concerned' (Shafir 1989: 172).

The national ownership of land for co-operative settlement was mainly implemented by the Jewish National Fund (JNF), which by its own codex drew on decisions initially made by the First Zionist Congress of 1897, namely that land purchased in Palestine for the settlement of Jews could not be resold, 'as it was held in trust for the whole nation' (Shafir 1989: 155).[16] These material steps were the opening salvos in an effort to realise the growing distinction between 'Jews' and 'non-Jews' (Davis 2003: 39) – a distinction that coded the flows of capital in the growing land and labour markets, and started to carve up the open Palestinian spaces into ethnic enclaves. This method, as Shafir explains, accomplished three complementary tasks, since 'not only did it . . . exclude non-Jews from control of land once acquired by the JNF, but in one fell swoop abolished private ownership of land, replacing it with hereditary land leasing'. It also assured, through the prohibition of subletting, the Jewish usufruct of the land (Shafir 1989: 155). Ultimately, 'land bought by Zionist organizations . . . was effectively removed from the open market by virtue of being held in perpetual trust for the Jewish people. No non-Jews could be employed on this land, which was leased to Zionist settlers' (Smith 1993: 135). The appropriation of the land was the necessary condition 'for the cultivation of another culture' (Young 1995: 172), bestowing upon the landed territory the quality of selective ethnicity, a quality that was to shape the collective unconscious. In this way the deterritorialising appropriation of land and work preceded the subsequent Zionist monopoly realised as economic comparison – a capture that imposed itself as the unit of measure within Palestine economy and society, from which every form of discrimination is now understood (Deleuze and Guattari 1987: 441–4). As Shafir explains, the territorial accumulation of land during Zionist colonisation changed the nature of acquisition from the end of the British Mandate period onwards, from 'money to sword', to achieve and ensure the 'completion of the transformation of Palestine' (Shafir 1989: 43).[17] The turning point cementing the use of force to appropriate land was undoubtedly during the ethnic cleansing of Palestine, planned by senior Jewish political officials and undertaken by Israeli military forces, taking place during the war of 1948–9 (Pappe 2006). From that point onwards, the 'Jewish Fist' became the currency of Zionist politics and the essence of Jewish life in Israel, as the Israeli philosopher Yeshayahu Leibowitz repeatedly maintained in interviews and public articles during the 1980s.

Zionist practices subdivided and striated Palestinian spaces by overcoding those new flows of land, work and people that had been created. The subdivision of material flows parcelled land and work from existent wholes, to create an increasing congruency between land, work and ethnicity. These captures produced a dynamic of *displacement* and *replacement* that was subsequently wrapped up in nationalist ideology. Therefore, the fundamental problem of this particular form of colonisation is not merely jurisprudential, nor does it concern only 'the manner in which the territorial domains of the prior inhabitants become transformed into a uniform space of landed property', as Patton states regarding Australian or American colonialism (Patton 2000: 124). Rather, for Zionist settler colonialism, the fundamental problem concerns the economy of the progressive division of the land as far as it may be ethnically reterritorialised.

The 'ways in which the Jewish workers used the lessons they learned from the labour market conflict, [shaped] Israeli nationalism and the Israeli-Palestinian conflict in general' (Shafir 1989: 55). Indeed, the accumulative strategy of 'making room' on the land for uniform and separated production becomes the nucleic mechanism of the Jewish state.[18] Against the argument that this separatism evolved in response to the escalating conflict between the Zionists and the Palestinians, the separatist logic instead played a crucial role in the making of the conflict (Shafir 1989; Smith 1993: 3).[19] Beyond Mandatory colonial policies that encouraged separatism through economic and administrative facilitation, the decision to create a separate culture and education system based on Hebrew for Jews only, was crucial in establishing a separate Jewish enclave (Smith 1993: 12).

Terra Nullius: Active and Productive Desiring-Machines

'Desire begins with connections' (Colebrook 2002: 91): body with body with land with land; elements pushing forward energies invested in different forms and movements. As a form of writing geography (Young 1995), three basic complementary operations characterise the Zionist desiring-machines. Firstly, depopulation deterritorialises places and sites, draining energy from the soil. The libidinal connection is established between human subjects and in this case it is plastic energy (between bodies) that produces the emptiness of the space (Holland 1999: 26); every human expulsion displaces flows of energy from one point to another, as a result of libidinal investment. This is *displacement*. Secondly, if depopulation is the investment of anti-matter, Judaisation is the material investment of human subjects – as parts of a collective entity – who connect themselves to the sockets of spatial emptiness and fill the depletion through free kinetic movement: housing, sexual reproduction, forests, routes and roads, everything 'replacing' that which had been drained. These are the infinite libidinal connections, disruptions and conjunctions that cement the imported collective body – the microphysics of the unconscious that explains the macroscopic social formations (Buchanan 2008: 89). As Deleuze and Guattari point out, 'civilized societies . . . *what they deterritorialise with one hand, they reterritorialise with the other*' (Deleuze and Guattari 1983: 257; original emphasis), since 'these two processes go hand in hand' (Buchanan 2005: 29), continuously carving the face of earth (Deleuze and Guattari 1987: 509), expressing cycles of flow and 'referring to the detachment and reattachment of the energies of production in general' (Holland 1999: 20). This is *replacement*. Thirdly, ethnic segregation is produced by fencing space as a means of further reterritorialisation. This involves an investment in the new means of desiring-production that binds together the vectors of reterritorialisation and ethnic expansion; by fencing, the collective body is given a silhouette – a path of disjunction from former connections – which makes tangible the boundaries of existence and defines the praxeological terms against the other. This is *fencing*: the circumscribing of flows of people, culture and wealth. Relationships with the soil and the surroundings are redefined, and collective desire is disciplined and socialised to produce a lasting exclusion (Buchanan 2008: 93). At this point the time-space is accessible for investments of segregation within different social areas of life, such as education, housing, the work-place and so forth. As a result, a discriminatory regime of multiple and hierarchical citizenship emerges (Peled and Shafir 2002).

Deterritorialisation destroys existent lifestyles and removes bodies from the earth, preparing for the violent constitution of new assemblages, and subsequently the political capture of the space to subdivide it into new, ethnic grids. For this reason, colonial Zionism is a negative form of relative deterritorialisation; the deterritorialised element is immediately subjected to forms of territorialisation and reterritorialisation that enclose or obstruct lines of escape. More explicitly, it deterritorialises in order to reterritorialise through ethnic capture (Deleuze and Guattari 1987: 508–10; Patton 2000: 106–7). Alternatively, deterritorialisation might have a more positive political function; desiring-machines may create revolutionary growth by reshaping the subjects' modes of connections to the world (within the Zionist-Palestinian structure), changing striation and transforming the infrastructure itself through a process of 'appropriation', namely transcending the conditions of reality and participating in creative acts (Buchanan 1999: 106–7), as occurs nowadays in various intercultural interactions in certain areas of Israeli education, civil society and politics where intersectionality feeds new connective syntheses (Svirsky 2008; Svirsky et al. 2007).

The colonial fabric destroys and reconstructs spaces and cultures, by implementing, as Young describes, 'the violent physical and ideological procedures of colonisation, deculturation and acculturation by which the territory and cultural space of an indigenous society must be disrupted, dissolved and then reinscribed according to the needs of the apparatus of the occupying power' (Young 1995: 169–70). The transformation of the geo-cultural landscape of Palestine illustrates how Zionism has redefined the relationship to the land. Since the advent of Zionism, the porous and open relationship of the Palestinian settled communities with the land has been marked by increasing ethnic segmentation of its surface. The landscape formed by the traditional Palestinian villages comprised open spaces 'with their natural stone houses and accessible, unhindered, approaches to the nearby fields, orchards and olive groves around them' (Pappe 2006: 30). The surroundings and setting of Palestinian villages and towns remain very much the same today; their characteristic features of multiple entrances and lines of construction that are homologous with the topography of the land and proximity of agricultural fields sit oddly with the layout of the Zionist countryside settlements. During the pre-state period, the Zionist settler colonies in the rural areas 'were built like military garrisons rather than villages: what inspired their layout and design, were security considerations rather than human habitation' (Pappe 2006: 30). In addition, demographic-security concerns have motivated the infamous *yehud hagalil* ('Judaisation of the Galilee') enterprise since the late 1970s. At the heart of 'Judaisation' is the premise that the Palestinian presence in specific areas within Israel must be counterbalanced demographically with Jewish citizens. This includes eroding the land resources of Arab villages and surrounding them with new Jewish communities.[20] The project brought about the construction of a new type of community settlement for Jews only – the *mitzpeh*. This literally means an outpost, a high lookout point situated topographically above the immediate space in order to keep it under observation. This typical Israeli military mode of discourse defines Arab areas as spaces that must be subject to surveillance. The panoptic organisation of space and the institution of a Foucaultian gaze as a means of control, frames the Arab as an object to be watched and guarded against, while defining the Jewish settler as his guardian. This guardian-inmate relation reflects the way in which the state has always perceived the Arab population, as a 'fifth column' that needs to be watched over. These small towns clearly segment the geo-cultural landscape. Enclosed within iron fences, they have electric coded gates, a security officer, a squad composed of residents and a flagpole with the national flag waving right near the only gate-entrance. These physical artefacts and practices in a human settlement decivilise the community by adopting a paramilitary character that deepens its physico-cultural distance from the immediate environment. This visible architecture of the Jewish communities stresses a 'construction of boundaries and borders that differentiate between those who belong and those who do not, and determines the meaning of the particular belonging' (Yuval-Davis et al. 2005: 521). These social regimes produce what Pappe calls a *White Fortress Israel* in which people become 'prisoners of their own warped reality' (Pappe 2006: 248–56), attesting to the illegitimate modality in which the collective Zionist unconscious synthesises the workings of desire and infuses the Real with a violent bipolar ethnic landscape, specific alliances and fixed and segregated subjects (Buchanan 2008: 72–3).

For almost a century, such forces have created a complex plane of collective libidinal production which manufactures the *ethnic disappearance of the other* – displacement-replacement-fencing. This is how the machines of *terra nullius* work. The statistical aggregations of these operations of desire 'eventually form social wholes; when bodies connect with other bodies to enhance their power they eventually form communities or societies' (Colebrook 2002: 91). Social bodies such as the Zionist collective form according to the way in which 'the libido . . . invests the social field with unconscious forms, thereby hallucinating all history, reproducing in delirium entire civilisations, races, and continents, and intensely "feeling" the becoming of the world' (Deleuze and Guattari 1983: 98). In a successive series of collective connections, desiring-machines are immanently constructed and changed over time, differentiating themselves in multiple ways within the actual order of things and beings. It is from this productivist perspective that we need to understand the realms of the obvious and the evident in our societies. Although normalising practices are developed through discipline and control, they are created, sustained and transformed by desire and passion. As one researcher of Zionism has observed regarding the protective practices of exclusive Jewish employment, '[T]his issue left its imprint on all social relations in the *Yishuv*, and excited the passions more than any other single question' (Shafir 1989: 215). Upon this virtual past, from these ontological settings, life patterns in the real were shaped and are perceived as natural, as expressions of instinctive acts which – at the collective level – are maintained as morally right; this explains the depth and the general acceptance of contemporary forms of oppression and discrimination.

We are captives of our past – not deterministically, but within the given forms that have emerged from the production of life. As May explains, '[T]o live is to navigate the world immersed in a historically given context . . . the past exists within me, and appears at each moment I am engaged with the world' (May 2005: 51). Indeed, we can still perceive 'the consequences of colonisation . . . in social life as well as in the memories of those affected, long after the initial acts of settlement' (Patton 1997: 5). This past is not just our personal past, but the entirety of the past itself, and in these engagements the actualisation of the virtual occurs. 'A person, through action, memory, or perception, brings the past to bear upon the present moment. In all these cases, past and present are mingled: the past unfolding, the present creating and inventing' (May 2005: 52). Power structures are not explained by a particular historical happening, but by the whole of the past that is reincarnated in living moments through the machinic operations of desire. The denial of the Palestinian community may be understood as the result

Terra Nullius and the Zionist-Palestinian Conflict 241

of an unconscious collective wishfulness, still prevalent among the vast majority of Israelis Jews, acting as an engine producing an exclusionist public space. The desiring-machines of *terra nullius* may plausibly explain practicalities within the Zionist-Palestine structure, for example the planning and execution of the ethnic cleansing of Palestine, and the collective amnesia in the aftermath of events such as the traumatic displacements and ruination of 1948–9 in Palestine:[21]

> [O]n a cold Wednesday afternoon, 10 March 1948, a group of eleven men, veteran Zionist leaders together with young military Jewish officers, put the final touches to a plan for the ethnic cleansing of Palestine. The same evening, military orders were dispatched to the units on the ground to prepare for the systematic expulsion of the Palestinians from vast areas of the country. The orders came with a detailed description of the methods to be employed to forcibly evict the people: large-scale intimidations; laying siege to and bombarding villages and population centres; setting fire to homes, properties and goods; expulsion; demolition; and, finally, planting mines among the rubble to prevent any of the expelled inhabitants from returning. Each unit was issued with its own list of villages and neighbourhoods as the targets of this master plan. Codenamed Plan D (*Dalet* in Hebrew), this was the fourth and final version of less substantial plans that outlined the fate the Zionists had in store for Palestine and consequently for its native population . . . This fourth and last blueprint spelled it out clearly and unambiguously: the Palestinians had to go . . . Once the decision was taken, it took six months to complete the mission. (Pappe 2006: xii-xiii)[22]

This was undoubtedly the most striking formative event in the crystallisation of the relationship between Zionism and the Palestinian people. As Pappe summarises, '[W]hen it was over, more than half of Palestine's native population, close to 800,000 people, had been uprooted, 531 villages had been destroyed, and eleven urban neighbourhoods emptied of their inhabitants' (Pappe 2006: xii–xiii). The villages 'had not only been depopulated but obliterated, their houses blown up or bulldozed' (Khalidi 1992: xv).[23]

We must remember that the ontological memory serves as the foundation for the unfolding of time (Deleuze 1991: 59), which is produced through the operations of the unconscious and its desiring-machines. 'How do these machines, these desiring-machines work – yours and mine?' ask Deleuze and Guattari (1983: 109). These machines work collectively to develop and incarnate the planes of immanence into socio-political ways of life. The social planes, the actual relations between peoples, are both the end products of desire and new syntheses that feed desire. In this way dwelling is mingled with production. Zionist formations are characterised by various enduring forms of differenciation into specific modes and features: the persistence of the 'Jews-only' mindset in the labour market; the connections that gave birth to the exclusionist agricultural settlement; the persistent pressure of Zionist organisations on the British administration 'to ensure that revenue attributable to the activities of the *Yishuv* should be spent for the exclusive benefit of the settler movement' (Smith 1993: 60); the economic policies during the formative years of the Jewish society according to which 'Jewish production was designed primarily for Jewish consumption and export and not for the majority of the Palestinian population' (Smith 1993: 179); and ultimately, the ethnic cleansing of Palestine and the continuing erasure of the Arab other. In Zionism, it is all our past which co-exists with each present (Deleuze 1991: 59). And every act of recollection involves a movement adapting the past to the present – a useful move coalescing into an image that intersects the demands of the specific condition of the moment and the virtual structure of the past (Deleuze 1991: 63–5). The proverbial pioneer of the first waves of immigration, arising again from the entire past of the Zionist-Palestinian structure, deports, dispossesses and destroys the Palestinian villages in the present, while reincarnating himself through the specificity of the given circumstances. Not only soldiers carry out such acts: the famous political slogans of 'Conquest of Labour and Land' are also implicated, insinuating within contemporary contexts that continue to segregate Jewish citizens from their prospective Palestinian partners.

Indeed, within the constructive Zionist libido we find explanations for the nature of the political and socio-economic relationship between the State of Israel and its Palestinian minority: in the divided and separated character of the economy, in the social life and politics of Palestine throughout the years of the British Mandate, and in the displacing and exclusionist Zionist life forces. In this respect, since 1948 the distance of the Palestinian community from the locus of control and prosperity parallels – and is an extension of – the separation that formed between the communities before that time. Pervasive attitudes to Palestinians indicate it is still the nature of Zionist politics to expand through contractions of time, allowing the operations of *terra nullius* to imprint new forms of the *disappearance of the other*, either by 'improving' the demographic ratio, or by explicit displacement and ethnic cleansing. With respect to the Palestinian citizens of Israel, the contemporary tactic is to enfeeble life through systematic discrimination, the nearest thing within democracy to formalising non-existence.

In this light we are better placed to understand Israeli ethnic policies, such as the Judaisation projects of areas populated predominantly by

Israeli Arabs (Yiftachel 1994; Yiftachel and Yacobi 2003); the kinship-oriented changes made recently in the Israeli Citizenship Law, aimed at limiting the right of marriage between Israeli Arabs and West-Bank/Gaza Palestinians;[24] or the increasing use of the architecture of walls to separate and isolate populations (Yacobi and Cohen 2006). The Judaisation of the Galilee programme is particularly illustrative. As Yiftachel and Carmon say, the 'leading goal of the new settlement in the Galilee was geo-political – the wish of the government . . . to populate larger parts of the Galilee with Jewish settlers and to halt an alleged continued Arab occupation of state lands' (Yiftachel and Carmon 1997: 219).[25] Again, the inter-coupling machine-elements of *terra nullius* impel and project further flows of reterritorialisation and deploy the desire of a land without the other, thus making clear that the forces sanctioning ethnic cleansing are still alive and continue 'to drive the inexorable, sometimes indiscernible cleansing of those Palestinians who live there today' (Pappe 2006: 259). The contact boundary between the ontological past and the actual present through which the desiring-machines operate worries us. This is the plane on which the perversity of *terra nullius* once again finds new circumstances and objects to apprehend, and mechanically 'ensures the proper utility of the whole and its performance in the present' (Deleuze 1988: 71), 'appearing at each moment in creative innovations' (May 1996: 52). Unfortunately, Zionist innovations reterritorialised Palestinian land according to a hostile coding of desire, which actualised the politics of erasure of Palestinians.

While Australian, New-Zealand and Canadian forms of colonialism in the past thirty years have transformed in becomings that may be regarded as democratic and multicultural, Zionism's *attention to the concrete life of the other* is remarkable for its pursuit of the nullification of the other's existence. For Deleuze, 'the other' is the very structure of alterity. It is 'neither an object in the field of my perception nor a subject who perceives me: the Other is initially a structure of the perceptual field, without which the entire field could not function as it does' (Deleuze 1990: 306–7). Beyond actualisations in concrete others, the other has 'pre-existence as the condition of organization in general' (Deleuze 1990: 307, 318–19), which Colwell refers to as *the pre-personal field* (Colwell 1997, 2000). Effectuating the desiring-machines of *terra nullius*, Zionism has embarked upon a 'Robinsonade', creating a 'world without Others' (Deleuze 1990: 319) by excluding otherness at the level of personal and collective experiences. This results in a repressive motorisation of the infrastructure against the multiplicity of the prepersonal. Perversion in Zionism is immanent:

> The world of the pervert is a world without Others, and thus a world without the possible. The Other is that which renders possible. The perverse world is a world in which the category of the necessary has completely replaced that of the possible . . . All perversion is an 'Other-cide' (Deleuze 1990: 320).

The pervert's behaviour always presupposes a fundamental absence of the others, a pure territory, explains Deleuze, and we see that Zionism has near perfected the art of perversion after a century of producing real absence. Like Deleuze (1990: 319), we may ask: 'Why does the pervert have the tendency to imagine himself as a radiant angel, an angel of helium and fire?'

Epilogue

The actual component of a given assemblage of desire is not a desire *for terra nullius* or *for* ethnic vacuum – '[T]here is no desire *for* revolution . . . no desire *for* power, desire *to* oppress or *to* be oppressed' (Deleuze and Parnet 2002: 133) – but the ethnic nullification of the *terra*, effectuated through specific movements of deterritorialisation and reterritorialisation. The settlers did not imagine the land to be empty; rather, they brought about its emptiness. Zionists do not merely discursively remove the local population through symbolic erasure, as has been suggested (Dalsheim 2004: 166). More importantly, the Zionist narrative is a product of the colonial libidinal fabric that creates reality.

When the municipality of Acre chose a sign that ignored the Arab presence, its functionaries genuinely believed they were not, in fact, ignoring anything, since you cannot ignore that which has been removed. '*They' are not supposed to be around 'us*' is the general feeling of most Israeli Jews. This is a feeling and an unconscious wish that underlies most state policies; this latent desire provokes the continuing displacement and the banal attitudes of uneasiness, such as when Arabic is spoken in public spaces, or when an Arab protest or demand for equality is raised in the face of discrimination. '*They are just not supposed to be here*' says the Zionist heart.

A machinic assemblage of *terra nullius* does not explain the essence or totality of Zionism. All socio-historical phenomena have a number of unconscious strands that come together in distinct but inter-connected planes of immanence. However, without the inception of new notions, the creation of new concepts, without political transformations or challenges of the old desires, *terra nullius* may continue to dominate the Zionist appetite for Palestinian displacement at all costs. This is not mere obstinacy – it is desire and its machines that explain the political inability to reach, in practice, a peaceable course in the inter-community relationship between Zionists and Palestinians. Only by changing the infrastructure, the workings of desire, can a collectivity change its attitude to life.

References

Ben-Porath, A. (1995), 'They Didn't Lay on the Fence', *Yunim be Tkumat Israel* 4: 278–98 (Hebrew).
Buchanan, I. (1999), 'Deleuze and Cultural Studies,' in I. Buchanan (ed.), *A Deleuzian Century?*, Durham: Duke University Press, pp. 103–19.
Buchanan, I. (2005), 'Space in the Age of Non-Place,' in I. Buchanan and G. Lambert (eds), *Deleuze and Space*, Toronto: University of Toronto Press, pp. 16–36.
Buchanan, I. (2008), *Deleuze and Guattari's Anti-Oedipus*, London: Continuum.
Colebrook, C. (2002), *Gilles Deleuze*, London: Routledge.
Colwell, C. (1997), 'Deleuze and the Prepersonal', *Philosophy Today* 41 (1): 160–8.
Colwell, C. (2000), 'Agencies of the Body', *International Studies in Philosophy* 32 (4): 13–22.
Dallmayr, F. (1996), *Beyond Orientalism*, New York: State University of New York Press.
Dalsheim, J. (2004), 'Settler Nationalism, Collective Memories of Violence and the "Uncanny Other"', *Social Identities* 10 (2): 151–70.
Davis, U. (2003), *Apartheid Israel*, London and New York: Zed Books.
Deleuze, G. (1988), *Bergsonism*, trans. H. Tomlinson and B. Habberjam, New York: Zone Books.
Deleuze, G. (1990), *The Logic of Sense*, trans. M. Lester, New York: Columbia University Press.
Deleuze, G. (1991), *Bergsonism*, trans. H. Tomlinson and B. Habberjam, New York: Zone Books.
Deleuze, G. (1994), *Difference and Repetition*, trans. P. Patton, New York: Columbia University Press.
Deleuze, G. and F. Guattari (1983), *Anti-Oedipus: Capitalism and Schizophrenia*, trans. R. Hurley, M. Seem and H. R. Lane, Minneapolis: University of Minnesota Press.
Deleuze, G. and F. Guattari (1987), *A Thousand Plateaus: Capitalism and Schizophrenia*, trans. B. Massumi, Minneapolis: University of Minnesota Press.
Deleuze, G. and F. Guattari (1994), *What is Philosophy?*, trans. H. Tomlinson and G. Burchell, New York: Columbia University Press.
Deleuze, G. and C. Parnet (2002), *Dialogues II*, trans. H. Tomlinson and B. Habberjam, New York: Columbia University Press.
Elster, J. (1983), *Sour Grapes: Studies in the Subversion of Rationality*, Cambridge: Cambridge University Press.
Falah, G. (1991), 'Israeli "Judaisation" Policy in Galilee', *Journal of Palestinian Studies* 20 (4): 69–85.
Goodchild, P. (1996), *Deleuze and Guattari – An Introduction to the Politics of Desire*, London: Sage.
Gur-Ze'ev, I. (1999), *Modernity, Postmodernity and Education*, Tel Aviv: Ramot (Hebrew).
Holland, E. (1999), *Deleuze and Guattari's Anti-Oedipus*, London: Routledge.

Humphries, I. (2005), 'From Gaza to the Galilee', *The Washington Report on Middle East Affairs* 24 (7): 12.
Khalidi, W. (1992), *All That Remains: The Palestinian Villages Occupied and Depopulated by Israel in 1948*, Washington: Institute of Palestinian Studies.
Kimmerling, B. (1983), *Zionism and Territory*, Berkeley: University of California Press.
Kletter, R. (2006), *Just Past – The Making of Israeli Archaeology*, London: Equinox.
Kretzmer, D. (1990), *The Legal Status of the Arabs in Israel*, Boulder: Westview Press.
Lustick, I. (1980), *Arabs in the Jewish State – Israel's Control of a National Minority*, Austin: University of Texas Press.
Masalha, N. (1992), *The Expulsion of the Palestinians – the Concept of Transfer in Zionist Political Thought, 1882–1948*, Washington: The Institute for Palestinian Studies.
Masalha, N. (1997), *A Land without a People – Israel, Transfer and the Palestinians 1949–1996*, London: Faber and Faber.
May, T. (1996), 'Gilles Deleuze and the Politics of Time', *Man and World* 29: 293–304.
May, T. (2005), *Gilles Deleuze: An Introduction*, Cambridge: Cambridge University Press.
Mercer, D. (1993), 'Terra Nullius, Aboriginal Sovereignty and Land Rights in Australia', *Political Geography* 12 (4): 299–318.
Metzer, J. (1998), *The Divided Economy of Mandatory Palestine*, Cambridge: Cambridge University Press.
Morris, B. (1989), *The Birth of the Palestinian Refugee Problem, 1947–1949*, Cambridge: Cambridge University Press.
Morris, B. (1990), *And After 1948: Israel and the Palestinians*, Oxford: Clarendon Press.
Pappe, I. (2006), *The Ethnic Cleansing of Palestine*, Oxford: Oneworld Publications.
Patton, P. (1996), 'Sovereignty, Law and Difference in Australia: After the Mabo Case', *Alternatives* 21: 149–70.
Patton, P. (1997), 'The World Seen from Within: Deleuze and the Philosophy of Events', *Theory and Event* 1 (1). Viewed at http://muse.jhu.edu/journals/theory_and_event/toc/
Patton, P. (2000), *Deleuze and the Political*, London: Routledge.
Peled, Y. and G. Shafir (2002), *Being Israeli: The Dynamics of Multiple Citizenship*, Cambridge: Cambridge University Press.
Peteet, J. (2005), 'Words as Interventions: Naming in the Palestine-Israel Conflict', *Third World Quarterly* 26 (1): 153–72.
Rabinowitz, D. (1997), *Overlooking Nazareth – The Ethnography of Exclusion in a Town in Galilee*, Cambridge: Cambridge University Press.
Rapoport, M. (2007), 'The Operation to the Detonation of the Mosques', *Haaretz* (6 July), The Supplement, pp. 22–8. Viewed at: http://www.haaretz.co.il/hasite/spages/878239.html
Said, E. (1979), *The Question of Palestine*, London: Routledge and Kegan Paul.
Shafir, G. (1989), *Land, Labour, and the Origins of the Israeli-Palestinian Conflict, 1882–1914*, Cambridge: Cambridge University Press.
Smith, B. J. (1993), *The Roots of Separatism in Palestine*, London: Tauris.
Svirsky, M. (2008), 'The Politics of Familiarity: An Intercultural Alternative to the Politics of Recognition', *HaMerhav HaTziburi* 2: 39–80 (Hebrew).
Svirsky, M., A. Mor-Sommerfeld, F. Azaiza and R. Herz-Lazarowitz (2007),

'Bilingual Education and Practical Interculturalism in Israel: The Case of the Galilee', *The Discourse of Sociological Practice* 8 (1): 55–81.

Yacobi, H. (2001), 'From Urban Panopticism to Spatial Protest: Housing Policy, Segregation and Social Exclusion of the Palestinian Community in the City of Lydda-Lod', Conference Paper, Cambridge MA: Lincoln Institute of Land Policy.

Yacobi, H. and S. Cohen (2006), *Separation: The Politics of Space in Israel*, Tel Aviv: Xargol and Am Oved.

Yiftachel, O. (1994), 'Spatial Planning, Land Control and Arab-Jewish Relations in the Galilee,' *Ir Ve'ezor* (City and Region) 23: 35–55 (Hebrew).

Yiftachel, O. (1995), 'The Internal Frontier: Territorial Control and Ethnic Relations in Israel', *Regional Studies* 30 (5): 493–508.

Yiftachel, O. (1996), 'The Internal Frontier', *Regional Studies* 30 (5): 493–508.

Yiftachel, O. (1999), 'Ethnocracy: The Politics of Judaizing Israel/Palestine', *Constellations: International Journal of Critical and Democratic Theory* 6 (3): 364–90.

Yiftachel, O. (2006), *Ethnocracy*, Philadelphia: University of Pennsylvania Press.

Yiftachel, O. and N. Carmon (1997), 'Socio-Spatial Mix and Inter-Ethnic Attitudes: Jewish Newcomers and Arab-Jewish Issues in the Galilee', *European Planning Studies* 5 (2): 215–38.

Yiftachel, O. and H. Yacobi (2003), 'Urban Democracy: Ethnicisation and the Production of Space in an Israeli 'Mixed' City', *Environment and Planning D: Society and Space* 21 (3): 322–43.

Young, R. J. C. (1995), *Colonial Desire*, London and New York: Routledge.

Yuval Davis, N., F. Anthias and E. Kofman (2005), 'Secure Borders and Safe Haven and the Gendered Politics of Belonging: Beyond Social Cohesion', *Ethnic and Racial Studies* 28 (3): 513–35.

Notes

The author especially thanks Paul Patton and Simone Bignall who have contributed to this article with their patient reading and meaningful observations on previous drafts. I also wish to thank Offer Parchev for our mutually interesting, endless discussions which have undoubtedly contributed, directly and indirectly, to this chapter.

1. For a map of discrimination against the Arab-Palestinian population in Israel see the reports of *Sikkuy*, an Arab-Jewish NGO working for equality in Israel: http://www.sikkuy.org.il/english/home.html. On socio-economic gaps, see reports of the Adva Centre – http://www.adva.org/indexe.html; the Association for Civil Rights in Israel – http://www.acri.org.il/english-acri/engine/index.asp; the Arab Centre for Alternative Planning –http://english.ac-ap.org/; Bimkom – http://www.bimkom.org/aboutEng.asp; and the Mossawa Centre website – http://www.mossawacenter.org/en/about/about.html, which criticises various forms of Israeli racism towards Arab citizens.
2. I prefer to label the conflict between these two nations as 'Zionist-Palestinian', instead of the more conventional 'Israeli-Palestinian', because I do not perceive the conflict as a confrontation between Palestinians and the Israeli public as a whole, but more specifically as the historical result of Zionist political thought and practice.
3. Nonetheless, it is important to notice that social production and desiring production 'differs only in modality (social production is molar whereas

desiring-production is molecular – this is a difference in function not scale, the molar can reside in the individual just as the molecular can reside in the collective)' (Buchanan 2008: 96).
4. In this context, the term *Nakbeh* indicates the national tragedy of the ethnic cleansing during the war of 1948–9.
5. See the interview (in Hebrew) at http://www.televizia.net/
6. There were two main patterns of land tenure in Palestine: at the end of the nineteenth century, most of the lands were under a collective-village form of ownership (the *Mushaa*), which enabled Palestinian communities to prevent their lands from going onto the market. This form of common ownership declined during the 1930s, converting most of the *Mushaa* lands into private property that could be sold to Jewish settlers (Kimmerling 1983: 32). 'The second major form of land tenure in Palestine was private ownership of large estates by mainly urban dwellers: in part the land was cultivated by the owners (with hired labourers) and leased to tenants and sharecroppers who had been the previous owners (and remained attached to the land by reason of work and sentiment) . . . 'This type of land was among the most fluid, and the owners' willingness to sell it was dependent on its price on the market' (Kimmerling 1983: 33). There were other types of land ownership such as the *Waqf* lands which, in market terms, was the most enduring type of ownership. These lands were considered sacred by Muslims and comprised mosques, schools, charities and Muslim bureaucracy. Another type, *Miri*, was owned *de jure* by the government, but in practice by settlers and cultivators, for as long as it was cultivated. For a complete classification of land tenure in the pre-Zionist period of Palestine see Kimmerling (1983: 34–6) and Smith (1993: 90–4).
7. While most Western colonialism grew out from a metropolis that emanated, wave-like, upon territories and cultures of the earth (Young 1995: 171), in Ottoman and Mandatory Palestine local immigrants unfolded these waves without an overseas locus of control.
8. For a list of publications providing a critical reading of Zionist development in Palestine, see: on its colonialist forming, Kimmerling 1983; Shafir 1989; Smith 1993. On the events of the 1948–9 war and the *Nakbeh* see Masalha 1992; Khalidi 1992; Pappe 2006.
9. '[A] a small stratum of organized Eastern European Jewish agricultural workers who reached Palestine in the Second *Aliyah* between 1904 and 1914 shouldered the major burden of Israel's creation. Their leaders . . . and their political heirs from the Third *Aliyah* of 1918–1923, gave determinate shape to emerging Israeli society' (Shafir 1989: 1). *Aliyah* literally means 'ascension', since for Zionism immigration to *Eretz* Israel (The Land of Israel) is an act of ideological and moral elevation quite distinct from immigration to any other country. Emigration of Israeli Jews from Israel is ideologically defined by Zionists as *yeridah*, an act of treasonous descending, lowering oneself morally.
10. '[O]n the one hand there was the steady concentration of, and encroachment by, an immigrant Jewish presence, accompanied by the relentless consolidation of its control over the natural resources of the country. On the other hand, there was the corresponding marginalization, dispersal, thinning out, and beleaguering of the indigenous Palestinians who until 1948 constituted the vast majority of the population. (Khalidi 1992: xxxi)
11. In Hebrew, the name used to describe the nascent Jewish collective entity in Palestine, means 'the Settlement' or 'the inhabited place'.
12. During the fifty years of Jewish immigration to Palestine leading up to the 1920s, the Palestinian economy gradually acquired certain capitalist characteristics – such as the apparatus of capture of profit (from labour) and taxation, a significant

expansion of agriculture (without modernisation), a partial integration in the international market through exports (mainly of wheat and oranges) and achieving a surplus of exports over imports (Shafir 1989: 29–30).
13. The feudal conditions that greeted the Jewish immigrants explain their historical choice for agriculture and land – and not industry – as the initial base of the new society, rather than the romantic notion of 'returning to the land' that characterizes the Zionist discourse (Ben-Porath 1995: 294).
14. Two other critical changes took place in the party-political arena and in the creation of the first Zionist paramilitary groups. All three experiments 'followed a similar logic' and were 'attempts to bypass the dynamic of the labour market' (Shafir 1989: 123–34). On the collectivist genesis and initial transformations of the *kibbutz*, see Shafir (1989: 168–86).
15. This archetypical colonial model was developed by prominent Zionist activists, drawing on German responses to the German agrarian crisis around the end of the nineteenth century and to frontier conflicts with the Slavic peoples (Shafir 1989: 154).
16. This codex is still in practice. Its effects have been challenged only in the last few years by civil-rights NGOs. Since the inception of the Israeli state, the JNF and the Jewish Agency enjoy a legal status that entitles the state to discriminate between Jews and non-Jewish citizens concerning the allocations of land and housing. See Davis 2003: 39–42; Yiftachel 2006: 103–10 and Kretzmer 1990: 49–77.
17. The modes of national land acquisition continued to transform after the establishment of a whole Israeli land system which nowadays owns, control and manage approximately 93 per cent of Israeli territory, either through the state or Jewish agencies in co-operation with the state, backed up by law. As Yiftachel explains, '[T]he making of a new land system was based on several key principles: physical seizure, nationalization, Judaisation, establishment of tight central control, and uneven distribution' (Yiftachel 2006: 136–42).
18. This does not mean that Israel emerged solely out of a series of co-operatives; by 'nucleic' I mean to indicate this as the most influential productive pattern which Zionism developed through experimentation. 'The significance of the *kibbutz* in the formation of the Israeli state and nation was much greater than its share of the *Yishuv's* population would indicate. Finally, quality did outweigh quantity' (Shafir 1989: 185).
19. Smith clearly exposes the role of the British Mandate in the production of a bifurcated economy in Palestine. Keeping peace and balancing the confronting interests and needs of the two communities was the apparent paradigm by which Britain operated in Palestine. In fact, 'British economic policy ... was a significant element in the divergent development of the Palestine economy following World War I' (Smith 1993: 3) and indeed helped Zionists build a national economic base. From 1921 onwards the British administration managed immigration policy on the principle of the country's 'economic absorptive capacity', limited 'by the numbers and interests of the present population'. But in fact, 'the concept of economic absorptive capacity was essentially a political tool, a useful slogan purporting to show Britain's government concern for the protection of Arab interests', since immigration was really determined by Zionist agencies and not according to the Mandatory Administration's ability to create employment and provide facilities for Jewish newcomers (Smith 1993: 68). The British administration adopted a *laissez-faire* approach to colonial land purchase that turned into a critical source of conflict and failed to protect the Arab peasantry from massive Zionist purchases that were accompanied by eviction of thousands of tenants from the land (Smith 1993: 87–115). Furthermore, the British administration made commercial monopolistic concessions to the Zionist movement in a bid to

exploit natural resources and operate public services and utilities (Smith 1993: 117), and adopted a protectionist industrial policy that included tax exemptions and regulations that favoured the growing Jewish industry (Smith 1993: 176). By not preventing the discriminatory 'Jews-only' employment policies of the private sector, 'the Civil administration clearly placed its commitment to promote the Jewish National Home above its obligation to protect the rights of the non-Jewish population' (Smith 1993: 159).

20. Now in its fortieth year of implementation, the 'Judaisation' project has evolved into the notion of a socio-territorial spatiality significantly characterised by an ethnic separatist mentality according to which Arab-Palestinians citizens remain confined to their villages and cities and continue to suffer from state discrimination in all areas of life, while Jewish newcomers into the region live apart within their small, enclosed and gated 'home and garden' communities, fully invested with new roads, well-equipped educational systems and cultural and sports centres, and wrapped in the warm mantle of governmental ideological and economic support (Falah 1991; Yiftachel 1996, 1999; Rabinowitz 1997; Humphries 2005)

21. Apologias based either on post-Holocaust nationalist drives or the inevitable consequences of war or insistence that all planning was motivated purely by ideology are misleading. Firstly, at the level of the state-machines of Israel, the Jewish Holocaust has never been more than a useful episode to be manipulated and mobilised for nationalistic functions (Gur-Ze'ev 1999); the ethnic cleansing of Palestine cannot be explained as the furious response of the Jewish people after the Holocaust, in a bid to secure a national home against any such recurrence in future. The state has had the significant opportunity to respond to the horrors of the Holocaust by ensuring the well-being of those survivors who reached Israel – this, however, has not been done, as attested by the protests of Holocaust survivors to this day. Secondly, ethnic cleansing is not an inevitable consequence of all wars, even when territorial conquest is involved. Thirdly, as was pointed out previously, ideology has played but a limited role in Zionist practice.

22. Pappe's *The Ethnic Cleansing of Palestine* is revolutionary, principally because he abandons the paradigm of war as explicative of the events of 1948, which served to justify atrocities against humanity as 'natural' outcomes of war – for example, in the work of the Israeli historian Benny Morris (1989). In its stead, Pappe adopts the paradigm of ethnic cleansing as the explanatory framework of analysis, a prism that enables a deeper understanding, not only of past events but also of their implications for the future.

23. Lately, researchers have discovered that the planned destruction of the Palestinian society, towns and culture also included a detailed scheme to destroy archaeological sites and mosques, at the instigation of the legendary Moshe Dayan (Rapoport 2007; Kletter 2006).

24. See: *The Citizenship and Entry into Israel Law (temporary provision) 5763 – 2003*, Knesset; http://www.knesset.gov.il/laws/special/eng/citizenship_law.htm

25. To this end, they add:

> The government of Israel and the Jewish Agency (a quasi-governmental body with development powers) created a range of incentives to attract the desirable population to the region: state land at very low cost, physical infrastructure at negligible cost, generous housing assistance, and high-quality municipal and educational services. The 'natural' process that aided the settlement activity was the increasing numbers of young middle-class Jewish families looking for semi-rural life style . . . These people were looking to improve their environmental and social residential settings, away from Israel's typically high density urban centres. (Yiftachel and Carmon 1997: 220)

Chapter 11
Virtually Postcolonial?

Philip Leonard

The idea, so popular among some commentators in the 1990s, that Information and Communications Technologies (ICTs) have steered political authority and cultural production away from the nation-state, has persisted in the twenty-first century. After the early pro-globalist rush to embrace the Internet as a truly supranational tool, new ICTs continue to be treated as a delocalising force, shifting the balance of power away from the organisational systems of the nation-state and placing it instead within a distributed informational network that operates outside of geographical and national space. With no spatial barriers to entry – and beyond the legislative structures that regulate activity within the nation-state – digital culture has allowed the individual to engage in open communication and to navigate information freely. We have become confident in our self-image as netizens and cybernauts who participate with unprecedented autonomy in an online democracy (Hauben and Hauben 1997; Rheingold 1993: 59ff.; Gore 2008: 245–70), rather than being subjected to information transmitted by governmental or national media organisations. More recently, the web's second incarnation has allowed it to graduate to greater heights of collaboration and interactivity, with online networks allowing groups to traverse the confines of space that have traditionally shaped social association. *Citizen Cyborg* (Hughes 2004), *The Cyborg Self and the Networked City* (Mitchell 2004), *The World is Flat* (Friedman 2006): such titles speak of the new *habitus* that transcends the imagined space of the nation-state, a digital (non-)place that can finally fulfil the promise of participatory citizenship because it is *globally* inclusive.

Many associated with postcolonial theory warn that such narratives of cultural inclusivity and social progress are deeply flawed. Reasserting a stubbornly colonial ethic, liberal – and libertarian – accounts of transnational participation have repeatedly assumed their right to universal representation by conjuring away any attachment to space and culture, celebrating the nation-state's transcendence while continuing to find a home in regions and nations whose authority is built on a colonial legacy. Too often, the 'we' invoked in discourses of cultural representation and political participation either excludes groups who do not identify with the new inclusivity, or tolerates those groups only at the margins of social life. Further, just as power and space remain organised around a recognisably colonial dynamic, so time and history here continue to be shaped by assumptions about reason and progress that postcolonial theory has compellingly challenged (see Prakash 1995; Spivak 1999; Young 2004). Placing global populations *sub specie aeternitatis*, declarations of our shared departure from the confines of the nation-state are certainly premature in their celebration of a collective emancipation, but they also risk reinforcing the historiographic privileging of colonial authority and Western modernity. However, although new technologies have become fused to an old Enlightenment narrative of development, the persistence of a technological divide is becoming increasingly apparent, with what might variously (and problematically) be termed first world, developed, or industrial nations continuing to benefit from the uneven distribution of information (and other) technologies. Governments and international organisations are beginning to attend to the issue of the digital divide across nations,[1] but social and cultural theory has been alert to this imbalance for some time, emphasising the resonances of this divide with an established colonial-developmental ethic.[2]

Deleuze too would find unsatisfactory and unconvincing the libertarian transnationalism that now frames orthodox readings of technology's place within globalisation. The relationship between technology and globalisation is not considered by Deleuze in terms that we might recognise today, and he writes only obliquely about postcoloniality and globalisation. But he does rethink the concepts of technological production and territorial location in ways that offer an antidote both to the notion that new technologies necessarily overcome the uneven distribution of power that has continued to shape postcolonial cultures and to the idea that a new virtuality has initiated a smooth space of global community. The familiar tropes that guide technolibertarian readings of globalisation – the claim that materiality has become subordinated to the informational or the notion that we have successfully separated ourselves from location and become technomigrants – can be seen, after Deleuze, as rooted in a misrecognition of subjectivity, agency, cultural location, materiality and transcendence. The nation-state is not so easily swept away in the information age as we might suppose, Deleuze cautions, but neither can territorial location or national consciousness be conceived as possessing an interior integrity that can endure threats from outside. As social and cultural theorists are now observing, national governments are reasserting themselves by developing strategies which, in both cultural and legal terms, are designed to re-establish national identity against the acceleration of transborder technologies;[3] the consequence of this reaction to globalisation is a kind of territorial schizophrenia, since governments are continuing to invoke narratives of national sovereignty while simultaneously positioning themselves within a wider social and political economy. After Deleuze, this schizophrenic condition can be understood as a functional, unstable and impermanent simultaneity.

Attempts have often been made to conceive Deleuze as a prototheorist of cyberculture, and he has been particularly associated with the idea that the Internet is ushering in an era of disembodied consciousness and rhizomatic multiplicities. This incorporation of Deleuze into cybertheory is being increasingly resisted, however, and several commentators have drawn attention to the disquiet that he felt about the collapsing together of technology and utopian posthumanism. John Marks, for example, observes that 'although there are elements in Deleuze and Guattari's work that undeniably connect with the creative and liberating aspects of cyberspace, there is also much which indicates a resistance to, and a critique of, what might be termed the "imaginary" of cyberspace' (Marks 2006: 195). This essay undertakes a related questioning of Deleuze's association with cybertheory by considering the ways in which he provokes a rethinking of technology's connection to national identity. While Deleuze certainly claims (albeit in a circumlocutory fashion) that technology can transform the social sphere and that the concept of the nation-state is inadequate, he does not, this essay argues, adopt either a technoculturalist or a globalist perspective. Beginning with Deleuze's concept of virtuality, it will dissect the two overlapping misconceptions that have grown up in both social theory and popular culture: the idea that digital culture has allowed us to transcend our geophysical location, and the belief that globalisation has resulted in the smooth distribution of information across what used to be the confines of the nation-state. In this manner, Deleuze's work resonates powerfully with postcolonial theory: just as postcolonial theory's concerns lie broadly with invisible persistence of colonial structures in a world that seemingly rejects colonial rule, so Deleuze argues that the nation-state constantly reasserts itself against both internal and external threats. But if postcolonial theory is also concerned to expose the ambivalent contingency that constantly haunts narratives of the nation-state's fixity (Bhabha 1993), then

Deleuze too argues that it is the incessant reshaping of territorial space that allows oppressed groups and minorities to interrupt the functioning of the majoritarian nation-state (see Deleuze and Guattari 1986: 16–27). And if postcolonial theory has displaced modernity's subject as the agent of resistance, then Deleuzian thought – and, to an extent, Deleuze himself – similarly finds in technology new modes of intervention that are effective precisely because they short-circuit regulatory mechanisms that operate at the national level.

The Digital Code

Deleuze, Keith Ansell-Pearson observes, 'is widely taken to be a philosopher of the virtual' (2005: 1121). However, while the virtual has been harnessed to other concepts in the Deleuzian lexicon (becoming, the machinic and the assemblage) to result in his catachrestic appropriation by anarchist technoevolutionism, this concept for him does not signify technological forms of simulation, disembodied immersion or artificial environments. Neither does it point to the recent and more elaborate sense of an interface between users and the devices that are associated with the information age – the mode of technological interaction that Katherine Hayles (1999: 92) names as 'virtual subjectivity', that Gonzalo Frasca (2006) refers to as 'outmersion', or that Mark Hansen describes as 'the deep correlation between embodiment and virtuality' (2006: x). Virtuality, for Deleuze, requires consciousness to be understood according to an alternative temporality from the one attributed to it by technoevolutionism, and his reassessment of virtuality challenges attempts to detach the integrity of the real from its imaging by mere representations. Bergson's account of the image-making function of memory – in which memory is not seen to retain or render present the past, but is an inert, non-individuated and extra-psychological condition from which consciousness is concretised as perception – provides Deleuze with the conceptual resources for rethinking virtuality as a space of unthought and unrealised multiplicities. For Bergson, Deleuze tells us, memory *is* the past: being before and beyond any act of conscious preservation – a subsisting primordiality – it is a condition of 'pure recollection' (Deleuze 1991: 55). It exists, in other words, in a virtual state. And yet, Deleuze emphasises, Bergson's metaphysics is not as recognisable as it might seem, since he refuses to consign pure recollection to a domain that is wholly exterior to the real. Instead, both memory and matter, both the image and the real, come together in a state of perpetual exchange. In this transactional interplay, the virtual exists not in state of transcendental seclusion, but in an undifferentiated and immanent space of energies from which individuated experience (consciousness, subjectivity, matter) appears. While it is the source of creativity and production, the virtual is, then, constantly actualised by thought which cannot fully or finally capture its smooth unity. What flows from this condition of unformed, non-determining and generative multiplicities is not a perception of the virtual, but instances of actualisation which subject virtuality to a logic of systematic differentiation:

> It is difference that is primary in the process of actualization – the difference between the virtual from which we begin and the actuals at which we arrive, and also the difference between the complementary lines according to which actualization takes place. In short, the characteristic of virtuality is to exist in such a way that it is actualized by being differentiated and is forced to differentiate itself, to create its lines of differentiation in order to be actualized. (Deleuze 1991: 97)

Rather than forming an ordered system, these lines of differentiation can come together only in a series of disjunctive syntheses: 'There is here no longer any coexisting whole,' Deleuze writes, 'there are merely lines of actualization, *some successive, others simultaneous*, but each representing an actualization of the whole in one direction and not combining with other lines or other directions' (Deleuze 1991: 100; original emphasis). The virtual therefore manifests itself in the actual only as an irritant to stasis, provoking an incessant renegotiation of the actual and preventing the process of differentiation from hardening into an ossified sense of the real.

For Manuel DeLanda, the concept of the assemblage provides a point of departure for conceiving actuality's status as a differentiated and differentiating condition. References to this concept are scattered throughout Deleuze's writing, as DeLanda observes in *A New Philosophy of Society*, its sense lying in an uncertain and exterior connection to other concepts – in other words, the concept of the assemblage is itself an assemblage. 'Taking into account the entire network of ideas within which the concept of "assemblage" performs its conceptual duties,' DeLanda writes, 'we do have at least the rudiments of a theory . . . part of a definition may be in one book, extended somewhere else, and qualified in some obscure essay' (DeLanda 2006: 3). Animated by Deleuze's thinking, rather than seeking exegetically to extract from Deleuze's work a fully-articulated theory,[4] DeLanda expands the concept of the assemblage into a more comprehensive ontology that aims to account for the constitutive processes that shape and reshape social entities. One of DeLanda's principal reference points when sketching out the loose shape of the assemblage is Deleuze's claim, in *Dialogues II*, that the combinatorial relationships that have produced all entities (whether organisms, ecosystems or social networks) need to be understood as relations of exterior association, not of interior attachment (such as biological inheritance, genetic bond or community affiliation). Deleuze writes:

> What is an assemblage? It is a multiplicity which is made up of many heterogeneous terms and which establishes liaisons, relations between them, across ages, sexes and reigns – different natures. Thus, the assemblage's only unity is that of co-functioning: it is a symbiosis, a 'sympathy'. It is never filiations which are important, but alliances, alloys; these are not successions, lines of descent, but contagions, epidemics, the wind. (Deleuze and Parnet 2002: 52, cited in DeLanda 2006: 121, n.9)

From such ephemera, *A New Philosophy of Society* is concerned primarily to build an alternative ontology of both nature and the social in order to arrive at a framework which sees all entities as the product of combination, interaction and association. This involves not only an effort to chart the processes that Deleuze elsewhere describes as the 'variable connections and positions' (DeLanda 2006: 93) by which assemblages come together and are actualised, but also the establishment of the virtual as a force which constantly initiates new actualities and different assemblages.

It is perhaps because DeLanda is concerned with establishing a broad ontology that he does not comment on the subsequent remarks in *Dialogues II*: 'An assemblage is never technological,' Deleuze writes, 'if anything, it is the opposite' (Deleuze and Parnet 2002: 52). Deleuze's distinction here points to the reductionist definition of technology as technical instrumentality – technology conceived as a set of engineered devices that are external to the human body, accessorising it either to aid its functional efficiency or to interrupt its capacity for self-governance. Such a sense of the technological is an insufficient one for Deleuze, since for him all entities (including technological devices) need to be located within the larger apparatus of the assemblage. 'Tools always presuppose a machine, and the machine is always social before being technical'; he elaborates: 'There is always a social machine which selects or assigns the technical elements used' (Deleuze and Parnet 2002: 52). Technological devices do not, then, possess the determining character with which they are often credited; to treat them as the motor of economic, demographic or communicational change would be a mistake, since they represent one constituent element of larger social and cultural systems. Rather than providing a route to the virtual, technological systems therefore need to be viewed as part of the order of actualisation and differentiation that is itself affected by virtuality.

Incorporating tools and instruments into the wider system of the assemblage in this way does not, however, preclude a Deleuzian model of social change from attaching some transformative potential to technological devices. Deleuze elsewhere continues to challenge the notion that technology drives modernity, introducing the now familiar concept of 'the machinic' as an alternative to that of the technological. Most often associated with Deleuze's redefinition of the body as an uncertain, shifting and externally dependent entity, the machinic 'relates not to the production of goods but rather to a precise state of intermingling of bodies in a society, including all the attractions and repulsions, sympathies and antipathies, alterations, amalgamations, penetrations, and expansions that affect bodies of all kinds in their relation to one another' (Deleuze and Guattari 1988: 90).[5] Less frequently considered is the way that this concept also questions a prevailing trend in Western historiography. Working against attempts to define 'primitive' societies as somehow pre-technological (since these societies as much as others need to be seen as processes of connection and disjunction), the machinic cannot, as a corollary, be understood in terms of social development, as the motor of civilised society, or as the marker of the West's advanced status. Instead, A *Thousand Plateaus* argues, the sense of a progressive (and, traditionally, Western-centred) entry into technological modernity precludes analysis of the particular machinic processes that shape and cut across social formations:

> We define social formations by machinic processes and not by modes of production (these on the contrary depend on the process). Thus primitive societies are defined by mechanisms of prevention-anticipation; State societies are defined by apparatuses of capture; urban societies, by war machines; and finally international, or rather ecumenical, organizations are defined by the encompassment of heterogeneous social formations. (Deleuze and Guattari 1988: 435)

Importantly, although the machinic signifies a departure from notions of corporeal integrity or social development, this concept is also built on the corresponding claim that entities *function* (albeit haltingly and without autonomy) as artificial apparatuses. What Deleuze challenges is not technology as such, but the impoverished perception of it as detached from a corporeally self-identical human. The machinic does not require a rejection of the technological (as *Dialogues II* might seem to suggest when it claims that 'A tool remains marginal, or little used, until there exists a social machine or collective assemblage which is capable of taking it into its "phylum"' [Deleuze and Parnet 2002: 52]), but the relocation of it as a part of the social assemblage that is fed by connections and disjunctions between entities – entities which, while differentiated, cannot be fully separated from each other. More than this, *A Thousand Plateaus* further extends the role of technologies beyond that of the instrumental when it associates tools with the machinic, claiming that they 'exist in relation to the interminglings *they make possible* or that make them possible' (Deleuze and Guattari 1988: 90; emphasis added). That is, since technological devices move within the assemblage – since they cannot be consigned to some meta-human or extra-social space – they must also be affected by the interruptive substratum that is virtuality. In short, while technology cannot be seen as ushering in a new state of incorporeal virtuality, it can nevertheless be instrumental to the process of social change.

The Agony of Connection

The technocultural celebration of becoming digital, understood as the progressive loss of embodied consciousness and the entry into an unregulated and discarnate state, cannot therefore be accommodated by Deleuze's sense of the virtual. Indeed for him, rather than acting as the driving force of a culture of simulation or allowing human culture to evolve into a newly transcendent condition of material disconnection, technology is itself troubled by the smooth substratum of the virtual. We are not entering the virtual, in other words, but are – and have always been – continuously negotiating our anxious relation to it. As *A Thousand Plateaus* reveals, this rethinking of technology's non-virtuality has dramatic consequences not only for our understanding of human embodiment, but also for understanding its place in the transformation of the nation-state: if it is no longer possible to assume that we are moving from the human to the virtual, then it seems similarly problematic to believe that technology is forcing us to lose our territorial location, to leave the national and become global.

Casual, cursory and superficial readings of Deleuze might seize upon moments in which he appears to promote the idea that national boundaries are not only precarious but also unsustainable and in a state of terminal decline. For example, in the opening section of the 'Geophilosophy' chapter of *What is Philosophy?* he states that 'the earth constantly carries out a movement of deterritorialization on the spot, by which it goes beyond territory: it is deterritorializing and deterritorialized' (Deleuze and Guattari 1994: 85). And in 'Schizophrenia and

Society' Deleuze claims that schizophrenic delirium releases history from the ordered perception of differentiated time, allowing a wider series of social intersections to become visible: 'Races, civilizations, cultures, continents, kingdoms, powers, wars, classes, and revolutions are all mixed together' (Deleuze 2007a: 26). Moments like these might, when isolated, suggest that Deleuze slips easily from mapping conceptual geographies or considering a particular psychosocial dynamic to exposing national and ethnic distinctions as unstable artifices which ultimately dissolve into an underlying condition of undifferentiated multiplicity. And yet, Deleuze is careful not to slide so easily into a celebration of diversity and difference that attenuates territorial location or to claim that pure detachment from the assemblage that is national location – and the power that resides within it – is possible. The strident naming of Deleuze the anarchist collapses not because he is a closet metaphysician who falls victim to the thinking of being he supposedly denounces (his 'fundamental problem', Alain Badiou [2000: 10] tells us, 'is most certainly not to liberate the multiple but to submit thinking to a renewed concept of the One'). Rather, it breaks down because it disregards Deleuze's attention to the reassertion of social bonds in the wake of crises. Examples of this other Deleuze proliferate: in the Preface to Henri Gobard's (1976) *L'Aliénation linguistique*, he draws attention to micropolitical responses to majoritarian representation, such as the 'resurgence of regional languages', the 'other languages and dialects' of African Americans within English, or the acts of linguistic mimicry which challenge English as 'the recognized vehicular language of the world' (Deleuze 2007b: 69). Paul Patton points to Deleuze's subtle (and often neglected) account of the version of colonialism that Palestinian and Native American people have experienced. While a significant distinction needs to be made between the ethnic location of both populations (since 'Palestinians, unlike Native Americans, do have an Arab world outside of Israel from which they can draw support'), they are both nonetheless subject to a colonialism that turns them into 'peoples who are often displaced from their traditional homelands, but who, whether displaced or not, remain captives of the colonial state established on their territories' (Patton 2006: 108). *A Thousand Plateaus* insists, against ethnography's treatment of nomadism as boundless movement and a departure from place, that the nomad is not an endlessly mobile and destratified drifter. Rather, the nomad 'has a territory; he follows customary paths; he goes from one point to another; he is not ignorant of points' (Deleuze and Guattari 1998: 380). And, despite its opening emphasis on processes of deterritorialisation, much of 'Geophilosophy' is given to charting philosophy's emergence within a particular configuration of social, historical and geographical forces: '[T]hinking takes place in the relationship of territory and the earth', Deleuze and Guattari observe (Deleuze and Guattari 1994: 85).

'Schizophrenia and Society' further emphasises the significance of location, arguing that schizophrenia needs to be seen as an unruly and agonising connectedness – 'an almost unbearable proximity with the real' – and not, as is often assumed, as a separation from the real or a disaggregated perception of self (Deleuze 2007a: 27). The schizophrenic's delirium arises because proper names become overburdened with signification, because spatial order becomes a process to be invested in and navigated intensely, rather than a deceptive simulation to be decoded and transgressed: 'It's as if the zones, the thresholds or the gradients of intensity which the schizophrenic traverses on the organless body . . . are designated by the proper names of races, continents, classes, persons' (Deleuze 2007: 26). Conspicuously dismissing the sense of spatial dislocation or transnational flows that we might now associate with globalisation, Deleuze therefore finds ethnic, national and territorial location to be overemphasised and hyperactualised by those who are seen to be incapable of perceiving it. What the schizophrenic draws attention to is not the unsustainable artificiality of national borders, but the connections that allow borders to function, fail and be re-formed around established modes of belonging, such as the nation-state. Reading Deleuze as an advocate of our liberation either by technology or into universal citizenship is, therefore, doubly problematic. Just as the virtual cannot, for him, be equated with the terminal dematerialisation of the real and the arrival of a new informationalism, so deterritorialisation cannot be understood in terms of transnational or multicultural flows that have recently emerged successfully to replace national belonging. It would therefore seem appropriate to read Deleuze not as an advocate of the historical decline of the nation-state and the consequent emergence of postcolonial or global cultures, but as someone who would view national, postcolonial and global cultures as actualised instances of an originary hybridity.

Technology and Space

As much as Deleuze establishes a functional similarity in the way that technology, territoriality and virtuality operate in the formation and transformation of social assemblages – and, as Marks (2006: 196) observes, although he is 'not unaware that contemporary societies are characterised by their dependence on information technology and computers' – Deleuze does not go on to examine the particular convergence of technology and transnationalism that is now associated with globalisation. Indeed, while convincing accounts of the transnational character of network culture remain relatively embryonic today, efforts are under way to resist the persistently technolibertarian and proglobalist claims that new communications technologies have allowed human culture to evolve into a harmonious, consensual, participatory and translocal virtuality. For instance, William Mitchell's *e-topia* moderates his earlier suggestion in *City of Bits* that the Internet 'is fundamentally and profoundly *antispatial*' by arguing that information flows in the digital age have resulted in a re-organisation of urban space (Mitchell 1995: 8). This condition he names 'renucleation', wherein

> [t]he electronic unravelling of traditional imperatives of adjacency may produce certain urban arrangements – perhaps major ones – but it is very unlikely to result in random scattering and galloping decentralization. We will continue to see a spatial division of labor, within which different localities perform varying specialized roles according to their comparative advantages. Things will still have their places. It will remain possible to describe neighborhoods, cities, regions, and nations in terms of their characteristic clusters of economic activities. (Mitchell 2000: 77)

Mitchell's emphasis falls primarily on the way that space has been iteratively reaffirmed, rather than abandoned, in the digital age; Geert Lovink's concern, in contrast, is with the reassertion of power by network culture. Network culture is now harnessed to official institutions and organisations, Lovink claims, since the early counterculturalist thrust of the Internet has been tamed by its conversion into a new space of market and governmental control. Indeed, for him, this development needs to be understood as yet another form of colonial capture: 'After discovery and colonization,' he writes, 'what remains is the socialization of cyberspace' (Lovink 2002: 2). Importantly, a discursive ruse needs to be identified in this 'electronic gold rush' (Lovink 2002: 330), since the concept of the Internet as an open and unregulated space has been successfully appropriated and mobilised by a narrative of free – supranational – exchange which nevertheless remains rooted resolutely in an established distribution of economic power and cultural authority. Network culture no longer facilitates the internationalist ethic of a digital avant-garde, Lovink argues, because 'a global economic model has replaced the libertarian-hippie model of a network architecture and culture that was so prominent in the early to mid 1990s.... There are hardly any signs left of cyberspace as an autonomous, supranational, transgender sphere' (Lovink 2002: 330).

Manuel Castells, too, believes that territorial space has been reasserted, rather than transcended, by network culture, although Castells is less impressed than Lovink by the utopianism of the 1990s technocultural counter-culture, and he is less convinced than Mitchell by the potential for digital technologies to usher in evenly structured urban spaces. Castells' *The Internet Galaxy* (2001) contests futurological pronouncements on the arrival of derealised informationalism and the attendant death of established modes of social organisation, describing techno-evangelists' claims that the Internet allows us to abandon materiality and to shape the social sphere as a digital inclusivity as irresponsible and ill-conceived. What we need to recognise, against the jubilant celebration of being online as a decentred immateriality, is that a different economic and spatial geography is being produced by networks of technological association:

> The Internet Age has been hailed as the end of geography. In fact, the Internet has a geography of its own, a geography made of networks and nodes that process information flows generated and managed from places. The unit is the network, so the architecture and dynamics of multiple networks are the sources of meaning and function for each place. The resulting space of flows is a new form of space, characteristic of the Information Age, but it is not placeless . . . it redefines distance but does not cancel geography. (Castells 2001: 207)

In what would have seemed to many in the 1990s a counter-intuitive move, Castells argues that the Internet reconfigures the movement of information as a differently spatialised flow, rather than allowing it to move entirely beyond spatial location. Metropolitan areas have become home to the majority of the world's populations, and the demographic shift towards urban living is, according to *The Internet Galaxy*, directly attributable to the explosion of information and communications industries and to the growth of a knowledge economy (comprising business, media and cultural industries) that is powered by the Internet. Importantly, though unsurprisingly for Castells, this migration of populations to urban and metropolitan areas is taking place because it is in such locations that network culture finds its most concentrated manifestation. It is in cities – notably, cities in 'developed' countries – that the Internet is being produced: it is in Finland, Japan, Sweden and the US that the corporate giants of the Internet are located; Helsinki, Tokyo, Stockholm, San Francisco, San Jose, Seattle and Washington are among the many 'technopoles' from which network culture radiates. This is '[n]o undifferentiated spatial diffusion', he maintains, 'but highly selective, metropolitan concentration, and global networking' (Castells 2001: 213). For

Mitchell, Lovink and Castells, then, place has been replaced, rather than displaced, by a different spatiality; while neighbourhoods, communities, cities and nation-states have undergone significant transformation as a consequence of developments in information and communication technologies, they have successfully endured the translocal and transborder dislocations that appeared to be proceeding uncontrollably, and at breakneck speed, in the closing moments of the twentieth century.

Identifying the new demography that has emerged with digital and network culture is not wholly at odds with a Deleuzian sense of the multiplicities that provoke the reshaping of the social sphere. As 'Schizophrenia and Society', 'The Future of Linguistics', *A Thousand Plateaus* and *What is Philosophy?* attest, Deleuze is certainly attentive to the processes of actualisation – given in the territoriality of the nomad or the geophilosophical settlement of Europe, for example – that produce social specificity and result in particular cultural topologies. But the concepts that Deleuze leaves us with do point to an understanding of the assemblage that is network culture, which differs from the ones offered by Mitchell, Lovink and Castells. Against Mitchell's suggestion that such transformation is driven – perhaps even determined – by technology, Deleuze finds technology to be part of an assemblage that is both shaped by and enables multivalent connections. In contrast with Lovink's nostalgic portrait of a now-deceased – authentic and libertarian – technoculture, Deleuze avoids equating resistance with an intentionalist politics of intervention. And, unlike Castells, Deleuze is concerned not so much with analysing the sociological and geopolitical dimensions of a particular social formation, but stresses instead the transformative force that produces new actualities and new assemblages. Indeed, while Deleuze does not advocate the notion of an 'undifferentiated spatial diffusion' that Castells castigates, he does remind us that it is virtuality – the underlying and undifferentiated condition of spatial dispersion – that incessantly resists the drive to fix systems and structures.

'A Politics of the Unrepresentable'

Although Deleuze himself left only a fragmentary sense of the precise relationship between virtuality, transnationalism and technoculture, commentators on his work have subsequently started to piece these fragments together in order to think more rigorously the relationship between technology and sociocultural transformation. Claire Colebrook observes that against 'all those modernist thinkers who regarded technology as a fall into lifelessness and mechanization', Deleuze finds 'the potential to free thought and perception from technology *through technology*; the very machines that extend life allowing for the reduction of effort can also open up new problems and new creations' (Colebrook 2006: 13; original emphasis). DeLanda picks out communications technologies as features of the assemblage that render the internal co-ordinates of spatial structures uncertain. Not just those of modernity and later modernity, such technologies as writing, the postal service, telegraphy and telephony (as well as computers) 'blur the spatial boundaries of social entities by eliminating the need for co-presence: they enable conversations to take place at a distance, allow interpersonal networks to form . . . and give organizations the means to operate in different countries' (DeLanda 2006: 13).

If, for commentators such as Colebrook and DeLanda, Deleuze provokes us into confronting the critical contribution that technologies can – must – make to sociocultural change, then for McKenzie Wark this critical role needs to be understood as one that falls outside of the traditions of deliberative interventionism. And, rather than considering the ways in which particular technologies might effect change, Wark argues that an indefinable and uncontainable process of transformation underlies and crosses different technologies, as well as other social entities. This process he terms 'hacking', though Wark's concept bears little relation to the acts that this term tends to signify (most recognisably, exploiting vulnerabilities in computer systems to access sensitive or supposedly secure data). Taking its theoretical inspiration from Deleuze (as well as Debord), Wark's *A Hacker Manifesto* (2004) is concerned to critique the emergent class that seeks to govern information in the age of global networks. Wark conceives this newly dominant group as a 'vectoralist class', since – above all else – it seizes possession of the instruments with which information is produced and the routes through which it flows. The successor to capitalism's proprietary ethic, the new vectoralist class eschews the equation of materiality with commodification, instead locating value in (and, as a consequence, seeking control of) the virtual and the informational. The power of this class, Wark writes, 'lies in monopolizing intellectual property – patents, copyrights, and trademarks – and the means of reproducing their value – the vectors of communication. The privatization of information becomes the dominant, rather than a subsidiary, aspect of commodified life' (Wark 2004: §032).[6] Were *A Hacker Manifesto* confined to identifying the shift towards the informational dominance in the new political economy then it would add little to existing analyses of global culture. But, just as Deleuze describes actualisation as a process that remains uncertain in the moment of its production, so Wark finds the vectoralist class vulnerable to the virtuality – what he calls the 'productive abstractions' – that it seeks to own and control (Wark 2004: §041).[7] Abstraction functions simultaneously as cure and poison for the network economy, providing it with information that it can commodify, but also allowing an alternatively motivated class to mobilise information in the pursuit of social transformation. Alongside and against the ascendance of a new dominant, this class 'hacks politics itself' (Wark 2004: §043), challenging regimes of disciplinary knowledge and refusing to respect the legislative codification of information as property:

> To hack is to express knowledge in any of its forms. Hacker knowledge implies, in its practice, a politics of free information, free learning, the gift of the result in a peer-to-peer network. Hacker knowledge also implies an ethics of knowledge open to the desires of the productive classes and free from subordination to commodity production . . . . When knowledge is freed from scarcity, the free production of knowledge becomes the knowledge of free production. This may sound like utopia, but the accounts of actually existing temporary zones of hacker liberty are legion. (Wark 2004: §070)

Plugging into abstraction and freeing itself from state surveillance, this ethic of open knowledge is perhaps felt most acutely at the national level. But, just as for Deleuze deterritorialisation should not be equated with dislocation, it would be a mistake to equate hacker politics with globalisation. Instead, vectoralism is built on a principle of uneven development and an imbalanced distribution of power that is now organised along developmental, rather than more-recognisably national lines. We have 'a new global division of labor', Wark observes in a recent essay on Marxism and information:

> Manufacturing becomes the specialty of the underdeveloped world; the overdeveloped world manages the brands, husbands the patents and enforces the copyrights. Unequal exchange is no longer between a capitalist economy in the north and a pastoralist economy in the south; it is between a vectoralist economy in the north and a capitalist economy in the south. But the vectoralist goes one better: it scrambles the once relatively homogenous economic spaces within various nation states. One can find the underdeveloped world now in Mississippi, and the overdeveloped world in Bangalore. (Wark 2006: 176)

Within this economy, regions of 'the overdeveloped world' seek to shore up their threatened sense of bordered identity by increasing barriers to immigration and employment, and imposing greater restrictions on the circulation of commodities and resources; the effect of this is to force those in underdeveloped regions to turn to nationalist politics, and to encourage 'the productive classes of the underdeveloped world to embrace their own rulers as representing their interests' (Wark 2004: §377). Such a strategy, as the history of decolonisation testifies, forces minority populations into the constraints of representation, acquiring a narrative of national identity that cannot fit, not only because it remains shaped by images and ideas imposed by majoritarian culture, but also because narratives of national belonging can only fail in a development-orientated system that no longer privileges the political economy of the nation-state.

Assuming what Eyal Amiran (2006: 197) describes as 'a Deleuzian refusal of representation itself', Wark (2004: §231) describes hacking as 'a politics of the unrepresentable', which cuts through this regime of identification. Providing minority populations and the underdeveloped world with alternatives to the imagined homeland of the nation – and, correlatively, denying overdeveloped nations the sense of ethnic and regional belonging that has secured their sense of cultural authority and ensured their economic prominence – hacking 'seeks to use international flows of information, trade or activism as the eclectic means for struggling for new sources of wealth or liberty that overcomes the limitations imposed by national or communal envelopes' (Wark 2004: §246). These claims might suggest that *A Hacker Manifesto* adopts a version of anarcho-globalism for the information age – that Wark promotes the death of the nation-state, as well as other forms of association and identification – but a rejection of such a position is central to his understanding of hacking's relationship to the nation-state. Just as Deleuze maintains that the spectre of the virtual can be read only through the social entities that it haunts – just as the nomad's peregrinations can be understood only in terms of the territoriality to which it remains strangely attached, just as schizophrenia is a condition that overdetermines sociocultural location – so hacker culture for Wark is not essentially disengaged from the nation-state. 'This expressive politics does not seek to overthrow the state, or to reform its larger structures, or to preserve its structure so as to maintain an existing coalition of interests,' Wark writes. 'It seeks to permeate existing states with a new state of existence' (2004: §257). Hacking, in other words, promotes neither a denial of praxis nor departure from the nation-state; rather, it produces new modes of association and intervention in the moment that it departs from representative politics, and it remains shaped by the nation-state in the moment that it moves across national frontiers.

The Assemblage: Global and Postcolonial

The relationship between postcoloniality and globalisation is an uncertain one, as Revathi Krishnaswamy observes:

> It is unclear . . . whether contemporary globalization has been made possible by the postcolonial challenge to older Eurocentric forms of globalization premised on the centrality of the nation and narrated in terms of modernization or whether postcoloniality is itself the consequence of a globalization premised on the marginalization of the nation in the economic and cultural domains. (Krishnaswamy 2007: 3)

No such uncertainty exists for Michael Hardt and Antonio Negri, who find in postcolonial theory inadequate models for contemporary cultural analysis. While for them postcolonial theory has indeed developed critical resources for challenging the structural persistence of colonial ideas and practices, it remains hypnotised by this legacy and fails to realise that the foundations of social institutions and cultural power have shifted dramatically. 'Postcolonial theory is a very productive tool for rereading history,' they write, 'but it is entirely insufficient for theorizing contemporary global power' (Hardt and Negri 2000: 146).

Wark too appears to move away from reading power in terms of postcoloniality when he claims that the underdeveloped and overdeveloped worlds are no longer organised according to a recognisable geopolitical order. Wark's account of the challenge that hacking poses to the overdeveloped world does indeed beg questions about the changing shape of the nation-state that are not conventionally associated with postcolonial theory. And yet, there is repetition in this rupture, since concepts developed by postcolonial theory lie palimpsestically behind his reading of the reshaping of national cultures by hacker politics. The claim that hacking refuses models of representative politics certainly echoes the sense that postcolonial intervention works through a displacement of the intending subject's agency. And, in the tracks of postcolonial theory's challenge to the kind of epochal historiography that would detach colonial oppression from postcolonial liberation, Wark warns that the structural logic of the nation-state persists in the supposed singularity of the global present. What Wark perhaps reveals, then, is that since globalisation and postcoloniality are not as distinctive as they may appear to be, cultural theory can most productively read power and resistance when it avoids an exceptional sense of the present.

This rewriting of theoretical vocabularies develops more overtly in Saskia Sassen's claim that the social sphere needs to be understood as a system of connected and fluctuating socio-cultural forces – or, as she terms it, an 'assemblage' – that cannot be adequately explained by the categories of the national and the global. What she recommends is not that social theory abandons these categories, but that it situates them within a series of interdependent processes that take on a specific character in different places and at different times. For this reason, she resists reading technoculture as an assemblage that either overcomes the nation-state or allows it to be confirmed as a fixed entity that can remain uncontaminated by the transborder exchange of commodities, populations or information; digitalisation, she writes, 'has enabled the strengthening of older actors and spaces and the formation of novel ones capable of engaging the competence, scope, and exclusivity of state authority' (Sassen 2006: 328). Sassen regards the status of the assemblage as a 'profoundly untheoretical' thread in her work, differentiating it from the more elaborate – 'important and illuminating' – treatment of this concept in Deleuze's thinking (Sassen 2006: 5, n.1). But these two versions of the assemblage are not so different, especially considered in the global *and* postcolonial context of how we are to understand national location and global dislocation. Beyond the schismatic reading of place and displacement, which has tended either to defend the durability of the nation-state as an organisational principle or declare a new condition of global community, the assemblage (for Deleuze as well as for Sassen) allows us to realise that the *habitus* has never been unequivocally national and is not yet (indeed, might never be) fully global.

References

Amiran, E. (2006), 'Revolution in Abstraction', *The Minnesota Review* 65–6: 193–202.

Ansell-Pearson, K. (2005), 'The Reality of the Virtual: Bergson and Deleuze', *MLN: Modern Language Notes* 120: 1112–27.

Badiou, A. (2000), *Deleuze: The Clamor of Being*, trans. Louise Burchill, Minneapolis: University of Minnesota Press.

Bhabha, H. K. (1993), *The Location of Culture*, London: Routledge.

Castells, M. (2001), *The Internet Galaxy: Reflections on the Internet, Business, and Society*, Oxford: Oxford University Press.

Colebrook, C. (2006), *Deleuze: A Guide for the Perplexed*, London: Continuum.

DeLanda, M. (2006), *A New Philosophy of Society: Assemblage Theory and Social Complexity*, London: Continuum.

Deleuze, G. (1991), *Bergsonism*, trans. H. Tomlinson and B. Habberjam, New York: Zone Books.

Deleuze, G. (2007a), 'Schizophrenia and Society', in *Two Regimes of Madness: Texts and Interviews 1975–1995*, trans. A. Hodges and M. Taormina, New York: Semiotext(e), pp. 17–29.

Deleuze, G. (2007b), 'The Future of Linguistics', in *Two Regimes of Madness: Texts and Interviews 1975–1995*, trans. A. Hodges and M. Taormina, New York: Semiotext(e), pp. 67–72.

Deleuze G. and F. Guattari (1986), *Kafka: Toward a Minor Literature*, trans. D. Polan, Minneapolis: University of Minnesota Press.
Deleuze, G. and F. Guattari (1988), *A Thousand Plateaus: Capitalism and Schizophrenia*, trans. B. Massumi, London: Athlone.
Deleuze, G. and F. Guattari (1994), *What is Philosophy?*, trans. G. Burchell and H. Tomlinson, London: Verso.
Deleuze, G. and C. Parnet (2002), *Dialogues II*, trans. H. Tomlinson and B. Habberjam, London: Continuum.
Frasca, G. (2006), 'Immersion, outmersion & critical thinking', *DREAM*, (accessed 8 August 2008) http://www.dream.sdu.dk/index.php?page=0116&lang=Dansk
Friedman, T. (2006), *The World is Flat: The Globalized World in the Twenty-first Century*, London: Penguin.
Gore, A. (2008), *The Assault on Reason: How the Politics of Blind Faith Subvert Wise Decision-Making*, London: Bloomsbury.
Hansen, M. B. N. (2006), *Bodies in Code: Interfaces with Digital Media*, London: Routledge.
Hardt, M. and A. Negri (2000), *Empire*, Cambridge: Harvard University Press.
Hauben, M. and R. Hauben (1997), *Netizens: On the History and Impact of Usenet and the Internet*, Los Alamitos: Wiley-IEEE Computer Society.
Hayles, N. K. (1999), 'The Condition of Virtuality', in P. Lunenfeld (ed.), *The Digital Dialectic: New Essays in New Media*, Cambridge: MIT Press, pp. 69–94.
Hughes, J. (2004), *Citizen Cyborg: Why Democratic Societies Must Respond to the Redesigned Human of the Future*, Cambridge: Westview Press.
Krishnaswamy, R. (2007), 'Connections, Conflicts, Complicities', in R. Krishnaswamy and J. C. Hawley (eds), *The Postcolonial and the Global*, Minneapolis: University of Minnesota Press, pp. 2–22.
Lovink, G. (2002), *Dark Fiber: Tracking Critical Internet Culture*, Cambridge: MIT Press.
Marks, J. (2006), 'Information and Resistance: Deleuze, the Virtual, and Cybernetics', in I. Buchanan and A. Parr (eds), *Deleuze and the Contemporary World*, Edinburgh: Edinburgh University Press, pp. 194–214.
Mitchell, W. J. (1995), *City of Bits: Space, Place, and the Infobahn*, Cambridge: MIT Press.
Mitchell, W. J. (2000), *e-topia: 'Urban life, Jim – but not as we know it'*, Cambridge: MIT Press.
Mitchell, W. J. (2004), *Me++: The Cyborg Self and the Networked City*, Cambridge: MIT Press.
Patton, P. (2006), 'The Event of Colonisation', in I. Buchanan and A. Parr (eds), *Deleuze and the Contemporary World*, Edinburgh: Edinburgh University Press, pp. 108–25.
Prakash, G. (1995) (ed.), *After Colonialism: Imperial Histories and Postcolonial Displacements*, New Jersey: Princeton University Press.
Rajchman, J. (2000), *The Deleuze Connections*, Cambridge: The MIT Press.
Rheingold, H. (1993), 'A Slice of Life in My Virtual Community', in L. M. Harasim (ed.), *Global Networks: Computers and International Communication*, Cambridge: MIT Press, pp. 57–80.
Sardar, Z. (1995), 'alt.civilizations.faq: cyberspace as the darker side of the west', *Futures* 27 (7): 777–94.
Sassen, S. (2006), *Territory, Authority, Rights: From Medieval to Global Assemblages*, Princeton: Princeton University Press.
Schech, S. (2002), 'Wired for Change: The Links between ICTs and Development Discourses', *Journal of International Development* 14: 13–23.

Spivak, G. C. (1999), *A Critique of Postcolonial Reason: Toward a History of the Vanishing Present*, Cambridge: Harvard University Press.
Wark, M. (2001), 'Elsewhere: Antipodean Space', *Literary Review* 45 (1): 98–106.
Wark, M. (2004), *A Hacker Manifesto*, Cambridge: Harvard University Press.
Wark, M. (2006), 'Information Wants to be Free (But Is Everywhere in Chains)', *Cultural Studies* 20 (2–3): 165–83.
Young, R. J. C. (2004), *White Mythologies: Writing History and the West*, 2nd edn, London: Routledge.

Notes

1. In June 2008, for example, Ban Ki-moon restated Kofi Annan's 2002 commitment to narrowing the digital divide, http://www.un.org/News/Press/docs/2008/sgsm11577.doc.htm (accessed 5 January 2009).
2. See, for example, Ziauddin Sardar's (1995) claim that cyberspace emerges in the 1990s as a new territory that serves the West's colonial appetites ('alt.civilizations.faq: cyberspace as the darker side of the west'): and Suzanne Schech's claim that the World Bank's 'recipe for development through knowledge delivered via new ICTs sits comfortably with a long tradition in western thought that seeks the solution to the world's ills, and ultimately salvation, in technological breakthroughs' (Schech 2002: 19).
3. See, for example, the opening paragraph of the UK government's Department for Culture, Media, and Sports' 2009 report *Digital Britain*, which states that:

    Around the world digital and broadband technologies are reshaping our Communications, Entertainment, Information and Knowledge industries, the wider economy, and the way of life for all of us. We are at a point of transformation. The success of our manufacturing and services industries will increasingly be defined by their ability to use and develop digital technologies. A successful Britain must be a Digital Britain.

    http://www.culture.gov.uk/images/publications/digital_britain_interimreport-jan09.pdf, (accessed 29 January 2009), p. 3.
4. 'Readers who feel that the theory developed here is not strictly speaking Deleuze's own are welcome to call it "neo-assemblage theory", "assemblage theory 2.0", or some other name' (DeLanda 2006: 4).
5. John Rajchman, for example, alerts Deleuze's readers to the dangers of viewing the machinic as an encounter between bodies and machines. The machinic, he argues, does not point to a once-pre-technological subject that is becoming supplanted in its encounter with prosthetic devices; instead, it 'supposes another sense of machine', wherein '[i]nstruments are always part of larger sorts of "arrangements" or "assemblages" that then allow for "machinic connections" of another, noninstrumentalized, even improbable, sort, which may then be taken up by thought' (Rajchman 2000: 7).
6. Wark provides a clearer sense of what he means by 'vector' elsewhere, in 'Elsewhere':

    To me, a vector is a technology that moves something from somewhere to somewhere else, at a given speed and cost and under certain specified conditions. They come in two kinds: those that move mostly physical objects about the place, and those that move only information. Transport and communication were once one and the same thing. Now communication moves at a faster rate, and is able to model and coordinate movements of ever more intricate design over great distances. (2001: 100)

7. 'To abstract', Wark writes in the tracks of Deleuze, 'is to express the virtuality of nature, to make known some instance of its possibilities, to actualize a relation out of infinite relationality, to manifest the manifold' (2004: §008).

Chapter 12
In Search of the Perfect Escape: Deleuze, Movement and Canadian Postcolonialism

Jennifer Blair

> For us time is space and even when we desire to have an experience of time our preference is for the remembrance of things past rather than the search for lost time. (Ansell-Pearson 2002: 162)

In late-nineteenth-century Canada, fire was a given. Buildings were being constructed as quickly as possible as a result of the newly established dominion's aspirations to develop, grow and modernise. As a result of this speed of construction, these buildings were haphazardly planned and composed of the most readily available – and also highly flammable – materials. In an 1887 address to the Royal Society of Canada, Quebecois architect Charles Baillairgé identified the frequency of the devastating fires occurring in Canada at the time as a phenomenon that marked Confederation-era Canadian architecture as distinct from that of its colonial past. These fires, he stated, 'are waxing more numerous than of old, due to the increasing consumption of light and resinous woods in the construction of buildings of all kinds'. Baillairgé went on to point out that in France 'where oak and other hard grained woods, as elm and the like, are almost exclusively employed or have been for years, a disastrous fire is of the rarest occurrence' (Baillairgé 1887: 1). Canada, deeply engrossed in physical, cultural and governmental nation-building activities in the late nineteenth century, faced a threat that was by this point in time minimal in its 'mother countries' – and this threat required the ingenuity and industry of its own architects to respond to it. In his many writings and speeches on fire safety, Baillairgé insisted that his colleagues treat fires as 'eventualities that might never occur', as if fire was a real presence in the buildings they designed, even if it would never become actualised in the future of each and every building (Baillairgé 1887: 2).

This chapter reads this curious labelling of fires as 'eventualities' in early Canada as an indication of Deleuze's notion of the virtual at work in Canada's nation-building period. It focuses on early Canadian fire escape designs in order to explore the various ways in which fires obliged early Canadians to become aware of and respond to the role of the virtual as it informed their lived environment. In attending to these designs as expressions of a Deleuzian virtuality, I hope to highlight the materially based affectivity within this Canadian post-colonial event of nation-building – an event that has, until now, most often been understood by critics as a primarily discursive phenomenon. Whether it reinforces or aims to deconstruct the institution of the nation, this critical conflation of nationhood with discursivity limits the scope of the analyses of the processes of nation-building we currently have at our disposal. Postcolonial criticism, when it understands the nation as a linguistic process, limits itself to an analysis of just this process, with little to no consideration of the ontological factors that gave rise to them and that exist alongside them and affect the construction of the nation. Most often this form of criticism concludes in an assessment of the nation's coherences vs incoherencies, presences vs absences and unities vs fragmentations, which it finds to be symptomatic of the linguistic material that represents it. In such a dualist model, time is left out of the equation – things either are or are not there, or things displace other things, but they do not move; they do not change through the process of time. The result is that Canadian postcolonial criticism has little in its repertoire with which to address the highly time-conscious and uniquely mobile nature of material culture in one of the key periods it addresses. In particular, it has little to offer an analysis of early Canadian fire escape designs, which turned the most formidably static of material objects (buildings) into mobile affective entities that expressed and multiplied the differentiated nature of time – in other words, they enacted the very kind of mobility, that, for Deleuze, demonstrates the unfolding of the virtual.

In response to Baillairgé's and other such similar calls for fire-conscious building design, architects, engineers and city planners searched for the information and inspiration that would enable them to design the ideal fire escapes for their buildings. At this time the building fire escape was something new. Prior to 1860 a 'fire escape' was not part of a building, but a separate extension-ladder unit with a base and wheels. Just a few of these mobile ladder escapes served an entire city. They were kept in apparently 'convenient' central locations and taken to a building when it was on fire.[1] People would wait on their balconies for this remote escape to arrive, or else they would wait on the roof, which they accessed through a hatch in the ceiling called a 'scuttle', specially designed for this purpose (Wermiel 2000: 190). Dangerous time spent waiting for these remote escapes caused people to invent supplementary escapes that were already somehow 'at', or part of, a building. The new on-site fire escapes that they came up with changed the way that people could respond to a fire: it meant they no longer had to wait in the windows or on the rooftops of their burning buildings, scanning the streets for signs of escapes making their way to them. But in the designs for the new escapes something of this eventual aspect of the fire escape itself remained in the sense that these designs treated the fire escape as something that would be required only in the event of a building fire, not something that was a constantly desired presence in a building. In some cases the new fire escapes kept the mobility of their predecessor remote models, even though they were also somehow attached to the building. If fires were an eventual presence in the building, now fire escapes were too. Their designers were searching for ways to make up for the time lost by the remote fire escapes without disturbing the buildings' facades. The best solutions were found in escapes that could themselves move, in addition to producing new pathways and enabling new types of movement for the building's inhabitants to engage in should they need to exit the burning building.

The fact that there were several types of fire escape invented and in use in the late nineteenth century suggests that at this time some questions remained unanswered regarding where a fire escape would be located in a building, what it would be made of, what escape route it would utilise or produce, and, most importantly, what aspect of the fire escape would enable the actual escaping and what modes of movement would be employed in the escape action. Several architects, including Baillairgé, swore by the design that became a convention by the twentieth century: the stationary staircase affixed to the exterior of a building. This is the design that makes the most 'sense' to us in the twenty-first century because it understands the 'escape' as something enacted by people, people engaging in their own self-propelled movements (walking, descending stairs), while the material structure itself stays still. But other architects did not immediately adopt this conventional alignment of the escape action with human movement and structure with fixity when they designed their fire escapes. Nor did they treat the eventuality of a building fire as a strictly spatial problem, where the goal attained was simply to produce a new space upon and through which people could put more distance between themselves and the burning building. Instead, they invented escapes that did the moving, in conjunction with, or instead of the people. Some of the more interesting examples of these include: the Burrows Escape, in which a basket on a pulley system delivered people safely to ground level; the Harris System, in which rope ladders uncoiled on the exterior wall of a building offering passage to the ground; and the Pardessus Escape, in which people slid down a spiral ramp inside a brick tower situated adjacent to a building. There were, of course, several others as well, but most followed the basic principles embodied within these three types of escape.

To argue for the significance of these escapes as an illustration of the material grounding of postcoloniality in Canada, and as evidence of the role of the virtual in Canada's nation-building era, this chapter proceeds in three sections. The first reviews the trend toward discourse analysis in Canadian postcolonial criticism and its associated enactment of a linguistic displacement of the material processes of nation-building. The second and third analyse the fire escape designs through Deleuze's philosophy of movement. Overall, these nineteenth-century escapes are worth considering, not just as historical curiosities, but as engagements with the material environment that open up several important questions about the extent to which Canadian postcolonial criticism, which has been so caught up in the issue of 'nation-building,' has considered the relation between time, memory, affectivity and movement in the construction of the nation. If the preoccupation with nation-building remains a defining feature of postcolonial analysis, even if 'the nation' itself has suffered a *deconstruction* of sorts (with increased attention now paid to multinationals, transnationals, nations within and First Nations), then it is important to take a broader and much more interdisciplinary inventory of the efforts to build Canada in the fields of architecture and urban planning. The upshot of such an approach is not just a wider-ranging scholarship. A reading of the nation that focuses on the material – and in drawing from Deleuze, the affectivity of the virtual in the course of material events – reveals the becoming of the Canadian nation as something much more heterogeneous and open-ended in character than has yet been acknowledged in our critical rendering of the nation as a primarily discursive phenomenon. Early Canadian mobile fire escapes are unique products of this key moment in Canadian cultural history because they identify the situation of a building fire as a multiplicity of mobilities and mobile bodies, and then they enhance this multiplicity by adding new types of movement to the eventual building-fires they imagine. In so doing, their treatment of the notion of 'escape' – and, more generally, their expressed understanding of how change operates in the world – accords with Deleuze's notion of the indeterminate affective potential of the virtual. In this context, fire escapes offer Canadian Postcolonial Studies some key examples of becoming in time and movement, examples that stand to expand upon our notions of causality, agency, responsibility and embodied subjectivity.

Nation-Building: From Discourse Analysis to Multiplicity

The hyphenated term 'nation-building' has been one of the most important and frequently used in postcolonial criticism, especially in the context of postcoloniality in places like Canada, where the colonising settlers sought to remove themselves from their colonial status by identifying as a nation, separate (if not always absolutely independent) from their imperial authorities in Europe. As Alan Lawson (1995) has pointed out, much of the post-colonial in Canada has to do with such nationalising acts and articulations of separateness by 'invader-settler subjects' – those whose 'nation-building' efforts involved (and in fact continue to involve) a displacement of both First Nations populations and culture, and also the culture of the coloniser.[2] This nation-building has been – *is* – a long-term process, perhaps by nature a never-ending one. Attaching the term 'building' to the term 'nation' has served to signify this nation-as-process condition of post-colonial Canada, and that this process is, or wants to be, progressive. Ideally the achievement of nationhood is something that can be mapped on a single line of time – what Imre Szeman (2000) has called the 'isochronic' construction of Canadian nationality – such that it is easily understandable according to the conventions of history and of narrative literature. In addition to this figuration of time-as-linear-progress into the ideology of nationhood, the term 'building' has also served to identify the variously combined discursive constructions that, in effect, produce this concept of the nation as something that seems to be naturally coherent. Here the term 'building' becomes the symptom identified by ideology critique, the symptom that exposes the constructedness of the nation, realised as a linguistic phenomenon. These two critical approaches to nation-building achieve two related effects: they treat the temporal and material aspects of nation-building as a spatial phenomenon (a timeline), and they make the nation a 'discursive-construction' rather than a phenomenon of shifting ontological and epistemological components.

Since the publication of Homi Bhabha's *Nation and Narration* in 1990, postcolonial criticism has worked to destabilise 'the nation' by identifying the 'ambivalences' which are to be found through reading the post-colonial as a form of narrative discourse (Bhabha 1990: 3). Understanding the nation as narrative is not new to us in Canada: since the Confederation era, politicians and writers alike have argued that the establishment of a national literature in Canada was essential to the establishment of the nation. As Jonathan Kertzer has written, '[V]irtually all critics, following [Northrop] Frye, have commented on the prominent role of language and conflicting styles to articulate a vision of Canada. The nation is created in, as, and through words' (Kertzer 1998: 86). However, it remains questionable what our efforts to identify the ambivalences in this narrative have achieved. For example, books like Kertzer's *Worrying the Nation: Imagining a National Literature in English Canada* (1998) employed tactics like 'worrying' to destabilise the apparent solidity of the nation. But such tactics have since been found to be inadequate. Kertzer's book, for example, received much criticism for the presence-absence logic behind 'worrying'. In one review published in 2000, Diana Brydon argued that *Worrying the Nation* seems to reproduce the 'nostalgic evocation of a lost authenticity [of the nation] that never, in truth, existed', and also that it 'demonstrates the bankruptcy of the old ways of thinking but cannot move beyond their terms of reference' (Brydon 2000: 17, 20). The problem, as Brydon goes on to note, is the way in which the emotionally affective aspects of Canadian nation-building become negated by virtue of being treated as literary phenomena: 'English Canadian guilt and ambivalence about Canada's foundation on conquest are part of what gets "disappeared" or converted into the literary in Canadian literature' (Brydon 2000: 20).[3]

Why is it that when we talk about 'nation-building' we are making the nation a linguistic phenomenon before we have looked at the various components and processes of the nation-building era? When we do so, we lose the potential for a more thorough understanding of this era, and we also lose the potential for the incorporation of a more complex and diversified set of ontological operations into our critical field of vision. Most importantly, we are actively conflating space and time into a single presence that is understood to have no 'other' but its own negation. In other words, as soon as we take it as our object of study, we predetermine the possibilities 'the nation' has for revealing and resisting colonial power, and therefore we forfeit any power that the postcolonial might have to enact actual difference, actual change, in our thinking and in our lived lives. We did not go wrong when we focused on 'building' as a term with a certain fertile potential for analysing postcolonialism in Canada. But we may have unnecessarily limited our project when we took this term that clearly connotes an event, an action expressing the passage of time, and then robbed it of its vital material and temporal aspects. Under postcolonial criticism, 'building' has become understood as a progressive process on a single, spatialised line of time, and as a sign of the ideological constructedness of the nation.⁴ And yet, as we observe in the example of early Canadian fire escapes, not all of the building practices in the nation-building era were so quick to subsume time into space and being into signification.

From Bhabha's suggestion to read for ambivalences in the narrative of the nation, to related criticism that adheres to analyses of linguistic processes, postcolonialism has taken its cue from the work of Michel Foucault and particularly his theory of 'discursive formations'. But if Foucault's discourse analysis was key to the development of postcolonial criticism, then Deleuze saw its contribution in largely contrasting terms. For Deleuze, discourse analysis was a theory that notably surpassed that of its predecessors, in so far as it promoted the acknowledgement of multiplicity. Tracing the divergences in these two interpretations of Foucault's work is useful in terms of locating Deleuze's possible entry into postcolonial criticism. Nancy Armstrong, the well-known critic of Victorian literature, recently championed Foucault's discourse analysis as a method which 'turns culture's every aspect into language in order to identify the metaphoric repetitions and metonymic connections by which that language creates the very objects and causal sequences it claims to be about' (Armstrong 2007: 11). For Armstrong, Foucault's 'simple move' of turning the world into discourse 'inverts the empirical world and transforms the material of cultural history into the subject matter of literary analysis' (Armstrong 2007: 11). This move to turn away from the empirical and toward literary analysis has been popular with Canadian postcolonialists who are quite rightly disturbed by the way in which scientific empiricism served (and still serves) to legitimate key acts of colonial oppression, including the African slave trade and the conquest of First Nations. But from a Deleuzian perspective this approach sidesteps the very possibilities for criticism that Foucault's discourse analysis opened up, even if Foucault did not follow through on these in his own writing.

In Deleuze's reading, Foucault's discourse analysis does not, in fact, let us become quite so disciplinary; nor does it let us do away with the empirical. Deleuze argues that Foucault's ultimate achievement was to show us how discourse operates on and is affected by 'non-discursive' forces, which occur outside of language and subjectivity. While Deleuze saw *The Archaeology of Knowledge* as 'the most decisive step yet taken in the theory-practice of multiplicities' (Deleuze 1988: 14), he also pointed out the limitations of this step when he wrote that the book 'marked a turning point: it posited a firm distinction between the two forms but, as it proposed to define the form of statements, it contented itself with indicating the other forms in a negative way, as the "non-discursive"' (Deleuze 1988: 31). In his own work, much of it completed by the time he published his book on Foucault, Deleuze went beyond this treatment of multiplicities based on presence and absence, to develop a complex philosophy that takes into account the ontological processes involved in becoming. Deleuze repeatedly insists upon the need to acknowledge the different types of processes occurring within the one composite, such as discourse, which cannot be reduced to a single schematic. For Keith Ansell-Pearson, this Deleuzian shift beyond the discursive was an attempt to solve the 'contradictions and problems – indeed, the antinomies of modern thinking' that 'stem in large measure from our imposition of symbolic diagrams upon the movement of the real, which serve to make it something uniform, regular and calculable for us, but which also cover it up and comes to constitute our only experience of the real' (Ansell-Pearson 2002: 162). I will turn now to a discussion of this 'movement of the real' as it was highlighted and augmented (rather than 'covered up') by nineteenth-century fire escape designers – those involved in the real material processes of Canadian nation-building and who, most tellingly, refused to reduce these processes to a symbolic realm.

Fire Escapes, Movement, Virtuality

If the conflation of space and time is a convention of modern thought, then it is not surprising that the fire escape model that we take to be the most 'common sense' approach to fire safety – the stationary staircase – works according to this convention. Figure 3 shows a nineteenth-century example of this staircase model, designed by E. T. Barnum and Iron Work.

In this model, one's escape can be measured according to how far and how fast one could remove oneself from a building – in other words, how fast one could move in a given, constant and contained spatio-temporal field. If the building's inhabitants were not fast enough to outrun the fire, or if their movement was halted in any way, the escape was not successful. Given the power and force of fire, this 'common sense' model seems illogical in its belief that a whole building full of people could keep ahead of the advance of a fire. Clearly recent history is full of events that offer evidence to the contrary. Even though we pride ourselves on our technological advances, it remains factual that no building is adequately equipped to guarantee its inhabitants safe exit from a fire. It is as if in this particular aspect of modern society we have sided with the ancient philosopher Zeno, when he argues that the tortoise will always

280 Deleuze and the Postcolonial

Figure 3 E.T. Barnum Fire Escape.

stay ahead of Achilles, provided that it is given a head start. This is the logic we resort to when we theorise the complex processes of affectivity through space.

The mobile fire escapes refuse this logic in favour of one focused on time and movement. Resonating with Henri Bergson's philosophy of movement, these escapes are designed upon and demonstrate the principle that movement does not stay constant, but changes in type in each new step, or other such interval, of action. This is not to say that the moveable fire escapes preclude the possibility of people catching on fire, but at least they do not try to reduce or deny the distinctions between the movement of the fire and the movement of people escaping the fire. Rather than adopting the logic of the stationary fire escapes, they highlight the necessity of understanding the complex event of a building fire – with so many constituent factors both human and non-human – as the interrelation of multiplicities. They reject the legitimacy of reducing the processes of all bodies involved to accord with the movement of one body, or to a single measure of time in which individual movements can be made relative according to speed.

Take, for example, the 'Burrows Escape.' In this model (see Figure 4), a moveable basket attached to metal cords on a pulley system travelled from window to window, picking up the people inside and delivering them to safety on the ground.

The basket was able to carry about four or five people at a time, and so it would need to take many trips from the upper-storeys to street-level before the building was evacuated (and one can only imagine what would determine priority in the order of rescue). This escape was noted by Halifax city planner Edward Henry Keating when he toured the eastern US looking for fire escape design ideas to bring back to Canada. In his report, Keating included this comment from a local newspaper reporting on a demonstration of the Burrows Escape at the Riggs' Hotel in Washington: 'The perfection attained by this invention in delivering a person from any window of a building to the ground in a few seconds, makes it the most efficient fire escape yet produced' (Keating 1883: 25). The report goes on to comment that 'Every one seemed delighted with the experiment, and the gentlemen having charge of the apparatus received many congratulations of their success.' It concludes, however, by noting that the 'chief engineer prefers fixed outside ladders' (Keating 1883: 26).

The Harris System offers an example of two other types of movement that nineteenth-century fire escapes were capable of – portability and 'automatic' movement. The Harris System was simple. It involved

Figure 4 Burrows Escape.

a coiled rope-ladder that could be thrown out of a window at any moment. The coil was to be hooked to the interior of a wall just below the window sill, and it came with a decorative case such that it could blend in with the room's decor (see Figure 5).

All in all, the beauty of the Harris System was in its inconspicuousness, as an advertisement noted: 'There is no visible suggestion of a Fire Escape – nothing whatever to mar the architectural beauty of a

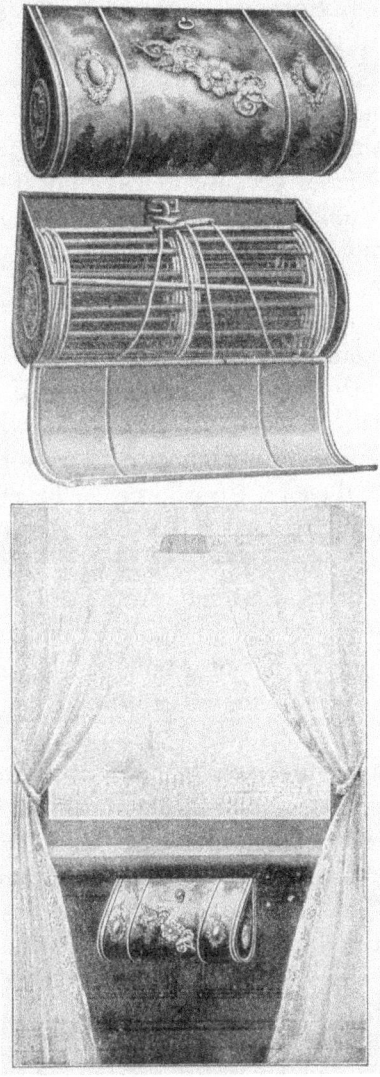

Figure 5 Harris Portable Fire Escape.

structure.' While the Harris Safety Company did not explain in detail just how 'portable' the ladders were intended to be, one assumes that they were meant to travel with residents as they moved from dwelling to dwelling. Harris also offered a 'built-in' model, where the coiled ladder was actually inside the wall (that is, in between the interior and exterior of the building, completely invisible from both inside and outside). This model was 'automatic' in the sense that, in the event of fire, the resident had only to push a button and a panel on the exterior of the building would open, and the ladder would spring out and uncoil offering passage to the ground (see Figure 6).

There were various rope ladder-type fire escapes in use in the nineteenth century, but there were also critics who felt that this style of escape was not adequate because it was only useful to agile adults, mostly men, and it would be nearly impossible for a parent to descend a ladder carrying a child.

The Pardessus Fire Escape claimed to solve all of the previous difficulties regarding the various health and modesty requirements of residents needing to escape from a fire (see Figure 7). The Pardessus model did not involve ladders or stairs. Instead it comprised a spiral ramp inside a fireproof tower. The tower was to be built adjacent to a building, or in between two buildings and connected to them by passageways that allowed it to serve as the escape for both. The benefit of this system was that it could be used by women and also by the young and the infirm, who, as the advertisement suggests, could slide down the ramp on their mattresses and bedclothes. Certainly, what the Pardessus model gained in safety and utility it lost in cost and cosmetics. It could not be put inconspicuously at one corner of a building, like the Burrow's basket model, and there was no way to make the tower invisible, like the Harris ladder system.

Although the data we now have of these escapes are entirely discursive (except for a few remaining rope-ladder and slide escapes in existence), the plans and texts that express these escapes do not seek, to return to Ansell-Pearson, an 'imposition of symbolic diagrams upon the movement of the real'. They cannot even pretend to do so, because the fact that the escapes work by moving means that their defining function could not begin to be expressed in the symbolic realm. To analyse their escape operations we need to make time (speed, movement, change) the basis of the affective event of a building fire. In terms of an analysis of nation-building, this means going beyond the dualistic analysis of the nation (where the nation is present or absent, coherent or fractured) that has dominated Canadian postcolonial criticism, to consider the realm of the ontological espoused by Deleuzian thought. Deleuze's writing offers a developed method for thinking about movement, especially in his early book on the metaphysical philosopher Henri Bergson, which is particularly useful in this project.[5]

Deleuze's interest in movement as the primary condition and expression of the affective world comes largely from Bergson. In his book *Matter and Memory*, Bergson theorised the nature of affectivity in an

The Harris Automatic-Mechanical "Built-in" Exterior Fire Escapes

The Fire Escape is compactly rolled and concealed within a case with ornamental front corresponding to style of building and is "built in" underneath the cornice or in the gable. There is no visible suggestion of a Fire Escape—nothing whatever to mar the architectural beauty of the structure.

To the case is attached a wire cable running perpendicularly through interior of building to the basement, and which may be extended along ceiling as far as desired to the furnace, boiler-room, laundry, or any point of greatest danger, with numerous fusible links exposed, which melt and separate at 160 degrees, thus automatically opening the door of the case containing Fire Escape (or the Fire Escape may be released by pulling the starting cord) simultaneously and loudly ringing the Fire Alarms, one located within the case and one on end of reel. The door of the case opens on its hinges to a slanting or inclined position, permitting Fire Escape to freely unwind at an angle sufficient to avoid any projections, balconies, awnings, etc., and momentarily checking descent of Escape when within 7 feet of ground (rendering impossible any accident to passers-by); then the door drops flatly against the building and the Fire Escape is made taut by a ratchet device attached to side of building or in pavement.

PRICE-LIST of Harris Automatic-Mechanical "Built-in" Fire Escape.

No. 1 Case and Mechanism for all lengths of Fire Escapes to 75 feet, $50.00
No. 2 Case and Mechanism for all lengths of Fire Escapes from 75 feet to 100 feet............ 75.00
No. 3 Case and Mechanism for all lengths of Fire Escapes from 100 feet to 125 feet............ 100.00

To above add 50c. per foot for steel cable ladders of length required.

Cost of installation extra.

Conduit system of concealed wiring if desired.

Estimates furnished on application, with scale drawings for architects.

Figure 6 Harris Built-In Fire Escape.

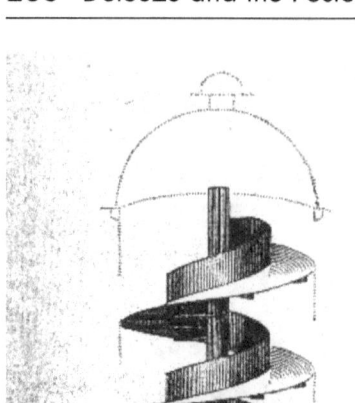

Cut A shows the exterior in outline and the interior arrangement of the tower fully, with the combined inner cold air duct, and open, or ladder-footing for firemen's use, and the outside *easy inclined roadway*, resulting from *not winding immediately about the centre shaft*, that persons fleeing may not experience difficulty. Blank places in the outline of the wall or casing, indicate the location of doorways or passages into the tower from a building in connection at each story.

At the apex of the roof, a dome exhaust-ventilating cap is placed.

The outer passage being without steps or landings, makes it feasible to remove aged people or the sick, unable to help themselves, by drawing them on bedding all the way down, without jar or injury. The partition separating the two passages is not so high but that firemen may vault over it if they desire, for the purpose of rescue, and afterward using the hose and water connection at the centre shaft (as shown in cut B), or wherever otherwise placed, as shown in the succeeding illustrations.

Figure 7 Pardessus Fire Escape.

example in which one perceives the movement of the bodies around oneself according to the potential for danger to be experienced from these bodies:

> The distance which separates our body from an object perceived really measures, therefore, the greater or less imminence of a danger, the nearer or more remote fulfilment of a promise. And, consequently, our perception of an object distinct from our body, separated from our body by an interval, never expresses the anything but a *virtual* action. (Bergson 1991: 56–7; original emphasis)

In this field of mutually affecting bodies, 'distance' is not a measurement of space but a potential of affective encounter. Bergson's 'interval' between 'our body' and the 'object' is more temporal than it is spatial in the sense that the potential for the components involved in this relation to affect one another has to do with their different speeds, and moreover with the different types of movement they bring to the situation.

For Bergson, it is important to present that separation or 'interval' as the key feature of a scenario. He is interested in the way affect operates without direct contact because it is in such cases that the 'virtual' plays a prominent role. When bodies in the world *do* collide they produce what Bergson calls a 'real action' – the bodies move one another according to their material qualities, and the person's response is like a reflex action (see Bergson 1991: 56–7). 'Virtual' action, however, speaks to the potential for more variation in the responsive action generated by the person than can ever attain in a reflex action. This potential for variation Bergson reserves for living bodies, especially those bodies with complex systems of sensory perception, like people. Bergson argues that people perceive the movements of the world by engaging in movements of perception that are much like those external movements (the sensory receptors move like the moving objects in the world). Those initial perception movements, which occur at the level of the skin, then travel through the body and deliver their information to the centre of the nervous system – the brain. At the brain they acquire complexity, in part through interacting with other sense perceptions, and also through interacting with other memory perceptions, both in terms of bodily memory and psychological memory. The important point is that the response movement is generated at this complex, interactive domain of sense perception, and when that response movement is generated (say in the form of some kind of motor activity) and expressed, time has passed since the initial perception. It could be a very short amount of time, but still the response action is something that comes from the past. Bodily action in this sense – action that occurs as perception shifts into response – is an act of memory rather than immediate reflex or intention.

So affectivity always comes from the past. What Deleuze helps to clarify in Bergson's theory is that the past is not necessarily just the product of that time delay between perception and response, but the whole memory of the body. What's more, the response that the body generates can acquire character from a memory that exists deeper in the past than the perception itself. Upon the sounding of a fire alarm, for example, people in the building might feel like responding by running and screaming. But they will likely interrupt that urge with the more orderly and quiet movement of walking through an escape route, a movement they will recollect from having participated in a fire drill that could have occurred months before. This interrupting movement is not simply retrieved from cognition or psychological memory; it also comes from bodily memory (which is why we need physically to practise fire drills, not just have the procedure explained to us). William E. Connolly notes that on many occasions, including emergencies, body memory comes before conscious action: '[I]n an emergency it is not only that explicit recollection gives way to virtual memory, *explicit image formation gives way to rapid information processing without image*' (Connolly 2002: 26–7; original emphasis). Even in cases when the memory that affects the responsive action is psychological, it is important to remember that it was produced initially from the body's material, sensory perception. The virtual domain of memory exists as movements in the past, not as recollected images.

For Bergson, movements rather than psychological images or pictures are primary affective agents, but he insists that the responsive movements that draw from the virtual are different in kind from perception movements. This is where the true 'interval' is to be found: between different acts in different kinds of time. The bodies that affect one another perceive one another's movements, and as part of the initial act of perception, they will respond with respect to one another. But they are still different bodies, whose different types of movement reflect their own unique types of dwelling in time and their own condition as always being affected by the past. Another word that Bergson uses for this condition of bodies in time, affected by their own pasts, is 'duration'. He sees the past as divided into various levels of duration. The body's movements in the present are shaped by events and movements of response that exist at levels more and less deep into the past, into memory, and all are qualitatively different from one another. These past movements affect the body's contemporary response to a given perception, actualising a new motor movement in the present. In the realm of duration, these memorised movements, these levels of the past, are so richly interpenetrating, so impossible to separate, that their capacity to affect one another is impossible to trace, their future actions and effects impossible to predict. They are examples of bodily features that Bergson calls 'intensive', a term that helps to express how different this field of durational affectivity is from the 'extensive' field, which is comprised of bodies, of movements, that are separated, that are outside of one another, and that therefore affect one another externally, generating 'actual' and not 'virtual' actions. In his examination of Bergson's work, Deleuze arrives at the conclusion that this is a theory not just about human perception and response, about how affectivity is an effect of time and movement, but also about the whole universe as it continues to become as an endless series of intensifications that actualise in always indeterminate ways, in ways that create change.

It is remarkable that Bergson could launch such a wide-ranging and complex philosophy of the virtual from the initial example that he offers of a body –'our body' – being affected by other bodies in the world. Yet, clearly all of the processes and implications of the virtual are given in that one simple example of an affective environment. This example has much in common with the scenario that was considered by the early fire escape designers, who were in fact contemporaries of Bergson. The job of the fire escape designers was to consider fire's potential danger to human bodies, and what they realised in doing so was that in the particular event of a building fire, time mattered more than space in terms of the affective potential of fire to injure people. These designers did not only take into account the building structure when they considered escape possibilities. That is, they did not merely treat their escapes as additions to this structure, as if their task was to impose spatial and material fixity upon this fire-event that was characterised and complicated by so many mobilities. They also had to take into account the speed with which a fire might travel through the building in question, what direction it might take, the nature of the fire (its temperature, its manifestation into smoke and flames), how fast its smoke would permeate available air space, and the state of the building materials and how fast they would burn. They considered these factors all in relation to how fast and by what type of movement people could escape it, and how quickly the fire fighters could arrive at the fire with hoses and other such rescue equipment to combat the fire and save the people. Thus, in considering and responding to these movements enacted by fire, and also by the people escaping it, fire escape designers called attention to this event as a composite, as one composed of real multiplicities of different potential movements. They responded to these movements, not by attempting to make them manageable by locating them within a single spatial location (for example, by making their escapes stationary), but instead by introducing yet new forms of movement (sliding, uncoiling, descending through the air), into this perceived eventuality of the building fire. In this sense these escape designers are particularly Deleuzian and Bergsonian, because they did not succumb to the convention of modern thought, which seeks to ignore or dissipate internal differences of a composite by making them relative, or like in kind, by forcing them to conform to the dualist conventions of representation:

> Bergson is aware that things are mixed together in reality; in fact, experience itself offers us nothing but composites. But that is not where the difficulty lies. For example, we make time into a representation imbued with

space. The awkward thing is that we no longer know how to distinguish in that *representation* the two component elements which differ in kind, the two pure *presences* of duration and extensity. We mix extensity and duration so thoroughly that we can now only oppose their mixture to a principle that is assumed to be both nonspatial and nontemporal, and in relation to which space and time, duration and extensity, are now only deteriorations. (Deleuze 1991: 22; original emphasis)

Rather than reduce time to the singularised realm of 'representation imbued with space', and rather than treat duration and extensity as 'deterioriations', these early Canadian fire escapes highlighted the differences within and between time and space by focusing upon and multiplying the types of movement people and buildings could enact. In the three mobile fire escapes I have considered here, people acquire new modes of moving (including modes that intervene in and redirect immediate reactive movements in which people might initially feel compelled to engage), part of a building moves in a new way, and/or a building enacts a shift (again, a kind of movement, although perhaps a temporary one as in the case of the Harris Built-in model) to adapt to the new situation of its being on fire. Through this process of adding movement to the event of a building fire, these escapes constitute one example of Deleuze's interpretation of the virtual as 'duration' in so far as 'duration divides up and does so constantly' and 'in the course of being actualized . . . is inseparable from the movement of its actualization' (Deleuze 1991: 42, 42–3). As well, in their explicit focus on differences in speed and time, these escapes constitute 'a nonnumerical multiplicity by which duration or subjectivity is defined', and, as such, they 'plung[e] into another dimension, which is no longer spatial and is purely temporal' (Deleuze 1991: 43). The remaining portion of this essay reads these escapes for their mobilities, and the variety of means by which they tend toward or express qualitative difference in time: becoming escapes through the acquisition of movement; creating new forms of movement in the human bodies doing the escaping; expressing the multiplicity of durations of bodies involved in a building fire; and finally by addressing the role of both the extensive and the intensive in the virtual.

Escape: To Differ, to Divide, to Move Anew

Early Canadian mobile fire escapes are uniquely Deleuzian because they express the virtual nature of the many potential actualisations that could take place in the event of a building fire. They differ, therefore, from the conventional stationary escapes which favour the space-oriented, determinable world of the possible becoming real. As we have seen, through the writings of Baillairgé, the building fire was understood as an 'eventuality'. Architects could not know in advance what a fire would be like, nor could they know whether or not a fire would actually occur in a given building. Unlike the stationary fire escapes that carried out their function of providing the means of escape even when the building was not on fire, these moveable fire escapes only became escapes when the fire occurred. In acquiring movement they became something other, something different, from what they had been. It is this movement that makes them differ, makes them incomparable to the more static objects they once were when there was no fire. This addition of new movement further divides the already pluralised and differentiated mixture of movements that constituted the event of the building fire. It enhances duration because as it 'moves from the virtual to its actualization, it actualizes itself by creating lines of differentiation that correspond to its differences in kind' (Deleuze 1991: 43).

In addition to their becoming actual escapes when people engaged them in a type of movement that they had not previously been activated with, the escapes themselves produced new capacities for movement in the people that were escaping. The Burrows Escape, for instance, enabled people to glide through the air, while the Pardessus Escape made it possible for people to slide away from the fire. What characterises the escape movements in both of these scenarios is the fact that they express a radical difference in the very being of the bodies engaging in these movement actions. These movement scenarios express something different from the conventional notion of movement in which a body remains constant with itself while travelling through a space that also remains constant. Instead, they express the type of movement espoused by both Deleuze and Bergson, in which, as Constantin Boundas explains, to move 'is not to go through a trajectory which can be decomposed and recombined in quantitative terms; it is to become other than itself, in a sense that makes movement a qualitative change' (Boundas 1996: 84). In fact, in all of the mobile fire escape scenarios I have discussed here, the instances in which the fire escapes enable people to engage in new forms of motion may be the most interesting. The Burrows Escape 'at rest' still quite clearly signals what its potential for movement is, but the building inhabitants going about their everyday lives do not immediately seem capable of, say, sliding or gliding through the air. The movement they acquire with the aid of the escape is truly new, and its progress largely indeterminable.[6] Brian Massumi discusses this indeterminable nature of potential movement as follows:

> When a body is in motion, it does not coincide with itself. It coincides with its own transition: its own variation. The range of variations it can be implicated in is not present in any given moment, much less in any position it passes through. In motion, a body is in an immediate, unfolding relation to its own nonpresent potential to vary. (Massumi 2002: 4)

Some of the mobile escapes, the Burrows Escape in particular, offer this intensively affective movement that Massumi describes, both where the body's movement is affected by its own potential for internal variation, and also where the material object of the escape differs from itself by moving according to a potentiality that is quite identifiable in the still object.

By introducing new forms of movement into the fire escape scenario, the early Canadian fire escape designers sought to express and contribute to the multiplicity of movements occurring in the event of a building fire. But this expression and enactment of difference could only take place because many different bodies were involved. It is only by attending to the nature of the escape's movements that we can begin to acknowledge the first multiplicity that concerns Bergson: the multiplicity of time. If the sole objects of our consideration were the permanently stationary staircase escapes, we would not necessarily need to take duration into account – we would perhaps not need to consider the multiplicity of pasts affecting the actions of a given body, and especially the human body. Instead we would likely remain satisfied with Zeno's analysis, based on a single space and single form of movement that produces the possibility of comparing relative speeds. What makes duration identifiable, Bergson argues, is being in the presence of other durations, durations that are different from ours. He gives the well-known example of the commonplace event in which a person waits for a lump of sugar to dissolve in water. For Deleuze, this event 'signifies that my own duration, such as I live it in the impatience of waiting, for example, serves to reveal other durations that beat to other rhythms, that differ in kind from mine' (Deleuze 1991: 32).[7] When the fire escapes move, they call into question our own capacity to move effectively in a situation, therefore making us aware of other durations (durations that could catch up with our movements), and also of the potential for us to become a part of durations that are outside of us (for example by being in the Burrows basket). To 'escape' in these early Canadian apparatuses is to change, not to traverse a certain amount of space but in fact to change one's capacity for movement.

If the virtual affectivity of human bodies in the processes of their becoming is most interesting to Bergson, why does he insist on a scene in which there are other types of bodies in the field of affect? What is the role of matter, of the extensive, in the virtual? The nineteenth-century moveable fire escapes serve well to document Bergson's concept of the role of human consciousness, which, as Elizabeth Grosz writes, is 'not to produce images or to reflect on them, but to put images directed from elsewhere, from the world, into the context of bodily action' (Grosz 2004: 168). In one sense the mobile fire escapes seem to preclude 'bodily action' since they often replaced walking with a different kind of movement that is not quite proper to human motor function. (People standing in the Burrows basket were not actively engaging the movement of their own bodies through space.) On the other hand, what they express is a consciousness of a world in action, where that consciousness is 'directed from elsewhere'. From Bergson's initial description of affectivity we see the virtual enacted only when the human body perceives other bodies in extension – bodies that are spatially separate from that body, material bodies whose movements generate the initial and extensive perceiving movement by the human body's sensory receptors. As Grosz explains, it is the 'interposition' of bodies and objects that makes them 'become "enlivened" and capable of being linked to nascent actions, drawn out of their inertia. Through them, objects are put into new contexts, utilized in new ways, produce new effects. Inventiveness is introduced into the rigid determinacy of matter's relations to itself' (Grosz 2004: 169). While so much of the contemporary interest in affect and virtual philosophy focuses on the realm of the intensive, it is important to remember, as Bergson and Deleuze insist, that memory always exists on a continuum with matter, and depends upon it for its existence. The escapes are the product of designers who were very much aware, it seems, of this interposition of moving bodies to effect further movement, and also to produce new movement, and their escapes articulated and multiplied the durations present in the many bodies involved.

These nineteenth-century mobile fire escapes express the multiplicity of movement that is the nature and condition of material affectivity and of ontological being in the world. They consider movement as both an extensive, spatialised phenomenon and as an effect of the virtual past that informs responsive movements and affects eventual outcomes. In so doing they maintain an awareness of the virtual world that unfolds, or divides up, as a series of qualitatively differentiated movements. Fire escapes are important in the context of early Canadian nation-building activities at the level of the material, lived environment because fires posed such a significant threat to these activities and yet at the same time generated such unique responses – responses that highlighted rather than sought to minimise their virtual nature. Of particular importance is these escapes' emphasis on the significance of temporality evident in the event of material movement and change, and their incorporation of actual qualitative difference into the escape actions they enabled. The mobile fire escapes I have considered here comprise a material archive of nation-building, one that is composed of plans and rhetoric signifying movement, but that still, in its focus on mobilities, resists the conflation of material events and eventualities into the realm of representation. All in all, the designers of these fire escapes made the creative, unpredictable and non-representable force of virtual duration the foundation of their safety technology. Perhaps contemporary postcolonial criticism can learn from this persistent expression of the virtual that once gave not just shape, but also time and motion, to nation-building in Canada.

References

Ansell-Pearson, K. (2002), *Philosophy and the Adventure of the Virtual: Bergson and the Time of Life*, London: Routledge.

Armstrong, N. (2007), 'Professing Disciplinarity', *Victorian Review* 33 (1): 11–14.

Baillairgé, C. (1887), *A Practical Solution of the Great Social and Humanitarian Problem: Escape from Buildings in Case of Fire*, paper read to the Royal Society of Canada, Quebec, CIHM 90206.

Bergson, H. [1896] (1991), *Matter and Memory*, trans. N. M. Paul and W. S. Palmer, New York: Zone Books.

Bhabha, H. (1990), 'Introduction: Narrating the Nation', in H. Bhabha (ed.), *Nation and Narration*, London: Routledge, pp. 1–8.

Boundas, C. (1996), 'Deleuze-Bergson: an Ontology of the Virtual', in P. Patton (ed.), *Deleuze: A Critical Reader*, Oxford: Blackwell, pp. 81–107.

Brydon, D. (1995), 'Introduction: Reading Postcoloniality, Reading Canada', *Essays on Canadian Writing* 56: 1–19.

Brydon, D. (2000), 'It's Time for a New Set of Questions', *Essays on Canadian Writing* 71: 14–25.

Brydon, D. (2007), 'Dionne Brand's Global Intimacies: Practicing Affective Citizenship', *University of Toronto Quarterly* 76 (3): 990–1006.

Connolly, W. E. (2002), *Neuropolitics: Thinking, Culture, Speed*, Minneapolis: University of Minnesota Press.

Deleuze, G. (1988), *Foucault*, trans. S. Hand, London: Athlone Press.

Deleuze, G. (1991), *Bergsonism*, trans. H. Tomlinson and B. Habberjam, New York: Zone Books.

Devereux, C. (2003), 'Are We There Yet? Reading the "Post-Colonial" and *The Imperialist* in Canada', in L. Moss (ed.), *Is Canada Postcolonial? Unsettling Canadian Literature*, Waterloo: Wilfrid Laurier University Press, pp. 177–90.

E. T. Barnum and Iron Work, (1883), *Builders' Wire, Iron and Brass Work: Iron Stairs, Fire Escapes, Sash Bars, Window Guards . . .* Detroit: E. T. Barnum.

(The) *Fourteenth Annual Report of the Royal Society for the Protection of Life from Fire, for Maintaining an Organised Body of Men, Provided with,*

and Instructed on the Use of Public Fire Escapes . . . (1850), London: Richards.
Grosz, E. (2004), *The Nick of Time: Politics, Evolution, and the Untimely*, Durham: Duke University Press.
Harris Safety Company (1900), *Harris System Portable Fire Escapes*, Philadelphia: Harris Safety Company.
Ivison, D. (2003), '"I too am a Canadian": John Richardson's *The Canadian Brothers* as Postcolonial Narrative', in L. Moss (ed.), *Is Canada Postcolonial? Unsettling Canadian Literature*, Waterloo: Wilfrid Laurier University Press, pp. 162–77.
Keating, E. H. (1883), *Fire Departments, Fire Apparatus, and Fire Escapes: A Report on the Means of Preventing the Loss of Life and Property by Fire*, Halifax: Morning Herald Printing and Publishing Company.
Kertzer, J. (1998), *Worrying the Nation: Imagining a National Literature in English Canada*, Toronto: University of Toronto Press.
Lawson, A. (1995), 'Postcolonial Theory and the "Settler" Subject', *Essays on Canadian Writing* 56: 20–36.
Massumi, B. (2002), *Parables for the Virtual: Movement, Affect, Sensation*, Durham: Duke University Press.
Pardessus, S. J. (1883), *Pardessus' Double-Passage Quick Fire Reach and Practical Fire Escape*, New York: S. J. Pardessus.
Slemon, S. (1990), 'Unsettling the Empire: Resistance Theory for the Second World', *World Literature Written in English* 30 (2): 30–41.
Szeman, I. (2000), 'Belated or Isochronic? Canadian Writing, Time, and Globalization', *Where Is Here Now? Special Issue of Essays in Canadian Writing* 71: 186–94.
Wermiel, S. E. (2000), *The Fireproof Building: Technology and Public Safety in the Nineteenth-Century American City*, Baltimore: Johns Hopkins University Press.

Notes

1. The *Fourteenth Annual Report of the Royal Society for the Protection of Life from Fire* (1850) claimed on its cover that public escapes were 'kept in readiness at various convenient stations throughout the metropolis' in London, England.
2. For more on second-world nation-building as an important and productive example of postcoloniality see Slemon (1990); Brydon (1995); Devereux (2003); and Ivison (2003).
3. Brydon is one of only a very few critics who have argued for a re-evaluation of what gets lost in the 'linguistic turn' that informed 1990s Canadian postcolonialism, and her most recent work argues for the use of affect theory in this field. See, for example, Brydon 2007.
4. In a related comment, Kertzer calls 'nation-building' an 'oxymoronic' phrase since, '[a]ccording to the romantic-nationalist project . . . nations, which should issue from nature, are not supposed to be "built" at all. They are supposed to grow organically without contrivance. Consequently, nation builders are obliged to efface their own artifice . . .' (Kertzer 1998: 63)
5. As Constantin Boundas pointed out in a 1996 article, this work has received relatively little attention. It is Deleuze's latter collaborative works with Félix Guattari that have gained some popularity in cultural criticism (Boundas 1996: 81). Postcolonial criticism has focused on the concept of 'deterritorialisation', especially as it is explored in *A Thousand Plateaus*. In terms of Canadian criticism, for example, the term has been useful for articulating the fluidity of immigrant

subjectivities in contemporary Canadian urban environments. When it comes to considering second-world postcolonialism in early Canada, however, we can gain at least as much from Deleuze's analysis in *Bergsonism*, which offers methods through which to analyse the temporal aspects of processes like nation-building.
6. S. J. Pardessus, for example, claimed that his escape 'secure[d] orderly flight', but one would assume that the movement described by a building full of people sliding down a ramp could never be orderly (Pardessus 1883: 2).
7. Consider also the following: 'The attempt to bring our duration in relation to other durations . . . constitutes for Deleuze the very meaning of philosophy since it is only through an adequate thinking of time *qua* duration that we can hope to attain a level of precision in our thinking' (Ansell-Pearson 2002: 10).

Notes on Contributors

Réda Bensmaïa is Professor and Chair in the Department of French Studies at Brown University. He is the author of *Experimental Nations, or the Invention of the Maghreb* (Princeton University Press 2003), and the Editor of the special issue of *Lendemains* on Gilles Deleuze's work (1989). Part of his correspondence with Deleuze – a letter from Deleuze on Spinoza – is published in *Negotiations* (Columbia University Press, 1995).

Timothy Bewes is Associate Professor in the Department of English at Brown University. He is author of *Cynicism and Postmodernity* (Verso, 1997), *Reification, or the Anxiety of Late Capitalism* (Verso, 2002) and articles in journals such as *New Left Review*, *Genre*, *Cultural Critique* and *Differences*. He is also an editor on the journals *New Formations* and *Novel: A Forum on Fiction*. His book *Postcolonial Shame* is forthcoming from Princeton University Press.

Simone Bignall is a Visiting Fellow in the School of History and Philosophy at the University of New South Wales. Her research interests include postcolonialism and feminism, particularly in relation to issues of transformative agency. She has published a number of scholarly articles on Deleuze, Guattari and postcolonial politics. Her book *Postcolonial Agency* is forthcoming from Edinburgh University Press, and she is currently working on a project titled *Ethics Beyond Enjoyment*.

Jennifer Blair is Assistant Professor of English at the University of Ottawa, specialising in Canadian Literature. Her work focuses on architectural design and representational practices in early Canadian texts. Jennifer has published articles in *English Studies in Canada* and *GLQ*, and she is co-editor of *ReCalling Early Canada: Reading the Political in Literary and Cultural Production* (University of Alberta Press, 2005).

Rey Chow is Andrew W. Mellon Professor of the Humanities at Brown University, where she holds appointments in Comparative Literature, English and Modern Culture and Media. She is the author of many essays and a number of books, the most recent of which include *The Age of the World Target* (Duke University Press, 2006) and *Sentimental Fabulations, Contemporary Chinese Films* (Columbia University Press, 2007). Her work has been widely anthologised and translated into major European and Asian languages.

Grant Hamilton is Visiting Assistant Professor of English Literature at the University of Hong Kong. He is the author of a forthcoming book titled *On Representation: Deleuze and Coetzee on the Colonised Subject* (Rodopi Press). He has also published a number of articles on African literature and is currently working on his second book, *Deleuze and African Literature*.

Philip Leonard is Reader in Literary Studies and Critical Theory at Nottingham Trent University. He is the author of *Nationality between Poststructuralism and Postcolonial Theory: A New Cosmopolitanism* (Palgrave, 2005), as well as articles on contemporary literature and theory. He is currently writing a book on technology, literature and culture, and is co-editor of the online journal *Writing Technologies*.

Nick Nesbitt is Senior Lecturer in French in the Centre for Modern Thought at the University of Aberdeen, Scotland. He is the author of Voicing *Memory: History and Subjectivity in French Caribbean Literature* (University of Virginia Press, 2003) and *Universal Emancipation: The Haitian Revolution and the Radical Enlightenment* (University of Virginia Press, 2008). He is also the editor of *Toussaint Louverture: The Haitian Revolution* (Verso, 2008), and co-editor with Brian Hulse of the volume *Sounding the Virtual: Gilles Deleuze and the Theory and Philosophy of Music* (Ashgate, 2009).

John K. Noyes is Professor of German at the University of Toronto. He is the author of books and articles on the cultural history of colonialism, postcolonial theory and the history of sexuality, including *Colonial Space* (Harwood, 1992), *The Mastery of Submission* (Cornell University Press, 1997), and *The Paths of Multiculturalism* (with Maria Alzira Seixo, Edições Cosmos, 2000). His current research is on intellectual responses to imperialism in late Enlightenment Germany.

Paul Patton is Professor of Philosophy at the University of New South Wales in Sydney, Australia. He is the author of *Deleuze and the Political* (Routledge, 2000) and *Deleuzian Concepts: Philosophy, Colonization, Politics* (Stanford, 2010). He edited *Deleuze: A Critical Reader* (Blackwell, 1996), (with Duncan Ivison and Will Sanders) *Political Theory and the Rights of Indigenous Peoples* (Cambridge, 2000) and (with John Protevi) *Between Deleuze and Derrida* (Continuum, 2003).

Patricia Pisters is Professor of Film Studies at the University of Amsterdam. Her research focuses on film and screen theory, particularly in relation to multiculturalism, interculturality and transnational media, focusing on the encounters between Western and Arab (media) worlds. Her publications include: *The Matrix of Visual Culture: Working with Deleuze in Film Theory* (Stanford University Press, 2003) and *Shooting the Family: Transnational Media and Intercultural Values* (ed. with Wim Staat; Amsterdam University Press, 2005). See http://home.medewerker.uva.nl/p.p.r.w.pisters

Andrew Robinson is an independent researcher and activist affiliated to the Centre for the Study of Social and Global Justice, University of Nottingham, UK, where he completed his BA, MA and PhD before being awarded a Leverhulme postdoctoral research fellowship. He has diverse interests and has published widely on themes such as oppressive discourse, Rawls, higher education, movements in the global South, utopianism and neo-Lacanian political thought.

Marcelo Svirsky is a Marie-Curie post-doctoral fellow at the Centre for Critical and Cultural Theory at Cardiff University. He is currently working on a theoretical elaboration of an intercultural politics from a Deleuzian perspective. He has published on intercultural political theory and on intercultural theory and bilingual education.

Simon Tormey was until 2009 Professor of Politics and Critical Theory at the University of Nottingham before joining the University of Sydney as Professor and Head of the School of Social and Political Sciences. He has published numerous books and articles including, most recently, *Key Thinkers from Critical Theory to Postmarxism* (Sage, 2006); *Anti-Capitalism: A Beginner's Guide* (Oneworld, 2004) and *Agnes Heller: Socialism, Autonomy and the Postmodern* (Manchester University Press, 2001). He is an associate editor of *Contemporary Political Theory*.

Index

abstract machine, 65–6, 222, 300
Abu Ghraib, 62–3, 74
action-image, 205, 208, 219
active/reactive, 22–6, 29–30, 38, 47, 85, 88–91, 110, 117
activism, 70, 266
actual-virtual, 7, 19, 105, 108–13, 127, 133, 136, 157(n. 11), 161(n. 26), 173, 203–11, 214, 240, 243, 255, 256, 257, 263, 272, 289–91, 294
actualisation, 12, 14, 15, 97, 108–10, 113, 127, 133, 157(n. 11), 204, 225, 229, 240, 243, 255, 257, 263–4, 291
aesthetics, 73–4, 106, 114, 143, 160(n. 23), 210, 211, 213
affectivity, 13, 16, 74, 82, 84–9, 93, 96–100, 227, 273, 275, 277, 281, 284, 287–9, 292–4
affirmation, 11, 22–3, 35–6, 69, 189
agency, 2, 4, 8, 16, 24, 26, 45, 71, 79, 84, 91, 205, 252, 267, 276
Algeria, 2, 14, 121, 131, 138, 140–2, 145, 148, 160–1, 215–16
alienation, 37–8, 71, 112–14, 220, 231

Althusser, Louis, 27–30, 36, 39(n. 3)
ambivalence, 81, 193, 276–8
anti-colonialism, 42, 47, 69, 117(n. 7)
Anti-Oedipus, 28, 36, 42, 44–5, 47–8, 51, 55–6, 129, 137, 151
apology 78, 82, 101(n. 3), 250(n. 21)
Appadurai, Arjun, 4, 20, 29, 36
Arendt, Hannah, 153
art, 36, 38, 73, 90, 201, 202, 211–12, 214–16
association, 52, 94–5, 168, 191, 196–7, 199(n. 3), 251, 256, 262, 266
assemblage, 6, 12–13, 44, 65, 67–9, 75, 79, 83–5, 87, 91, 93, 96, 99, 100, 139, 147–8, 152, 186, 189, 193, 199, 221–2, 225, 231, 234, 238, 244, 254–60, 268, 270(n. 4, 5)
assimilation, 7, 78, 92
Australia, 13, 78–9, 81–2, 86, 89–91, 101(n. 2, 3), 224, 236, 243
authenticity, 2, 5, 24, 31, 35, 71, 134, 141–2, 215, 263, 277

Badiou, Alain, 104–11, 114, 116(n. 3), 117 (n. 6, 10), 118 (n. 12), 127, 133–5, 157 (n. 10, 11), 259
Baillairgé, Charles, 272–4, 291
Barbarians, 48, 184–99
becoming, 3, 4, 8, 11, 12, 14–16, 19(n. 1), 22–5, 30, 32, 34–5, 37–8, 69, 75, 80, 88–9, 92–3, 97–8, 105, 108, 118(n. 12), 124, 128, 132, 137–8, 140–2, 148, 156(n. 8), 159, 161(n. 27, 29), 165, 167, 170, 183, 191–3, 198, 201–2, 208, 210, 213–14, 221, 243, 254, 275, 279, 293
Bergson, Henri, 122, 136, 172, 174, 176, 204, 232, 254, 281, 284, 287–90, 292–3
Bhabha, Homi, 11, 19(n. 1), 69, 127, 158(n. 14), 219(n. 2), 276, 278
binaries, 34–5, 37, 41–3, 53, 211; see also dualisms
black hole, 12, 126, 189, 198
body, 48, 51, 71, 79, 80, 82–9, 91–4, 97–9, 107–9, 112–13, 118(n. 12), 133–4, 164, 184–5, 211–13, 215, 222, 237, 257, 287–9, 291–3
body-without-organs, 48, 61(n. 3), 129, 213
Boudjedra, Rachid, 138
Buchanan, Ian, vii, 165, 222, 233
bureaucracy, 140, 159(n. 23), 248(n. 6)

capitalism, 20, 23, 25–6, 42–4, 46, 48–58, 71, 90, 108, 114, 130, 134, 159(n. 18), 203, 230, 231–2, 235, 248(n. 12), 264–5
capture, 3, 5, 6, 8–10, 13, 22, 24, 63, 73–5, 77(n. 2, 6), 122, 130, 183, 189, 197, 222, 224, 229, 231, 236, 238, 248(n. 12), 257, 261
cartography, 45, 47, 48, 52, 130, 144–5, 156(n. 8), 247(n. 1), 259, 276
causality, 12, 16, 26, 42, 44–5, 83–5, 89–92, 94, 108, 118(n. 12), 136, 159(n. 20, 23), 163, 166, 190, 228, 231–2, 234, 276, 278
Cazier, Jean-Philippe, 123
Césaire, Aimé 103, 106–7, 127
change, 14, 26, 55, 83, 87–8, 104–5, 107, 128, 142–3, 174, 178, 203, 223, 234, 236, 240, 245, 256–8, 264, 275, 277, 281, 284, 289, 292, 293, 294
Chaplin, Charlie, 205–6
cinema, 4, 15, 72–4, 77(n. 6), 123, 157(n. 12), 162(n. 30), 166–7, 171, 173–81, 201, 204–16
class, 28, 58, 70, 72, 106, 109, 114, 117(n. 5), 137, 234, 250(n. 25), 259, 260, 264–6
Clastres, Pierre, 33, 198
coding, 34, 48–9, 51–2, 144, 146–8, 161(n. 29), 176, 191, 210–11, 213–14, 233–6, 243, 254, 260, 265
Coetzee, J. M., 15, 164, 183–200, 298
colonial policy, 13, 78, 81, 227, 249(n. 19)
compatibility, 79, 88–90, 95
communitarianism, 80–3, 93, 102(n. 6), 126
community, 16, 78–82, 88, 98, 139, 158, 221, 239, 240, 242, 245, 252, 256, 268

conceptual personae, 124
confinement, 62–3, 68–9, 73–5, 187, 189, 192, 250(n. 20), 251–3
conflict, 9, 53, 70–1, 80, 90, 92, 105, 137–8, 213, 220–50
connectivity, 16, 17, 22, 25–6, 47, 65–6, 73, 88, 118(n. 12), 124, 134, 143, 144, 146, 161(n. 29), 175, 223, 231, 233, 237–8, 240, 242, 256–8, 260, 263, 267, 270(n. 5)
consensus, 16, 61(n. 8), 192, 194, 261
consistency, 6, 7, 83, 84, 88, 93, 99, 110, 136, 179, 229
constructivism 8, 26, 222–3, 242
cosmopolitanism, 20, 82; *see also* globalisation
counter actualisation, 4, 37, 105, 109–11, 178
creativity, 2, 6, 8–9, 11–12, 14, 17, 26, 31, 37–8, 39(n. 3), 55, 69, 85, 90, 93, 99–100, 105, 110, 123, 128, 223, 238, 243, 253, 255, 294
culturalism (multi-; counter-; agri-; techno-), 114, 190, 253, 261
Cusset, François, 122, 157(n. 9), 158(n. 16); *see also* 'French Theory'
cyberspace, 253, 261, 270(n. 2)

death, 53, 69, 110–11, 138, 150–2, 157(n. 11), 190, 215, 262, 266
decolonisation, 1, 2, 3, 103, 107, 111–12, 115, 117(n. 6), 121, 137, 159(n. 21), 160(n. 24), 168, 169, 208, 216, 266
deconstruction, 3, 11, 16, 43, 60(n. 1), 69, 152, 219(n. 2), 226, 273, 275

Deleuzism, 121, 135, 159(n. 18)
Deleuze's names, 6, 17, 120–39, 157(n. 11), 158(n. 14), 159(n. 15), 259
democracy, 96, 102(n. 4), 106, 165, 222, 242–3, 251
Derrida, Jacques, 32, 35–6, 43, 122, 127, 134, 152, 157(n. 9), 219(n. 2)
desire, 3, 11–13, 15, 22–30, 35, 38, 41, 43, 44–50, 52, 55–6, 61(n. 2), 99, 151, 165, 176, 202, 219(n. 2), 221–50
de/reterritorialisation, 15, 23, 47, 51, 69, 105, 133, 140–3, 148, 153, 160(n. 26), 161(n. 29), 170, 183, 185–99, 221–4, 236–8, 244, 259–60, 265, 296(n. 5)
diagram, 65–6, 223, 279, 284
dialectic, 41–2, 46–7, 49, 54, 61(n. 4), 67, 106–7, 117(n. 5), 135, 160(n. 24), 164, 170, 176, 205, 224
dialogue, 8, 13, 21, 119, 130–1, 133, 143
diaspora, 4, 158(n. 16)
differentiator (Deleuze as), 14, 131–6
Dirlik, Arif, 43, 46, 58
disciplinary forces, 13, 34, 44, 62–3, 67–8, 225, 238, 240, 265, 278
discourse analysis, 275–6, 278
dispositif, 125, 127, 133, 137
dispossession, 15, 78, 80–2, 94, 99, 224, 227, 231
domination, 5, 22, 24–6, 49, 95–6, 112, 130, 163, 179–80, 189, 229
doxa, 8, 121, 129, 139

dualisms, 37, 53–6, 273, 284, 290; see also binaries
duration, 83, 178, 288–94, 296(n. 7)

earth, 15, 48, 50–1, 142–3, 183, 185–7, 189, 229, 231, 237–8, 258, 260
economic development, 48, 58, 230, 248(n. 8), 249(n. 19), 250(n. 25), 252, 257, 261, 263, 265–6, 270(n. 2, 3)
emancipation, 22, 36, 67, 69, 71–2, 106–7, 116(n. 4), 227, 252; see also liberation
empire, 3, 20, 52, 55–7, 106, 184–88, 191, 194
encounter, 8, 9, 11, 14–15, 17, 20, 51, 69, 83–95, 103, 119–39, 148, 156(n. 6), 158(n. 15), 159(n. 17), 164, 175, 183, 208, 229–30, 270(n. 5), 287
enemy, 135, 169, 190–3
Engels, Friedrich, 42
enlightenment, 20, 55, 57–8, 63, 67, 252
essentialism, 7, 13, 21–2, 26, 98, 184
ethnocentrism, 32
ethnography, 15, 34, 166–7, 198, 259
Eurocentrism, 1, 2, 5, 20–1, 32–8, 64, 71, 202, 267
event, 4, 14, 17, 53, 62, 67, 71, 77(n. 6), 86, 105, 107–15, 117(n. 6), 117(n. 10), 118(n. 12), 122, 136–7, 148, 160(n. 26), 164–6, 170–1, 178, 205, 222, 229, 231, 272–5, 277, 281, 287–84
exclusion, 5, 13, 22, 32, 68–71, 82, 97, 113, 117(n. 8), 130, 177, 221, 234–5, 238, 240–3, 252, 268
experimentation, 47, 67, 69, 120, 156(n. 8), 157(n. 9), 171, 191, 211, 235, 249(n. 18)

fabulation, 12, 208–9
Fanon, Frantz, 9–10, 36, 69, 103, 117(n. 5), 127, 168–70, 177, 216
fantasy, 15, 33, 204, 225; see also ideal/real
Farès, Nabile, vii, 14, 138, 139–53, 159(n. 23), 160(n. 24), 161(n. 27), 162(n. 32)
Fascism, 23, 28–9, 38, 54, 126, 135, 161(n. 28), 200(n. 4)
feminism, 4, 42, 102(n. 6), 126
film see cinema
First Nations, 16, 275–6, 278
fold, 97, 107, 136, 152
forgetting history, 70, 226–7
Foucault, Michel, 4, 5, 13, 20–1, 25–7, 32, 35, 45, 62–74, 77(n. 2, 3), 97, 122, 125, 127, 134, 138, 158(n. 16) 219(n. 2), 239, 278–9
'French Theory', 20, 122, 126, 157(n. 9); see also Cusset
Freud, Sigmund, 37, 51, 69–70, 141, 151–2, 199(n. 3)

gaze, 95, 108, 148, 164, 175–6, 179, 186–7, 191, 239
geography, 44, 51, 54, 149, 160(n. 24), 183, 237, 262
Gilroy, Paul, 69
Glissant, Édouard, 3, 4, 14, 103–14, 116(n. 2), 117(n. 5), 127, 151
globalisation, 16, 20, 41, 43, 46, 49, 130, 134, 150, 208, 251–3, 260–1, 265–7

Guattari, Félix, 3, 21, 35, 37, 49, 103, 121, 125–7, 129, 157(n. 10), 158(n. 15)
Guha, Ranajit, 34–5, 127

habitus, 251, 268
haecceity, 14, 53, 137–9, 141; *see also* event
Hall, Stuart, 41, 43–6, 69, 208
Hallward, Peter, vii, 104–7, 109, 114, 116(n. 3), 117(n. 5, 8, 9), 203, 219(n. 2)
harmony, 80, 91, 156(n. 8), 159(n. 20), 174, 176, 179
Hegelian thought, 35, 36, 42, 80, 110, 117(n. 5), 134, 135, 144, 159(n. 18)
hegemony, 13, 21, 27, 30–1, 38, 64, 144, 160(n. 23), 220
heterogeneity, 5, 6, 16, 25, 75, 131–2, 136, 145, 147, 148, 161(n. 29), 256–7, 275
history, 5, 28, 33, 36, 42, 44, 46–51, 53, 55, 61(n. 3), 68, 74, 78–9, 98, 108, 112, 138, 141–2, 146–7, 151–3, 159(n. 21), 160(n. 24), 163–4, 178, 193, 203, 221, 229, 232, 240, 252, 259, 266–7, 275–6, 278
Holland, Eugene, 39(n. 2), 50, 54
homogeneity, 25, 191, 231, 265
humanism, 2, 23, 33, 37, 52, 55, 63–5, 67, 69, 78, 80–2, 95–6, 106, 108, 127, 164, 170, 172, 174, 176–7, 253, 258
humour, 205–6, 210, 213–14
hybridity, 3, 11, 90, 260

ideal/real, 15, 55, 167, 173, 204, 265–6

identity formation, 4, 11, 87–9, 93–4, 99, 104–5, 109, 132, 136, 153, 157(n. 9), 158(n. 16), 164–5, 167, 173, 180, 205, 216, 227
identity politics, 11, 28, 69–70, 80–2, 104–14, 117(n. 6), 126, 130, 147, 153, 205, 216, 227, 253, 265–6
ideology, 13, 21, 27–31, 37, 46, 49, 54, 56, 118(n. 10), 173, 202, 204, 214, 228–9, 232–3, 236, 250(n. 21), 276
imperialism, 3, 4, 6, 8, 32, 44, 50–4, 70; *see also* empire
image (media), 13, 62, 71–5, 77(n. 6), 173–9, 201, 204–14, 219(n. 6)
image of thought, 4, 7, 9, 28, 29, 49, 215
imagination, 63, 82, 145, 204, 209–14, 225, 227
immanence, 15, 66, 75, 118(n. 12), 179, 201, 204–6, 208, 215, 222, 229, 240–1, 243–4, 255
indigenous, 1, 4, 13, 21, 33–4, 37, 47, 60(n. 1), 78–82, 86, 89–99, 147, 202, 210, 223–4, 230, 231, 238, 248(n. 10)
inclusive politics, 95, 251–2, 262
incorporeality (of the virtual), 109, 111, 229, 258
indetermination, 137, 172–3, 179, 193–4, 275, 289, 292
intensive, 24, 67, 84, 95 118(n. 12) 124, 136–7, 143–4, 147 159(n. 19), 185, 196, 213–14, 260, 289, 291–3
interests, 28–9, 37–8, 45, 202, 223, 227–8, 233, 249(n. 19), 266
intersubjectivity, 87, 106, 163

invention, 3, 10, 17, 30, 44, 51–3, 97, 99, 103, 110, 133, 141, 161(n. 27), 174, 192, 201, 205, 210–11, 240, 274, 293
invisibility, 13, 21, 66, 68, 151, 204, 213, 253, 283, 284; *see also* visibility
Iraq, 62, 182(n. 3)
irrationality, 57, 63, 148, 162(n. 30)
Islam, 29, 34, 141–2, 160(n. 23, 24), 215–16, 219(n. 11)

joy, 82, 84–6, 89–91, 93–5, 98–9, 123, 173, 214
justice, 2, 13, 65, 70, 78–9, 82, 92–3, 97–8, 100, 102(n. 6), 104, 106, 116(n. 3), 193–4, 197, 205
jurisprudence, 96, 102(n. 4), 236

Kabyle, 140–7, 161(n. 27, 29)
Kant, Immanuel, 20, 44, 55, 61(n. 2), 122, 128
Khatibi, Adelkébir, 138

labour, 32, 53, 57, 71, 175, 230–6, 242, 248(n. 6, 12), 249(n. 14)
Lacan, Jacques, 22, 29, 35–7, 133, 134, 151, 153, 158(n. 16)
lack, 29, 31, 35–8, 45–6, 80, 95, 112, 132, 136
Lacoue-Labarthe, Philippe, 153
land, 47–8, 78, 82, 90, 92, 94, 175, 190, 209, 213, 223–5, 227, 230–44, 248(n. 6), 249(n. 13, 16, 17), 250(n. 25), 259, 266
language, 3, 6, 38, 49–50, 65–6, 69, 94, 99, 111, 122, 124, 130, 139, 145–7, 151–3, 161(n. 29), 167–8, 175, 259, 277–8

law, 54, 56, 92, 94, 117(n. 6), 159(n. 20), 197, 212, 224, 243, 249(n. 17)
liberalism, 29, 81–2, 93, 102(n. 6)
liberation, 3, 9, 13, 26, 45, 69, 70, 72, 110, 112, 130, 137, 160(n. 26), 166, 174, 177, 180, 186, 228, 253, 259, 260, 267; *see also* emancipation
line of flight, 37, 126, 141, 144
Lionnet, Françoise, vii, 4
listening, 5, 10, 17, 31, 69, 94–5, 100, 124
literature, 3, 14, 123, 129, 150, 163, 166, 168–9, 276–8

machines, 3, 15, 22–3, 26, 37, 45, 49, 50, 51–2, 55, 65–6, 73, 125–6, 129–30, 135, 148, 171, 180, 189–90, 194–5, 197–9, 199(n. 2), 211, 222–3, 228, 230–45, 254, 256–8, 264, 270(n. 5)
macropolitics, 97
Maghreb, 3, 138, 140, 143, 147, 161(n. 28)
magic, 57, 212, 225, 227
majoritarian, 3, 16, 22–4, 26, 32, 139–42, 159(n. 22), 160(n. 23), 165, 254, 259, 266; *see also* molar
mapping *see* cartography
marginalisation, 32–3, 139, 143, 189, 198, 211, 248(n. 10), 267
Marks, Laura U., 4
Martinique, 4, 103, 112, 118(n. 14)
Marxism, 11, 20, 27, 30, 41–2, 46–9, 51, 61(n. 3), 71, 105, 169, 232, 265
master, 10, 31, 129, 135, 164
materialism, 3, 11, 13, 16, 41–8,

52–8, 78, 108, 118(n. 10), 252, 260, 262, 264
Mbembe, Achille, 20, 36, 127, 157(n. 11)
Meddeb, Abdelwahab, 138
mediation (mediator),12–13, 16–17, 92, 119, 124–5, 127–35, 158(n. 15), 166, 168, 204
Mehta, Uday Singh, 20
Memmi, Albert, 69, 127
memory, 4, 16, 19(n. 1), 74, 141, 146, 172, 174, 176–7, 209–10, 225–7, 240–1, 254, 275, 287–8, 293
micropolitics, 97, 122, 130, 144, 259
milieu, 36, 80, 83–4, 86–7, 89, 93, 96, 144, 230
Miller, Christopher, vii, 50, 157(n. 10), 202
mimesis, 11, 75, 144, 259
minoritarian, 3, 23–6, 30, 32–3, 37, 105, 109, 139–43, 159(n. 22), 165, 190, 202, 211, 213; *see also* molecular
molar, 22, 23, 25, 30, 126, 141, 232, 247(n. 3); *see also* majoritarian
molecular, 22–4, 26, 30, 35, 141, 232, 234, 247(n. 3)
multiplicity, 23, 25, 38, 68, 84, 132, 137–8, 144, 147, 156(n. 5), 199(n. 3), 243, 256, 259, 275–6, 278, 290–2, 294
mutuality, 1, 8–9, 12, 68, 79, 82, 86, 89–98, 287

Nancy, Jean-Luc, 153
nation, 16, 17, 106–7, 149, 159(n. 21), 225, 235, 249(n. 18), 251–4, 258, 260, 263, 265–8, 272–3, 275–9, 284, 294, 296(n. 4)
natives, 10, 33–4, 90, 92, 224, 230–1, 241, 259; *see also* indigenous
Native Americans, 34, 259
native title, 92, 224
negativity, 29, 35, 38, 44, 47, 63, 196, 238, 279; *see also* lack
negotiation, 8–12, 16, 80, 255, 258
neo-colonialism, 106, 111, 112, 131
Nietzsche, Friedrich, 20, 50–3, 55, 109, 112, 122, 124, 132, 136, 211, 213–14
nomads, 2, 3, 7, 54–8, 148, 186, 192, 195–6, 198–9, 201–2, 210–11, 214, 224, 230
nomadology, 1–4, 15, 24–5, 28, 30, 32, 35, 49–58, 69, 125, 129–30, 132, 134, 148–9, 183–4, 186, 191–3, 195–9, 201–2, 210–16, 259

Oedipus, 3, 26, 29, 31, 36, 38, 69–70, 107, 134, 151
ontology, 11, 14–15, 19(n. 1), 36, 38, 80–3, 88–9, 91, 93, 96, 99–100, 105, 109, 116(n. 3), 118(n. 12), 152–3, 163–5, 169–70, 173, 183, 232, 240–1, 243, 255–6, 273, 276–7, 279, 284, 294
orientalism, 70, 219(n. 2)
outside *see* exclusion

paganism, 141–2, 160(n. 23, 24)
Palestine, 2, 3, 15, 19(n. 2), 121, 201–13, 219(n. 7, 11), 220–50, 259
paranoia, 22, 23, 29, 197

Parnet, Claire, 46, 128, 136, 155(n. 1)
Patton, Paul, 4, 61(n. 5), 102(n. 4), 104, 111, 155(n. 2), 219(n. 8), 224, 229, 231, 236, 259
perception, 14–15, 77(n. 6), 164–6, 168, 172–4, 176–7, 180, 184–5, 209, 215–16, 240, 243, 254–5, 257, 259–60, 264, 287–9
periphery-centre, 20, 23, 32, 42, 46, 52
perversion, 69, 88, 106, 243, 244
Pieraggi, Ange-Henri, 123
pleasure, 93, 94, 124, 153, 185, 206, 217
policy, 13, 78, 81, 227, 249(n. 14)
political economy, 11, 27–9, 42, 44, 47, 52–8, 69, 71, 105, 114, 203, 230 232–7, 242 247(n. 1), 248(n. 12), 249(n. 19), 250(n. 20), 253, 261–7, 270(n. 3)
politics of the impersonal, 15, 110–11, 132, 137, 177–80, 201, 203, 205–6, 208, 210, 214–17, 243
postcolonial theory, 1, 4, 6–8, 11–14, 17, 20–1, 39(n. 2), 41–4, 48, 50, 52–4, 57–8, 69–70, 72, 104, 120–2, 127, 129–31, 157(n. 9), 158(n. 16), 251–4, 267
primitive societies, 50, 53, 257

race, 54, 70, 72, 106, 109, 139, 147, 159(n. 21), 240, 259, 260
racism, 54, 78, 81, 228, 247(n. 1)
recognition (politics of), 64, 80, 220–24
reconciliation, 45, 78, 224
reductive analysis, 7, 29–30, 36, 49, 147, 228, 256

repetition, 11, 28, 34, 71, 79, 108, 112, 151, 171, 175, 188, 192, 193, 205, 267, 278
representation (in politics), 5, 11, 12, 22–5, 27–8, 30, 45–6, 52, 62, 64, 70–1, 96, 105, 202, 204–5, 208–16, 220, 225, 252, 259, 266
repression, 13, 26, 28, 70–2, 126, 142, 146–7, 227–8, 243
resistance, 2, 3, 5, 9–13, 15, 23–7, 36–7, 47, 52–3, 55–6, 58, 70–2, 90, 97–8, 122, 127, 134, 169, 183, 189, 193, 206, 254, 263, 267, 277
respect, 81, 95, 99–100, 194, 265
responsibility, 5, 16, 78, 82, 92, 157(n. 13), 170, 262, 276
revolution, 23, 44, 52, 106, 108, 110, 112, 117(n. 10), 125, 160(n. 23), 160(n. 24), 169, 184, 188, 191, 194, 199, 238, 244, 250(n. 22), 259
rhizome, 3, 24, 29–30, 47, 69, 75, 104, 107, 126, 129, 144, 156(n. 8), 157(n. 9), 161(n. 29), 196–8, 200(n. 4), 219(n. 2), 253
rights, 2, 13, 70, 72, 78–82, 88, 92–7, 99, 106, 118(n. 14), 189, 227, 231, 247(n. 1), 249(n. 16), 250(n. 19)
Rimbaud, Arthur, 215–6

Said, Edward, 50, 55, 58, 69, 127, 158(n. 14), 219(n. 2), 232
Sanbar, Elias, 2
Sartre, Jean-Paul, 80, 107, 164, 168–71, 173, 177, 180
satisfaction, 80, 82, 85, 95, 114, 167

savage, 48, 164
schizoanalysis, 26, 31, 203, 222, 232
segmentation, 26, 34, 40(n. 5), 126, 130, 144, 190–1, 198, 221, 238–9
self-deception, 225–8
settlers and settlement, 78–9, 990, 94, 157(n. 13), 164, 185, 221, 223–5, 230–44, 248(n. 6, 11), 250(n. 24), 263, 276
shame, 14–15, 79, 163–73, 177–80, 181(n. 3), 228
singularity, 24, 26, 34, 48, 55, 65, 111, 127, 131–2, 137, 143, 151, 187, 193, 205, 233, 267, 290
slavery, 23, 108–12, 117(n. 10), 164, 278
smooth space, 15, 16, 24–5, 37, 183, 195, 231, 252–3, 255, 258
South Africa, 29, 159(n. 22)
sovereignty, 22–3, 35, 37, 50, 64, 157(n. 11), 170, 197, 221, 224, 253
Spinoza, Baruch, 79, 82, 84–6, 89, 91, 93, 99, 119–20, 122, 126, 136
Spivak, Gayatri Chakravorty, 4–5, 7–8, 10, 12–13, 20–38, 43, 45, 49, 69, 127, 201–2
state, 3, 16, 25–6, 34, 50–6, 78, 82, 95, 126, 148, 182(n. 3), 183, 186–99, 200(n. 4), 209, 221, 225, 227, 239, 242, 249(n. 16, 17), 250(n. 21), 266
stolen generations, 13, 78–82, 93–5, 97
strata, 8, 126, 144, 191, 209–10
subalternism, 4–5, 6, 8, 10, 20, 21–5, 31–3, 36–8, 70, 96, 120–2, 126; *see also* indigenous

subtraction, 15, 104–6, 109–11, 116(n. 3, 4), 171–6, 179, 186
surveillance, 62–3, 73, 75, 239, 265

taboo, 57
technology, 16, 62, 73–4, 77(n. 6), 168, 190, 212, 251–64, 270(n. 3, 5, 6), 279, 294
teleology, 20, 53, 232
temporeality *see* duration
Terra Nullius, 220–50
time-image, 72, 74, 173, 178–9, 208–9
tool (theory as), 4, 56, 105, 125, 249(n. 19), 267
transcendence, 13, 16, 21, 30, 105, 108, 110, 113, 117(n. 6), 118(n. 12), 122, 132, 136–7, 160(n. 23), 233, 252, 254, 258
transnationalism, 16, 144, 208, 212, 251–2, 260, 261, 263, 275; *see also* cosmopolitanism; globalisation
transparency, 21–6, 30–1, 35, 125, 139, 141, 143, 161(n. 27)
trauma, 78, 133–4, 241; *see also* wound

unity, 23, 48–9, 54, 92, 255–6
universalism, 20, 46, 54, 70, 105–7, 114, 117(n. 7), 192, 203, 210
utopia, 27, 69, 77(n. 5), 105, 142, 253, 262, 265

variation, 7, 107, 192, 287, 292
violence, 32–3, 47, 63, 70, 88, 110–11, 159(n. 22), 186, 190, 202, 204, 206–7, 211–17, 227, 238, 239
Virilio, Paul, 149, 162(n. 31), 188

virtual, 105, 109–10, 202–14, 240, 254–6, 258, 260, 264, 266, 272–3, 275, 287–94; *see also* actual-virtual; actualisation
visibility, 13, 63–76, 80, 104, 138, 143, 151–2, 188, 195–7, 239, 259; *see also* invisibility
vitalism, 75, 107, 109, 118(n. 12), 203, 205, 214, 227

war machine, 3, 15, 49, 50, 52, 125, 129, 130, 148, 190, 194–9, 199(n. 2), 211, 257
Western ('the West'), 3–6, 8, 13, 14, 20–2, 24, 29, 32–7, 42, 56, 58, 60(n. 1), 70, 79, 83, 97, 99, 163, 167, 174–6, 179–80, 203, 210, 224, 248(n. 7), 252, 257, 270(n. 2)
whiteness (as majoritarian), 24, 53, 71, 108, 138–40, 159(n. 22, 23), 168–70, 239
wound, 98, 108–13, 143, 146, 160(n. 26), 199(n. 1)
Wuthnow, Julie, 60(n. 1), 219(n. 8)

Yacine, Kateb, 127, 138
Young, Robert, 3, 47, 50, 69, 219(n. 2), 238
YouTube, 62, 74–5, 207

Zionism, 16, 220–50
Žižek, Slavoj, 36, 80, 105, 114, 133–4, 157(n. 10), 159(n. 18)

EUP JOURNALS ONLINE
Deleuze Studies

Editor
Ian Buchanan, Cardiff University

Executive Editor
David Savat, University of Western Australia

Co-editors
Claire Colebrook, Penn State
Tom Conley, Harvard University
Gary Genosko, Lakehead University
Christian Kerslake, Middlesex University
Gregg Lambert, Syracuse University

Deleuze Studies is the first paper based journal to focus exclusively on the work of Gilles Deleuze. Published triannually, and edited by a team of highly respected Deleuze scholars, *Deleuze Studies* is a forum for new work on the writings of Gilles Deleuze. *Deleuze Studies* is a bold journal that challenges orthodoxies, encourages debate, invites controversy, seeks new applications, proposes new interpretations, and above all make new connections between scholars and ideas in the field. The journal publishes a wide variety of scholarly work on Gilles Deleuze, including articles that focus directly on his work, but also critical reviews of the field, as well as new translations and annotated bibliographies. It does not limit itself to any one field: it is neither a philosophy journal, nor a literature journal, nor a cultural studies journal, but all three and more.

A 2010 subscription will include a free supplementary issue of the journal Deleuze and Political Activism, guest-edited by Marcelo Svirsky.

ISSN 1750-2241   eISSN 1755-1684   Three issues per year
Find *Deleuze Studies* at www.eupjournals.com/DLS

Register to receive Table of Contents Alerts at www.eupjournals.com

EU representative:
Easy Access System Europe
Mustamäe tee 50, 10621 Tallinn, Estonia
Gpsr.requests@easproject.com

www.ingramcontent.com/pod-product-compliance
Lightning Source LLC
Chambersburg PA
CBHW070016010526
44117CB00011B/1594